Cultural Heritage and Tourism

ASPECTS OF TOURISM TEXTS
Series Editors: Professor Chris Cooper (*Oxford Brookes University, Oxford, UK*),
Dr C. Michael Hall (*University of Canterbury, Christchurch, New Zealand*)
and Dr Dallen J. Timothy (*Arizona State University, Phoenix, USA*)

This new series of textbooks aims to provide a comprehensive set of titles for higher level undergraduate and postgraduate students. The titles will be focused on identified areas of need and reflect a contemporary approach to tourism curriculum design. The books are specially written to focus on the needs, interests and skills of students and academics. They will have an easy-to-use format with clearly defined learning objectives at the beginning of each chapter, comprehensive summary material, end of chapter review questions and further reading and websites sections. The books will be international in scope with examples and cases drawn from all over the world.

Full details of all the books in this series and of all our other publications can be found on http://www.channelviewpublications.com, or by writing to Channel View Publications, St Nicholas House, 31–34 High Street, Bristol BS1 2AW, UK.

ASPECTS OF TOURISM TEXTS
Series Editors: Chris Cooper (*Oxford Brookes University, UK*),
C. Michael Hall (*University of Canterbury, New Zealand*)
and Dallen J. Timothy (*Arizona State University, USA*)

Cultural Heritage and Tourism
An Introduction

Dallen J. Timothy

CHANNEL VIEW PUBLICATIONS
Bristol • Buffalo • Toronto

Library of Congress Cataloging in Publication Data
A catalog record for this book is available from the Library of Congress.
Timothy, Dallen J.
Cultural Heritage and Tourism: An Introduction/Dallen J. Timothy.
Aspects of Tourism Texts: 4
Includes bibliographical references and index.
1. Heritage tourism. I. Title. II. Series.
G156.5.H47D35 2011
338.4′791-dc22 2011015350

British Library Cataloguing in Publication Data
A catalogue entry for this book is available from the British Library.

ISBN-13: 978-1-84541-177-0 (hbk)
ISBN-13: 978-1-84541-176-3 (pbk)

Channel View Publications
UK: St Nicholas House, 31–34 High Street, Bristol BS1 2AW, UK.
USA: UTP, 2250 Military Road, Tonawanda, NY 14150, USA.
Canada: UTP, 5201 Dufferin Street, North York, Ontario M3H 5T8, Canada.

The policy of Multilingual Matters/Channel View Publications is to use papers that are natural, renewable and recyclable products, made from wood grown in sustainable forests. In the manufacturing process of our books, and to further support our policy, preference is given to printers that have FSC and PEFC Chain of Custody certification. The FSC and/or PEFC logos will appear on those books where full certification has been granted to the printer concerned.

Typeset by The Charlesworth Group.
Printed and bound in Great Britain by Charlesworth Press.

CONTENTS

LIST OF FIGURES

LIST OF TABLES

LIST OF PLATES

PREFACE

As a child I always enjoyed school field trips to heritage sites where history came alive. I loved learning and still do. By age nine, I had planned my first two-week trip to Europe, precisely to see castles, cathedrals, ancient ruins and lederhosen, although I clearly didn't have the means or ability to undertake such a journey from the United States. My awareness of my own heritage has also deepened with age and somehow drives an interest in my personal patrimony. Now, many years later and after having visited more than 120 countries, I can safely say that I have seen or experienced nearly every type of cultural heritage resource, but I still have not had my fill of it. Much time is spent before each journey learning about local history and living cultures, so that no visit is wasted simply on conferences, meetings or seminars, for there is heritage to explore and places to understand! My interest in the cultural past is not casual; I am, unashamedly, a self-proclaimed heritage fanatic.

For thousands of years people have traveled in search of the past. Even in ancient days, travelers sought out places that by then were ancient! Today, built and living culture is perhaps the most salient draw for tourists the world over. Even some of the most devout sun, sea and sand worshippers will, on occasion, peel away from the beach just long enough to gaze upon built patrimony or immerse themselves in local cultures, or some version thereof. Sport tourists, many of them on a pilgrimage-like journey from one event and venue to another, inadvertently become heritage consumers based on the sport they sample or the arenas they visit. The same could be said of any other sort of tourist as well – there is likely to be some element of heritage and culture to almost every journey taken.

The tourism economies of some places are based entirely on cultural heritage. Other destinations have secondary or tertiary heritage appeal. On a global scale, however, far more than half of all journeys away from home have some connection to living and built culture, or the arts. With a growing realization of the importance of cultural heritage-based tourism on the world stage, increasing numbers of tourism, geography, cultural studies, history and museology programs at colleges and universities are beginning to offer courses, modules and even entire programs in cultural and heritage tourism.

My personal interest in cultural heritage, recognition of the salience and ubiquity of the past as a tourism resource, and the recent boom in academic programs and professional training geared toward the cultural industries, including heritage tourism, are the impetus for this book. This work endeavors to build a critical awareness of cultural and heritage tourism and its manifold expressions that will help direct scholars in their academic pursuits of knowledge and practitioners in their quest for more effective heritage management.

Dallen J. Timothy
Gilbert, Arizona, USA

CHAPTER 1

CULTURAL HERITAGE AND TOURISM

LEARNING OBJECTIVES

After reading this chapter, you should be able to:

1. Identify some of the earliest manifestations of heritage tourism.

2. Understand the meaning of heritage and what it entails.

3. Understand the characteristics of cultural tourism and heritage tourism.

4. Recognize the commonalities between cultural and heritage tourism.

5. Be familiar with tangible and intangible elements of culture.

6. Be aware of the difference between serious and casual cultural heritage tourists.

INTRODUCTION

Since the beginnings of human history, people have journeyed away from home for a multitude of reasons. The world has undergone many phases of human development, including long-distance travel. One of the earliest forms of travel was hunters following their prey and trading with other hunters and gatherers nearby. Transhumance, or the seasonal migration of pastoral peoples with their herds, was an early demonstration of longer-distance travel away from the village or family. Eventually, trade in foodstuffs, furs and other animal products, precious metals, spices, textiles and other important commodities led merchants further afield in search of consumer items and profits. In Asia, religious devotion to early forms of Hinduism and Buddhism was manifested in pilgrimages long before the Christian pilgrimage movement to the Holy Land began during the first few centuries after Christ. The widespread Christian pilgrimage phenomenon began shortly after the death of Jesus and was facilitated by the already well developed shipping routes of the Mediterranean and the expansive Roman highway system. During the medieval period, global explorations and colonization began, leading to yet more areas of the globe being 'discovered' by outsiders.

All human eras have contributed to the common understanding we have today of travel and tourism. For example, roads and highways were developed along ancient paths and trade routes. Road signs and roadside inns grew along important routes. And the notion of different types of tourism began early on with pilgrimage, educational travel, and cultural tourism already being well established by the 15th century. Travel for strictly leisure or pleasure purposes began in the post-industrial era of the 20th century, and contemporary patterns of human mobility are marked by increasing levels of independent travel, more off-the-beaten-path destinations, and a wider variety of experiences.

Today, hundreds of millions of people travel each year in search of pleasure, relaxation, enjoyment, education, love, curiosity, and a whole range of other internal motives. The cultural heritage of humankind is one of the most important resources upon which travel is based and appeals to many underlying motives for travel, including those noted above. The experiences of tourists and the heritage resources they utilize are the focus of this book. This chapter provides an initial understanding of the relationships between cultural heritage and tourism, establishes a set of definitions and concepts that helps readers understand better the discussions in subsequent chapters, and lays out the contents of the book as a valuable resource for students and scholars interested in cultural and heritage tourism.

THE HISTORY OF HERITAGE TOURISM

As already noted, one of the earliest forms of heritage tourism was pilgrimage. Early pilgrims – people who travel in search of spiritual experiences or for religious reasons – visited places that were important from religious or spiritual perspectives. Burial sites of famous leaders, locations where miracles occurred, or places of mystical importance, believed to have healing powers, were all seen as salient destinations for religious travelers. The earliest pilgrims, therefore, visited places of spiritual heritage importance, many with global appeal.

Biblical and other ancient accounts provide evidence of the noble classes traveling to view sites that were already old. The seven wonders of the ancient world were popular attractions in the ancient days of the Greek and Roman empires. The earliest Greek guide books were known to have included reviews of the Pyramids of Giza, the Hanging Gardens of Babylon, the Temple of Artemis at Ephesus, the Colossus of Rhodes, the Statue of Zeus at Olympia, the Mausoleum of Maussollos at Halicarnassus, and the Ishtar Gate (later the Lighthouse of Alexandria replaced Ishtar Gate on the list of Seven Wonders), which were all well-known attractions at the time but only within reach of merchants, traders, soldiers and the aristocracy.

The Grand Tour is another important historical phase of heritage tourism. From the 1600s until the mid-1800s, it was common for young men of social and financial means in Europe to travel with tutors and other entourage to the classical art cities and architectural wonders of Italy, France, Switzerland, Belgium, Germany, Austria and the Netherlands. They often traveled for months or years at a time with the purpose of becoming cultured nobility. Learning languages, art, history, and architecture was among the main objectives. Their journeys took them to Paris, Rome, Venice, Florence and other historic cities known for their architectural wonders and great works of art. The Grand Tour is among the earliest known examples of pre-packaged and mass-produced cultural tours of Europe.

Perhaps the best-known modern origins of heritage tourism were the experiences of Thomas Cook, the father of modern travel agents, tour operators, and group tours. Cook lived in England and began his career as a travel agent and tour operator in 1841, when he arranged a 15km train trip for more than 500 people to attend a special event in England. Five years later he led a group of 350 English people on a tour of Scotland. In the 1860s he began offering ship- and train-based tours of Europe, Egypt, Palestine and the USA, the contents of which were largely cultural heritage-oriented. The Great Pyramids were a major selling point of Cook's Egyptian tour, and the American itineraries included Civil War battlefields and important historic sites in New York and Washington.

Today, heritage properties and living cultures are among the most popular attractions everywhere. Few countries have tourism industries devoid of cultural heritage products. Even the most ardent sun, sea and sand destinations (e.g. some Caribbean and Pacific islands) also offer elements of cultural heritage for tourist consumption. Nearly all package tours include heritage sites, and cultural areas are among the most prized destinations among independent travelers as well. It is safe to assume that a majority of tourist attractions and destinations in the world today are based on elements of cultural heritage.

A MATTER OF DEFINITION: CULTURAL AND HERITAGE TOURISM

Heritage scholars agree on one basic concept that defines heritage – it is what we inherit from the past and use in the present day. Simply stated, history is the past, whereas heritage is the modern-day use of the past for tourism and other purposes (e.g. education and community development). In broad terms this includes both natural and cultural heritage. Natural heritage includes naturally-occurring phenomena, such as canyons, rain forests, lakes, rivers, glaciers, mountains, deserts and coastlines. Cultural heritage, on the other hand, is the past created by humankind and its various manifestations. While natural heritage is an important part of tourism, particularly in the growing realm of nature-based tourism, this book is concerned with the human past as a tourism resource.

The cultural heritage we use today includes both tangible and intangible elements. It comes in the form of material objects such as buildings, rural landscapes and villages, cities, art collections, artifacts in museums, historic gardens, handicrafts and antiques, but it also encompasses non-material elements of culture, including music, dance, beliefs, social mores, ceremonies, rituals and folklore. All of these are important components of heritage that are used for tourism and other purposes.

Heritage tourism: What is it?

Some people define heritage tourism simply as people visiting heritage places or viewing historical resources. Others suggest that a personal connection to the objects or places being viewed is what defines heritage tourism. Even more specifically, some observers argue that heritage tourism is based on visits by people who want to learn something new or enhance their lives in some way. All of these perspectives are important elements of heritage tourism, but it is not as simple as any one of these definitions alone. In fact there are many definitions of heritage tourism, but they all include elements of the human past as a resource, and entail a variety of motives on the part of the tourists.

For the purposes of this book, heritage tourism refers to travelers seeing or experiencing built heritage, living culture or contemporary arts. Its resources are tangible and intangible and are found in both rural and urban settings. Visits are motivated by a desire to enhance one's own cultural self, to learn something new, to spend time with friends and family, to satisfy one's curiosity or simply to use up excess time. In short, heritage tourism encompasses a multitude of motives, resources and experiences and is different for every individual and every place visited.

It is worth noting, however, that a heritage tourist is somewhat more difficult to define because he or she may have very little interest in cultural heritage, or conversely a great deal of interest. One effective way of viewing heritage visitors is their level of interest in elements of the past. Stebbins (1996) noted that serious cultural tourists are people who visit heritage places or cultural events because it is their hobby; they want to learn something new or expand their personal skills, and they are enthusiastic about heritage. For serious heritage tourists, the visit is more than a laid-back stopover at a castle or a happenstance run-in with an art museum. Instead, these opportunities are desired and actively pursued. Casual heritage tourists, on the other hand, are people who do not necessarily plan to visit a heritage site or museum while on vacation but decide to attend once they discover it, while in the destination for other purposes. They might be curious about the attraction but are not active seekers of heritage places and cultural experiences. In some cases, they might even have to be convinced to visit a historic environment or cultural setting by relatives or friends in the destination who drag them along. Between these two extremes lie many levels of devotion as regards culture and heritage, but what is important to note for this discussion is that people do in fact visit heritage places and participate in cultural displays for a variety of reasons, with a wide range of outcomes. Regardless of an individual's level of interest in visiting cultural attractions, his/her visits are part of the larger whole of heritage tourism.

Cultural tourism: What is it?

The terms 'cultural tourism' and 'heritage tourism' are often used in the industry and in scholarly writing as being two separate but related, or overlapping, phenomena (see Figure 1.1). Cultural tourism is sometimes used to refer to people visiting or participating in living cultures, contemporary art and music or other elements of modern culture. Some observers suggest that heritage tourism is based upon antiquated relics; it tends to occur in rural areas and is more place-bound, while cultural tourism is dominant in urban areas

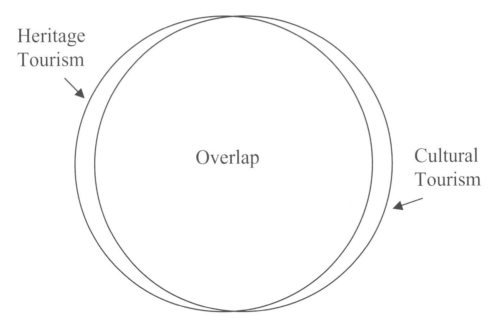

Figure 1.1 Common view of cultural and heritage tourism

Source: After National Trust for Historic Preservation (2010)

and is less place-bound, so that the '*content* is the same while the *context* is different' (National Trust for Historic Preservation, 2010). Still other scholars have suggested that cultural tourism is more about people trying to edify their cultural selves and satisfy their cultural needs by visiting places and observing built heritage, arts, performances, and living cultures.

Interestingly, none of these elements differs significantly from the meaning of heritage tourism. Casual observers or serious hobbyists 'consuming' living and built culture in rural or urban contexts and their own personal experiences, including education and cultural edification, are an important part of the heritage tourism experience (see Figure 1.2). Even contemporary art and living culture are important constituents of heritage, because they are based upon past (recent or distant) creative and social values and because they become historical while they are being produced. Some of the world's premier performing arts centers, such as the Sydney Opera House and the Grand Ole Opry, have become important heritage sites in their own right, and the performances that take place within them are an essential part of the world's intangible artistic heritage. The same is true of art museums and galleries such as the Louvre, the Hermitage and the Metropolitan Museum of Art. Assuming that heritage is based solely on remnants of a distant past illustrates a misunderstanding of cultural resources. Even artifacts and artworks created during the past decade should be considered important cultural heritage resources just as a temple built a millennium ago should be.

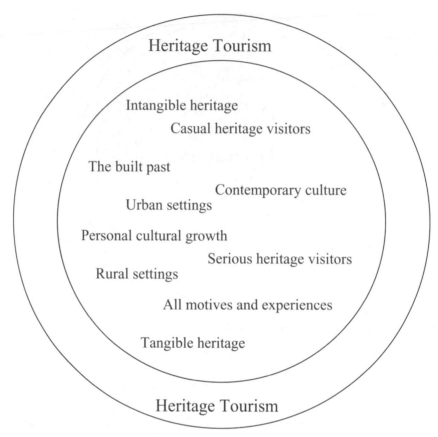

Figure 1.2 Definition of heritage tourism

Cultural heritage tourism

In summary, then, cultural heritage tourism encompasses built patrimony, living lifestyles, ancient artifacts and modern art and culture. While some authors prefer to draw distinctions between cultural tourism and heritage tourism based on people's desires or the currency of resources, the differences, if they exist at all, are rather subtle, and both terms will be used interchangeably throughout this book.

STRUCTURE AND CONTENTS OF THE BOOK

This book is divided into two primary sections. In addition to this brief introduction, the first section includes 12 chapters that cover general concepts and issues related to heritage tourism, many of which are scholarly or theoretical questions, but it also includes management implications for heritage sites and cultural destinations. In the next eight chapters, the second section examines several subtypes of heritage tourism and the ways in which many of the concepts discussed in the first section manifest in real life.

Chapters 2 and 3 examine the importance of demand for, and supply of, heritage tourism products and experiences. The demand chapter (Chapter 2) looks at the growth in global demand for tourism, and cultural tourism in particular. It points out some of the most influential demand shifters, or forces that alter demand for heritage, and details the primary markets for cultural products, including tourist and non-tourist cohorts. Finally, this chapter considers heritage consumers' socioeconomic, demographic, and geographic characteristics and their experiences while visiting historic sites. The supply chapter (Chapter 3) delves into the wide range of resources and support services that are utilized in the cultural tourism system, including attractions, heritage transportation, shops and heritage lodging. Related to this, the implications of spatial perspectives related to scale, form and function, contextual setting (urban and rural areas), location and geographical relativity are at the core of Chapter 4.

The authenticity debate in heritage tourism studies lies at the core of Chapter 5. The chapter examines tourists' perceptions of authenticity and whether or not it can be measured objectively, or if it simply depends on each individual's experience. Several types of inauthenticity are considered in the realm of heritage and examples of each one are provided. These include relative authenticity, contrived places, cultural imposters, uncertain pasts and unknown pasts.

Chapter 6 highlights the multidimensional and complicated political issues surrounding heritage, its conservation, its interpretation and its use in tourism. Concepts of power and exclusion are among the most salient in this regard, and the chapter looks at how these play out in an everyday context through social amnesia and the deliberate erasure of some histories, contested pasts and heritage dissonance, the propagandized manipulation of heritage for political gain and the effects of war and other conflict on cultural resources and heritage tourism.

Chapters 7–9 contend with the complicated issue of preserving the past. The negative and positive impacts of cultural tourism on the physical, social and economic environments are examined in Chapter 7 to establish the need for sound conservation policies and practices. Chapter 8 describes heritage protection legislation in several key destination countries and looks at supranational trade alliances (e.g. the EU and the Association of Southeast Asian Nations (ASEAN)) and how these address the needs of cultural heritage conservation. It also introduces the notion of non-supranational global organizations (e.g. United Nations Educational, Scientific and Cultural Organization (UNESCO) and the International Council on Monuments and Sites (ICOMOS)) that establish practices and policies related to the listing and conservation of historic environments. The ninth chapter discusses why heritage conservation is important, the ways in which it is approached and the primary obstacles to its success.

Chapter 10 focuses on one of the most important management and political aspects of heritage: the interpretation of the past or the revealing of the importance of places, people and events. Interpretation is an extremely important management tool for various social, economic, educational, and ecological reasons – most of which are discussed in the chapter. The most common interpretive media are reviewed, the need for considering special populations is highlighted and the interpretive planning process is described.

Physical planning and more recent views of sustainable tourism planning form the core of Chapter 11. Following a discussion of the important tradition of physical, or land-use, planning at heritage sites and cultural places, a sustainable tourism planning model is identified (participatory, incremental and cooperative planning) and applied to the cultural heritage setting to emphasize the need for effective and sustainable development.

Chapter 12 provides an overview of marketing opportunities, implications and challenges. Scale is important in this chapter, too, as it examines destination branding and marketing, as well as the promotion of individual sites. The marketing planning process is described, and the use of authenticity as a competitive advantage is highlighted. In addition, the principles of sustainability are applied to the marketing context to understand how heritage can be marketed in more sustainable ways that diverge from the ineffective traditions of mass tourism growth and boosterism.

Management concerns continue in Chapter 13 with an overview of handling visitors to minimize impacts and maximize efficiency. Given the tight financial constraints of the modern day for managing and protecting the past, the issue of revenue generation is also underscored in this management chapter.

Chapters 14–21 in the second part of the book delve more into supply and demand, conservation, planning, politics, interpretation, visitor management, marketing and authenticity in real-world contexts. Although space constraints necessarily limit the number of heritage tourism contexts that can be examined chapter by chapter, several have been selected to illustrate the management problems and conceptual issues described in the first section of the book. The chapters provide insight into museums, archaeological sites and ancient monuments, ordinary landscapes and landscapes of the extraordinary, industrial heritage, religious sites and pilgrimage, roots or diaspora tourism, living culture and indigenous heritage, and sites associated with death and human suffering (dark tourism).

SUMMARY AND CONCLUSION

Cultural heritage, whether built or living, is one of the most salient elements of the global tourism system. Many destinations rely almost entirely upon art, culture and built patrimony for their economic well-being, and even the most devout non-heritage destinations have some elements of culture that can be shared with visitors as part of the tourism product mix. More places, such as some Caribbean islands, are beginning to realize heritage as a potential tool for diversifying their tourism economies.

Heritage tourism encompasses all elements of the human past and the visitor experiences and desires associated with them. Serious heritage tourists seek meaningful, educational or spiritual experiences, or a combination of these. Casual heritage visitors tend to look more at museums, art galleries, archaeological sites and other cultural attractions as ancillary to their primary attractions of interest or their other motives. Nevertheless, both ends of the continuum, and those who fall in between, are an important part of the long-established and fast-growing phenomenon of cultural heritage tourism.

REVIEW QUESTIONS

1. In what ways has cultural tourism existed since ancient days? What are some examples of ancient and medieval forms of heritage tourism?

2. Is everything in the environment around us part of our heritage, or does it only include buildings and archaeological sites? What parts of our surroundings should be considered heritage?

3. What are some world-famous examples of intangible culture that are important heritage attractions?

4. Do cultural tourism and heritage tourism differ from one another? If so, how?

5. How do serious cultural tourists differ from casual cultural tourists?

RECOMMENDED READING

Ashworth, G.J. and Graham, B. (eds) (2005) *Senses of Place: Senses of Time*. Aldershot: Ashgate.

Ashworth, G.J. and Larkham, P.J. (eds) (1994) *Building a New Heritage: Tourism, Culture and Identity in the New Europe*. London: Routledge.

Boniface, P. and Fowler, P. (1993) *Heritage Tourism in 'the Global Village'*. London: Routledge.

Breathnach, T. (2006) Looking for the real me: Locating the self in heritage tourism. *Journal of Heritage Tourism* 1(2), 100–120.

Chambers, E. (ed.) (1997) *Tourism and Culture: An Applied Perspective*. Albany: State University of New York Press.

Corsane, G. (ed.) (2005) *Heritage, Museums and Galleries: An Introductory Reader*. Abingdon: Routledge.

Craik, J. (2001) Tourism, culture and national identity. In T. Bennett and D. Carter (eds) *Culture in Australia: Policies, Publics and Programs* (pp. 89–113). Cambridge: Cambridge University Press.

Dann, G.M.S. and Seaton, A.V. (eds) (2001) *Slavery, Contested Heritage and Thanatourism*. New York: Haworth.

Diamond, H.A. (2008) *American Aloha: Cultural Tourism and the Negotiation of Tradition.* Honolulu: University of Hawaii Press.

Di Giovine, M.A. (2009) *The Heritage-Scape: UNESCO, World Heritage and Tourism.* Lanham, MD: Lexington Books.

du Cros, H. and Lee, Y.S.F. (2007) *Cultural Heritage Management in China: Preserving the Pearl River Delta Cities.* London: Routledge.

Graham, B., Ashworth, G.J. and Tunbridge, J.E. (2000) *A Geography of Heritage: Power, Culture and Economy.* London: Arnold.

Graham, B. and Howard, P. (eds) (2008) *The Ashgate Research Companion to Heritage and Identity.* Aldershot: Ashgate.

Hanley, K. and Walton, J.K. (2010) *Constructing Cultural Tourism: John Ruskin and the Tourist Gaze.* Bristol: Channel View Publications.

Howard, P. (2003) *Heritage: Management, Interpretation, Identity.* London: Continuum.

Ivanovic, M. (2008) *Cultural Tourism.* Cape Town: Juta.

Knudsen, B.T. and Waade, A.M. (2010) *Re-Investing Authenticity: Tourism, Place and Emotions.* Bristol: Channel View Publications.

Leask, A. and Fyall, A. (eds) (2006) *Managing World Heritage Sites.* Oxford: Butterworth Heinemann.

McKercher, B. and du Cros, H. (2002) *Cultural Tourism: The Partnership between Tourism and Cultural Heritage Management.* New York: Haworth.

McKercher, B. and du Cros, H. (2003) Testing a cultural tourism typology. *International Journal of Tourism Research* 5, 45–58.

Navrud, S. and Ready, R.C. (eds) (2002) *Valuing Cultural Heritage: Applying Environmental Valuation Techniques to Historic Buildings, Monuments and Artifacts.* Cheltenham: Edward Elgar.

Ooi, C. (2002) *Cultural Tourism and Tourism Cultures: The Business of Mediating Experiences in Copenhagen and Singapore.* Copenhagen: Copenhagen Business School Press.

Poria, Y., Biran, A. and Reichel, A. (2006) Tourist perceptions: Personal vs. non-personal. *Journal of Heritage Tourism* 1(2), 121–132.

Prideaux, B. (2009) River heritage: The Murray-Darling River. In B. Prideaux and M. Cooper (eds) *River Tourism* (pp. 165–180). Wallingford: CAB International.

Prideaux, B., Timothy, D.J. and Chon, K.S. (eds) (2008) *Cultural and Heritage Tourism in Asia and the Pacific.* London: Routledge.

Richards, G. (1996) *Cultural Tourism in Europe*. Wallingford: CAB International.

Richards, G. (ed.) (2001) *Cultural Attractions and European Tourism*. Wallingford: CAB International.

Richards, G. (ed.) (2007) *Cultural Tourism: Global and Local Perspectives*. New York: Haworth.

Richards, G. and Munsters, W. (eds) (2010) *Cultural Tourism Research Methods*. Wallingford: CAB International.

Sigala, M. and Leslie, D. (eds) (2005) *International Cultural Tourism: Management, Implications and Cases*. Oxford: Butterworth Heinemann.

Singh, L.K. (2008) *Indian Cultural Heritage: Perspective for Tourism*. Delhi: ISHA Books.

Smith, L. (2006) *Uses of Heritage*. London: Routledge.

Smith, M.K. (2003) *Issues in Cultural Tourism Studies*. London: Routledge.

Smith, M.K. and Robinson, M. (eds) (2006) *Cultural Tourism in a Changing World: Politics, Participation and (Re)presentation*. Clevedon: Channel View Publications.

Timothy, D.J. (2009) River-based tourism in the USA: Tourism and recreation on the Colorado and Mississippi Rivers. In B. Prideaux and M. Cooper (eds) *River Tourism* (pp. 41–54). Wallingford: CAB International.

Timothy, D.J. and Boyd, S.W. (2003) *Heritage Tourism*. Harlow: Prentice Hall.

Timothy, D.J. and Prideaux, B. (2004) Issues in heritage and culture in the Asia Pacific region. *Asia Pacific Journal of Tourism Research* 9(3), 213–223.

Walle, A.H. (1998) *Cultural Tourism: A Strategic Focus*. Boulder, CO: Westview Press.

Waters, A.M. (2006) *Planning the Past: Heritage Tourism and Post-Colonial Politics at Port Royal*. Lanham, MD: Lexington Books.

Winter, T. (2007) *Post-Conflict Heritage, Postcolonial Tourism: Culture, Politics and Development at Angkor*. London: Routledge.

RECOMMENDED WEBSITES

Cultural Heritage Tourism – http://www.culturalheritagetourism.org/

Cultural and Heritage Tourism Alliance – http://chtalliance.com/

Heritage Tourism (National Trust for Historic Preservation) – http://www.preservationnation.org/issues/heritage-tourism/

Heritage Tourism (Society for American Archaeology) – http://www.saa.org/forthepublic/resources/heritagetourism/tabid/90/default.aspx

SECTION 1

CHAPTER 2

CONSUMPTION OF CULTURE: HERITAGE DEMAND AND EXPERIENCE

LEARNING OBJECTIVES

After reading this chapter, you should be able to:

1. Review the global magnitude of tourism.

2. Understand the significance of cultural heritage in global trends.

3. Identify various types of demand for heritage experiences and places.

4. Be familiar with various demographic, geographic and psychographic characteristics of cultural consumers.

5. Recognize other heritage consumers besides tourists.

6. Understand heritage consumers' motives.

7. Develop knowledge about different types of demand.

8. Appreciate the social, ecological and economic variables that affect demand for cultural heritage.

INTRODUCTION

Based on the definitions of heritage presented in Chapter 1, every place has heritage, although not all heritage resources appeal to tourists, even if they are important for local residents. Nevertheless, the past and its resources lie at the core of much of global tourism today, and people by the hundreds of millions travel worldwide each year to seek out and experience places of historical significance. Many others happen upon such places while traveling for other purposes and opt to pay a visit to heritage places while in the destination. Regardless of the original motives, it is a well-established fact that heritage tourism is big business, and demand for it continues to grow, especially as the world becomes more complicated and people desire to get back to their roots and experience times when life was simpler and much less complex, even if it is in a sometimes superficial tourism context. Some authors have suggested that people need the past to be able to cope with the frenetic life of today; the world is so complex that people look to the past, in part by visiting heritage places, as a way of finding a footing in an evolving and unstable world.

There are likely as many reasons or motives to visit heritage places as there are people who visit, but this chapter aims to examine at least some of the multitudinous motivations for visiting heritage sites. It also highlights several other aspects of demand, such as types of demand, tourist and non-tourist use of the past, and various socio-economic forces that act as demand shifters.

TOURISM AND THE DEMAND FOR HERITAGE

In tourism studies, we often speak of demand as consumers of the tourism product – the tourists. From an economics perspective, tourism is seen as an 'invisible export industry' because the product of tourism (i.e. the travel experience) is intangible, paid for by outsiders who bring new money into the region and exported from the destination where it is created. The consumption of the product of tourism by travelers themselves or by various intermediaries is referred to as demand.

There are many ways to understand various aspects of demand for heritage tourism, but it is important to remember that tourists are not the only consumers of heritage products. Likewise, researchers are interested in what is usually referred to as current demand, but latent, or potential, demand is also important. This first section examines the tourism demand for heritage, followed by a brief examination of other consumers of heritage.

General patterns of tourism demand

To contextualize heritage tourism in the larger framework of international travel, this section describes current demand for international and domestic travel. Global tourism has grown significantly since the Second World War, from an estimated 25 million international trips in 1950 to nearly a billion cross-border trips in 2010 (see Table 2.1). The World Tourism Organization predicts that this remarkable growth will continue into the foreseeable future, with international arrivals expected to exceed a billion in 2010–2011 and reaching 1.6 billion by 2020 (UNWTO, 2009). Every year tourists spend hundreds of billions of dollars directly, and their expenditures induce trillions of additional dollars in indirect spending by employing people directly or indirectly in tourism. Tourism and its related sectors are typically considered one of the largest industries in the world in terms of consumer expenditures, and as a result, nearly every place is clamoring for a piece of the tourism pie because of its potential to generate employment, earn taxes for local and national governments, and stimulate destination economies through increased regional income.

Table 2.1 Growth of international tourist arrivals since the Second World War

Year	Number of international tourists	Year	Number of international tourists
1950	25 million	1990	457 million
1960	69 million	2000	698 million
1970	166 million	2010	935 million
1980	288 million		

Source: UNWTO (2011)

Much of this growth is attributed to technological advances, particularly in the realm of transportation. More efficient aircrafts, the popularization of the personal automobile, the development of highway systems and growing affluence throughout the world have spurred an increase in international travel heretofore unseen. While annual growth rates of international travel during the 1990s and early 2000s ranged from 4–7% per annum, tourism's growth by 38 times since 1950 is remarkable.

There are some salient geographical patterns associated with these trends in global growth. One of the most notable is that the top 15 destination countries in 1950 were responsible for some 98% of all international arrivals. By the 1970s, this figure had declined to 75%. In 2009 the top 15 countries accounted for only 56% of all arrivals (UNWTO, 2010). This pattern indicates the spread of tourism to new destinations beyond the traditional top 15, especially in less-developed and newly-industrialized countries. When new destinations open up, demand is redirected away from the traditional destinations in favor of places that might have been closed or otherwise inaccessible for many years. This is especially notable as tourists become more sophisticated in their demands for experiences and places on the world's periphery or where tourism is in an early stage of development, such as in many isolated or peripheral countries in Latin America, Africa and Asia.

The World Travel and Tourism Council (WTTC) (2008) highlighted several countries as 'emerging destinations' that are expected to experience rapid tourism growth. Table 2.2 illustrates the top ten countries expected to undergo the most relative economic growth through tourism (as proportion of GDP) in 2008. While the final accounting is not yet known, it is interesting to note that countries such as Azerbaijan and Angola demonstrate characteristics of development potential to the degree that they could become major tourist destinations in the near future. Clearly both countries have a lot to offer potential visitors, but it remains to be seen whether or not political conditions and efforts by their respective governments to welcome tourists and promote the industry will result in the desired dividends.

Table 2.2 Countries expected to grow their tourism economies fastest after 2008

Rank	Country/Region	Real tourism GDP growth %
1	Macau	23.8
2	Montenegro	17.0
3	Seychelles	14.1
4	Angola	13.7
5	Reunion	13.7
6	United Arab Emirates	13.5
7	Libya	13.2
8	Azerbaijan	11.4
9	China	11.3
10	Romania	9.3

Source: WTTC (2008)

The WTTC also forecasts that between 2008 and 2018 other countries that traditionally have not been top-tier destinations will be among the fastest growing and largest tourism-based economies, based on arrivals, employment and relative growth in tourism GDP. Countries on this list include Vietnam, Vanuatu, Romania, Sao Tome and Principe, Chile, Cape Verde, Brunei, Qatar, Montenegro, Namibia and Rwanda. Clearly these countries, most of which have not been counted among the world's leading destinations, have considerable potential for further growth.

In 2007, the fastest growing tourism regions in the world were the Middle East, South-east Asia, Northeast Asia and Central America, as measured by international arrivals. Table 2.3 illustrates global growth patterns before the onset of the current worldwide recession. The Middle East experienced a remarkable growth of 16.4%, with most of this being shored up by increased arrivals to Egypt, Saudi Arabia and the United Arab Emirates. Southeast Asia's tourist arrivals grew by 12.2%, reflecting in part the increasing popularity of Vietnam, Cambodia and Malaysia as tourist destinations. Arrivals in 2007 in East Asia exceeded 2006's numbers by nearly 11%, with Macau demonstrating the highest growth – an astonishing 21%. Japan experienced a 13% growth in one year, and a 10% growth was recorded for China. Central America's extraordinary 10% growth reflected notable enlargement in demand for Costa Rica, Honduras and Panama. With the economic crisis of 2007–2011, most regions of the world saw a decrease in international arrivals in 2008–2009. Africa was the only region to see a net growth during this difficult economic period, with 3.1% growth between 2008 and 2009, while other regions experienced a 2–6% decrease in arrivals (UNWTO, 2010).

Table 2.3 International arrivals by sub-region

Sub-region	International arrivals (millions)					Growth between 2006 and 2007 (%)
	1990	1995	2000	2005	2007	
EUROPE						
Northern Europe	28.6	35.8	43.7	52.8	57.6	2.2
Western Europe	108.6	112.2	139.7	142.4	154.9	3.6
Central/Eastern Europe	31.5	60.6	69.4	87.8	95.6	4.5
Southern Europe	93.9	102.7	140.8	157.3	176.2	7.0
ASIA AND THE PACIFIC						
Northeast Asia	26.4	41.3	58.3	87.5	104.2	10.6
Southeast Asia	21.1	28.2	35.6	48.5	59.6	12.2
Oceania	5.2	8.1	9.2	10.5	10.7	1.7
South Asia	3.2	4.2	6.1	8.1	9.8	8.2
AMERICAS						
North America	71.7	80.7	91.5	89.9	95.3	5.2
Caribbean	11.4	14.0	17.1	18.8	19.5	0.1
Central America	1.9	2.6	4.3	6.4	7.7	9.6
South America	7.7	11.7	15.3	18.2	19.9	6.4
AFRICA						
North Africa	8.4	7.3	10.2	13.9	16.3	7.9
Subsaharan Africa	6.8	12.8	17.7	23.3	28.2	7.1
MIDDLE EAST						
Middle East	9.6	13.7	24.4	37.8	47.6	16.4

Source: UNWTO (2008)

It is also interesting and useful to examine where the demand for tourism comes from, not just where it goes. Table 2.4 shows the origins of people who travel for personal/leisure reasons in order of how much is spent on travel. American tourists spend more than any other individual nationality, exceeding the second ranked nationality, the Japanese, by more than three times. China's position in the top ten demonstrates its burgeoning middle class, which can now afford to travel and which has benefited from the Chinese government's Approved Destination List – countries the Chinese are permitted to visit on holiday vacations, which continues to expand each year. Mexico's inclusion on the top ten list also testifies to growing affluence in that country and the high priority Mexicans place on international travel. Table 2.5 similarly shows expenditures on business-related travel. Not surprisingly, most nations on the personal travel top ten list also have a place on the business travel top 10 list. There has always been a positive relationship between pleasure- and business-oriented travel, as one tends to support the other.

Table 2.4 Top 10 personal traveler origin countries by expenditures, 2008

Rank	Country	$ US (billions)	Rank	Country	$ US (billions)
1	United States	889.5	6	China	167.5
2	Japan	274.4	7	Italy	127.1
3	United Kingdom	208.1	8	Spain	123.9
4	Germany	201.8	9	Canada	95.8
5	France	170.9	10	Mexico	77.1

Source: WTTC (2008)

Table 2.5 Top 10 business traveler origin countries by expenditures, 2008

Rank	Country	$ US (billions)	Rank	Country	$ US (billions)
1	United States	190.1	6	France	43.3
2	Japan	70.2	7	Italy	40.3
3	China	65.8	8	Spain	21.7
4	Germany	62.1	9	Canada	20.2
5	United Kingdom	51.1	10	Brazil	15.5

Source: WTTC (2008)

In addition to international travel, domestic tourism is very significant in most parts of the world. Some observers suggest that domestic trips even exceed international travel by more than ten times. While there is no way to measure domestic tourism accurately, because it often involves people driving their own cars and staying in the homes of friends or relatives, industry estimates do acknowledge that it is a staple of the tourism industry. Logically, domestic travel is most visible in larger countries, such as the USA, Canada, Mexico, China, Australia, France and the United Kingdom, although by no means is it negligible in small countries. As with international tourism in general, there is also a tendency for domestic tourism to be of a larger scale in the developed portions of the world, although it is important everywhere.

The significance of people traveling within their own country can be seen in a USA-based 2007 study (TIA, 2007) by the Travel Industry Association (now the US Travel Association), which concluded that 2.001 billion domestic person-trips were taken in the US compared to 1.034 billion household trips in 2006. Leisure travel accounted for almost three quarters (74%) of all US domestic trips, with 26% representing various forms of business travel, such as conventions, training, sales and meetings. Travel inside the USA by Americans has grown significantly since 2000, which, according to Ioannides and Timothy (2010), can be explained partially by a widespread reluctance to travel abroad, new passport requirements to enter the US (only 27–30% of US citizens possess a valid passport), and the current economic crisis, which has caused people to spend their holidays closer to home.

Cars have long been the favored mode of transportation for domestic travelers in the US (84%), followed by airplane (8%) and other (8%), which includes trains and motor coaches. The top domestic destinations in the USA are California, Texas, Florida, New York, Pennsylvania, Michigan, Ohio, North Carolina, Illinois and Missouri. More than half of all US domestic travelers stay in commercial lodging establishments (52%). The second most popular accommodation is staying with friends and relatives (34%), followed by camping (4%) and other (12%), including second homes and timeshares. These broader patterns of tourist demand are important to understand when considering the heritage sector specifically.

Heritage tourism consumption

As already noted in the first chapter, we generally consider heritage tourism to be the use of cultural resources (tangible and intangible) as attractions. This involves a wide network of consumers, including tourists, travel agents, tour operators, information brokers and other service providers. This first section examines tourists as consumers of cultural heritage.

While cultural heritage is an important part of the tourism product throughout the world, most countries do not keep or tabulate data specifically related to heritage tourism. The primary reason for this is that heritage tourism is difficult to measure or differentiate from other forms of tourism. One of the main reasons for this is a lack of conceptual clarity in defining who is a heritage/cultural tourist and what constitutes heritage tourism. This is especially difficult when travelers indulge in many activities during a single trip, including museum visits, sunbathing on the beach and shopping. Because of this confusion regarding who is a heritage tourist and who is not, as Chapter 1 noted, we sometimes look at heritage tourists as being hard-core/serious heritage visitors or casual heritage visitors. Serious heritage tourists travel specifically to visit cultural sites and do so frequently. Heritage is their hobby and provides an important travel stimulus. Casual visitors are those who might happen upon a museum or archaeological site and visit while they are in the area; they are not necessarily cultural enthusiasts. In this sense, the cultural sites become secondary attractions and perhaps only one of several days (or even a few hours) is spent visiting a heritage site (see Plate 2.1).

According to Gail Lord (1999), a cultural heritage planning consultant, the demand for heritage can be subdivided even further (see Figure 2.1). She noted that some 15% of the general population would not visit heritage sites and events under any circumstances, which leaves approximately 85% of the traveling public who would attend if conditions were right and can therefore be classified as potential cultural/heritage tourists. Hard-core heritage enthusiasts, whom Lord refers to as 'greatly motivated' visitors, actually comprise

Plate 2.1 Cruise passengers are casual visitors at this nutmeg plantation in Grenada

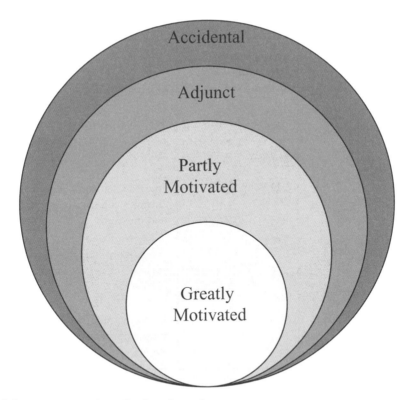

Figure 2.1 Four categories of cultural tourists

Source: After Lord (1999)

the smallest part of the cultural tourist market, estimated to be about 15%. These are people who travel to a specific destination purposefully to experience the culture and heritage of the region. The second group, the partly-motivated cultural tourists, travel both because of the heritage appeal of the destination and other reasons, such as playing golf or visiting relatives. This group represents the largest market segment at approximately 30%. Third, comprising some 20% of heritage demand, are the 'adjunct' visitors, who are motivated primarily by other factors, such as trekking in a rainforest, relaxing at a beach resort or attending a sporting event, but will also plan a side-visit to a cultural site while they are in the area. Accidental cultural tourists comprise some 20% of heritage tourists. These people have no plans to visit historic sites or cultural events but might stumble onto an opportunity or accompany friends or relatives who insist on going. As these classifications indicate, there is huge demand for heritage tourism products and experiences.

Current demand refers to the present use of a product in terms of its volume and size. As already noted, there is a glaring lack of information specifically about global patterns and trends in the area of heritage and cultural tourism. However, the World Tourism

Table 2.6 Cultural heritage tourists in select countries

Country	Year of data	No. of heritage site and cultural visits by tourists	Comments/Explanation
Australia	2008	12.36 million	International and domestic tourists. Includes arts, heritage sites, aboriginal cultural tourists
Canada	2008	11.66 million	International and domestic tourists. Includes cultural events, historic sites and museums
New Zealand	2006	2.27 million	International and domestic tourists. Includes museums and Maori cultural events
United States of America	2003	216.80 million	Domestic tourists only. Includes arts, museums, heritage sites and cultural events

Sources: Canadian Tourism Commission (2009); New Zealand Ministry of Tourism (2008a, 2008b); Travel Industry Association of America (2003); Tourism Research Australia (2009)

Organization suggests that approximately half of all international trips every year involve visits to cultural heritage sites (UNWTO, 2006). In most cases, national-level heritage data are also non-existent, although there are a few exceptions, primarily from the developed portions of the world. Table 2.6 illustrates some basic heritage/cultural tourist numbers for a selection of English-speaking developed countries where heritage is an important part of the tourism product.

In the USA, heritage site visits are an important travel pastime. Table 2.7 shows 2010 visitor numbers at US National Park Service (USNPS) properties that focus exclusively or largely on cultural heritage. The US Travel Association is also active in monitoring heritage sector trends. A few other countries, too, are trying to understand current uses of heritage resources better (e.g. the United Kingdom), but the most comprehensive nationwide study was done in 2003 by the US Travel Association, which at the time was known as the Travel Industry Association (TIA). While the data in that study are becoming outdated and focus only on domestic tourism, it is one of the only comprehensive, nationwide studies to attempt to understand the dynamics and characteristics of the heritage tourism market and therefore is an important baseline information source for this section.

Table 2.7 Visitation at select US National Park Service heritage properties, 2010

Property type	Visitation in 2010	Property type	Visitation in 2010
National Battlefield	1,765,207	National Memorial	30,799,674
National Battlefield Park	2,255,096	National Military Park	4,565,799
National Historic Site	9,747,040	National Monument	23,012,207
National Historical Park	28,135,991	National Park	64,623,855

Source: US National Park Service (2011)

Between 1996 and 2003, heritage tourism in the USA grew by 13% as Americans became more interested in their own personal pasts and their national heritage; approximately one quarter of all domestic heritage visitors in the US consider themselves to be frequent or devoted heritage tourists. Some 81% of American travelers (118.1 million) who undertook a trip away from home in 2002 visited at least one heritage site or participated in a cultural activity, with more than 216 million trips being taken to heritage sites or heritage events, comprising 21% of all domestic person-trips. In addition, the US Department of Commerce estimates that in 2004 more than 10.6 million overseas tourists visited cultural events and historic sites during their stay in the USA (US Department of Commerce, 2005).

There are several reasons for this growth and for the high ratio of avid heritage enthusiasts. One explanation is the rapid pace of modernization, which often causes people to become more nostalgic for certain elements and periods of the past, where life was simpler and more unassuming. Related to this is an aging population of baby-boomers, who are said to become more nostalgic for the past as they get older and who are more economically secure and therefore better able to travel for cultural purposes. Another impetus is the terror tragedy of September 11, 2001, which instigated an increased sense of patriotism and appreciation for America's national past and augmented heritage-based travel to places and historic sites of nationalistic significance.

The tourism industry of Great Britain is also heavily dependent on heritage sites and cultural events, and is enthusiastic about understanding demand for its heritage products. The heritage portion of Britain's tourism industry is estimated to be worth approximately £4.5 billion a year, directly supporting some 100,000 full-time jobs (VisitBritain, 2010a). The national tourism agency responsible for marketing Britain as a destination, VisitBritain (2008), conducted a study similar to the 2003 TIA study, which also reveals interesting and similar patterns of domestic heritage consumption. This and many other studies provide some foundational data for understanding basic patterns of heritage tourism demand in the UK. Some 42% of the 28,117 domestic travelers surveyed claimed to have visited a museum or gallery in the previous year. Almost three quarters (70%) visited an historic site during the same period, and 67% attended some kind of arts event. The most visited sites included historic cities or towns, historic parks or gardens, monuments (e.g. castles or ruins), heritage buildings, historic places of worship, industrial heritage sites, archaeological sites and sport-related heritage sites. The most common arts events were theater, live music, carnivals, craft exhibitions, dance events, ballets and operas.

VisitBritain also tracks the popularity of heritage attractions and categorizes them into two types: paid admission and free admission sites. The most popular admission-charging heritage attractions in England for domestic visitors were the Tower of London, St Paul's Cathedral, Canterbury Cathedral, Westminster Abbey, Windsor Castle, York Minster, Stonehenge and the Roman Baths in Bath. The most popular free attractions were Tate Modern, the British Museum, the National Gallery, the Natural History Museum, the Science Museum, the Victoria and Albert Museum, the National Portrait Gallery, Tate Britain, Oldway Mansion, the National Railway Museum, the Lowry and St Martin-in-the-Fields (VisitBritain, 2008).

Foreign tourists in Great Britain also view heritage attractions with a great deal of enthusiasm and, in fact, heritage is among the most important pull factors to the UK for travelers from North America, Australia, New Zealand, Continental Europe and Japan. Some observers even suggest that almost all forms of tourism in the UK have some element of heritage and culture at their foundation. According to VisitBritain's (2010b) study of international holiday visitors, dining out is the most common activity undertaken by foreign leisure tourists (70%), which is not surprising. In conjunction with this, approximately 46% visited a pub (itself an important part of British heritage!). Shopping is the second most popular activity with between 53 and 60% of all tourists shopping for clothes, accessories or souvenirs. Experiencing cultural heritage comes in third. More than half (59%) of all foreign vacationers visited historic houses, famous monuments, churches and castles; 41% visited museums and art galleries in the UK. Other heritage-related activities besides stopovers at historic buildings included researching ancestry (2%); visiting literary, music or film locations (3%); and visiting gardens and parks (41%). A similar study from the late 1990s among incoming tourists found that visiting heritage places played a critical role in the decision to visit Britain for 37% of arrivals (Nurick, 2000).

Cultural heritage is a component of the tourism resource base for most countries of the world. Some of the most famous heritage destinations on earth today are located in the developing world, including Machu Picchu (Peru), Angkor Wat (Cambodia), the Great Wall of China (China), and the Pyramids of Giza (Egypt). Unfortunately, most of these countries have very limited, if any, data specifically associated with cultural tourism, except on a site-specific scale. Nonetheless, it is certain that tens of millions of people visit these most famous heritage sites and other less well-known attractions in both the developing and developed worlds each year. The few traditional exceptions to this pattern have been small island nations, for example in the Caribbean, whose natural amenities and beachfront developments overshadow their indigenous and colonial heritage. This is beginning to change, however, as even the most sun, sea and sand-dependent destinations are beginning to consider the importance of diversifying their product bases with historic sites, because they realize demand exists for heritage places even among day trippers from resorts and cruise ships.

Characteristics of heritage tourists

To understand demand and market attributes, marketing and management specialists have traditionally segmented tourists according to three sets of characteristics: demographics, psychographics and place of origin. Heritage tourist characteristics can also be classified in the same manner, which makes their experiences and behaviors easier to understand and evaluate.

Demographic segmentation results when visitors are classified by certain social and socio-economic characteristics. The most common of these are age, gender, employment, marital status, education and income. There are several reasons why it is important for heritage managers to understand visitor demographics. For example, pricing policies are often established in part based on what visitors are willing to pay for the experience being offered. There are direct correlations to income and education levels, and willingness to pay. Other reasons are so that interpretive media and even structural design might be geared toward specific markets to be able to meet visitors' needs better and cater to their desires and expected outcomes.

A great deal of research has been done to understand heritage visitor demographics and several patterns have emerged during the past 30 years. As a general rule, heritage tourists are younger and middle aged, with the majority being between 30 and 50 years of age. However, this trend differs from place to place; in the USA, heritage tourists tend to be older and more likely to be retired.

Education is a prominent characteristic of heritage tourists. In general, they are college or university graduates, with many having post-graduate degrees as well. Serious heritage tourists tend to be the best educated, with a strong personal interest in various aspects of history, such as culture, migration, museums and various manifestations of heavy industry such as mining or railroads. Many devoted heritage tourists prepare for their visits ahead of time by reading about, and researching, the places they will visit. In addition, literary tourists, one type of heritage tourist, tend to be especially well versed in various genres of literature, which contributes to their desire to visit the places they have read about or where their favorite authors lived and wrote. Education can be seen as a stimulus for opening people's eyes to various elements of the past and increasing a desire to experience historic places and cultural events.

Along with education usually comes more affluence. Heritage tourists are more affluent than other types of tourists and most are employed in white-collar jobs. In a comprehensive study of European cultural tourism, Richards (2001) found that 70% of cultural tourists were occupied in professional or managerial positions, and an additional 25% were employed in sales and other services. Most heritage tourists' socio-economic position allows them to travel to relatively exotic destinations or to travel domestically more frequently, and it affects their behavior in the destination. For instance, heritage tourists tend to spend more money on shopping, lodging and food than many other types of tourist. Likewise, they can afford to stay longer in the destination and do so, on average, by at least a few days. Besides being able to afford lengthier stays, their personal interests in culture and history provides excuses to explore places in more depth and seek out sites that interest them, thereby extending their stays in the destination. In Australia, foreign heritage tourists spent on average $6,355 per trip, compared to $4,000 spent by other international tourists in 2008. Similarly, domestic Australian travelers who visited heritage sites, or participated in cultural events, spent an average of $994 per trip, whereas non-heritage domestic travelers spent $576 per trip (Tourism Research Australia, 2009).

There is some evidence to suggest that more women than men are involved in heritage tourism, with the exception of some types of museums. This, according to Richards (2001), might be a result of women's propensity to consume cultural activities more than men.

Psychographic segmentation is based on visitors' attitudes and behaviors, which are often conditioned by their home surroundings, lifestyles, and social networks. Adventurous travelers and risk takers are one way of classifying people psychographically. Outgoing personalities, shy demeanors or workaholics are other ways people can be seen from a psychographic perspective. All of these, and many others, have a salient influence on the types of travel people undertake and their expectations and desires from a vacation experience. One of the best-known models for classifying tourists in a psychographic context is Plog's (1991) allocentric-psychocentric model. Plog's conceptualization argues that tourists, their behavior, and their choices of destinations lie somewhere along a spectrum from less-adventuresome, conservative (psychocentric) travelers who desire the comforts of home and familiar environments on one end to very adventurous travelers (allocentrics), who seek exotic experiences in unusual places on the other end of the scale. Most tourists, he argues, fall somewhere in between these two extremes.

Psychographic models are also useful in understanding the types of heritage experiences people desire or the cultural destinations they elect to visit. For instance, we could say that a Japanese individual traveling to spend time immersed in and learning about the culture of an isolated tribe in the jungle of central Africa, where little tourism exists, would fall under the category of allocentric heritage tourist. By the same token, a Swedish tourist involved in a motorcoach-based castle and cathedral tour in Great Britain might well be viewed as a psychocentric heritage tourist. In a similar vein, workaholics might choose to visit historic properties close to home because they do not want to 'waste time' traveling long distances. Individuals who have withdrawn personalities might also opt for isolated cultural destinations with few other tourists, or they might favor less-popular museums instead of those that attract large masses.

The third category often used to understand visitor characteristics is geographic segmentation. This involves two primary perspectives: where guests are from and where they go (and what they do) while in the destination. Both of these perspectives are important. Knowledge about the origins of tourists allows destination and site marketing planners to know where their promotional budget might be put to the best use. As well, knowing where people go and what they do while in the destination helps monitor visitor impacts, can help measure the effectiveness of tourism planning and can help determine which areas or attractions are most popular.

In New Zealand there are some interesting geographical trends related to overseas visitors participating in Maori cultural tourism. Maori heritage tourists come primarily from overseas (80%), although 20% live in New Zealand. From an international perspective, Chinese were the most inclined to experience Maori heritage, with 51% in 2006. This was followed by Germans, Koreans, Canadians, British, Taiwanese, Americans, Japanese, Singaporeans and Australians. Even though Australians comprise New Zealand's largest foreign market, Maori culture-based tourism is considered important by only 11% of Australian tourists. Two thirds (65%) of New Zealand's domestic cultural tourists come from the Auckland area, followed by other large cities (e.g. Wellington), owing to a large urban immigrant population and the desire among city dwellers to explore rural New Zealand and its indigenous cultures (New Zealand Ministry of Tourism, 2008a).

Although Australia's heritage market is primarily domestic, European visitors had the highest propensity to visit heritage and cultural sites, including people from Switzerland (85%), Germany (73%), Italy (71%) and the Netherlands (68%). Asians are less inclined to participate in heritage/cultural tourism (Tourism Research Australia, 2009), instead favoring to spend more time at shopping centers and natural areas.

As already noted, it is also essential to understand where tourists go to enjoy cultural products. The top destinations for heritage tourists in the USA are California, Texas, New York, Florida, Pennsylvania, Virginia, Illinois, Tennessee, North Carolina and Georgia (TIA, 2003). Several of these states are home to some of America's most significant heritage attractions, such as the Alamo in Texas, Colonial Williamsburg and Arlington National Cemetery in Virginia, and Gettysburg Battlefield, the Amish Culture, and the USA's first capital, Philadelphia. In Australia, New South Wales is the most popular state for international and national heritage tourists, followed by Victoria for domestic tourists and Queensland for foreigners (Tourism Research Australia, 2009).

Rural areas are popular heritage destinations all over the world because of their alluring agricultural landscapes and historic villages. Terraced rice fields in the Philippines and

Indonesia, villages in southern and eastern Africa, and the plantation landscapes of Sri Lanka, India and the USA for instance, wield a significant appeal to tourists who have an interest in seeing traditional life and agrarian lifestyles. Cities, however, especially capital cities, tend to be the most popular heritage destinations in terms of visitor numbers, as these are viewed as centers of culture, the arts and national treasures. Most well-known museums, stadiums, churches and mosques, historic homes and monuments are located in or very near urban areas, which, together with the role of cities as important transportation nodes and gateways for arriving tourists, sets cities apart as important clusters of heritage resources.

A final perspective on heritage tourism characteristics is where they get their information about which cultural sites to visit. Information searching and trip planning are an important aspect of tourism demand. Understanding information sources can help site marketers and managers make more informed decisions about how best to approach their potential markets. When planning their trips, the majority of frequent heritage travelers utilize the internet as their primary source of information, followed closely by recommendations from friends and relatives (see Table 2.8). They also use brochures, guide books, magazines, newspapers, television ads and travel agencies as important sources of information regarding heritage sites and cultural events. While less devoted heritage tourists use the same sources, they rely on them much less than avid heritage tourists, with the exception of word of mouth. Although it will be discussed in more depth later, it should be noted here that these differences tend to reflect the socio-economic and demographic profiles of heritage visitors, suggesting that the people more inclined to use the internet and printed sources of information for planning a trip are more educated and have higher incomes (TIA, 2003). Nearly half (40%) of heritage tourists in the USA plan their cultural activities before their trip; 38% plan site visits only after arriving in the destination, and 22% plan heritage visits both before and during the trip.

Table 2.8 Sources of information about heritage and cultural activities among US domestic travelers

Information source	Frequent heritage tourists (%)	Infrequent heritage tourists (%)
Internet	58	33
Friends and relatives (word of mouth)	48	49
Brochures	33	23
Guide books	26	20
Magazines	24	14

Hotel visitor guide	17	11
Television	13	11
Newspaper	15	9
Travel agency	12	11

Source: TIA (2003)

Other consumers of heritage tourism

There are other people and agencies that comprise part of the demand for heritage tourism, besides the tourists themselves. These include travel agents, tour operators, destination management organizations, transportation companies and other service providers. In fact, demand is a force that stimulates the production of various products, including heritage tourism, so anyone or any organization that also requires cultural products to sell to other consumers may be considered heritage consumers that form part of the broad spectrum of demand.

Heritage tour operators are manifold, and a casual browse on the internet will reveal thousands of companies offering a variety of package tours that focus on various elements of heritage. Among the most common are personal heritage packages, or genealogy tours, that take groups of people to the homelands of their ancestors to experience the lands where their forebears lived and worked, to conduct genealogical research in archives, churches, libraries and cemeteries, and help descendents locate the villages, farms and even farmhouses where their ancestors once lived. Another common heritage tour is the religious tour, of which there are many, especially Christian package trips to important religious sites in the USA, the Middle East and Europe, including Bible-based cruises (e.g. In the Footsteps of Paul) through the Greek Islands and Turkey. A third type of heritage tour is comprised of visits to sites of nationalist or patriotic importance. American heritage tours that visit Boston, Philadelphia, Washington, DC, Revolutionary War sites and Civil War sites are very popular. Many other countries have similar tours that highlight the colonial past and freedom/independence movements from the colonizing power. Fourth, there are tours that specialize in certain heritage-related hobbies, such as Second World War enthusiasts (or participants) or railway aficionados traveling to see important sites associated with the world wars or the development of trains. A fifth type of heritage tour is the kind that visits multiple living cultural areas, such as Native Americans or ethnic villages in southern China. Companies providing these experiences cater to travelers who want to experience living cultures different from their own. Hill trekking in Thailand or in the Himalayas of Nepal is as much cultural tourism as it is nature-based tourism and provides a good example of this unique phenomenon. Finally, nearly all of the most basic comprehensive tours of individual

31

countries (e.g. France or Germany) or regions (e.g. the British Isles or the Iberian Peninsula) include many cultural and heritage experiences and locations, such as castles, cathedrals, synagogues, museums, archaeological parks and ancient monuments.

While the frontline consumers of these experiences are the tourists themselves, the tour operators, motorcoach companies, hotel chains and even food services are also consumers of heritage, because they use it for their own financial gain.

NON-TOURISM DEMAND FOR HERITAGE

While they are not strictly tourists by official definition because they do not spend a night away from home, day-trippers are an extremely important part of heritage demand, and their activities are in fact a salient part of the broader tourism phenomenon. In Australia, it is estimated that 8.5 million domestic day visitors attended cultural events or went to see historic sites in 2008 – almost four times the number of international tourists undertaking the same activities (Tourism Research Australia, 2009). Museums in small towns and local monuments rely almost solely on the patronage of local residents, who make substantial economic contributions to the historic sites themselves through admission fees and donations.

To encourage visits by local residents, many heritage properties and museums, particularly those in the less-developed world, operate a dual pricing system. In this system, foreign or non-local tourists pay a higher admission fee than local residents or domestic tourists. For instance, the entrance fee at Bhaktapur, an ancient city in Nepal and a World Heritage Site, now swallowed up by Kathmandu, costs less than one dollar for tourists from South Asia (South Asian Association for Regional Cooperation (SAARC) countries), but for non SAARC citizens the charge is $10; for Nepalese admission is free. While many foreign tourists are surprised by this, and some have even been known to express discontent over being charged sometimes more than 20 times what locals have to pay, heritage managers still believe this to be an equitable solution that encourages local residents to appreciate their own heritage as well. Even if locals never visit their own heritage places, the knowledge alone that such sites exist builds community pride and continuity.

Journalists

Journalists and other media reporters are also important heritage consumers. While some of them, if they are from out of town, are tourists, local journalists are not. Nonetheless, they are crucial from a heritage perspective as they write travel stories that provide information about heritage places and cultural events for others. In doing so, they directly or indirectly promote certain destinations or attractions, or they might hurt an establishment's reputation if they have a negative experience. The media is extremely influential in tourism development and heritage visitation otherwise, and in this sense is also an important consumer of the heritage product.

School and youth groups

The formal educative role of historic sites is perhaps best seen in school group visits. In most parts of the world it is a common sight to see groups of school children on field trips at historic sites and cultural centers (see Plate 2.2). In places where heritage sites are an important part of the historic landscape and sense of place, these field excursions are often written into the school curriculum and contribute to students' experiential learning. In common with school groups, other youth organizations, such as boy scouts, hobby groups or sports teams, often utilize the past as a resource for learning and experiencing common interests.

Governments

Governments often use heritage places, historic buildings and monuments to build patriotism and ensure their citizenry's loyalty. Often the past is used as a propaganda tool to disseminate information that will help develop devotion to the state or its leaders. In fact, most countries of the world use heritage for this very purpose. In the USA, history and national heritage are often used to influence public opinion and sway decision makers and voters.

Plate 2.2 Young Israeli students visiting Jerusalem's Old City

Plate 2.3 Heritage symbols of *Juche* doctrine dot the landscape of North Korea

Various administrations in Finland have been successful in developing landscapes of war heritage throughout the country that commemorate the country's win against its much larger Soviet neighbor during the Winter War (part of the Second World War). In reproducing a patriotic landscape that is frequented by many Finns, a nostalgic and patriotic sense of place has been created and a Finnish national identity formed at purpose-built sites that never were in fact part of the original landscape of war.

In North Korea, the communist government uses heritage places to ensure that its citizens remain connected to the country's unique *Juche* form of communism that dictates every aspect of social, economic and work life. Visits by North Koreans to monuments built to memorialize great revolutionary leaders, and extol the virtues of the *Juche* ideology, are not only considered a favorite pastime but are also a requirement in the school curriculum, during leisure time and even domestic holidays (see Plate 2.3).

Community leaders and local businesses

At the local level, community leaders and businesses often utilize heritage for a variety of reasons. First, community leaders use the past to encourage people to move into a community. For instance, boasting of an industrious past or a unique ethnic heritage is one tool frequently utilized to add appeal to communities. Second, historic buildings, parks, theaters, schools or churches are commonly documented on websites and in town brochures as these are seen to validate people's claims of a high standard of living or quality of life in any given place. Potential employers frequently use this approach as a way of convincing potential new employees that their location is trendy and is a worthwhile place to live and work. Third, from the business perspective, it is a common practice to adopt heritage or elements of heritage in their names, because heritage sells. Some real-life examples include, Heritage Bank, the Heritage Residential Center, the Old Waterwheel Café, Cliff Castle Casino and the Old Town Reception Center.

There are myriad ways in which communities and business people within communities form part of the demand for the heritage product. Finally, towns, cities and villages will often establish local holidays or special events, such as fairs and festivals, to commemorate founding pioneers or unique traditions endemic to the area. From this perspective, heritage is used as a way of building community pride and socio-psychological empowerment of residents.

VISITOR MOTIVES AND EXPERIENCES

People visit historic places for a variety of reasons. Many studies have been undertaken to understand people's heritage motives. Most observers agree that there are social/personal and educative reasons involved. Socializing with others, such as family members and friends, is one of the most often-cited reasons for visiting heritage places. Developing relationships during leisure time is crucial for many people, and visiting museums and monuments is seen as a good use of time with loved ones. Other personal motives include exercise (walking), sightseeing, gaining emotive or spiritual experiences, relaxing or for business-related reasons when their work has something to do with culture. Nostalgia is another motivation and can be seen from two perspectives: nostalgia for their own past and societal nostalgia. Visiting places that relate to their own past, such as museums they visited when they were younger, is a common reason for people to take their own children. Societal nostalgia refers to a desire to visit places (and times) that are rooted in the simpler life of the past, when life was not as fast-paced and unpredictable as it is today.

From the educational perspective most people visit heritage sites and museums to learn something new about history and culture, to increase their knowledge skills in relation to a certain hobby (e.g. history, coin collecting or antiques), to encourage their children to learn or to put their knowledge to use. Most heritage visitors agree that experiences wherein they learn something new are more satisfying and memorable. Many people find that their hobbies and personal interests determine where they choose to travel and what heritage/cultural activities they undertake.

There are other sundry reasons why people visit cultural sites. These include using up spare time, getting out of bad weather, completing school assignments, getting out of the house and showing guests around.

UNMET DEMAND

One of the primary concerns of tourism managers, including heritage site administrators, is the notion of unmet demand. Simply stated this is the number of people who do not utilize heritage resources but who potentially could. This includes people who do not visit but probably would if they had an opportunity. This is known as latent demand and refers to potential demand that remains unmet because of a variety of factors including a lack of information or a lack of money. All forms of unrealized demand can involve people who rarely visit, people who used to visit but no longer do or individuals who have never visited. A knowledge of latent demand for heritage can help managers understand how they might change their programs, cater to infrequent guests, devise ways to attract new visitors or entice back those who have visited in the past.

There are several primary reasons why people do not visit heritage sites or participate in cultural events. The leisure constraints literature suggests that participation barriers come in three main forms: intrapersonal, interpersonal and structural. Perhaps the most common intrapersonal constraint is a lack of interest or desire. For a significant part of the population, historic buildings, archaeological sites, cultural festivals and museums are uninteresting and uninviting. In this case, other activities, or none at all, take up their leisure time.

For some individuals, a lack of education and experience keeps them away. As noted above, heritage tourists tend to be more educated and aware of the world around them than the average person. Many people are unable to relate intellectually to museum exhibits or archaeological areas, and there is a connection between being socially con-ditioned in childhood to visit historic places and behavior later in life. People who were not socialized into site and museum attendance while they were young will be less likely to visit these places as an adult.

People with disabilities may also be restricted by a number of intrapersonal, inter-personal and structural constraints. Structurally speaking, physical barriers, such as rocks, trees, steep inclines or difficult building structures, prevent the wheelchair-bound visitor from accessing all of a heritage area. From an interpersonal viewpoint, there may also be a physical dependence on someone else or a fear of negative reactions towards them by other visitors. Intrapersonal constraints include skill gaps, health problems, social fears and a lack of knowledge about places.

For some latent visitors, a lack of money and time is a salient reason for not visiting. Fiscal deterrents include high admissions costs and transportation expenses. It is difficult for people earning low wages, barely making ends meet, to spend $20–25 on an admission ticket to a living museum or historic monument. For others a lack of time overshadows a lack of money.

DEMAND SHIFTERS

The discussion above on unrealized demand pertains more to individual constraints than to general global patterns. On a macro scale, demand for cultural tourism, like demand for all forms of tourism, is inconsistent and volatile, and it changes with political, environmental, economic and social changes across the globe. These macro-types of forces that alter demand for products and destinations, both up and down, are known as demand shifters. While site-specific demand can be best understood by examining current and latent demand, demand in general for the heritage product should be seen from a larger perspective.

Demand shifters are typically viewed from two perspectives: those emanating from the tourists' home region or place of origin, and forces occurring in the destination or globally that affect departures and arrivals. From the first perspective, demographic changes are one of the most influential forces to affect consumption.

Demographic changes

The aging and retirement of large cohorts of retirees in the western world, who are healthier and more affluent than previous generations, increases demand significantly as people are living longer and possess more disposable income than their predecessors. These two variables are resulting in heritage-related travel throughout the world, especially to places associated with individuals' own heritage (i.e. ancestral homelands) or destinations where they can learn about different peoples and cultures.

Ethnic composition of tourist-generating societies also influences demand. Increased immigration and cultural diversity in traditionally homogenous societies creates awareness of foreign countries, which might spark an interest in traveling abroad, but it also means that in most cases the new émigrés have an abiding interest in visiting their homelands as often as possible. This is particularly evident among African immigrants in Western Europe and among migrants from Latin America and Asia in the USA and Canada. Changes in the ethnic makeup of origins also determine which destinations are viewed more favorably. People of African descent might gravitate more noticeably toward historic sites associated with famous black people or slave-related attractions. Immigrants in North America, Australia and Western Europe from less-developed parts of the world have a stronger propensity to return to the homeland on vacation to visit relatives and friends.

The smaller average family size, which has been most notable since the 1960s, is another important demographic trend. This, together with the increasing affluence associated with two family incomes, allows people to travel more often to more distant places. Much of this involves visitors to national shrines and other cultural destinations.

Economic variables

In terms of economic trends, it is fairly obvious that when unemployment rates rise, travel declines. Travel is considered a dispensable luxury during times of economic hardship. The current global economic crisis (2007–2011) is illustrative of this, as many people have cut travel completely out of their budgets until the fiscal climate begins to stabilize. Millions of people have recently lost their jobs and their homes; in these dire circumstances, travel is one of the first items to be trimmed from the family budget. As well, there is a direct correlation between currency exchange rates and international travel. When rates are favorable people will travel abroad. When exchange rates become unfavorable, travel slows down. Personal holiday travel is the most elastic in relation to exchange rates; business travel tends to remain fairly constant during periods of currency devaluation.

The global economic crisis has caused more people to stay home, and many cultural destinations have suffered the consequences. However, this has given rise to a new concept known as 'staycations' wherein people 'vacation' closer to home, in their own communities and regions. Thus, they behave like tourists but spend like locals. Visiting museums, historic houses, gardens and other cultural attractions at home has, to some extent, replaced the vacation abroad.

Political climate

Political circumstances have a profound influence on demand for tourism as well. As already noted, an extreme example is terrorism and war. These have obvious downturn effects not only in the countries where the conflicts occur but in their broader regions and throughout the entire world. One of the most momentous political shifters during the past two decades was the collapse of state socialism (communism) in Eastern and Central Europe. With the fall of communism in countries like Poland, the Czech Republic, Bulgaria, Romania, Serbia, Albania and the successor states of the former Soviet Union, there has been a huge influx of tourists to these countries. This trend elevated several of them to the World Tourism Organization's list of top 20 destinations because of the newfound freedom to visit there. People of Polish or Romanian decent living abroad could now visit their homelands freely without fear of detainment or government harassment. Many emigrants from the region who left following the Second World War were not permitted to return or they might face imprisonment in some cases. The disintegration of the communist system has created a huge global demand for the countries of Eastern Europe. Mongolia, China, Vietnam and Cambodia, all rich in heritage, have faced similar changes in Asia. Even though China, Cambodia and Vietnam remain communist states, they have adopted economic systems that resemble capitalism; they welcome foreign visitors and encourage tourism growth, something the European communist states did not do.

Other political issues relate to travel restrictions, passports and visas. In 2003, the Department of Homeland Security began requiring a transit visa for all passengers transferring between flights in American airports, even if they do not leave the airport building. This is only one of several new regulations initiated to fight the threat of terrorism. This has been a point of contention between the USA and some of its allies. Citizens of most Latin American, Caribbean, Asian, African and Pacific Island countries must now obtain a transit visa just to change airplanes in a US airport.

As part of its national security measures, the US government recently ratified a law that requires passports for all travel into and out of the USA, including by foot and car to Mexico and Canada. Canadians have always been permitted to enter the USA with only proof of citizenship (e.g. a birth certificate) and vice versa. Americans have long been able to visit Mexico without a passport. Now passports (or passport cards) are required of everyone when entering the USA. The governments of Canada, Mexico and several Caribbean islands have protested against the US government's decision, suggesting that such a passport requirement (only about one quarter of Americans possesses a valid passport) will create a huge drop in American arrivals. For many Americans, travel to Canada, Mexico and the Caribbean before 2009 was appealing because passports were unnecessary.

Seasonality

Periodic variations in demand for tourism products are known as seasonality. There are two general types of seasonality: natural and institutional. Institutional seasonality occurs as a result of human variables, including school breaks, public holidays and special events. Natural seasonality results from naturally-occurring phenomena, including weather and climate (see Plate 2.4). While heritage tourism tends to see lower levels of seasonal variation than beach-based, nature-based and sport-based tourism, it does indeed experience varying degrees of demand throughout the year. Figure 2.2 illustrates clear seasonal changes in demand at Independence National Historic Park in Philadelphia, Pennsylvania, USA, where visitation is highest during the summer months when children are out of school. Visitor numbers are especially high in July owing to the fact that America's Independence Day is celebrated on July 4, and Philadelphia, as the first capital of the USA, is a desirable place to be on that day.

Special events and holidays are important causes of institutional seasonality and are common demand shifters. These can include festivals, public holidays, school breaks, sporting events or other periodic occurrences that increase demand for places and products. Mega sporting events, such as the World Cup, the Olympics, the World Series (baseball) and the Super Bowl (American football), are extremely popular events that

Plate 2.4 Signs of natural seasonality on a heritage trail in New Brunswick, Canada

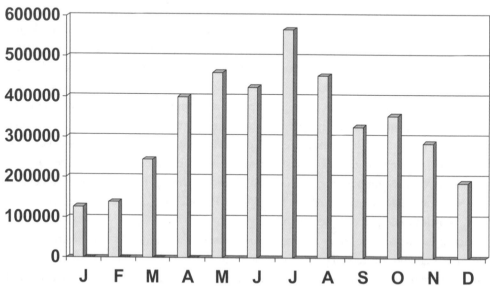

Figure 2.2 Monthly visitation at Independence National Historic Park, Philadelphia, USA, 2009

draw tens of thousands of people physically to a place and deliver considerable media exposure to others. Communities throughout the world compete to host such large-scale events because of the numbers of tourists they produce.

Religious and public holidays cause notable shifts in travel patterns. Easter in Jerusalem and Christmas in Bethlehem are the Holy Land's busiest times of the year, and both relate to important heritage events in the lives of Christians. Labour Day, Thanksgiving, Remembrance Day, Anzac Day, Independence Day and other such public holidays provide larger blocks of leisure time, which are often used to visit cultural festivals and heritage places.

Climate and weather are important demand shifters that also create seasonal patterns of high and low demand. The cultural attractions of Europe receive most of their annual visitation during the summer months (June–August) when the weather is warm and sunny. The religious sites in northern India for Buddhists and Hindus are busiest during the dry season and winter months, October–April. Summer monsoon season is unbearable for many pilgrims and cultural tourists, particularly because at outdoor sites walking is the primary means of getting around.

Low season is when demand for cultural attractions is reduced. From a purely economics perspective this is seen negatively by the destination because it translates into less regional income, fewer jobs and reduced tax income for governments. Heritage sites can attempt to counteract the effects of low season by hosting special events, such as plays, concerts, weddings and antique shows. They can also reduce their entrance fees to be more inviting to residents and tourists.

SUMMARY AND CONCLUSION

Hundreds of millions of people travel every year in search of cultural experiences. Many travel specifically to visit cultural areas and heritage sites, while others simply stumble upon them while traveling for other purposes. Serious cultural tourists have a desire to learn or enliven their hobbies. Casual heritage visitors are less inclined to engage deeply with historic places but enjoy spending time with loved ones or having a relaxing experience.

Estimates suggest that approximately 85% of the general population can be considered current or potential heritage tourists. Many different factors determine demand for heritage products at global and personal levels. Among these are socio-economics, worldwide political relations, demographic characteristics, climatic variations, physical abilities or disabilities, temporal constraints and available leisure time. Demand for heritage tourism is growing rapidly, as people realize the importance of the past in their current lives and the value of sharing it with others. There is no doubt it will continue to grow as long as there are cultural resources to satisfy the need.

REVIEW QUESTIONS

1. In what ways do political conflict and economic instability affect the growth of tourism? How in particular do they influence consumption of cultural heritage tourism?

2. Why would it be important for destination planners and marketers to understand where heritage consumers come from?

3. How might domestic demand for cultural resources differ from that of international visitors?

4. What marketing or research value is there in dividing heritage consumers into different types based upon their person interest in the past?

5. Demographically and socio-economically how do heritage tourists differ from other tourists? Can you explain why they differ?

6. Are there other tourism-based and non-tourism consumers of culture besides tourists? In what way can they also be considered heritage consumers?

7. We know heritage managers want to understand current demand for cultural experiences. Why is it important for them to understand latent or unmet demand as well?

8. Identify at least three demand shifters from each of the categories of political, economic and demographic. How do these influence current and future demand for heritage?

RECOMMENDED READING

Alzua, A., O'Leary, J.T. and Morrison, A.M. (1998) Cultural and heritage tourism: Identifying niches for international travelers. *Journal of Tourism Studies* 9(2), 2–13.

Apostolakis, A. (2003) The convergence process in heritage tourism. *Annals of Tourism Research* 30, 795–812.

Balcar, M.J.O. and Pearce, D.G. (1996) Heritage tourism on the west coast of New Zealand. *Tourism Management* 17, 203–212.

Ballantyne, R., Packer, J. and Hughes, K. (2008) Environmental awareness, interests and motives of botanic gardens visitors: Implications for interpretive practice. *Tourism Management* 29, 439–444.

Beeho, A.J. and Prentice, R.C. (1997) Conceptualizing the experiences of heritage tourists: A case study of New Lanark World Heritage Village. *Tourism Management* 18, 75–87.

Cameron, C.M. and Gatewood, J.B. (2008) Beyond sun, sand and sea: The emergent tourism programme in the Turks and Caicos Islands. *Journal of Heritage Tourism* 3(1), 55–73.

Chandler, J.A. and Costello, C.A. (2002) A profile of visitors at heritage tourism destinations in east Tennessee according to Plog's lifestyle and activity level preferences model. *Journal of Travel Research* 41(2), 161–166.

Davies, A. and Prentice, R. (1995) Conceptualizing the latent visitor to heritage attractions. *Tourism Management* 16, 491–500.

Falk, J.H. and Dierking, L.D. (2000) *Learning from Museums: Visitor Experiences and the Making of Meaning.* Lanham, MD: AltaMira.

Fodness, D. (1994) Measuring tourist motivation. *Annals of Tourism Research* 21, 555–581.

Garrod, B. and Fyall, A. (2001) Heritage tourism: A question of definition. *Annals of Tourism Research* 28, 1049–1052.

Giusti, E. (2008) Improving visitor access. In L. Tallon and K. Walker (eds) *Digital Technologies and the Museum Experience* (pp. 97–108). Lanham, MD: Rowman and Littlefield.

Goodall, B., Pottinger, G., Dixon, T. and Russell, H. (2004) Heritage property, tourism and the UK Disability Discrimination Act. *Property Management* 22(5), 345–357.

Goodall, B., Pottinger, G., Dixon, T. and Russell, H. (2005) Access to historic environments for tourists with disabilities: A compromise? *Tourism Review International* 8, 177–194.

Goodall, B. and Zone, R. (2006) Disabled access and heritage attractions. *Tourism, Culture and Communications* 7(1), 57–78.

Hewison, R. (1987) *The Heritage Industry: Britain in a Climate of Decline.* London: Methuen.

Hood, M.G. (2004) Staying away: Why people choose not to visit museums. In G. Anderson (ed.) *Reinventing the Museum: Historical and Contemporary Perspectives on the Paradigm Shift* (pp. 150–157). Walnut Creek, CA: AltaMira Press.

Jansen-Verbeke, M. and van Rekom, J. (1996) Scanning museum visitors: Urban tourism marketing. *Annals of Tourism Research* 23, 364–375.

Kerstetter, D.L., Confer, J.J. and Graefe, A.R. (2001) An exploration of the specialization concept within the context of heritage tourism. *Journal of Travel Research* 39(3), 267–274.

Krakover, S. and Cohen, R. (2001) Visitors and non-visitors to archaeological heritage attractions: The cases of Massada and Avedat, Israel. *Tourism Recreation Research* 26(1), 27–33.

Light, D. (1996) Characteristics of the audience for 'events' at a heritage site. *Tourism Management* 17, 183–190.

Light, D.C. and Prentice, R.C. (1994) Who consumes the heritage product? Implications for European heritage tourism. In G.J. Ashworth and P.J. Larkham (eds) *Building a New Heritage: Tourism, Culture and Identity in the New Europe* (pp. 90–118). London: Routledge.

Lowenthal, D. (1994) Indentity, heritage and history. In J. Gillis (ed.) *Commemorations: The Politics of National Identity* (pp. 41–59). Princeton, NJ: Princeton University Press.

Masberg, B.A. and Silverman, L.H. (1996) Visitor experiences at heritage sites: A phenomenological approach. *Journal of Travel Research* 34(4), 20–25.

Mazanec, J.A. (1992) Classifying tourists into market segments: A neural network approach. *Journal of Travel and Tourism Marketing* 1(1), 39–60.

Mazzanti, M. (2003) Valuing cultural heritage in a multi-attribute framework microeconomic perspectives and policy implications. *Journal of Socio-Economics* 32, 549–569.

McIntosh, A. (1999) Into the tourist's mind: Understanding the value of the heritage experience. *Journal of Travel and Tourism Marketing* 8, 41–64.

McKercher, B. and du Cros, H. (2003) Testing a cultural tourism typology. *International Journal of Tourism Research* 5(1), 45–58.

Nyaupane, G., White, D.D. and Budruk, M. (2006) Motive-based tourist market segmentation: An application to Native American cultural heritage sites in Arizona, USA. *Journal of Heritage Tourism* 1(2), 81–99.

Okrant, M. (2006) *Heritage and Nature-Based Tourism in the Northern Forest Region: A Situation Analysis.* Bethlehem, NH: North Country Council and Northern Forest Center.

Poria, Y., Butler, R. and Airey, D. (2003) The core of heritage tourism. *Annals of Tourism Research* 30, 238–254.

Poria, Y., Butler, R. and Airey, D. (2004) Links between tourists, heritage and reasons for visiting heritage sites. *Journal of Travel Research* 43(1), 19–28.

Poria, Y., Reichel, A. and Biran, A. (2006) Heritage site perceptions and motivations to visit. *Journal of Travel Research* 44(3), 318–326.

Powe, N.A. and Willis, K.G. (1996) Benefits received by visitors to heritage sites: A case study of Warkworth Castle. *Leisure Studies* 15, 259–275.

Prentice, M.M. and Prentice, R.C. (1989) The heritage market of historical sites as educational resources. In D.T. Herbert, R.C. Prentice, and C.J. Thomas (eds), *Heritage Sites: Strategies for Marketing and Development* (pp. 143–190). Aldershot: Avebury.

Prentice, R.C. (1989) Visitors to heritage sites: A market segmentation by visitor characteristics. In D.T. Herbert, R.C. Prentice, and C.J. Thomas (eds) *Heritage Sites: Strategies for Marketing and Development* (pp. 1–61). Aldershot: Avebury.

Richards, G. (1996) Production and consumption of European cultural tourism. *Annals of Tourism Research* 23, 261–283.

Richards, G. (2001) The market for cultural attractions. In G. Richards (ed.) *Cultural Attractions and European Tourism* (pp. 31–53). Wallingford: CAB International.

Timothy, D.J. (1997) Tourism and the personal heritage experience. *Annals of Tourism Research* 34, 751–754.

Timothy, D.J. (2010) Highways and byways: Car-based tourism in the United States of America. In B. Prideaux (ed.) *Drive Tourism: Trends and Emerging Markets* (pp. 172–193). London: Routledge.

Timothy, D.J. and Boyd, S.W. (2003) *Heritage Tourism*. Harlow: Prentice Hall.

US Department of Commerce (2005) *Cultural and Heritage Tourism in the United States*. Washington, DC: US Department of Commerce.

RECOMMENDED WEBSITES

Canadian Heritage – http://www.pch.gc.ca/eng

Cultural Heritage Tourism Factsheet – http://www.preservationnation.org/issues/heritage-tourism/additional-resources/2010-CHT-FactSheet.pdf

History Field Trips – http://www.mnhs.org/school/images/fieldtrips_2008.pdf

New Zealand Ministry for Culture and Heritage, Demand for Cultural Tourism – http://www.mch.govt.nz/publications/cultural-tourism-research/CulturalTourimResearchP1.html

The Heritage Council – http://www.heritagecouncil.ie/

UNESCO Patrimonito – http://whc.unesco.org/en/patrimonito

US National Park Service Statistics – http://www.nature.nps.gov/stats

World Travel and Tourism Council – http://www.wttc.org/

CHAPTER 3

THE HERITAGE SUPPLY: ATTRACTIONS AND SERVICES

LEARNING OBJECTIVES

After reading this chapter, you should be able to:

1. Identify the wide array of heritage resources used in tourism.

2. Understand the scientific and marketing value of classifying attraction types.

3. Realize that other services besides attractions can also be important heritage resources.

4. Recognize that almost every element of the human past can be utilized for tourism purposes.

5. Discover that tangible heritage and intangible heritage are both important elements of the cultural tourism offering.

INTRODUCTION

Heritage tourism is a unique sector, for supply usually precedes demand; in most other industries, including some types of tourism, demand typically precedes supply. Heritage supply includes material objects, most notably historic buildings, vehicles, cities and towns, rural cultural landscapes, cemeteries and memorials, historic sites, museums and portable artifacts. It also encompasses intangible elements of culture and history that are passed down from previous generations and appreciated, used or consumed in some form in the present day. Some of the best examples of intangible patrimony include religious beliefs, music and dance, cultural traditions, social mores, political ideologies, language, social networks, foodways and cuisine, worldviews, immigration and cultural diversity, lifestyles, folkways and folklore, poetry and art and literature. These intangible and tangible features of the past combine to make one of the most salient attraction bases for tourism, and indeed embody much of the tourism product.

The heritage sector is also exceptional in that the resources marked for use range from the most ancient archaeological remains to locations where atrocities or cultural mega-events have recently occurred. As noted in the first chapter, heritage is whatever we inherit from the past and utilize for some purpose in the present day. The sites of the bombings and shootings of tourists and residents in Mumbai, India, in 2008, are as much a heritage site of atrocity as Ground Zero in New York City is with regard to the 2001 terrorist attacks, the World War Two Jewish concentration camps in Europe, and the 15th and 16th century slave trading forts along the coast of Ghana.

In addition to attractions, there is also a range of amenities and services that must exist for tourism to succeed. This chapter introduces several main types of cultural attractions and briefly describes additional services and resources upon which heritage tourism depends, including transportation, accommodation and shopping.

TYPES OF HERITAGE ATTRACTIONS

Heritage attractions are an important part of the tourism system. As already noted in Chapters 1 and 2, they provide a significant appeal for much of the traveling public. In 1990, Neil Leiper developed a view of tourist attractions to debunk the conventionally accepted notion that attractions, as inanimate objects, somehow exude an appeal or magnetism that draws people to them. He argued, instead, that attractions are a subsystem of travelers, central nuclei and markers that reveal information about the nucleus and persuade travelers to want to visit (see Figure 3.1). The traveler, according to Leiper, goes somewhere to satisfy a need or desire, and the decision about what destination or attraction (i.e. nucleus) to visit is heavily influenced by generating markers – information sources that exist at home before the trip begins (e.g. travel agents, the internet and TV ads). This information provides the motives for visiting a specific attraction.

The second part is the nucleus, or the central element of the attraction system. This can be any characteristic or feature of the destination a person desires to visit. In most cases there is more than one nucleus, creating clusters or lines of nuclei that can be visited on a single trip. Historic city centers with concentrations of historic homes, museums, shops and government buildings are a good example of clustered nuclei. Stopping at a museum on the way to an amusement park is an example of a linear set of nuclei. Some of the nuclei experienced on one trip may be more important than others and are seen as primary, secondary or tertiary attractions.

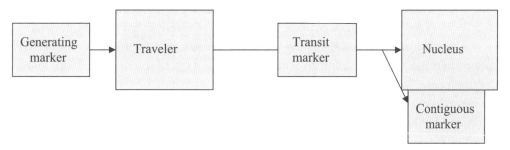

Figure 3.1 Model of tourist attractions

Source: After Leiper (1990)

The third main element of Leiper's (1990) model is the markers, which are the information sources about the nuclear elements of the attraction. Markers, he argues, link the humans to the nucleus to form the attraction system. Generating markers were noted above. Transit markers are important, too, in motivating travelers to visit a nucleus or set of nuclei. These include billboards, radio commercials and TV ads seen along the way that push the traveler further toward the destination. The final marker type is the contiguous marker, which refers to information and its source located at the nucleus.

This unique way of viewing tourist attractions suggests that the object itself (e.g. castle, church and cemetery) does not intrinsically draw people to it. Instead, there are social conditions and 'markers' (information and information sources) that cause people to visit a site as a way of fulfilling a need or want, and thus the 'attraction' is more than the nucleus being visited.

Leiper's concept is also useful in understanding tourism types. Based on a combination of the nature of tourist attractions and visitors' motives and experiences, researchers and the industry often categorize general heritage tourism into various subtypes. These types are helpful in providing theoretical frameworks for academic research, understanding people's motives and experiences, and marketing and managing sites more effectively. Industrial tourism, dark tourism and literary tourism are three prominent examples that are all part of cultural tourism but motivated and managed differently. Each of these subtypes of tourism is defined holistically by the nucleus of the journey and the traveler's own world view and influences of 'markers'.

While the model is helpful in interpreting cultural destinations and tourists' experiences, in the remainder of the book the terms 'attraction' and 'resource' will be used to refer to Leiper's 'nucleus' or object of tourist attention.

In general, heritage resources are divided into various broad categories for ease of understanding, measuring and managing. The broadest way of classifying heritage resources is by whether they occurred naturally or were human made. If heritage includes all elements inherited from the past, the concept is very broad and includes the natural realm as well. Rainforests, mountain peaks, canyons, rivers, rocky coastlines, redwood forests and desert landscapes all fit within the far-reaching scope of natural heritage. Most tourism associated with natural heritage is referred to as nature-based tourism, ecotourism or outdoor recreation. The other broad form of heritage, and the focus of this book, is cultural heritage, referring simply to artifacts, places and traditions associated with human development.

Cultural heritage can also be compartmentalized into several forms. As noted at the beginning of this chapter, cultural patrimony can be seen as tangible (having physical form) or intangible (having no physical form). A similar way is to view heritage as either built or living, which differentiates buildings or other structures from living traditions, such as ways of life, folklore and religious ceremonies.

Heritage sites may be viewed in terms of scale of notoriety, as was noted in the first chapter. For instance, some attractions are world-renowned sites that draw significant international attention. The Terracotta Warriors (China), the Pyramids of Chichen Itza (Mexico), Neuschwanstein Castle (Germany) and Great Zimbabwe (Zimbabwe) are just a few examples. Further down the scale are local museums, heritage festivals or monuments commemorating town pioneers. These places are typically of primary interest to local people or non-locals who have a personal connection.

Finally, cultural heritage may also be classified by type of attraction; typologies of heritage attractions are commonplace, and could include hundreds of different classes (see Figure 3.2). However, the discussion that follows highlights several main types of heritage attractions that have become important for tourism. Individual types of tourism, based on attraction type and tourists' experiences and motives, as well as detailed

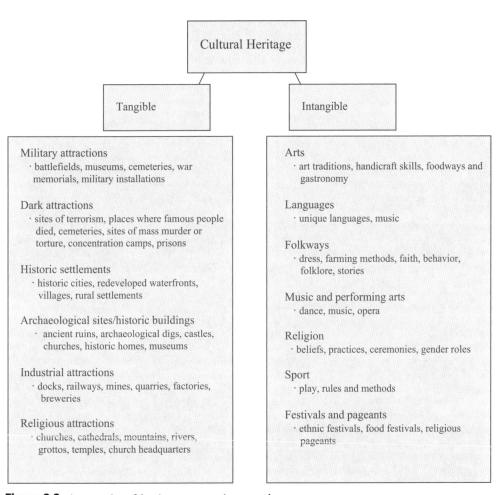

Figure 3.2 A sample of heritage attractions and types

information about various attraction types are covered in much more depth in the second half of the book and will not be elaborated on in great depth in this chapter.

Museums

One of the most pervasive types of heritage attraction is the museum – an establishment that houses collections of artifacts (see Plate 3.1). Almost every city, town and village of any consequential size in the developed world has a local heritage museum that depicts the rise of the community and commemorates important milestones in its development. In most cases, local museums have primarily a local audience and depend largely on volunteer labor. In rural regions, local museums often have an agriculture focus, while in towns and cities they sometimes focus more on the industrial past. Many of the artifacts on display are donated by residents or loaned to the museum for an extended period of time. In the USA, a common element of local museums is a room dedicated to the men and women from the community who served in the military during times of war.

National heritage museums tend to focus on patriotic elements of the past that will appeal to domestic tourists and satisfy the educational or curiosity needs of foreign visitors. National museums are very common in the developing parts of the world or in

Plate 3.1 A popular opium museum in northern Thailand

smaller countries. In the largest countries, there may be multiple national museums. Military, science, colonization and indigenous heritage are among the most important themes associated with national museums. Some museums are world famous and draw visitors from the local region, as well as from overseas. Such famous institutions as the Smithsonian, the Vatican Museums and the British Museum are examples that draw millions of visitors each year from all corners of the globe.

Besides historical museums, there are several other types of museums whose mandates fit within the broader concept of heritage. Heritage visitor centers, popular in Britain, can be seen as one type of museum or other interpretive center. Sports museums house memorabilia pertaining to various sports and athletes, and usually include uniforms, balls, awards and trophies plus famous players' personal mementos. Music museums also possess the personal belongings of famous musicians and trace the development of certain genres of music through the ages. Science centers are typically located in large cities with large catchment areas and are especially popular among children and youth. Some of them market themselves as children's museums and offer activities and experiments, and involve learning opportunities beyond just sedentary displays of relics. Art museums are another part of the heritage milieu, especially those that house the world's most beloved paintings. The Metropolitan Museum of Art in New York City, the Hermitage Museum in St Petersburg, Russia, the Louvre in Paris and the Guggenheim in Spain are among the best-known art museums in the world, containing some of the most impressive artworks of the great masters and drawing millions of visitors each year.

Historic theme parks/folk life museums

A unique type of museum that has become more salient in the past half century is the historic theme park or folk life museum. These are outdoor, living museums that aim to highlight everyday life during some set period of time and are not as concerned about housing collections of artifacts or authentic period articles. They are usually staffed with live interpreters dressed in period or cultural costumes, and in most cases the actors keep the character of the era or culture they represent.

The purpose of these types of attractions is to educate people about how life might have been during an earlier period of history or presently in different regions of a country. Homes, streetscapes, agricultural patterns, food preparation, clothing and economic activities are depicted and demonstrated to tourists. In most cases, managers try to be as authentic in their reproductions as possible but, as will be noted in the chapter on authenticity, this poses considerable challenges.

Thousands of these folk life museums have been developed all over the world since the 1800s. Most of them can be categorized into one of two types: historic villages that are frozen in time or cultural villages that depict recent or current cultural patterns throughout a region or country. In some cases these two modes overlap, perhaps with demonstrations of colonial heritage and current indigenous cultures. A well-known example of the first type is Plimoth Plantation, USA, which attempts to depict life in 17th century colonial America. In addition to its educational role, it also attempts to instill a sense of national pride and patriotism in its visitors.

Taman Mini Indonesia Indah is a good illustration of the second type of living museum. Located just outside Jakarta, Indonesia, Taman Mini strives to represent natural and cultural life in the country's islands and provinces. Architecture, dress, language and cultural performances of music and dance are the highlights of visits to the park, which is staffed by people from around Indonesia. The concept of developing a 'miniature Indonesia' was conceived in the early 1970s and has become one of the country's most important attractions for domestic and foreign tourists. The Kalevu Cultural Centre in Fiji and the Polynesian Cultural Center in Hawaii are two well-known examples of folk life parks that have become extremely popular tourist attractions for international visitors. There are also a growing number of these centers in various parts of China, which aim to display the living cultures of the country's 55 officially recognized minority groups through music and dance (see Plate 3.2). While they are becoming a more important part of the foreign tourist circuit, they are especially popular among domestic Chinese tourists.

Plate 3.2 Minority cultural center/ethnic village in Yunnan Province, China

Performing arts

Performing arts, and art in general, are a crucial part of the cultural heritage product. There are dozens of world-famous opera houses, theaters and concert halls, for example, where artists perform a variety of artistic trades (see Plate 3.3). Many of these are important historic architectural wonders on their own, even some of the more recent ones (e.g. the Sydney Opera House). These are usually located in large cities, and can be found in all parts of the world. Compared to some Asian societies, the European concept of performing arts and the facilities that developed around them are of a more recent vintage, even if they are centuries old, while there are many venues in places such as China, Japan and Korea that are home to ancient traditional dance and music forms.

Generally the arts and art centers are classified as heritage in two ways: the buildings and the performances/artworks. In the first case, the buildings themselves are historic structures that contribute importantly to the heritage milieu of urban areas. The ruins of several ancient Greek and Roman theaters in Greece, Israel and Italy are still used today as backdrops to operas, concerts and other theatrical performances. Examples include the Roman Coliseum, where contemporary concerts are performed in an ancient setting. Several ancient theaters in Greece are also used today for concerts and plays, including the Theatre of Dionysus (4th century BC) and the Herodeion (2nd century AD).

Plate 3.3 Sydney Opera House, one of the world's iconic performance centers

Although not as ancient as these, there are many more modern theaters, concert halls and opera houses that are important heritage buildings for tourists and are usually included on city tours, even if performances are not attended. The Teatro alla Scala in Milan, Italy, for instance is one of the most celebrated historic opera houses in the world (built 1778) and adds a considerable heritage value to the city of Milan. Likewise, the Royal Opera House (current structure built 1857–1858) is an important heritage site in London, England (see Table 3.1). Many tourists visit these theaters because of their remarkable architecture, elaborate décor and historic role in the development of the cities where they are located.

Table 3.1 Famous performing arts centers that are popular cultural heritage attractions

Opera house/theater	Year built	Location
Bolshoi Theater	1824	Moscow, Russia
Royal Opera House	1858	London, England
Teatro alla Scala	1778	Milan, Italy
Metropolitan Opera House	1903	New York City
Théâtre de l'Académie Royale de Musique	1821	Paris, France
Sydney Opera House	1959–1973	Sydney, Australia
Victoria Theater and Concert Hall	1905	Singapore
Wiener Konzerthaus	1913	Vienna, Austria
Vigadó Concert Hall	1859	Budapest, Hungary
Teatro Colón	1908	Buenos Aires, Argentina
Opéra de Paris	1875	Paris, France
Wiener Staatsoper	1869	Vienna, Austria
Croatian National Theatre	1895	Zagreb, Croatia
Národní Divadlo	1881	Prague, Czech Republic
Saigon Opera House	1897	Ho Chi Minh City, Vietnam
Palacio de Bellas Artes	1934	Mexico City, Mexico

The second way in which performing arts centers are heritage attractions is the performances presented in them. Beloved operas by Rossini, Mozart, Gluck and Handel have been passed down through the generations, as have musical pieces by Beethoven, Handel, Vivaldi, Bach and Brahms. Plays written by Shakespeare, Molière and Tennessee Williams have also gained international notoriety and, like operas and musical scores, are salient parts of the world's intangible, artistic heritage.

Archaeological sites and ancient monuments

Most archaeological sites are of ancient origin, although some are from more recent periods of time. These are among the most valued heritage sites everywhere; there are very few places in the world today that do not have some kind of archaeological site set aside for heritage consumption. These types of attractions are unique from others, such as historic houses and museums, in that they are generally hundreds if not thousands of years old, and many are currently in ruins, or have been in ruins at one point in time and have been restored.

These types of places range from archaeological digs where little is visible to the untrained eye, to huge mega-monuments that are well known the world over and even inscribed on UNESCO's World Heritage List. In this regard there is an important element of scale as well, for the tendency is that the larger a monument is the more famous it becomes. In fact, many of UNESCO's listed sites and the various so-called 'wonders of the world' are among the most grandiose ancient monuments on earth. For many people heritage tourism is synonymous with visits to legendary sites of international acclaim, with smaller attractions and more mundane elements of the archaeological past often not recognized.

In the USA and Canada, archaeological sites focus on the built patrimony of North America's indigenous peoples, although Civil War and Revolutionary War camps in the USA are important archaeological locations as well. Remnants of ancient cities dot the landscape of Latin America in countries such as Mexico, Belize, Guatemala, Honduras and Peru (see Plate 3.4). Colonial forts and other administrative buildings are commonplace in the Caribbean, South America and Asia. Ancient Buddhist and Hindu temples in South and Southeast Asia are important tourist attractions in those regions, especially in Indonesia, Cambodia, Laos, Vietnam, Thailand, Myanmar, India, Nepal and Sri Lanka. Monasteries, cathedrals and churches, cave dwellings, cemeteries, castles, villages and ancient megaliths are among the most common ancient monuments in Europe. Slave forts dot the coast of West Africa; antiquated religious sites have the potential to draw tourists to Ethiopia; and remnants of ancient civilizations are critical elements in the cultural landscapes of Zimbabwe, Ghana, Benin and Mali. Likewise, the Middle East is full of religious sites for Muslims, Jews and Christians, as well as locations that exemplify remnants of successive conquering empires. These are only a few of the millions of archaeological settings that exist on every continent on earth (see Table 3.2), most of which are not major tourist attractions but many of which are among the most visited places in the world.

Table 3.2 Examples of renowned ancient monuments that are important tourist attractions

Site	Location	Characteristics
Rapa Nui National Park	Chile (Easter Island)	300 AD monumental sculptures and architecture
Machu Picchu	Peru	Remnants of an ancient Incan city
São Miguel das Missões	Brazil	Ruins of 17th century Jesuit missions
Stonehenge	United Kingdom	Ancient megalithic circular structures
Pyramids of Giza	Egypt	Royal tombs and ancient wonder of the world
El Jem Amphitheatre	Tunisia	Ancient Roman amphitheater with capacity for 35,000 people
Teotihuacan	Mexico	Pre-Hispanic city temples and pyramids
Acropolis	Greece	Classic Greek architecture and temples in Athens
Borobudur	Indonesia	8th century Buddhist temple in Central Java
Mont-Saint-Michel	France	Gothic abbey on small islet surrounded by an historic village
Brimstone Hill Fortress	St Kitts and Nevis	17th century colonial fortress overlooking St Kitts
Bahla Fort	Oman	Ruins of large fort, 12th–18th century
L'Anse aux Meadows National Historic Site	Canada	Remains of an 11th century Viking village – first Europeans in America
Golden Temple of Dambulla	Sri Lanka	2,200 year old pilgrimage monastery built in a cave
Red Fort of Agra	India	16th century Mughal fort made of red sandstone
Megalithic Temples	Malta	Giant bronze-age structures on the islands of Gozo and Malta
Painted Churches of Troodos	Cyprus	Ten Byzantine churches in the Troodos Mountains
Tikal	Guatemala	Ancient temples and pyramids, remnants of large Mayan city

La Fortaleza	Puerto Rico (USA)	15th century colonial fortress built to protect the Bay of San Juan
Sukhothai	Thailand	Ancient Buddhist temples and early capital of Thailand
Petra	Jordan	Cave and rock city at the crossroads of ancient trade routes
Litomyšl Castle	Czech Republic	16th century Renaissance castle

Plate 3.4 Ancient pyramid at Tikal National Park, Guatemala

Living culture

Living culture cannot always be pinpointed at a specific location, although some places are known for the cultures that inhabit them. This category of heritage includes elements of everyday life that either individually or compounded with other elements fall prey to the tourist gaze. This is sometimes referred to as 'ethnic tourism', as the primary attraction is an ethnic or cultural group and its way of life. The living, breathing culture of a unique ethnic or cultural group as it is presently lived becomes the attraction because of its unique imprint on the cultural landscape. This does not include the staged folk life museums discussed above.

North America is home to many good examples of ethnicity-based heritage tourism. For instance, the old-order Amish and Mennonite people of Ohio, Pennsylvania, and Indiana (USA) and Ontario (Canada) have become an important attraction in those states and provinces, often to their chagrin. Their unique faith, dress, language, horse and buggy transportation, and tidy farms comprise a landscape that many outsiders find irresistible. There is also a wide range of urban ethnic islands that attract many tourists. China-towns in San Francisco, Vancouver, Los Angeles, New York and Toronto are just a few examples. Chinatowns exist all over the world and appeal to tourists for their living heritage, food, Chinese ambience and architectural milieu. The following are some of the most tourism-dependent Chinatowns in the world:

- Australia: Melbourne, Sydney.
- Canada: Vancouver, Toronto, Montreal, Victoria, Edmonton.
- France: Paris.
- Peru: Lima.
- Philippines: Manila.
- Singapore: Singapore.
- Thailand: Bangkok.
- United Kingdom: Liverpool, London, Manchester.
- USA: Honolulu, San Francisco, Los Angeles, New York City, Chicago, Detroit.

Other tourism-oriented ethnic enclaves include Little Italies in Boston, New York and Toronto, as well as Little Havana in Miami, Florida. In addition to these immigrant patrimonies, native peoples are a very important part of the tourism product, and their traditional homes, villages, ways of life and ceremonies are a salient part of living culture. Indigenous heritage will be examined in more detail later in the book.

Some aboriginal people are happy to be seen as an attraction, while others would prefer not to be. In Egypt and Jordan the native Bedouins are involved in various aspects of tourism, including offering visits to their settlements to observe everyday life and over-night stays in their tents (see Plate 3.5). The Sami of Finland, Sweden and Norway, a traditional nomadic group whose livelihood depended on reindeer herding and hunting,

Plate 3.5 Bedouin tent for tourists in Israel

are involved in tourism in all three countries. Aboriginal Australians are an important part of that country's tourism and many offer guided tours of the desert or rainforest, participate in cultural performances or host tourists in their communities (see Plate 3.6).

Heritage festivals

Most towns and villages have something unique or special they want to share with outsiders. One way of doing this is to organize festivals and other special events. This is closely related to living culture, in that much of what takes place in these local festivals is cultural in origin, often based on local folklore and may reflect the cultural characteristics of populations, at least as they once were (see Plate 3.7).

While festivals exist almost everywhere, the Midwestern USA is home to thousands of festivals. The region has a rich heritage of agriculture and ethnic migration, and most festival events have this as their focus. Festivals based on themes of cheese, pickles, cherries, watermelon, corn, sausage, apples or onions are grounded in the region's agricultural heritage. Ethnic celebrations such as Czech Festival, Tulip Time, German Fest and FinnFest attest to the importance of the region's history of migration. The main focus of these celebrations is food, music, dance, artworks and dress. Cooking competitions,

Plate 3.6 Aboriginal cultural performer in Queensland, Australia

parades, language recitations and awards ceremonies are common elements of these ethnic festivities. Throughout the USA and Canada, hundreds of festivals and other cele-bratory occasions commemorate the arrival of the Dutch, Cubans, Africans, Danes, Finns, Swedes, Germans, Chinese, Vietnamese, Ukrainians, Poles, Italians, Russians, Irish, Icelanders, Basques, French, Mexicans and others. Throughout the entire world, music and dance festivals, religious festivals and art shows are important celebrations of culture that attract many local viewers and visitors from abroad.

Religious sites

Religious sites come in a wide variety of forms. Forests, caves, rivers or grottos tend to be important attractions for pilgrims and other religious tourists. Usually these natural features become attractions because of miracles or spiritual incidences that happened nearby. Churches, cathedrals and temples are important sacred structures for Christians, as are Holy Land sites associated with Jesus Christ or his apostles throughout the Mediterranean region. For Jews, synagogues, tombs and cemeteries are considered especially sacred spaces, but the Western Wall in Jerusalem is the holiest place on earth and the focal point for Jewish pilgrimage. Mosques, graves of famous imams and sites in

Plate 3.7 Water Festival performed by the Dai people of Yunnan Province, China

various holy cities associated with the life of the Prophet Mohammed are considered the most important sacred sites for Muslims, and for Buddhists sites associated with the life and teachings of Siddhârtha Gautama (Buddha) in Nepal and India are the holiest places, together with temples around the Buddhist world that have some connection to Buddha.

Millions of devout religionists travel the world each year to these sacred sites to participate in conferences, to pray or to undertake pilgrimage ceremonies. Religious attractions are among the most pervasive, not just for pilgrims but also for general cultural tourists. If we think about some of the most impressive buildings and other historic structures in the world, it is obvious that religious edifices and other locales are among the most pervasive heritage attractions in the world. St Peter's Basilica in the Vatican City is the largest Catholic church in the world and religious center for the world's one billion Catholics. It is visited every year by millions of religious pilgrims and other curious tourists (see Plate 3.8). Almost all tours of Rome include a stop at the Basilica. Likewise, the Bahá'í Faith's Shrine of the Báb with its terraces and gardens in Haifa, Israel, are a popular attraction not only for Bahá'ís, but for other tourists in the city of Haifa too.

Even Stonehenge, Machu Picchu and the Egyptian pyramids have ancient and modern spiritual connotations and attract many modern-day pilgrims. While the people who visit

Plate 3.8 St Peter's Basilica, Vatican City, a major pilgrimage destination

these sites are not traditional pilgrims, they are 'new age' pilgrims of a different sort, who travel to ancient places as a way of gaining personal peace and fulfillment, communion with nature and spiritual growth.

The industrial past

With the Industrial Revolution of the 19th century, urban areas grew rapidly and developed spatially as people moved from the countryside to the cities in search of work in new industries. However, this would not last long, as western societies moved through a series of socio-economic changes that de-emphasized heavy industry and emphasized non-extractive and non-manufacturing, service-oriented economies. This modernization process during the mid-20th century replaced primary economic sectors/extractive sectors (e.g. mining, fishing, forestry) and secondary sectors (known as Fordist activities) (e.g. manufacturing and processing) with service industries (e.g. tourism, banking, finance, insurance – often referred to as post-Fordism). Today, most economies of the developed world are more dependent on the service sectors than they are on extractive or manufacturing industries.

This transition has led people to bemoan the modern-day materialism and over-consumption that dominate the lifestyles of Europeans, Australians, North Americans,

Plate 3.9 Mine tours on offer to tourists in southern Arizona, USA

Japanese and others, with a longing for the days when an honest living was made farming the land or working in coal mines. Since the mid- and late-1900s, the industrial past of countries and regions is now seen as an important heritage that should be preserved and interpreted for future generations. Dockyards, mines, railways, factories, assembly plants, mills, fishing boats, breweries and distilleries, canals and canal locks are some of the most common elements of the industrial patrimony currently being preserved and promoted as heritage (see Plate 3.9).

An important element of this is the concept of gentrification or urban regeneration. This refers to the resurrection and reinvention of old city centers into heritage zones that tend to have a recreation and tourism slant. Shopping, dining, entertainment and museums dominate the landscapes of urban renewal. The overhauling of derelict landscapes and the revitalization of industrial zones is an important part of gentrification. Many examples exist of waterfronts that were at one time geared toward heavy industry, such as manufacturing and shipping, being rebuilt, renovated and renewed to create recreation space and add a tourist appeal to cities. Baltimore, Toronto, Sydney, Tel Aviv and London are just a few examples of this de-industrialization and reinvention process.

War and political patrimony

The heritage of war is one of the most popular forms of tourist attraction. Battlefields are extremely popular heritage sites in most places where there has been conflict. The battlefields of the First and Second World Wars in Europe and Japan are very popular destinations, especially among war heritage enthusiasts. In the US, Civil War, Revolutionary War and War of 1812 battlefields are scattered throughout the east and southeast and have become important attractions, many of which are conserved and managed by the National Park Service or various state parks services. The most famous battlefield in the USA is Gettysburg, where 51,000 soldiers were killed or injured in an 1863 decisive battle between the north and south in the Civil War (see Plate 3.10). Battlefields in Israel, Cambodia, the UK, France, Mexico and many other countries are being excavated, interpreted and managed. Other important war heritage sites include cemeteries, monuments, gravesites, hospitals and command centers.

Another type of political attraction is functioning government offices. Capitol buildings, houses of parliament, embassies, presidential residences and other such political edifices are popular attractions (see Plate 3.11). Embassy tours, or embassy hunting, in capital cities is a common activity where people track down various embassies with maps and cameras. There is some kind of excitement associated with seeing, and possibly even entering the compound of, a foreign embassy.

Nationalist monuments, or memorials that commemorate founding pioneers, glorify war heroes or stand for some political ideology are important attractions. Often these are considered sacred ground and are used for propaganda purposes both for foreign and domestic tourists.

Plate 3.10 Gettysburg National Military Park, Pennsylvania, USA

Plate 3.11 A political attraction in Buenos Aires, the Congress of the Argentine Nation

Sites of death and human suffering

Battlefields can be counted also as sites of human suffering and death. Thanatourism, and dark tourism, refer to visits to sites of suffering and death, of which there are many. Holocaust locations in Europe and museums in Israel and the USA are important places where the atrocities enacted upon Jews by the Nazis are memorialized. The prisons of South Africa (e.g. Robben Island) where freedom fighters and political prisoners were incarcerated during the apartheid era are salient political and dark attractions. One of the most significant attractions in Rome is the catacombs beneath the city streets. The monument at Lockerbie, Scotland, memorializing the terrorist air disaster there in 1988; the golden flame marking the location of the death of Princess Diana in Paris; Ground Zero and its new monument in New York City where the World Trade Center fell in 2001; and the 1982 war memorials on the Falkland Islands have all become important heritage sites that draw mourners and curiosity seekers.

Agritourism and foodways

Tourist activities based on agriculture, farming and viticulture are part of the broader category of agritourism. This is an important aspect of heritage tourism, as agriculture is an important socio-economic foundation for many regions of the world. It forms the basis for an agrarian heritage that intertwines nature and culture and which determines many aspects of living culture such as cuisine, dress and celebrations. The attractiveness of agritourism can be seen from several perspectives: staying on farms, u-pick farms, touring properties and facilities, and tasting.

Farmstays and dude ranches allow visitors to stay on farms or ranches, participate in the chores, ride horses, herd sheep or cattle and eat the fruits of their own labors. U-pick farms are especially popular in rural areas near large cities, as urbanites can travel to the countryside to pick their own fruits, vegetables or eggs. In most cases this is a day-trip activity, but it is nonetheless an important recreational pursuit. Farmstays and u-pick farms have become an important element of heritage owing to their nostalgic element. For many visitors, staying on a farm or picking their own fresh fruit takes them back to younger years when they might have grown up on a farm or visited grandparents on the farm. For many, self-pick activities are a way for young families to get out of the city and for parents to show their children the origins of the fruits and vegetable products they buy at the store.

Touring farms is another very salient tourist activity in many places. Pineapple plantations in Hawaii, papaya plantations in Jamaica, nutmeg farms in Grenada, olive orchards in Italy or sheep farms in New Zealand are important agro-heritage sites that are not only a part of the historic agricultural landscape, but in many cases they are a strategic part of the national image or identity associated with those places (see Plate 3.12). On such tours, visitors can observe processing and packaging for worldwide distribution. Tasting fruits or wines at wineries is another important activity that tourists enjoy and which contributes to the heritage ambience of the rural experience.

Plate 3.12 An important agro-heritage attraction is the Agrodome in New Zealand

Cuisine and foodways are a related heritage resource for tourism. Regional cuisines are an important part of the intangible heritage, as they reveal a great deal about a people's past, their cultural norms and values, relationships with nature, inter-generational passing of recipes and methods and the realities of place and geography. Many destinations have become famous in part because of their associations with important and widespread foodways – Italy, China, Mexico and Thailand being just a few examples whose food traditions have influenced international gastronomy.

Literary and film locations

Places associated with authors or characters in novels, short stories, plays, nursery rhymes and television series are destinations for what are often referred to as literary tourists. Literary heritage includes the homes of authors, the natural landscape of the region where they lived and worked, their studios, the settings (real or imagined) of the stories they created and museums associated with these places and events. The successful *Anne of Green Gables* novel series and subsequent television series (*Road to Avonlea*), which took place on Prince Edward Island, Canada, have been a critical force for the success of tourism in that province. The home (Green Gables) that inspired the concept still stands and the home of Lucy Montgomery (the author) and the created TV village of Avonlea

67

are all part of the tour circuit at Cavendish. Much of the island's tourism commercialization efforts revolve around *Anne of Green Gables*. Even gift shops and cafes in the capital city, Charlottetown, quite a distance from the Green Gables farm, are themed with Anne memorabilia and the characters feature prominently in the province's promotional campaigns.

Other popular places, many of them mythical, have become important literary heritage places. Sherwood Forest, the famed home of Robin Hood, is a popular attraction in the UK, and many places in the western USA associated with the novels of Louis L'Amour are reaping the benefits of being mentioned in his fictions.

Even the sets and locations of modern films have become a type of heritage attraction because of their popularity with successful movies. Several guidebooks, for instance, lead Lord of the Rings enthusiasts to various sites in New Zealand. Locations where scenes were filmed have become very important destinations, such as the remains of the set of Hobbiton, located near the town of Rotorua on the North Island (see Plate 3.13). The farmer who owns the land where the former set is located has established a lucrative business based on people's interest in the film and its locations. This film-induced tourism is widespread and benefits every time a place is highlighted in a popular motion picture.

Plate 3.13 The Hobbiton movie set, in New Zealand, is an example of literary heritage

Heritage trails

Tourist trails can be viewed from a number of different scales. Large, multi-nation trails, such as the Silk Road or La Ruta Maya, are important long-distance routes that are hard to traverse, but doing so in any degree of distance requires an automobile. Subnational routes are also important and may be large in scale. The Oregon Trail and Santa Fe Trail in the USA are good examples that appeal to history enthusiasts who are able to traverse the length of the trails by car or motorcycle. The Jesus Trail in the Holy Land traverses many of the locations Jesus was said to have walked 2000 years ago (see Plate 3.14). Smaller-scale urban or rural routes are also popular attractions, such as the Freedom Trail in Boston, which extends four kilometers inside the historic city and passes several important historic sites related to the early colonial settlement of the USA and its struggle for independence. The route is marked on the ground with a red brick trail, which is easy

Plate 3.14 The Jesus Trail and trail marker near Nazareth

for tourists to follow, and each site is well interpreted. The Hadrian's Wall Path National Trail is a popular countryside trail that runs a distance of 138 km in northern England along the Roman Hadrian's Wall.

What makes heritage trails particularly important is their ability to link individual sites together into a connected circuit that encompasses a single or double theme. Individually, small-scale attractions might not have the appeal to attract visitors from far away, but when linked with other sites on a themed trail or route, they support each other and encompass a larger product.

OTHER HERITAGE SERVICES

Leiper's (1990) attraction model acknowledged 'surrounds of a nucleus', which included commercial support services that add appeal to the attraction or facilitate tourism. Of course heritage tourists require the same services other tourists do, including lodging, food and transportation. However, there are perspectives on these elements of supply that are unique to cultural tourism. This last section describes the relationship between these tourist services and heritage.

Transportation

Global travel for the purpose of visiting historic sites and other cultural places is undertaken primarily by airplane. Once in the destination, however, the most common mode of transportation for heritage enthusiasts is personal car or rental car. Whether one drives his/her own vehicle to cultural sites nearby or flies into a destination and hires a car, personal automobiles afford the highest degree of flexibility and mobility of all types of transportation and are therefore the favored mode of travel among heritage tourists, many of whom tend to want to explore a series of sites, rather than just one or two. Someone following a wine route, or a long-distance pilgrimage trail would have a considerable advantage if traveling by car.

Trains, while popular in some parts of the world, do not offer the same degree of freedom to visit a multitude of heritage places in one day or on one circuit. Following the automobile, buses or coaches are the most important, a reflection of the role of heritage places in package tours. Most tours of Europe, for example, include a heavy dose of cathedrals, castles, churches, museums, Roman ruins, performing arts, archaeological sites and industrial areas. In essence, most package tours of Europe by companies such as Globus, Thomas Cook and Europa Tours are overwhelmingly heritage tours.

Perhaps of most relevance here, however, is the notion of transportation as heritage. The best example of this is historic railways and trains. Since the 1970s, there has been a substantial growth of heritage railways catering to tourists, especially those for whom railroads and trains are a hobby (see Plate 3.15). In any case, their popularity lies in the

Plate 3.15 Tourists riding the historic Kuranda Scenic Railway near Cairns, Australia

novelty of historic trains and renowned railway routes. While there are some lines that have functioned for many years (e.g. the Trans-Siberian Railway) and are therefore themselves historic in nature and become a heritage experience, in most cases heritage railways are old and famous lines that have been restored to offer heritage experiences in their own right.

One of the most famous of these is the Orient Express, which originally ran from London and Paris to Istanbul, Turkey, and was considered among the great luxury railway experiences of the world. During its lifetime, it has traversed several different routes, many of which have ceased to exist. Today, the route runs from Paris to Vienna, but there is talk of resurrecting the Istanbul portion in the near future.

Heritage railways are often linked to mining, frontier settlement and historic routes in areas of high cultural or natural amenity. One that fits the third definition is the Grand Canyon Railway, which was first established in 1901 for mining purposes. Soon, however, its owners realized the economic potential of transporting tourists to and from the Grand Canyon from Flagstaff, Arizona. The railway was highly instrumental in developing tourism at the Grand Canyon and in the state of Arizona more generally. In 1968, the operation ceased as people began to view cars as the best alternative. In 1989, however, a group of investors purchased the railroad and began offering passenger services. The

Table 3.3 A selection of heritage railways of interest to tourists

Name of heritage railway	Location
Isle of Man Railway	Isle of Man
Heber Valley Historic Railroad	United States
Ferrocarril Chihuahua al Pacífico	Mexico
Tarn Light Railway	France
Old Patagonian Express	Argentina
Östra Södermanlands Järnväg	Sweden
Kalka-Shimla Railway	India
Kuranda Scenic Railway	Australia
Darjeeling Himalayan Railway	India
Shangri-La Express	China
Čierny Hron Railway	Slovakia
Krøder Line	Norway
Port Stanley Terminal Rail	Canada
Glenbrook Vintage Railway	New Zealand
Mocăniţă	Romania
West Clare Railway	Ireland

trains and the train ride are viewed as an important heritage experience that allows passengers to view nature and culture in relative comfort.

Hundreds of heritage railways exist in all regions of the world. Table 3.3 highlights several of them in diverse locations. Most of these railways have become important tourist attractions.

Heritage transportation is not limited to railways. Cruises and other water-based transport are an important part of the heritage product. Nostalgic paddle-wheeled steamboat cruises on the Mississippi River in the USA are gaining popularity as a nostalgic element of travel. American author Mark Twain painted a romanticized picture of Mississippi riverboats and life on the river that is now essentially embedded in the

American psyche. Several cruise companies operate paddle-wheel boats on the Mississippi to capitalize on tourists' feelings of nostalgia for the past and rural Americana.

Cruises have developed in recent years as important heritage experiences. Cruises in the Mediterranean, Southeast Asia and Australia focus largely on heritage sites at various ports of call, and there is an increasing number of educational and cultural cruises focusing on the lives of great philosophers and ancient civilizations; they usually visit ports with a focus on art, history, archaeology and philosophy. One of the best examples of the juncture between the cruise sector and heritage are Panama Canal cruises. While much of the content of these cruises focuses on sun, sea and sand-type tourism at stops in Mexico, Aruba and Costa Rica, the canal experience itself is certainly one of an ultimate industrial heritage phenomenon – cruising through the canal and locks that took many years to build in the early 1900s.

Pilgrimage cruises are another interesting contemporary issue that form part of the religious heritage product. Christian cruises follow routes of the apostles of Jesus Christ. In the Footsteps of Paul is a good example of such a cruise, which traces the route of St Paul through the Greek Islands and Turkey, stopping at prominent locations mentioned in the New Testament. Some Christian cruises in the Mediterranean include stops in Egypt, Israel and Italy at prominent locations associated with the lives and ministries of Jesus and his disciples.

Accommodations

Like heritage railways, lodging facilities have the potential to become important heritage attractions. Historic hotels become famous by playing an important role in the history and development of a place; achieving notoriety through film, TV, or novels; being the location of an important or newsworthy event; or because they are representative of a unique architectural style or period of history. Table 3.4 illustrates examples of famous historic hotels that are attractions and lodging facilities.

Table 3.4 Examples of famous historic hotels

Hotel	Location	Year opened
Oriental Hotel	Bangkok, Thailand	1876
Raffles Hotel	Singapore, Singapore	1887
Goldener Hirsch	Salzburg, Austria	1671
Grand Hotel Europe	St Petersburg, Russia	1875
Hotel D'Angleterre	Copenhagen, Denmark	1755

Grand Hotel du Louvre	Paris, France	1855
Mena House	Cairo, Egypt	1886
Grand Hotel Royal Budapest	Budapest, Hungary	1896
Banff Springs	Banff, Canada	1888

Source: Timothy and Teye (2009)

One of the best examples of a heritage hotel is the Raffles Hotel in Singapore. The Raffles (built 1887) is a luxury colonial hotel with an important history pertaining to the British period of Singapore. It was constructed as a lodging facility for the British and other European guests, as Asians were not permitted even to enter the establishment far into the 20th century. The Raffles also had a role in the Japanese invasion and surrender during the Second World War. In addition to its role as a luxury accommodation property, the Raffles houses a variety of boutique shops, a museum and a Victorian theater.

The national park lodges and hotels in the USA and Canada are impressive examples of historic hotels. Park lodges exude an image of rustic and exotic surroundings, and they allow guests to be immersed in a natural setting. The world's first national park, Yellowstone (est 1872), in the USA, began a trend of conservation areas that has extended throughout the world. Besides camping, accommodation at national parks in the USA is synonymous with lodges. Many lodges were built in the late 1800s and early 1900s in the national parks of the west as tourism began to grow with the widespread ownership of personal automobiles. Well-known lodges such as El Tovar Hotel (Grand Canyon National Park, Arizona) (see Plate 3.16), Bryce Canyon Lodge (Bryce Canyon National Park, Utah), Ahwahnee Hotel (Yosemite National Park, California) and Old Faithful Inn (Yellowstone National Park, Wyoming) are still attractive heritage accommodations that provide a nostalgic and romanticized lodging option for park visitors.

Some of Canada's national parks have similar lodges, sometimes known as grand railway hotels, but they differ somewhat in their age (earlier than their American counterparts) and architectural style. These railway hotels were constructed by the Canadian National Railway and the Canadian Pacific Railway in the 1880s and 1890s. The majority were built before the surrounding areas were designated national parks. Prominent examples include Chateau Lake Louise (Banff National Park, Alberta), Banff Springs Hotel (Banff National Park, Alberta) and the Prince of Wales Hotel (Waterton Lakes National Park, Alberta).

In Canada and the USA, park lodges have a high esthetic and historical value, largely owing to their association with the early railways that were critical in the countries' westward settlement and establishment of the national parks. They are also unique architecturally and stand as proof of the early importance of tourism in the west. As such,

Plate 3.16 El Tovar historic lodge on the south rim of the Grand Canyon

they are important as tourist attractions just as they are as lodging facilities and are among the most popular tourist attractions within the park boundaries. In recognition of their historic significance, several of the American national park lodges have been listed as National Historic Landmarks on the National Register of Historic Places.

Finally, bed and breakfasts (B&Bs) provide yet another insight into the heritage nature of lodging from two perspectives: the building itself is historic or the location of the B&B is one of high amenity value. In a considerable number of cases, B&Bs are established in historic homes or schools that have a heritage ambience and are in many cases designated historic properties by local heritage preservation groups or even national registers of historic places.

Paradors and castles are a popular form of historic accommodation in Europe. *Paradors* are luxury accommodations housed in historic buildings such as monasteries, castles or mansion homes. These are especially popular in Spain and a few other Spanish-speaking countries. In Portugal these are known as *pousadas*. Rooms in castles and chateaus can be rented as lodging options, and their heritage value increases their appeal for potential guests. Many historic buildings have been transformed from their original use into tourist accommodations (see Plate 3.17); monasteries and churches in Italy, pilgrim rest houses in

Plate 3.17 A four-star historic hotel in Colonia, Uruguay

Israel and India and even old factories in some urban areas of Europe and North America. Underscoring the viability of all of these is their heritage appeal.

Heritage foods and shops

While the use of heritage in general is clearly a form of consumption, there are other forms of consumption that are more literal. Obviously, eating traditional foods and cuisines is an important manifestation of that, and in fact customary ethnic foodways are an important part of the heritage milieu. This is particularly the case in places that have become known for their foodways, ingredients and preparation methods. China, France, Mexico, Thailand and Italy are a handful of countries whose cuisines have become fashionable throughout the world and add allure to these countries as destinations. Many other places that are known for special ingredients or specialty foods radiate an appeal to food enthusiasts, including paprika in Hungary, cheese in Switzerland and humus and falafel in the Middle East. Food and foodways are a salient heritage product that are gaining influence in people's travel-making decisions.

Antique shops and antiquities vendors are another central element of the heritage supply. Antique stores are very pervasive in tourist destinations. In places associated with ancient cultures and built heritage, antiquities markets are more common (see Plate 3.18).

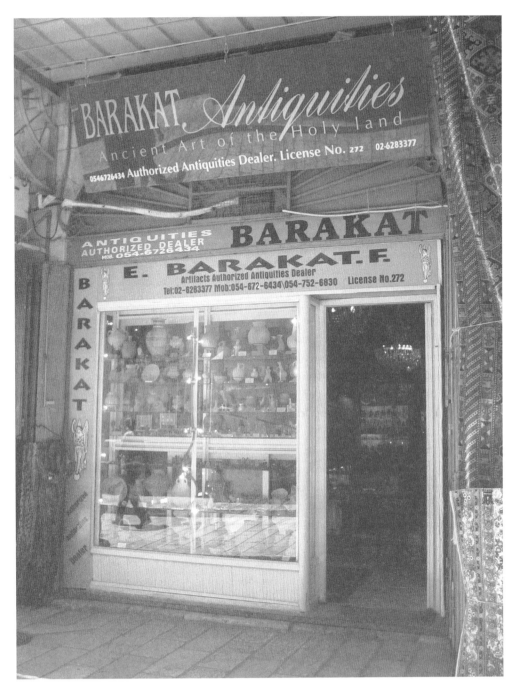

Plate 3.18 An antiquities shop in the Old City of Jerusalem

Antiques are old but not typically as old as antiquities, which tend to be hundreds of years old or older. Collecting and buying artifacts is an important pastime for many tourists. Collectors travel the world in search of ancient relics to enhance their collections. While there is a legal market for antiques, and even a limited number of antiquities, the most common antiquities trade is illicit. Western demand for artifacts fuels grave robbing, plundering from churches and other historic buildings and illegal excavations at archaeological sites. In terms of supply, this problem is most notable in the less-developed world where destitute farmers and fishermen try to supplement their paltry earnings by undertaking clandestine digs and plundering ancient tombs to forage for relics that can be sold to collectors and dealers. In just a few days, they can earn as much money as they would earn for working many months in the fields or on the fishing boat. Some indigenous people believe that harvesting ancestral riches from graves and tombs is justified because they are collecting the gifts left intentionally for them by their forebears.

SUMMARY AND CONCLUSIONS

Heritage is all around us. It comes in many sizes and forms, including intangible elements of culture that have been passed down from generation to generation. The past is a valuable commodity in the world of tourism, and many places depend on it for their economic well-being. As the heritage market continues to mature and grow, other services develop to cater to their particular needs, including lodging, transportation and food services, creating employment opportunities and other positive economic benefits in the destination.

There are many different types of heritage, ranging from sites of morbidity (e.g. death and disaster) to monuments commemorating the lives of famous authors and politicians. Living culture, built heritage and cultural landscapes are important elements of the attractiveness of most tourist destinations. As the last chapter indicated, demand for cultural experiences continues to grow. Parallel to this, new archaeological sites, historic homes and gardens, old prisons and schools, ghost towns, art forms, industrial zones and many more heritage resources are discovered, conserved and promoted. As communities all over the world begin to realize the importance of preserving their past, more and more resources will appear on the front lines of heritage tourism to be utilized by tourists and local residents.

REVIEW QUESTIONS

1. How can other tourist services, such as lodging or transportation, be viewed or utilized as heritage attractions?

2. How do attraction types and visitors' motives and experiences work together to create specific types of tourism?

3. Can you think of three world-famous museums that act as 'anchor' attractions and three local museums you might have seen that act as 'ancillary' attractions?

4. How can live performing arts and modern artworks be seen as heritage attractions?

5. Why might some cultural groups not want to become a tourist attraction?

6. In what ways and to what extent do you feel ethnic or heritage festivals can help create a sense of place or reinforce a cultural identity?

7. Explain the assertion that foods, cuisines and culinary traditions are important parts of national or regional heritage.

RECOMMENDED READING

Al-Oun, S. and Al-Homoud, M. (2008) The potential for developing community-based tourism among the Bedouins in the Badia of Jordan. *Journal of Heritage Tourism* 3, 36–54.

Ashworth, G.J. (1990) Swords into ploughshares: Defense heritage tourism as the peaceful use of the artefacts of war. *Visions in Leisure and Business* 9(1), 61–72.

Ashworth, G.J. and Hartmann, R. (eds) (2005) *Horror and Human Tragedy Revisited: The Management of Sites of Atrocities for Tourism*. New York: Cognizant.

Atwood, R. (2004) *Stealing History: Tomb Raiders, Smugglers, and the Looting of the Ancient World*. New York: St. Martin's Press.

Balcar, M.J.O. and Pearce, D.G. (1996) Heritage tourism on the West Coast of New Zealand. *Tourism Management* 17, 203–212.

Bos-Seldenthuis, J. (2007) Life and tradition of the Ababda nomads in the Egyptian desert, the junction between intangible and tangible heritage management. *International Journal of Intangible Heritage* 2, 31–43.

Boyd, S.W. (2002) Cultural and heritage tourism in Canada: Opportunities, principles and challenges. *International Journal of Tourism and Hospitality Research* 3, 211–233.

Brodie, N. (2003) Stolen history: Looting and illicit trade. *Museum International* 55(3/4), 10–22.

Bruner, E.M. (2005) *Culture on Tour: Ethnographies of Travel*. Chicago: University of Chicago Press.

Butler, R.W. and Hinch, T. (eds) (2007) *Tourism and Indigenous Peoples: Issues and Implications*. Oxford: Butterworth Heinemann.

Chang, T.C. (1997) Heritage as a tourism commodity: Traversing the tourist-local divide. *Singapore Journal of Tropical Geography* 18, 46–68.

Che, D. (2004) Reinventing Tulip Time: Evolving diasporic Dutch heritage celebration in Holland (Michigan). In T. Coles and D.J. Timothy (eds) *Tourism, Diasporas and Space* (pp. 261–278). London: Routledge.

Coles, T. and Timothy, D.J. (eds) (2006) *Tourism, Diasporas and Space*. London: Routledge.

Dinçer, F.I. and Ertuğral, S.M. (2003) Economic impact of heritage tourism hotels in Istanbul. *Journal of Tourism Studies* 14(2), 23–34.

Edwards, J.A. and Llurdés i Coit, J.C. (1996) Mines and quarries: Industrial heritage tourism. *Annals of Tourism Research* 23, 341–363.

Falk, J.H. and Dierking, L.D. (1992) *The Museum Experience*. Washington, DC: Whalesback Books.

Hall, C.M. and Zeppel, H. (1990) Cultural and heritage tourism: The new Grand Tour. *Historic Environment* 7(3/4), 86–98.

Halsall, D.A. (2001) Railway heritage and the tourist gaze: Stoomtram Hoorn–Medemblik. *Journal of Transport Geography* 9, 151–160.

Herbert, D.T. (ed.) (1995) *Heritage, Tourism and Society*. London: Mansell.

Herbert, D.T. (2001) Literary places, tourism and the heritage experience. *Annals of Tourism Research* 28, 312–333.

Homa, D. (2007) Touristic development in Sinai, Egypt: Bedouin, visitors, and government interaction. In R.F. Daher (ed.) *Tourism in the Middle East: Continuity, Change and Transformation* (pp. 237–262). Clevedon: Channel View Publications.

Ivanovic, M. (2008) *Cultural Tourism*. Cape Town: Juta.

Janiskee, R. (1996) Historic houses and special events. *Annals of Tourism Research* 23, 398–414.

Jansen-Verbeke, M. (1999) Industrial heritage: A nexus for sustainable tourism development. *Tourism Geographies* 1, 70–85.

Jansen-Verbeke, M., Priestley, G.K. and Russo, A.P. (eds) (2008) *Cultural Resources for Tourism: Patterns, Processes and Policies*. New York: Nova Science Publishers.

Kerstetter, D., Confer, J. and Bricker, K. (1998) Industrial heritage attractions: Types and tourists. *Journal of Travel and Tourism Marketing* 7, 91–104.

Krakover, S. and Cohen, R. (2001) Visitors and non-visitors to archaeological heritage attractions: The cases of Massada and Avedat, Israel. *Tourism Recreation Research* 26(1), 27–33.

Leask, A. and Yeoman, I. (eds) (1999) *Heritage Visitor Attractions: An Operations Management Perspective*. London: Thomson.

Lennon, J.J. and Foley, M. (2000) *Dark Tourism: In the Footsteps of Death and Disaster*. London: Cassell.

Makens, J.C. (1987) The importance of U.S. historic sites as visitor attractions. *Journal of Travel Research* 25, 8–12.

McKercher, B. and du Cros, H. (2002) *Cultural Tourism: The Partnership between Tourism and Cultural Heritage Management*. New York: Haworth.

McKercher, B., Ho, P., and du Cros, H. (2004) Attributes of popular cultural attractions in Hong Kong. *Annals of Tourism Research* 34, 20–25.

Prentice, R.C. (1993) *Tourism and Heritage Attractions*. London: Routledge.

Prideaux, B., Timothy, D.J. and Chon, K. (eds) (2008) *Cultural and Heritage Tourism in Asia and the Pacific*. London: Routledge.

Richards, G. (1996) Production and consumption of European cultural tourism. *Annals of Tourism Research* 23, 261–283.

Richards, G. (2001) *Cultural Attractions and European Tourism*. Wallingford: CAB International.

Sethi, P. (1999) *Heritage Tourism*. New Delhi: Anmol Publications.

Silberberg, K. (1995) Cultural tourism and business opportunities for museums and heritage sites. *Tourism Management* 16, 361–365.

Smith, L. and Akagawa, N. (eds) (2009) *Intangible Heritage*. Abingdon: Routledge.

Smith, M.K. (2003) *Issues in Cultural Tourism Studies*. London: Routledge.

Smith, S.L.J. (1988) Defining tourism: A supply-side view. *Annals of Tourism Research* 15, 179–190.

Timothy, D.J. (2006) Supply and organization of tourism in North America. In D. Fennell (ed.) *North America: A Tourism Handbook* (pp. 53–81). Clevedon: Channel View Publications.

Timothy, D.J. and Boyd, S.W. (2003) *Heritage Tourism*. Harlow: Prentice Hall.

Timothy, D.J. and Teye, V.B. (2009) *Tourism and the Lodging Sector*. Oxford: Butterworth Heinemann.

Tufts, S. and Milne, S. (1999) Museums: A supply-side perspective. *Annals of Tourism Research* 26, 613–631.

Weiler, B. (1984) Reusing our working past for recreation and tourism. *Recreation Canada* 42(2), 36–41.

Zeitler, E. (2009) Creating America's 'Czech Capital': Ethnic identity and heritage tourism in Wilber, Nebraska. *Journal of Heritage Tourism* 4(1), 73–85.

RECOMMENDED WEBSITES

American Association of Museums – http://www.aam-us.org/

Australian Heritage Council – http://www.environment.gov.au/heritage/ahc/index.html

Center for Heritage Resource Studies – http://www.heritage.umd.edu/

Cultural Heritage Tourism – http://www.culturalheritagetourism.org/

English Heritage – http://www.english-heritage.org.uk/

Heritage Conservancy – https://www.heritageconservancy.org/

Heritage Hotels and Resorts – http://www.hhandr.com/

International Council of Museums – http://icom.museum/

National Trust (UK) – http://www.nationaltrust.org.uk/main/

National Trust for Historic Preservation – http://www.preservationnation.org/

New Zealand Historic Places Trust – http://www.historic.org.nz/

Paradores de Turismo – http://www.parador.es/en/portal.do

Parks Canada – http://www.pc.gc.ca/

Taman Mini Indonesia Indah – http://www.tamanmini.com/index.php?modul=home&lang=eng

UK Heritage Railways – http://ukhrail.uel.ac.uk/

UNESCO World Heritage List – http://whc.unesco.org/en/list

US National Park Service – http://www.nps.gov/index.htm

CHAPTER 4

SPATIAL PERSPECTIVES AND HERITAGE RESOURCES

LEARNING OBJECTIVES

After reading this chapter, you should be able to:

1. Be aware of how location and place have a bearing on supply and demand for cultural tourism.

2. Recognize that the spatial form of some resources affects their manageability and how they can be conserved.

3. Know about the varying global, national, local and personal forms of heritage and how each of these manifests in heritage consumption.

4. Develop knowledge about urban heritage contexts and how cities are unique venues for heritage tourism.

5. Discover how rural regions provide unique contexts for heritage tourism.

6. Understand concepts of scale, spatial distribution, temporality, clustering and magnitude of appeal.

INTRODUCTION

Tourism is inherently a geographical phenomenon, and geographers are among the most avid researchers of tourism, one of their primary concerns being the industry's locational aspects. There are many unique spatial patterns associated with tourism, not least of which is market origins and the spread of tourism throughout the world. Of particular interest from a geographical perspective is scale and locational differences in supply and demand. This is especially true for tourism based on cultural heritage resources, as cultures vary considerably from place to place.

This chapter examines several spatial concepts in relation to the supply and demand sides of cultural tourism. First it describes the spatial forms of heritage attractions from linear, nodal and areal perspectives. It then highlights the implications of scale at global, national, local and personal levels of heritage, followed by an overview of the urban and rural contexts within which heritage resources are located. Finally the chapter identifies several additional geographical implications, such as spatial variation in supply and the principle of clustering.

SPATIAL CHARACTERISTICS OF HERITAGE ATTRACTIONS

The spatial arrangement of attractions and the components of heritage supply in a given area have long been of interest to tourism planners. Understanding these characteristics is critical for evaluating the impacts of tourism, visitor management and site maintenance and conservation. Wall (1997) contends that tourist attractions can be divided into three kinds based upon their physical-spatial attributes: points, lines and areas, with each one requiring a different approach to management, planning and commercial development.

Point resources, according to Wall, are stand-alone, individual sites where crowds of people congregate at one time in a small space. Some good cultural examples of this include ancient temples, archaeological sites, monuments, historic houses, forts, battle-fields, museums, festivals and theaters. Although there are dangers involved in this type of format, such as overcrowding, environmental degradation and a possible reduction in the quality of experience if the site is too crowded, it simultaneously creates management opportunities. For example, the concentration of customers in a small area lends itself to easier commercial exploitation and can be useful in controlling the flow of visitors and therefore the spread of ecological impacts to other areas of a site.

Stonehenge is a good example of how overcrowding required fast and controlled action to keep the monument from being damaged further. In the 1970s, thousands of people visited Stonehenge every day during the summer months, inflicting damage to the megalithic stones. Stones began to lean, they were scratched and dirty, and people had begun vandalizing them in other ways. In the late 1970s, however, the English Department of the Environment restricted entry into the stone circle itself. Today, visitors are filtered through a ticket booth and souvenir shop that are located a couple of hundred meters from the monoliths and relegated to Stonehenge's perimeter behind a small barricade. The advantage of this set-up from a point perspective is the ability to control tourists' movements in relation to the stones, to direct them along a set route via a ticket booth, shops and pathway, thereby minimizing the physical impact while still allowing the opportunity to fund conservation through admissions and concessions.

Linear attractions include lakeshores, coastlines, scenic routes, rivers and linear land-forms. Some of these have intrinsic linear properties, such as rivers, while others have been created to link point resources and to guide users along a specific path (e.g. scenic byways). Linear resources are characterized by visitors being concentrated along narrow strips of land or transportation corridors. Unlike point attractions, according to Wall (1997), these line attractions allow some degree of dispersal because they are two-dimensional, which breaks up the high concentration of visitors. Although, certain nodes along paths and shorelines still resemble point attractions and might suffer from overcrowded conditions while at the same time these nodes may also allow entrepreneurs or managing agencies to offer commercial services, such as cafes and restaurants, souvenir shops, equipment rental booths and gas stations. The danger in this, however, is that narrow strips of land can become too commercialized.

The most pertinent application of the linearity concept in cultural tourism is historic routes and heritage trails, although coastal areas and riverfronts also have considerable heritage appeal. Many nodes along long-distance trails (e.g. visitor centers, battlefields, encampments and historic buildings) are operated by public agencies or might be held in private ownership. In areas where there are multiple ownerships along a single trail, public-private collaboration is an absolute necessity. Many of the specific historic sites along the Mormon Trail and the Santa Fe Trail in the USA are managed by the National Park Service, as are several nodes along the much smaller Freedom Trail in Boston. Other trails, such as some of the rails-to-trails and scenic byways in the US, are largely on private or trust land.

Areas are larger resources that usually encompass many smaller attractions. They also attract many visitors but the spread of area resources allows visitors to be less concentrated in a single space. Examples of area attractions include historic city centers, parks and protected areas and scenic landscapes. Heritage cities are usually home to historic houses and buildings, libraries, churches, cemeteries, museums, theaters and monuments of various sorts. All of these working together create the cultural heritage milieu that appeals to locals and tourists. National parks often encompass historic cabins or homes, lodges, natural scenery, interpretive centers, hiking trails and other features that contribute to the overall ambience of the place. Like linear resources, areal destinations are sometimes comprised of nodal points where visitors congregate, such as information/interpretive centers and observation platforms. These can be key tools for destination managers to disseminate information, assist visitors in finding meals or lodging, or earn extra revenue by selling maps, souvenirs, posters, books, DVDs or other visitor-oriented merchandise.

SCALE

Related to the spatial characteristics outlined by Wall (1997), scale is an important geographical concept in understanding many aspects of heritage tourism, including demand, supply and impacts. The appeal of heritage and its resources may be viewed at different scales or dimensions of demand. Timothy (1997) introduced the concept of scale in relation to heritage attraction types and suggested that different scales of attractions appeal to different audiences – global, national, local and personal/individual, depending on the site characteristics and the visitor's degree of personal connection to the place (see Figure 4.1).

Global

Attractions that fall under the category of global heritage include sites and monuments that are well-known throughout the world and have come to symbolize certain regions, countries, ethnic groups or eventful periods of time that have impacted the entire world.

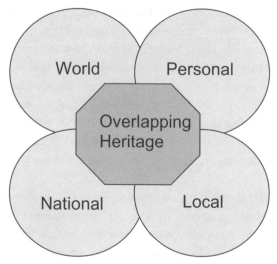

Figure 4.1 Scales of heritage resources and experiences

Source: After Timothy (1997)

Examples include the Great Wall of China, Hadrian's Wall, the Pyramids of Egypt, the Roman Coliseum, Machu Picchu and Stonehenge (see Plate 4.1). These are all iconic symbols of past societies and have achieved international visibility and distinction. They are on the 'must see' lists of many travelers and successfully draw visitors from all corners of the globe. In general terms one could hardly think of tourism in Egypt, Italy, Peru, England or China without identifying these sites as a major part of the attractiveness of the entire country or region. While these locations draw large numbers of people from around the globe, it is unlikely that they feel any kind of personal attachment to the site being visited; it is generally not connected to their own personal past.

In this case, the object of attention is of worldwide importance and may be recognized as such by being listed by UNESCO as a World Heritage Site (WHS), although not all world-scale historic sites have been inscribed by UNESCO, and not all of the WHSs listed are necessarily famous outside their own regions. In addition to being world-famous cultural attractions, many of the monuments at this scale might also be seen as national-level attractions. The Coliseum, for instance, while it might be considered an important part of the world's heritage, it also has an important role in the national past of Italy. Thus, from a scale perspective, there are many instances of overlapping or shared heritages.

National

At the national level are attractions and sites associated with the development of nation-states. Although these appeal primarily to citizens of the countries where they are located, because of a closer personal link to themselves, the sites might also attract foreign visitors who are already in the country for other reasons. These features have come to signify

Plate 4.1 An example of a global heritage site is the Roman Coliseum

national unity and patriotism. Monuments of this caliber symbolize a country's struggle for independence or a period of time that was crucial to the development of a national identity. Visits to these attractions can increase a nation's solidarity and often stir emotions that may be described as spiritual, patriotic or nationalistic; in many cases the past is manipulated by national governments to do just that.

The Tomb of the Unknown Soldier in Arlington National Cemetery (Virginia), the Vietnam Veterans Memorial in Washington, DC, and Independence Hall in Philadelphia are often cited as national attractions that instill a sense of pride and stir emotive responses in Americans (see Plate 4.2). The same can be said of battlefields, such as Gettysburg and even Ground Zero in New York City. Finland's defiant stand against the Soviet Union during the Winter War (part of the Second World War) is marked in several places by monuments and reconstructed battlefield landscapes. These are an important part of the national heritage recognized by Finns and have been established to encourage national pride.

Local/regional

Almost every place on earth wants to develop tourism. One way of doing this is by marking locations and buildings that have played an important role in the patrimony of a

Plate 4.2 National heritage includes the Tomb of the Unknown Soldier, Arlington, USA

region, town, village or other community, and promoting them as tourist attractions. Most of the time, however, these sites wield little allure for outsiders, but they can be important places to visit for locals. Most heritage sites in the world are local in their extent. They are not generally well known abroad, and they typically do not attract people from far away unless they are in the area already or there is a personal connection to the place.

Local-scale monuments have the potential to stir a sense of nostalgia or appreciation for the past in the local community. Memorials, statues or other markers raised to the memory of a community's early settlers, or historic houses and museums designated as historically important, provide a crucial foundation for local residents to appreciate their past – an experience most outsiders would likely not understand (see Plate 4.3).

By way of illustration, Texas declared its independence from Mexico in 1836 and functioned as a sovereign nation, even recognized through diplomatic relations with the USA, France and Great Britain, for 10 years, until it was admitted into the USA in 1846. The state's remarkable history as an independent country is a major point of pride for Texans. Considerable efforts have been made by the Texas Historical Commission, the Daughters of the Republic of Texas, Texas Parks and Wildlife Department and other conservation bodies to mark and interpret locations associated with the Republic's past.

Plate 4.3 This border marker between Dutch and French St Martin illustrates local heritage

In addition, the Texas Historical Commission has established a Texas Independence Trail which allows tourists to follow a route that links many of the most significant sites associated with Texas' independence from Mexico, including battlefields, Spanish missions and government buildings. This is a good example of a regional or local set of attractions. While such a trail and the marked sites are of vital importance for loyal Texans, most Americans are unaware that Texas was once an independent country.

Individual/personal

This scale of heritage is obviously the most meaningful personally to each individual. It features people, places and events associated with one's own familial past. Personal heritage travel is particularly important in the fast-paced modern world, where people seek out their own roots to lend stability and belongingness in a frenetic world fraught with insecurity and instability (Lowenthal, 1985). Members of diasporic groups traveling back to their homeland, individuals conducting family history or genealogy research away from home, people visiting friends and relatives or a person visiting places he/she lived at some point in the past are all manifestations of this type of heritage tourism.

Roots travel, or genealogy-based tourism, is becoming more commonplace today and encompasses visits to ancestral homelands, homesteads and farms, cemeteries, churches,

Plate 4.4 This 'House of Names' in Ireland illustrates a personal heritage attraction

temples, family villages, genealogy libraries, archives and libraries (see Plate 4.4). The Church of Jesus Christ of Latter-day Saints operates the world's largest genealogical library, which attracts hundreds of thousands of people each year from all over the world who come to seek out their roots. Many tour operators are now offering personal heritage tours for individuals, family groups or larger groups. Homeland heritage tours are popular products and include visits to clan lands and familial homesteads, family reunions, churches and cemeteries, meetings with distant relatives, and archival research sessions with genealogy specialists. National tourism offices, like those for Scotland, Wales, Hungary, Poland and Ukraine have done a good job of marketing themselves to their diasporic groups in North America, Australia, New Zealand and Western Europe.

SETTING

Heritage resources are found in a wide variety of physical and cultural settings. One of the most common ways of viewing heritage settings, however, is rural and urban locations. Cultural tourism occurs in urban or rural contexts, or a combination of both. Each venue has its own set of issues and implications for the resources it offers.

Urban context

Countries often have their own definitions and measures of what constitutes a city, but what they all have in common is a permanent and fairly densely populated area, a conglomeration of homes and services, and a functioning government body. Cities and towns are home to many heritage attractions, and collections of buildings and artifacts together help create a sense of place and urban milieu that emanates an unquestionable attraction for tourists.

Cities play several important roles in tourism. They are gateways, or entrances, to countries and regions via airports, train stations and bus depots. As gateways, cities function as transportation and accommodation hubs. Even people who spend most of their time in the wilderness or countryside typically use towns and cities as gateways, shopping venues and places to sleep at the beginning or end of a trip. Some wilderness enthusiasts even base themselves in a city at night, taking daytime excursions into the countryside. Thus, cities are important transit points or thoroughfares for people going from place to place.

Second, cities are major destinations. In fact, most tourism in the world today takes place in cities or sizable towns. Various subtypes of tourism exist in cities, including heritage tourism, sport tourism, health/spa tourism, beach resort-based tourism, shopping tourism, educational tourism and business travel. Because of their concentration in cities and towns, all of these sub-forms of tourism together comprise a broader classification known as urban tourism – or tourism that takes place in cities and towns. What characterizes urban tourism is its multiplicity of other forms of tourism and a wide array of attractions and services in one concentrated area.

A third role of cities is the seat of government, including not only capitols and legislative buildings but also ministries of tourism, heritage preservation bodies and other important administrative offices that develop policies and oversee the care of historic places. Laws and policies regarding the planning, development and protection of historic artifacts are usually enacted in cities. Various city-based levels of governance, such as municipal, county, state/provincial or national, establish safeguarding measures within their legal frameworks by establishing urban parks and museums, and certifying urban historic properties, such as homes, shops, hotels and factories.

Lastly, another metropolitan function is that of an economic engine for entire countries and regions. Cities are the main fiscal drivers in most parts of the world and play many economic roles, including centers of banking, stock market trading, export and import processing, manufacturing, retailing and education. These are all extremely important elements of the financial environment of places, which trickle into rural areas as well. Owing to their financial and administrative position, cities are also usually the favored location of large tour companies, travel agencies and other travel sector suppliers, including heritage tour operators and historic hotels.

Aside from these issues, what makes cities important from a heritage perspective is their assembly of historic buildings and environments (see Plate 4.5). Most urban environments include a mix of historic sports arenas or stadiums, factories, theaters and opera houses, historic houses and other buildings, statues and monuments, museums, parks, cemeteries and markets – all of which work together to create an appealing historic environment that gives cities much of their appeal. Clusters of individual structures create heritage zones that are often marketed specifically for tourism by destination marketing and management organizations. The urban cores of the world's oldest cities are usually replete with historic buildings, plazas, fountains, statues and historic markers and even archaeological sites. These are usually the most attractive part of the city from the perspective of leisure travel and esthetic environment.

Ashworth and Tunbridge (1990) conceptualized the notion of 'tourist-historic cities' (THCs), which they defined as an area of older cities where the urban structure, architecture and artifacts are used to create a place-based heritage product. The old historic centers of Rome, Amsterdam, Paris, Madrid and hundreds of other cities in Europe, Asia, the Middle East and Latin America are very good examples of THCs. These not only function as tourist settings, but they contribute to community pride, well-being and a

Plate 4.5 Tiny San Marino's capital city with museums, churches and government buildings

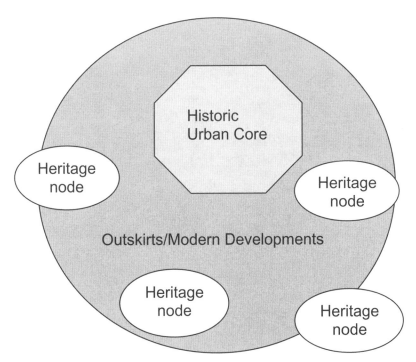

Figure 4.2 Historic urban core and peripheral heritage nodes in cities

sense of contentment. There are many overt linkages between these historic urban centers and shopping, tourist accommodation and fine dining.

In the majority of historic cities, heritage tourism is concentrated in the historic center, ignoring the shopping malls, residential areas, business buildings and industrial parks typically located in exurban zones or suburban residential districts. Nonetheless, there are often secondary and tertiary nodes on the outskirts, such as in areas where archaeological digs might be taking place or where nearby villages have been absorbed into an expanding urban agglomeration (see Figure 4.2). Jerusalem is a prime example, where the ancient historic nucleus is the primary attraction and the residential settlements and skyscrapers surrounding the ancient city are rarely visited by tourists, except for a few museums and government buildings. There are, however, areas of the city that were once villages located further away. Ein Karem, the ancient village of John the Baptist for instance, used to be several kilometers from Old Jerusalem, but now it has been annexed and is an integral part of the urban fabric of the city.

Rural setting

Rural landscapes are among the most valued heritage resources in the world (see Plate 4.6). While the majority of global tourism occurs in cities, in terms of visitor numbers, the countryside is not far behind. The rice terraces of Southeast Asia, the meeting of nature

93

Plate 4.6 Fascinating cultural landscape in rural Myanmar (Burma)

and culture on the steppes of Mongolia, small villages and pastures in the European Alps, native architecture in New Zealand, living culture in the Pacific Islands, castles in England, distilleries in Scotland, cemeteries in North America, archaeological ruins in Africa and Latin America, wineries in France and Italy and rural museums in nearly every part of the globe are important rural resources for heritage tourism. In fact, the majority of the most famous ancient monuments are located in rural settings. Like the cultural past, natural heritage is a vital part of the rural product, and most national parks in the world are located outside of urban areas, designated the protectors of rainforests or taiga forests, coastal zones, desert landscapes, fluvial systems, mountain ecosystems, grasslands or sub-oceanic environments.

The national park movement, which began in the USA in 1872, has spread throughout the world. Parks and other preserve areas can be found in nearly every country on earth, protecting nature and culture in all its forms. In the USA, the National Park Service protects and manages cultural and natural heritage and the majority of its properties are located in rural and/or wilderness settings, offering some of the most spectacular natural scenery in the world. National parks around the world have similar mandates and are favored destinations both for domestic and international tourists.

For many urbanites, rural life and landscapes are seen as something different, something beyond the 'ordinaryscapes' of everyday life and something that draws them in. Urban life itself is by definition frenetic, harried and stressful, causing many people to need to get away and unwind. In the more developed regions of the world, there is a prominent nostalgic sentiment associated with rurality, which some observers have labeled the 'countryside idyll'. This romanticized depiction of the countryside denotes that rural living is healthy living. It is wholesome and desirable, perceptually antithetical to life in large cities. For some, being immersed in the countryside away from the hustle and bustle of the city can be a hallowed experience.

Thousands of rural communities have capitalized on this notion of a countryside idyll and the experience it offers by selecting heritage to be the focus of their tourism development efforts. St Jacobs, Canada, is such a village. Located in rural Ontario near the Kitchener-Waterloo conurbation, St Jacobs was settled by Mennonite farmers. The area is still inhabited by Old-Order Mennonites, and their unique landscape of farm layout, architectural style, schools, churches and cemeteries, modes of transportation (horses and buggies), horseshoe shops, buggy repair shops and dress (conservative black) forms an attractive cultural landscape that in conjunction with handicraft, specialty food and antiques shopping attracts many day-trippers and tourists from further afield.

Similar examples can be found nearly everywhere – villages profiting from their heritage locations and built patrimony. Some base their tourism on historic farms, barns and silos. Others use covered bridges or old mills as the foundations for their tourism efforts. Many post-industrial villages that once depended on mining have become ghost towns, or near ghost towns, and are attempting to resurrect their economies via tourism. Nearly always, however, the historic ambience is accompanied by some form of retailing, such as antiques and handicrafts.

OTHER SPATIAL CONSIDERATIONS

There are more spatial concepts than there is room to include them, but several additional ones are worth mentioning in this chapter. The first of these is the spatial distribution of different types of heritage attractions. Worldwide there is an uneven utilization of the built past, which is primarily a result of political priorities, conservation legislation and lack of funding. Although cultural heritage is rife in the developing countries, it is not as well preserved or exploited for tourism as it is in the more developed parts of the world, owing largely to budget shortfalls, inadequate protective legislation and a lack of social and government will to protect elements of the past. These will be discussed in more detail later in the book as barriers to conservation. Heritage tourism has been successful in Western Europe, North America, Australia and New Zealand for many generations. However, with the exception of mega-monuments that have long featured prominently on the global stage (e.g. the Egyptian Pyramids and Machu Picchu), in most of the less-developed world, it has only come to the fore in recent decades, and many cultural sites in the developing world are still relatively inaccessible to tourists.

Even within an individual country, there might be differences in the distribution of resources. In the USA, for instance, most of the national parks are located in the western portion of the country, emphasizing the importance of natural heritage in that region. Likewise, cultural heritage in the western states tends to focus on Native American archaeological sites, living Native American culture, mining heritage (including ghost towns), cattle ranching and Spanish missions. Colonial patrimony, slave heritage, renovated industrial plants and Civil and Revolutionary War sites dominate the heritage landscapes of the east.

A second pattern is that age and antiquity are relative terms. What is considered very old and extraordinary patrimony in the USA might well be considered new and ordinary in Great Britain, Turkey, India or China. In some countries, there is so much heritage strewn about that only the oldest and most exceptional historic sites and relics can be selected for protection. This certainly is the case in India, for public monies and human resources are in short supply there, which usually results in only the best examples being emphasized in official heritage narratives. In newer countries, such as the USA, almost every archaeological site and historic building receives special attention and is listed for protection.

Third, as noted earlier under the concept of scale, there is a tendency for the magnitude and reputation of heritage places to draw crowds from varying distances. There are literally hundreds of thousands, if not millions, of small-scale historic sites all over the world. Most, however, remain unvisited by the majority of tourists, although they are still important in creating an historic environment that translates into a higher quality of life for community members. It is true that tourists have a tendency to associate certain destinations with an ensconced image or icon that identifies that place. In the mind of the tourist, the Eiffel Tower is synonymous with France; the Coliseum and Leaning Tower of Pisa define the boundaries of Italy; the Empire State Building and Statue of Liberty define New York City; the Taj Mahal is the romanticized image of India; the environments and cultures of the Sahara (Sahel) region of northern Africa are embodied in the ancient city of Timbuktu; and Rio de Janeiro would be almost meaningless without the Christ the Redeemer statue overlooking the city. This form of 'mental mapping', while grossly inaccurate, is what leads many people to make their travel decisions, favoring idealized, even stereotyped, destinations and ignoring thousands of other potential destinations of slightly less renown.

Finally, the principle of clustering is related to Wall's (1997) notion of areas mentioned earlier in the chapter. Although an individual building or monument might posses significant heritage appeal on its own accord, its overall social value increases when it is clustered with similar attractions. Buildings in historic urban zones, for instance, might appear to be rather run of the mill on their own, but when considered in the company of other historic buildings, they create part of an attractive historical setting. In this regard, clustered heritage artifacts and buildings have the potential to draw in more visitors and higher levels of expenditures. In most American and Canadian cities famous historic structures tend to be scattered amongst modern skyscrapers, with most tourists needing a route map to lead them from one significant locale to another. Quebec City and Montreal are two notable examples. Europe is somewhat different in that the oldest historic cities have a tendency to have remained more intact as a cohesive heritage zone. Cities such as Rome, Bern, Florence, Helsinki, Amsterdam and Paris have fairly distinctive historic cores that have not been as deeply penetrated, or replaced, by (post)modern edifices as their North American counterparts. In addition, many medieval towns in Europe, such as Rothenburg ob der Tauber, are remarkably well preserved. They have remained cohesive communities where the entire historic fabric is more consequential than the sum of its parts.

SUMMARY AND CONCLUSION

The spatial characteristics of heritage resources, whether a point, area or linear set of nuclei, are important in understanding the potential positive and negative impacts of cultural tourism. Likewise, scale in terms of the appeal of a particular attraction for individuals, communities, nations and global travelers can help determine markets and demand for a particular cultural destination or heritage product. Thus, these geographical aspects are of high utility for site and destination managers who desire to attract the right people and minimize their negative impacts.

REVIEW QUESTIONS

1. What makes point attractions more prone to negative impacts from tourist crowding than linear attractions?

2. Are there any global-scale heritage attractions in the region where you live? If so, what are their major characteristics that draw people from around the world?

3. Have you ever felt moved emotionally when visiting a national heritage site? What is it about such places that make visitors feel something emotional or spiritual while visiting?

4. Do you think it would be harder to promote personal heritage destinations or national heritage destinations? Why?

5. Can you explain why most cultural heritage attractions are located in cities rather than in rural areas?

6. What are some variables that determine an unequal spatial distribution of cultural attractions throughout the world?

RECOMMENDED READING

Alderman, D. (2003) Street names and the scaling of memory: The politics of commemorating Martin Luther King, Jr within the African American community. *Area* 35, 163–173.

Ashworth, G.J. and Larkham, P.J. (eds) (1994) *Building a New Heritage: Tourism, Culture and Identity in the New Europe*. London: Routledge.

Bahaire, T. and Elliott-White, M. (1999) Community participation in tourism planning and development in the historic city of York, England. *Current Issues in Tourism* 2(2/3), 243–276.

Bessière, J. (1998) Local development and heritage: Traditional food and cuisine as tourist attractions in rural areas. *Sociologia Ruralis* 38, 21–34.

Bromley, R.D.F. (2000) Planning for tourism and urban conservation: Evidence from Cartagena, Colombia. *Third World Planning Review* 22(1), 23–43.

Bunce, M. (1994) *The Countryside Ideal: Anglo-American Images of Landscape*. London: Routledge.

Butler, R.W. and Boyd, S.W. (eds) (2000) *Tourism and National Parks: Issues and Implications*. Chichester: Wiley.

Caffyn, A. and Lutz, J. (1999) Developing the heritage tourism product in multi-ethnic cities. *Tourism Management* 20, 213–221.

Caserta, S. and Russo, A.P. (2002) More means worse: Asymmetric information, spatial displacement and sustainable heritage tourism. *Journal of Cultural Economics* 26(4), 245–260.

Chang, T.C. (1999) Local uniqueness in the global village: Heritage tourism in Singapore. *Professional Geographer* 51, 91–103.

Chang, T.C., Milne, S., Fallon, D. and Pohlmann, C. (1996) Urban heritage tourism: The global-local nexus. *Annals of Tourism Research* 23(2), 284–305.

Cohen-Hattab, K. (2004) Historical research and tourism analysis: The case of the tourist-historic city of Jerusalem. *Tourism Geographies* 6(3), 279–302.

Coles, T. and Timothy, D.J. (eds) (2004) *Tourism, Diasporas and Space*. London: Routledge.

Curtis, S. (1998) Visitor management in small historic cities. *Travel and Tourism Analyst* 3, 75–89.

di Giovine, M.A. (2009) *The Heritage-Scape: UNESCO, World Heritage, and Tourism*. Lanham, MD: Lexington Books.

Frost, W. (2003) The financial viability of heritage tourism attractions: Three cases from rural Australia. *Tourism Review International* 7(1), 13–22.

Graham, B., Ashworth, G.J. and Tunbridge, J.F. (2000) *A Geography of Heritage: Power, Culture and Economy*. London: Arnold.

Griffith, T. and Hayllar, B. (2006) Historic waterfronts as tourism precincts: An experiential perspective. *Tourism and Hospitality Research* 7(1), 3–16.

Hall, C.M. (2002) Tourism in capital cities. *Tourism* 50(3), 235–248.

Hall, C.M. (2009) Tourists and heritage: All things must come to pass. *Tourism Recreation Research* 34(1), 88–90.

Hall, D. and Mitchell, M. (eds) (2005) *Rural Tourism and Sustainable Business*. Clevedon: Channel View Publications.

Henderson, J.C. (2002) Built heritage and colonial cities. *Annals of Tourism Research* 29, 254–257.

Hodges, M. (2009) Disciplining memory: Heritage tourism and the temporalisation of the built environment in rural France. *International Journal of Heritage Studies* 15(1), 76–99.

Hoffman, L.M., Fainstein, S.S. and Judd, D.R. (eds) (2003) *Cities and Visitors: Regulating People, Markets and City Space*. Oxford: Blackwell.

Hopkins, J. (1998) Signs of the post-rural: Marketing myths of a symbolic countryside. *Geografiska Annaler B: Human Geography* 80(2), 65–81.

Hovinen, G.R. (1995) Heritage issues in urban tourism: An assessment of new trends in Lancaster County. *Tourism Management* 16, 381–388.

Ioannides, D. and Timothy, D.J. (2010) *Tourism in the USA: A Spatial and Social Synthesis*. London and New York: Routledge.

Jansen-Verbeke, M. (1998) Tourismification of historical cities. *Annals of Tourism Research* 25, 739–742.

Jansen-Verbeke, M. and Lievois, E. (1999) Analysing heritage resources for urban tourism in European cities. In D.G. Pearce and R.W. Butler (eds) *Contemporary Issues in Tourism Development* (pp. 81–107). London: Routledge.

Judd, D.R. and Fainstein, S.S. (1999) *The Tourist City*. New Haven: Yale University Press.

Law, C.M. (1993) *Urban Tourism: Attracting Visitors to Large Cities*. London: Mansell.

Law, C.M. (2002) *Urban Tourism: The Visitor Economy and the Growth of Large Cities*. London: Continuum.

Leask, A. and Fyall, A. (eds) (2006) *Managing World Heritage Sites*. Oxford: Butterworth Heinemann.

Litvin, S.W. (2005) Streetscape improvements in an historic city: A second visit to King Street, Charleston, South Carolina. *Tourism Management* 26, 421–429.

MacDonald, R. and Jolliffe, L. (2003) Cultural rural tourism: Evidence from Canada. *Annals of Tourism Research* 30, 307–322.

Makhzoumi, J.M. (2009) Unfolding landscape in a Lebanese village: Rural heritage in a globalising world. *International Journal of Heritage Studies* 15(4), 317–337.

McKercher, B. and du Cros, H. (2002) *Cultural Tourism: The Partnership Between Tourism and Cultural Heritage Management*. New York: Haworth.

Montanari, A. and Muscarà, C. (1995) Evaluating tourist flows in historic cities: The case of Venice. *Tijdschrift voor Economische en Sociale Geografie* 86(1), 80–87.

Murphy, L., Benckendorff, P., Moscardo, G. and Pearce, P. (2010) *Tourist Shopping Villages: Forms and Functions*. London: Routledge.

Murphy, P.E. (ed.) (1997) *Quality Management in Urban Tourism*. Chichester: Wiley.

Nasser, M. (2003) Planning for urban heritage places: Reconciling conservation, tourism and sustainable development. *Journal of Planning Literature* 17, 467–479.

Orbaşli, A. (2000) *Tourists in Historic Towns: Urban Conservation and Heritage Management*. London: E & FN Spon.

Page, S. (1995) *Urban Tourism*. London: Routledge.

Page, S. and Getz. D. (1997) *The Business of Rural Tourism: International Perspectives*. London: International Thomson Business Press.

Page, S. and Hall, C.M. (2003) *Managing Urban Tourism*. Harlow: Prentice Hall.

Pearce, D.G. (1999) Tourism in Paris: Studies at the micro scale. *Annals of Tourism Research* 26, 77–97.

Pearce, D.G. (2001) An integrative framework for urban tourism research. *Annals of Tourism Research* 28, 926–946.

Prideaux, B. (2002) Creating rural heritage visitor attractions: The Queensland Heritage Trails project. *International Journal of Tourism Research* 4, 313–323.

Prideaux, B. and Kininmont, L. (1999) Tourism and heritage are not strangers: A study of opportunities for rural heritage museums to maximize tourism visitation. *Journal of Travel Research* 37(3), 299–303.

Rogerson, C.M. (2002) Urban tourism in the developing world: The case of Johannesburg. *Development Southern Africa* 19(1), 169–190.

Selby, M. (2004) *Understanding Urban Tourism: Image, Culture and Experience*. London: I.B. Tauris.

Setiawan, B. and Timothy, D.J. (2000) Existing urban management frameworks and heritage conservation in Indonesia. *Asia Pacific Journal of Tourism Research* 5(2), 76–79.

Shaw, B.J. and Jones, R. (1997) *Contested Urban Heritage: Voices from the Periphery*. Aldershot: Ashgate.

Smith, A. (2007) Monumentality in 'capital' cities and its implications for tourism marketing: The case of Barcelona. *Journal of Travel and Tourism Marketing* 22(3/4), 79–93.

Sommers, B.J. and Timothy, D.J. (1999) Economic development, tourism, and urbanisation in the emerging markets of Northeast Asia. In G.P. Chapman, A.K. Dutt, and R.W. Bradnock (eds), *Urban Growth and Development in Asia. Volume I, Making the Cities* (pp. 111–131). Aldershot: Ashgate.

Timothy, D.J. (2008) Genealogical mobility: Tourism and the search for a personal past. In D.J. Timothy and J. Kay Guelke (eds) *Geography and Genealogy: Locating Personal Pasts* (pp. 115–135). Aldershot: Ashgate.

Timothy, D.J. and Prideaux, B. (2004) Issues in heritage and culture in the Asia Pacific region. *Asia Pacific Journal of Tourism Research* 9(3), 213–223.

Timothy, D.J. and Wall, G. (1995) Tourist accommodation in an Asian historic city. *Journal of Tourism Studies* 6(2), 63–73.

van der Borg, J., Costa, P. and Gotti, G. (1996) Tourism in European heritage cities. *Annals of Tourism Research* 23, 306–321.

Vukonic, B. (2002) Historic cities and options for their tourism development. *Acta Turistica* 14(2), 85–96.

Xie, P.F. (2003) Visitors' perceptions of authenticity at a rural heritage festival: A case study. *Event Management* 8(3), 151–160.

RECOMMENDED WEBSITES

About the Family History Library –
http://www.familysearch.org/eng/library/FHL/frameset_library.asp

Catswhiskerstours – http://www.catswhiskerstours.co.uk/

Preserving America's Rural Heritage –
http://www.preservationnation.org/issues/rural-heritage/

Promoting Tourism in Rural America –
http://www.nal.usda.gov/ric/ricpubs/tourism.html

Rural Heritage Magazine – http://www.ruralheritage.com/

Rural Tourism International – http://www.ruraltourisminternational.org/

Scotland Heritage Tours – http://www.scotlandheritagetours.co.uk/

UNESCO – http://whc.unesco.org/

CHAPTER 5

LOOKING FOR SOMETHING REAL: HERITAGE, TOURISM AND ELUSIVE AUTHENTICITY

LEARNING OBJECTIVES

After reading this chapter, you should be able to:

1. Understand current thinking about the nature of tourists' authentic experiences.

2. Recognize that some researchers do try to measure authenticity objectively.

3. Be familiar with characteristics inherent in arts and cultures that contribute to visitors' sense of authenticity.

4. Realize that most scholars believe authenticity of place, artifact and experience is a subjective notion and differs between visitors.

5. Understand certain trends and patterns in heritage tourism and conservation that accentuate an attraction or destination's authenticity.

INTRODUCTION

There has been a long scholarly debate since the 1960s about tourists and their search for authentic places and experiences. There are many diverging ideas concerning authenticity, with some observers suggesting that it is intrinsic in the objects, artifacts or locations being visited. Others suggest that it lies only in the perceptions or experiences of tourists. Some people have even suggested that it matters very little whether a person has an authentic experience or not. What is important is that he/she has an enjoyable experience away from home. In fact, in most cases it is this sense of 'otherness' that people do desire, whether authentic or not. Playing off the important question of authenticity, many destinations utilize 'authenticity' (whether it is true or not) as a competitive advantage or unique selling proposition in their marketing efforts (see Chapter 12). Like the notion of green tourism, or sustainable tourism, authenticity sells.

This chapter begins by presenting the decades-old conceptual debate about the nature of authenticity and whether or not tourists are really seeking authentic experiences and places. It then looks at how people have tried to measure authenticity objectively, or if it can even be measured. Finally, several ways in which cultural attractions are rendered inauthentic are presented, including contrived places and people, relative authenticity, cultural imposters, uncertain pasts and overly-idealized pasts.

TRAVELERS' QUESTS FOR AUTHENTICITY

One of the earliest commentators on the notion of authenticity in the tourism context was the social historian Daniel Boorstin. In his book, *The Image: A Guide to Pseudo-Events in America*, Boorstin (1961) argued that people travel away from home for fun and excitement, not caring if the places they visit and the experiences they have are authentic. In fact he argued that nearly all touristic environments are inauthentic, fake and fabricated for the consumption of tourists, for this is the kind of contrived, artificial experience they seek. Over a decade later, MacCannell (1973; 1976) challenged the thinking of Boorstin by suggesting that tourists in fact are seekers of authenticity but are duped into experiencing simulated environments and phony settings that are created by the tourism machine to profit from visitors' naivety. In most cases, tourists are content with contrived, inauthentic places and objects because they are unable to see through the façade.

MacCannell (1973) contended that the ignorance of outsiders and the craftiness of destination residents and service providers have together resulted in a system of 'staged authenticity', whereby local lifestyles, living cultures and cultural landscapes are set up, or staged, for tourist consumption. The 'front stage', or areas where tourists most commonly visit, are fabricated to resemble the local cultures and living conditions, or some variation, that exist in the 'back stage' where real life is lived by destination residents. The back stage is devoid of the glitz of tourism. Locals are free to live their own lives in the back stage areas, and everyday life functions, for better or for worse, with limited intrusions by outside visitors. The front stage is carefully crafted to satisfy the needs of tourists and to resemble what they stereotypically think a place ought to be, even if it is far from the reality of modern living. In the back stage, residents can protect their space from intruding tourists and protect many elements of their true culture from the gaze of the tourist.

Some indigenous groups have utilized this spatial dichotomy by presenting to the tourists a front stage performance that will satisfy the desires of visitors but which will not reveal the deep spiritual or cultural meanings associated with rites and ceremonies. These are reserved for the back stage, for times and places where tourists are not allowed. There are many accounts of cultural groups all over the world who create artificial events and traditions for the gaze of tourists, in order to safeguard their real traditions.

In contrast to Boorstin and MacCannell, Urry (1995) insists that tourists do have the ability to discern the contrived nature of heritage places and in fact do so. Some tourists just simply seek out spurious experiences because what they really want is to have fun, not necessarily to learn anything or experience the reality of place and past. Urry (1995: 140) suggests that 'the post-tourist finds pleasure in the multitude of games that can be played and knows that there is no authentic tourist experience'. Thus, some people prefer to visit Paris Las Vegas or New York New York in Las Vegas rather than the real Paris or the real New York, not only because they are closer and cheaper (for Americans and Canadians), but because they do indeed provide a more counterfeit, unreal experience, which does not require mindfulness, thoughtfulness or effort (see Plate 5.1). Instead, these prefabricated environments require only a mindset of fun, fantasy and frivolousness. In this regard and in this context, tourists are looking for an entertaining experience rather than historical reality.

Other people, while not necessarily seeking fake experiences, are blinded by stereotypes and unsubstantiated traditions. This skews their perceptions of what is real and affects their travel behavior as they seek a stereotype or false image they have grown up with via movies, television or other media. The Vikings are a good example. In visiting sites in Europe associated with the Vikings, many tourists are disappointed to learn that not all Vikings were blood-thirsty plunderers, but rather most were merchants, farmers and traders who lived in relative peace. While some Norsemen did indeed engage in warfare and pillaging, many did not. Many accounts of invasions and plundering were blown out of proportion by Christian historians who despised the Vikings' pagan beliefs and whose communities were most affected by the pillagers. Movies, television and even comic strips (e.g. *Hagar the Horrible*) have been instrumental in perpetuating many myths about the Vikings. The fact that they were well-groomed and did not wear horned helmets debunks the traditional views many people still hold of the savage Norsemen, and there are many controversies regarding whether or not such misconceptions should continue to be promulgated at Viking historic sites in Britain and Europe. In most cases, Norse heritage site managers try to emphasize the less ferocious representation to create a more balanced view of the past. 'However, it is often still the more bloodthirsty image that initially inspires tourists to visit [the Viking] sites' (Halewood & Hannam, 2001: 566). Thus, the inauthentic is more titillating and exciting than the authentic.

Cohen (1979), like Urry, argued that tourists are able to discern between real and staged cultural environments and that objectively real situations exist. Cohen created a matrix (see Figure 5.1) that illustrates the level of awareness of tourists regarding the staged or real environment they are visiting. The first condition exists when tourists encounter 'objectively real' cultural environments outside the normal tourist areas, and they accept the situation as being real. The second situation is akin to MacCannell's front stage and occurs when tourists are presented with a staged situation and are unable to tell that it is inauthentic. In the third situation, the tourist doubts the authenticity of a site or setting, even if it is genuine, because of some previous experience with phony, staged cultural settings. Finally, in some places, the scene is openly staged and tourists are aware of the contrived nature of the setting. In this case, the commercialization and intentional re-invention of the past is authentic enough for the visitors. The examples from Las Vegas noted above are a good illustration of this last category.

Plate 5.1 The Eiffel Tower in Las Vegas, an inauthentic reproduction

	Tourists believe the experience is real	Tourists believe the experience is staged
Real scenes	1. Authentic experience	3. Denial of authenticity (suspect staging)
Staged scenes	2. Staged authenticity	4. Contrived authenticity (overt tourist space)

Figure 5.1 Degrees of authenticity in the tourist experience

Source: After Cohen (1979: 76)

The works of Boorstin, MacCannell, Urry and Cohen all confirm a wide range of different meanings associated with authenticity, suggesting that there is more to the concept than a simple objectivity, or that not all places and objects are authentic to everyone. Many different scholars have looked at various types and degrees of authenticity, but Reisinger and Steiner (2006) provide one of the most comprehensive overviews. According to Reisinger and Steiner, the authenticity of historical objects, events, places and settings can be examined from three conceptual viewpoints: realism/objectivism/ modernism, constructivism and postmodernism.

Realists, objectivists and modernists maintain that authenticity can be a known reality, that objects, sites and events do have a discernible and objective genuineness that can be delineated and measured. Considerable research has been done to examine the potentially innate characteristics of art, music, handicrafts, historic sites, rituals and events that make them authentic. Concepts such as objective, real, honest, unadulterated, genuine, accurate, original, untouched and legitimate garnish the thoughts and language of realists. In this line of thinking, authenticity of objects and sites can be measured and understood against factual criteria.

Museum curators, heritage site interpreters, National Trust and National Park Service workers, archaeologists, and many historians loathe the idea that authenticity could be anything but objective. To them, objects and places are inherently authentic by virtue of their own characteristics. For many their job is to substantiate the objective past through scientific and archival evidence. In most cases, curators frame and interpret what they believe to be true about the sites over which they have charge.

Constructivists contend that authenticity is subjective and variable. Relics, heritage places and historical occurrences have different meanings for different people, and their level of authenticity is negotiable between visitors, curators and service providers. Therefore, authenticity is not inherent in the properties or characteristics of objects and places but is simply based on judgments made about heritage places and relics by consumers. Contrary to the view of objectivists, constructivism sees authenticity as being constructed by individuals based on their social networks, their own pre-conceived notions of what is real and the context of their travel experience. Thus, genuineness is relative to the individual and the setting in which the encounter between the visitor and the visited takes place.

According to Jamal and Hill (2004) and other observers, this aspect of the heritage experience is a phenomenological one, wherein people's own heritage and emotional attachment to the places being visited are manifest in individuals' levels of experienced authenticity. Personal and group identity is therefore an important element in constructing the experience. Thus, for people of a specific diaspora, travel to the homeland, or visiting an ethnic festival or museum in the new land, can stir feelings of genuineness and nostalgia to which non-diasporic peoples cannot relate. Likewise, religious adherents visiting sites sacred to their own faiths will have a different experience from those not of the same faith visiting a site. For Roman Catholics a visit to St Peter's Basilica in the Vatican or a Buddhist's pilgrimage to a temple in Tibet or Thailand would be a very different spiritual (and therefore authentic) experience from that of non-Catholics and non-Buddhists visiting the same sites.

Under this constructionist umbrella is the idea that there are many stakeholders involved in created heritage experiences – all of which have different perspectives on authenticity. Governments, business leaders, tour guides, culture brokers, ethnic groups and the tourists themselves all have their own views of authenticity and have a part to play in creating genuine experiences.

Postmodernists believe that authenticity is irrelevant to most visitors (post-tourists), whose primary motive is entertainment, relaxation, pleasure or fun. Most 'post-tourists' are aware that places are inauthentic; they are suspicious of, or cynical about, site-specific authenticity and recognize that it is unnecessary for a satisfying experience. As noted above, Urry's (1995) recognition of this fact is indicative of a postmodern perspective. Post-tourists are content with fabrications because they live in a world of hyperreality anyway as tourism landscapes are Disneyfied and McDisneyfied (Ritzer & Liska, 1997), meaning they are grounded in inauthenticity rather than authenticity, everything is packaged specifically for mass tourism consumption and the tourist experience becomes standardized, predictable, controlled and efficient.

Post-tourists are less interested in visiting Mexico, for instance, than they are in visiting Mexicolandia. At the El Mercado mall in San Antonio, Texas, shops are stocked with products from Mexico, and buildings are designed to look like a traditional, albeit overly stereotypical, Spanish colonial village. Similarly, Sedona, Arizona, boasts a Mexico-themed outdoor/indoor shopping complex, which is extremely popular among tourists and day visitors. Many other examples abound in the US of popular themed Mexicolands, because they allow Americans and foreign visitors to 'visit Mexico' without actually having to go there. They can consume the Mexican experience via merchandise, food, dress, music, architecture and general ambience without enduring the poverty, smells, urban decay and peddlers south of the border (Arreola, 1999).

MEASURING AUTHENTICITY

For scholars who lean toward objectivist and constructivist approaches, measuring authenticity has been a valuable pursuit. Despite the fact that researchers do not agree on an objective definition or set of criteria that can define what is authentic and what is not, several studies have set out to identify criteria by which the content of places and material artifacts can be judged as real or fake from the tourist's perspective. Most academic research of this nature has focused on material cultural elements of heritage, while others have highlighted the characteristics of places and facts surrounding historic events and how these are perceived by visitors as real or not.

Many of the criteria that define authenticity from the visitor's perspective derive from research in the area of handicrafts and souvenirs. Handicrafts are an important part of the historical legacy of ethnic groups around the world, and it is reasonable to develop authenticity-defining characteristics from research on crafts and traditional artworks. Other research on visitors' perceptions of their experience at historic sites contributes to our understanding of what travelers consider authentic or not. The first criterion is esthetics, which is one of the most salient definers of authenticity. Colors, artistic design and overall visual attractiveness create an esthetic value that lends itself to authentic culture. Usually, tourist consumers determine what is authentic based on their own judgments, including what they deem to be beautiful.

Second, uniqueness of product and experience makes heritage places and artifacts genuine to many consumers. Uncommon places, one-of-a-kind crafts or relics, or exclusivity of experience are seen as being more authentic than run-of-the-mill, everyday places. The search for otherness described earlier is an indication of this way of thinking. When few such artifacts or places exist a scarcity value is created and often equated with authenticity.

Cultural and historical integrity is another variable that often lends a degree of authenticity to heritage places and experiences. Accuracy in telling the story and in conserving the built environment is crucial in this regard. One example is the expectation that indigenous pasts will be told by indigenous people, and that native handicrafts will come from a native area and reflect elements of culture that are important to the natives themselves. Museum displays, artifacts and historic sites must, according to this criterion, represent local identity and local history, and exude historical accuracy as much as possible. A documented history through archival and scientific evidence is an important part of this.

Fourth, workmanship is a salient condition in the definition of authenticity. Creative quality and attention to detail in the realm of handicrafts, and architectural and conservation excellence in the built landscape, increase the legitimacy of the place. In some cases, historical accuracy is less significant than quality and design as some people accept the fact that cultures change over time.

Crafts are more genuine when local artisans make them with their own hands, involving care and personal attention to detail. Mutual respect develops as visitors realize artisans are sharing their culture with outsiders. Works by artisans trained in traditional methods hold more accuracy value as well (see Plate 5.2). From a living culture perspective, heritage interpreters who are local and indigenous lend more credibility, and therefore authenticity, to heritage sites and events than those hired from the outside who are not personally connected to the historical location.

Sixth, meeting cultural performers or crafters is an important part of the authentic heritage experience. Tourists enjoy observing the production process in the places where the items are made. According to Markwick (2001: 34), buying handicrafts where and when they are produced 'heightens the authenticity of the tourist experience'. This is also

Plate 5.2 A traditional clog maker demonstrating his skills in the Netherlands

Plate 5.3 These Native American pots are 'certified' authentic by their creators

a salient variable for visitors to indigenous sites. For most, interacting and even being guided by native guides makes the place or event more authentic.

Current functionality and use by natives is another criterion. Many travelers believe that if the locals use an item (e.g. figurine, basket), a site (e.g. burial area, temple, market), or tradition (e.g. dance, music, performance, ritual), then it must be truly authentic. If the use or performance is still something done in the 'back stage' for locals, then it must be legitimate.

Finally, for some people a guarantee of authenticity via some kind of certification or contract is binding. Certificates, artisan names and signatures, labels, production dates and stated production locations all authenticate a handicraft. 'Made in ...' labels are an important verifier of genuineness. In this sense, the creator or curator is confirming to consumers and observers that the experience or product is real (see Plate 5.3).

Other trends in measuring authenticity

The multitude of research studies upon which these authenticity criteria are based uncovered additional interesting trends and patterns. One of these is age. Several studies confirmed that there is a direct link between age and perception of authenticity, suggesting that the older the person the higher the feelings of authenticity often turn out to be. There are other mitigating factors, however, such as personal identity/connection to the place being visited, which might also have a bearing on the visitor's experience. In the US context, age can relate to having lived through various wars, including the Second World War, the Korean War and the Vietnam War. Thus, visiting memorials, national cemeteries and other patriotic sites can invoke emotions and feelings that younger visitors might not be able to feel as readily.

Level of education also seems to have a bearing on people's perceptions of authenticity. Most people with higher levels of education are less inclined to feel their heritage destinations are authentic. This is likely a factor of today's educational environment, which trains students to think critically and not accept everything they are told at face value. Education, however, also causes people to seek out more authentic places and experiences, which are fewer in number, but which provide educational and deeper existential experiences.

Past experience has a bearing on people's perceptions of authenticity in cultural settings. Some studies show that as numbers of visits to heritage places increases, perceptions of authenticity tend to decrease. This can be illustrated by tourists' souvenir purchasing behavior. When people first travel to a destination, their initial reaction is to buy souvenirs that are stereotypical and overly touristy, because to them these represent their 'authentic visions' of the destination. However, with each subsequent visit they acknowledge the inauthenticity of the staged tourist setting and the kitschy nature of the souvenirs they have bought. It thus becomes more challenging with each successive visit to find locations and merchandise that are less commodified for tourist consumption.

There has also been a trend in discovering differences between perceptions of local users, domestic tourists and foreign tourists. In most cases, there is a marked difference between them, with a tendency toward local and domestic tourists being less concerned about objective authenticity than foreign tourists.

INAUTHENTIC PASTS

Timothy and Boyd (2003) identified several different forms of 'distorted pasts', which they argue are indicative of some of the ways in which authenticity at heritage places is called into question (see Figure 5.2). Such misrepresentations of the past are not usually intentional; they are rarely done to deceive heritage visitors but rather may result from a lack of historical information, a dearth of funds, the need to create jobs and regional income, human resource shortages or marketing efforts to build awareness of historic places and events. Clearly, distortions of heritage occur as a direct result of tourists' demand for authentic experiences and destination residents' and managers' efforts to stage cultures, events and places for outside consumption.

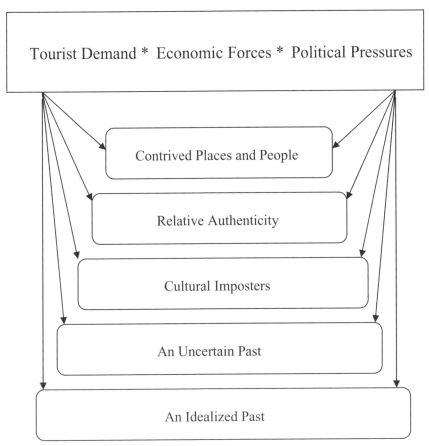

Figure 5.2 Manifestations of distorted heritage

Source: After Timothy and Boyd (2003: 245)

Contrived places and people

Economic necessity and political expediency frequently bring about places, people and events that never were, even though they are marketed as legitimate, original or historically accurate phenomena. The invention of heritage has been happening for many years and is closely linked with the notion of literary heritage. Places, events and people that come to life via fictional writings have become very important tourist destinations; places that never were, but which exist in the minds of literary fans.

A few places in Kansas (USA) claim to be the real-life location of Dorothy's fictional home and Land of Oz in the 1900 novel *The Wonderful Wizard of Oz* and the 1939 motion picture, *The Wizard of Oz*, competing with each other for tourist dollars and the distinguished recognition as the 'real' Oz. In Kansas, visitors can skip along the Yellow Brick Road, visit Dorothy's house and tour the Emerald City in Liberal. However, they can also visit the Oz Museum, the Oz Winery or the Emerald City Market in Wamego

Plate 5.4 'Ozification' of Wamego, Kansas, one of several 'authentic' locations of Oz

(see Plate 5.4). In Liberal, even the solemn mission statement of the Seward County Historical Society states that its purpose is to 'provide enrichment, enjoyment and education for residents and visitors through the preservation of regional history and the Land of Oz' (Seward County Museum, 2009).

Obviously there is no 'real' Land of Oz but the magic of the media has created such a place in the minds of fans, and they come seeking places they deem authentic, even places validated by official agencies, such as the Seward County Historical Society. Such places, including Mr McGregor's garden (in England), where Peter Rabbit was caught eating vegetables, and the fictional village of Avonlea in Prince Edward Island, Canada, where Anne Shirley (Anne of Green Gables) caused so much mischief, have become places of literary heritage importance, particularly for those visitors who grew up reading the novels of Potter and Montgomery. The Land of Oz, Avonlea and Mr McGregor's Farm are not real places, but their creation in fictional writing and television were inspired by the authors' real experience with real places. Nevertheless, for visitors these places come alive and 'lines blur as imagined worlds vie with real-life experiences' (Herbert, 1995: 33).

While many literary heritage locations are make-believe, there are many examples of real places with invented pasts. One of the best documented of these in the USA is

Leavenworth, Washington, a fabricated Bavarian village that was never settled by Bavarians. Once the timber industry of Leavenworth dried up, the town experienced a rapid out-migration of youth and a severe economic decline. In an effort to revitalize the local economy, town leaders looked to other communities in the USA and saw the potential of developing a themed ethnic village where one never existed. The theme of a Bavarian village was selected. Homes and storefronts were remodeled to resemble the traditional architecture of alpine Germany. Flower boxes and baskets were hung, German restaurants were built, streetscapes were changed and residents donned lederhosen and sang German songs in an effort to simulate a traditional, albeit stereotypical, Bavarian village environment. Today, Leavenworth is one of the most successful themed towns in America, celebrating one of the world's largest Oktoberfest celebrations and giving heritage enthusiasts an opportunity to see the Nutcracker Museum. Several other declining communities have followed suit using Leavenworth as a template. The notion of theming has become commonplace in many parts of the world and is often associated with 'invented authenticity' or the creation of themes, objects and places that never existed.

Relative authenticity

It is clear that historical truth is an elusive concept. History is written, told, acted out and preserved according to the whims and wishes of people in power – the winners of wars, not the defeated. The 'truth' about a single historical event can be seen from a multitude of viewpoints, some of which might not even resemble one another. Nonetheless, stories are perpetuated in different social circles, with some events taking on more significance with every passing generation. The European-American settlement of the West is a prime example.

Battles between white settlers and Native Americans are seen at polar opposite extremes of aggression. From the indigenous people's perspective, the Europeans came to steal their lands and disrupt the harmonious relations between humankind and nature. Thus, fighting was an absolute necessity to protect traditional dwelling places, hunting grounds and sacred sites. From the standpoint of the white settlers, the land was unoccupied and free for the taking. The religiously-grounded notion of Manifest Destiny determined that by divine decree the entire North American continent was to be subdued and integrated into the USA. Fighting with the Indians was necessary to keep them from attacking the settlers and their legally-obtained land claims. The American Indian Wars, therefore, are recorded and interpreted differently depending on who is telling the story and who comprises the audience.

Authenticity might also be place and context specific. While some historic sites might derive their claims to authenticity by the number of buildings that have been recon-structed or the number of archaeological digs undertaken, other sites are rendered more genuine by remaining in a ruined state. Ghost towns, for example, abound in the USA, Australia and Canada where authenticity is measured by the degree of deterioration. In some cases, such as Bodie, California, one of the best-known ghost towns in the USA, there is a policy of 'arrested decay', where efforts by California State Parks aim to 'keep it standing but make it look like it's still falling down' (DeLyser, 1999: 614). In this regard, Bodie is an 'authentic ghost town' – unrestored and left to ruin.

There is a tendency to place more heritage value on structures that are old or very old. Recently-abandoned homes or buildings, even if they have unique architectural designs or are otherwise culturally significant, tend to have less value to heritage interpreters and conservationists than ancient and long-abandoned structures. A 1950s home left to decay in rural Europe during the 1970s might be torn down or otherwise receive little conservation assistance, while an 18th century home abandoned in the 1970s would more likely be targeted for preservation as an historic house or a museum. A Swiss chalet built in the early 1800s is more likely to be viewed as an authentic chalet than one built in the 1960s of the same design, materials and by Swiss hands. This 'age factor' is an important issue as regards relative authenticity and relative heritage significance.

As noted early in the chapter, authenticity is also relative because it is a subjective experience. What is authentic to visitor A might not be authentic to visitor B. It depends on their degree of personal connection to the place and their own social baggage brought with them to the experience. Herbert (1995) proposes that heritage scholars should be less concerned about objective truth than whether or not a visitor has in his or her own mind an authentic experience. 'If visitors seek an experience … which is meaningful to them … should we be concerned whether that experience draws upon fact or reality, or whether or not the two can be distinguished? The answer to that question is "probably not". If the experience is authentic to the visitor, that is sufficient' (Herbert, 1995: 45).

Cultural imposters

The notion of ethnic intruders derives from the employment of non-natives or non-original people to play the roles of others, sometimes, although rarely, in a deceptive fashion. Although the Polynesian Cultural Center (PCC), in Hawaii, for example, makes no claims to provide a truly authentic experience (their role is to entertain and provide some factual knowledge about the islands), it has its share of authenticity critics. The critics argue that humorous interpretations of traditional cultures is out of line with genuine culture, seemingly forgetting that most islanders have a sense of humor and would no doubt demonstrate their humor if tourists were visiting them in Tahiti, Samoa or Tonga.

The legitimacy of cultural presentations is also called into question when non-natives play the role of natives. For example, Douglas and Douglas (1991) criticize the PCC for employing Samoan students to depict Tongan traditions, or Maoris to demonstrate Hawaiian culture. The blurring of traditional dress is also a point of contention, as Fijians might perform a dance donning a Samoan grass skirt. The PCC probably receives more criticism than other Polynesian cultural theme parks because of its location in the USA

Plate 5.5 Actors at the Kalevu Cultural Centre re-enact a kava ceremony in Fiji

and because of its large size and huge popularity among tourists. The Kalevu Cultural Centre in Fiji is smaller, but receives less criticism, even though almost all of its actors are Fijians depicting Maori, Tahitian, Samoan and Tongan cultural heritage (see Plate 5.5).

Authenticity is sometimes questioned as a result of increased foreign support for conservation efforts. Many heritage conservation movements in the less-developed portions of the world are spearheaded by foreign donors, agencies and non-profit groups. This, some people argue, is a problem in that cultural preservation loses its indigenousness, becoming controlled by outside elites without the grassroots advocacy needed to create a truly 'authentic' preservation effort and visitor experience.

An uncertain past

Many commentators have suggested that no heritage place or event can be truly authentic because, despite extensive writings, photographs, paintings and other documented descriptions of places, people and occurrences, we simply cannot know exactly what life was like in any period of history. Even within modern memory, or the span of recollection of people still alive (e.g. the Second World War), memories fade, records are inaccurate and details become nebulous. Thus, while some elements of the past might be somewhat genuine and truthful, the complete picture can never be painted in its totality. For many people this is not a major issue, and depictions of the past, even if they are incomplete, are encouraged for the education of posterity and preservation of a fading social memory. On the other hand, there are critics who argue that because any contemporary portrayal of history will be inaccurate, it should not be done, because history then becomes erroneous and falsified.

From the latter perspective, the past is always pictured through present-day eyes and therefore reflects power biases, socio-economic and political trends of today rather than those of the period being considered. In a sense, then the past can only be imagined, not re-lived. Several theorists contend that preserved places are frozen in time and reflect the preconceptions and social values of today and what current researchers believe life might have been like in the past. For the most part, observers laud the efforts of curators, conservationists, interpreters and managers of sites such as Plimoth Plantation, Massachusetts, and Jamestown Settlement, Virginia, as sound modern endeavors to present 17th and 18th century life in the American colonies. Critics, however, suggest these places seethe with inauthenticity because of their role in modern-day tourism and the minor elements within them that reflect modernity instead of olden-day values. The use of modern lawnmowers, fire hydrants, toilets and electric lights are examples of what many believe make such places inauthentic (see Plate 5.6).

In addition to the architectural elements, costumes, foodways, verbal communication and lexicon and streetscapes associated with folklife museums and other heritage places, managers must also consider the role of the natural and cultural landscape surrounding the site and its influence on the site and the lives of the people being depicted. The cultural landscape in general, including gardens, streetscapes, water supply, ditches and canals, pastures and fields, fences, coops and pens and common areas also form a salient part of the heritage experience of these places. Often, however, the buildings are recon-structed as authentically as possible, while the accuracy of the gardens and grounds is neglected, giving rise to additional criticism among many culture and heritage specialists.

An idealized past

There is a popular line of thinking that suggests if visitors at outdoor living museums were to experience truly authentic pioneer villages, they would be repulsed by the smells, dust, mud, horse manure, disarray and cold weather. In the words of Barthel (1990: 87), living folk museums are 'clean beyond reason. They also don't smell bad. The stench that would have permeated a whaling town like Mystic is totally absent'. Instead, historic theme parks such as these present a sanitized patrimony, unlike everyday life in times of old. Flushing toilets and drinking fountains are available for visitors at ancient castles and heritage villages, even though flush toilets were not widespread until the late 1800s and even into the 1900s in many areas. With few exceptions tourists of today would prefer a 'sanitized experience' over an 'authentic' one in these conditions.

Plate 5.6 Modern devices, such as this fire hydrant, in Colonial Williamsburg, draw criticism from some cultural observers

Another view of idealized pasts relates to societal amnesia (discussed in depth in the next chapter). Most heritage places and interpretive centers traditionally have overlooked the darker side of the past and presented the positive aspects of history. This, too, has received considerable criticism by critics who suggest that the entire past should be told; even the uncomfortable elements of history should be revealed as part of the heritage experience. Even today few living heritage museums depict what life was truly like in the distant past. Diseases, orphans, widows, beggars and class structures and even discussions of these are noticeably absent from the historic landscapes being portrayed and disseminated to visitors. Such things would indeed be controversial, albeit more accurate, aspects of life in bygone eras, but humans have a tendency to remember the good times or pleasantries from history as public memory of negative events diminishes.

Likewise, in the past there have been efforts in the USA to subdue revelations about the maltreatment of Japanese-Americans during the Second World War as they were rounded up and gathered into internment camps ('relocation camps') as prisoners in their own country. Many political historians have argued that this was necessary to gauge their allegiance during a time of war. However, mistakes were made, and the period of time between 1942 and 1945, when approximately 120,000 Japanese-Americans were interned in relocation camps (see Table 5.1), is now seen as a national disgrace.

Table 5.1 Japanese-American internment camps 1942–1945/46

Internment camp	Location	Peak population	Date of last detainee departure
Tule Lake	California	18,789	March 20, 1946
Poston	Arizona	17,814	November 28, 1945
Gila River	Arizona	13,348	November 10, 1945
Heart Mountain	Wyoming	10,767	November 10, 1945
Manzanar	California	10,046	November 21, 1945
Minidoka	Idaho	9,397	October 28, 1945
Jerome	Arkansas	8,497	June 30, 1944
Rohwer	Arkansas	8,475	November 30, 1945
Topaz	Utah	8,130	October 31, 1945
Granada	Colorado	7,318	October 15, 1945

Source: After Daniels (2004: 147)

Fortunately, this over-idealized past is breaking down to reveal truths about what really happened and why. As recently as the 1970s, as a result of lobbying by descendents of the 1940s imprisoned Japanese-Americans, several of the internment camps were listed on the National Register of Historic Places. In 1992, Manzanar, California, was approved by Congress as a National Historic Site. In 2001, Minidoka Camp, Idaho, became the second camp to be named a National Historic Site. The lateness in recognizing these ignominious circumstances reflects the ideal that the government could do no wrong in a time of war and that such deeds were a necessary evil. Luckily, a more accurate portrayal of this aspect of the past is being presented to the public with the admission that wrongs were committed in the 1940s. There is still a considerable way to go, however, as several of the camps still lie in ruins and are yet to be excavated and restored for a visiting audience.

As this case denotes, the idealization of history sometimes occurs because of embarrassment for past mistakes. It might also be a result of trying to cover up elements of the past that a community wishes not to share with the public, such as a thriving prostitution economy or the locations of mass murders. By 'covering up' or avoiding these facets of history, heritage destinations become purer, less controversial and more wholesome. In the eyes of destination and attraction managers, wholesomeness sells; decadence does not.

SUMMARY AND CONCLUSION

In spite of many recent efforts to try to define authenticity through empirical studies, we still know relatively little about the concept. What is becoming clear, however, is the idea that heritage authenticity can be seen as both objective and subjective. Examples of objective authenticity would be artifacts that are known to be from a certain period or known to have been owned by a certain person. This meaning of authenticity is rather straightforward and easy to measure and display, although there are some who would argue that even these interpretations are subject to scrutiny. Subjective authenticity, however, which is the more common idea being debated in heritage studies today, suggests that each person probably has his/her own different authentic experiences. This is typically a result of one's own personal connections to the site being visited or his/her perceptions of what makes an object authentic. For some people, a simple label designating an artifact as authentic is enough to make it so, while someone else might need to watch it being excavated or molded to consider it genuine.

REVIEW QUESTIONS

1. What are the current debates regarding tourists seeking authentic experiences? Do all tourists travel in search of authentic experiences, or do many of them want unreal experiences?

2. Can authenticity truly be verified if each person's own experience is different? Or, are there innate characteristics in artifacts, events and places that render them authentic?

3. How do realists and constructivists disagree with regard to objective authenticity in cultural settings?

4. What are some of the characteristics of certain cultural products that tourists have identified as being authentic to them?

5. How do past experience and level of education affect one's perception of heritage authenticity?

6. In what ways might researchers have gone too far in suggesting that places can be rendered inauthentic by cultural imposters or an idealized past?

RECOMMENDED READING

Alberts, H.C. and Hazen, H.D. (2010) Maintaining authenticity and integrity at cultural World Heritage Sites. *Geographical Review* 100(1), 56–73.

Alonso, A.D., O'Neill, M.A. and Kim, K. (2010) In search of authenticity: A case examination of the transformation of Alabama's Langdale Cotton Mill into an industrial heritage tourism attraction. *Journal of Heritage Tourism* 5(1), 33–48.

Anderson, L.F. and Littrell, M.A. (1995) Souvenir-purchase behavior of women tourists. *Annals of Tourism Research* 22, 328–348.

Apostolakis, A. (2003) The convergence process in heritage tourism. *Annals of Tourism Research* 30, 795–812.

Asplet, M. and Cooper, M. (2000) Cultural designs in New Zealand souvenir clothing: The question of authenticity. *Tourism Management* 21, 307–312.

Barthel, D. (1996) *Historic Preservation: Collective Memory and Historical Identity.* New Brunswick, NJ: Rutgers University Press.

Bruner, E.M. (1994) Abraham Lincoln as authentic reproduction: A critique of postmodernism. *American Anthropologist* 96, 397–415.

Bruner, E.M. (1996) Tourism in Ghana: The representation of slavery and the return of the black diaspora. *American Anthropologist* 98, 290–304.

Budruk, M., White, D.D., Wodrich, J.A. and van Riper, C.J. (2008) Connecting visitors to people and place: Visitors' perceptions of authenticity at Canyon de Chelly National Monument, Arizona. *Journal of Heritage Tourism* 3, 185–202.

Burnett, K.A. (2001) Heritage, authenticity and history. In S. Drummond and I. Yeoman (eds) *Quality Issues in Heritage Visitor Attractions* (pp. 39–53). Oxford: Butterworth Heinemann.

Chang, J., Wall, G. and Chang, C.L. (2008) Perception of the authenticity of Atayal woven handicrafts in Wulai, Taiwan. *Journal of Hospitality and Leisure Marketing* 16(4), 385–409.

Chhabra, D. (2007) Exploring market influences on curator perceptions of authenticity. *Journal of Heritage Tourism* 2(2), 110–119.

Chhabra, D. (2008) Positioning museums on an authenticity continuum. *Annals of Tourism Research* 35, 427–447.

Chhabra, D., Healy, R. and Sills, E. (2003) Staged authenticity in heritage tourism. *Annals of Tourism Research* 30, 702–719.

Cohen, E. (1988) Authenticity and commoditization in tourism. *Annals of Tourism Research* 15, 371–386.

Cohen, E. (2002) Authenticity, equity and sustainability in tourism. *Journal of Sustainable Tourism* 10, 267–276.

Daniel, Y.P. (1996) Tourism dance performances, authenticity and creativity. *Annals of Tourism Research* 23, 780–797.

Dann, G. (1998) 'There's no business like old business': Tourism, the nostalgia industry of the future. In W.F. Theobald (ed.) *Global Tourism* (pp. 29–43). Oxford: Butterworth Heinemann.

Edensor, T. (2001) Performing tourism, staging tourism. *Tourist Studies* 1(1), 59–81.

Ehrentraut, A. (1993) Heritage authenticity and domestic tourism in Japan. *Annals of Tourism Research* 20, 262–278.

Fawcett, C. and Cormack, P. (2001) Guarding authenticity at literary tourism sites. *Annals of Tourism Research* 28, 686–704.

Gable, E. and Handler, R. (1996) After authenticity at an American heritage site. *American Anthropologist* 98, 568–578.

Gordon, A. (2004) Heritage and authenticity: The case of Ontario's Sainte-Marie-among-the-Hurons. *Canadian Historical Review* 85(3), 507–532.

Hewison, R. (1987) *The Heritage Industry: Britain in a Climate of Decline*. London: Methuen.

Hitchcock, M. (2000) Introduction. In M. Hitchcock and K. Teague (eds) *Souvenirs: The Material Culture of Tourism* (pp. 1–17). Aldershot: Ashgate.

Hughes, G. (1995) Authenticity in tourism. *Annals of Tourism Research* 22, 781–803.

Jamal, T. and Hill, S. (2002) The home and the world: (Post)touristic spaces of (in)authenticity. In G.M.S. Dann (ed.) *The Tourist as a Metaphor of the Social World* (pp. 77–107). Wallingford: CAB International.

Jansson, A. (2002) Spatial phantasmagoria: The mediatization of tourism experience. *European Journal of Communications* 17(4), 429–443.

Kim, H.G. and Jamal, T. (2007) Touristic quest for existential authenticity. *Annals of Tourism Research* 34, 181–201.

Kim, S.S. and Littrell, M.A. (2001) Souvenir buying intentions for self versus others. *Annals of Tourism Research* 28, 638–657.

Lev Ari, L. and Mittelberg, D. (2008) Between authenticity and ethnicity: Heritage tourism and re-ethnification among diaspora Jewish youth. *Journal of Heritage Tourism* 3, 79–103.

Lindholm, C. (2008) *Culture and Authenticity.* Malden, MA: Blackwell.

Littrell, M.A. (1996) Shopping experiences and marketing culture to tourists. In M. Robinson, N. Evans, and P. Callaghan (eds) *Tourism and Culture: Image, Identity and Marketing* (pp. 107–120). Newcastle: University of Northumbria.

Littrell, M.A., Anderson, L. and Brown, P.J. (1993) What makes a craft souvenir authentic? *Annals of Tourism Research* 20, 197–215.

MacDonald, S. (1997) A people's story: Heritage, identity and authenticity. In C. Rojek and J. Urry (eds) *Touring Cultures: Transformations of Travel and Theory* (pp. 155–175). London: Routledge.

McIntosh, A. and Prentice, R. (1999) Affirming authenticity: Consuming cultural heritage. *Annals of Tourism Research* 26, 589–612.

Mehmetoglu, M. and Olsen, K. (2002) Talking authenticity: What kind of experiences do solitary travelers in the Norwegian Lofoten Islands regard as authentic? *Tourism, Culture and Communication* 4(3), 137–152.

Metro-Roland, M.M. (2009) A needle in a hay stack: Finding authenticity in local provenance at the John Hay Center, Salem, Indiana. *Journal of Heritage Tourism* 4, 145–156.

Moscardo, G.M. (2000) Cultural and heritage tourism: The great debates. In B. Faulkner, G. Moscardo and E. Laws (eds) *Tourism in the 21st Century: Lessons from Experience* (pp. 3–17). London: Continuum.

Moscardo, G.M. and Pearce, P. (1986) Historic theme parks: An Australian experience in authenticity. *Annals of Tourism Research* 13, 467–479.

Olsen, K. (2002) Authenticity as a concept in tourism research: The social organization of the experience of authenticity. *Tourist Studies* 2, 159–182.

Olsen, K. (2007) Staged authenticity: A *Grande idée? Tourism Recreation Research* 32(2), 83–85.

Onderwater, L., Richards, G. and Stam, S. (2000) Why tourists buy textile souvenirs: European evidence. *Tourism, Culture and Communication* 2(1), 39–48.

Prentice, R.C. (2001) Experiential cultural tourism: Museums and the marketing of the new romanticism of evoked authenticity. *Museum Management and Curatorship* 19, 5–26.

Price, T. (1996) *Miracle Town: Creating America's Bavarian Village in Leavenworth, Washington.* Vancouver, WA: Price and Rogers.

Quivik, F.L. (2008) Authenticity and the preservation of technological systems. *CRM: The Journal of Heritage Stewardship* 5(2), 26–36.

Reisinger, Y. and Steiner, C. (2006) Reconceptualising interpretation: The role of tour guides in authentic tourism. *Current Issues in Tourism* 9(6), 481–498.

Ritzer, G. (2008) *The McDonaldization of Society.* Thousand Oaks, CA: Sage.

Salamone, F.A. (1997) Authenticity in tourism: The San Angel Inns. *Annals of Tourism Research* 24, 305–321.

Schouten, F. (1995) Heritage as historical reality. In D.T. Herbert (ed.) *Heritage, Tourism and Society* (pp. 21–31). London: Mansell.

Silver, I. (1993) Marketing authenticity in third world countries. *Annals of Tourism Research* 20, 302–318.

Steiner, C.J. and Reisinger, Y. (2006) Understanding existential authenticity. *Annals of Tourism Research* 33, 299–318.

Taylor, J.P. (2001) Authenticity and sincerity in tourism. *Annals of Tourism Research* 28, 7–26.

Thomson, R.G. (2008) Authenticity and the post-conflict reconstruction of historic sites. *CRM: The Journal of Heritage Stewardship* 5(1), 64–80.

Timothy, D.J. (2005) *Shopping Tourism, Retailing and Leisure.* Clevedon: Channel View Publications.

Timothy, D.J. (2007) Introduction. In D.J. Timothy (ed.) *The Political Nature of Cultural Heritage and Tourism: Critical Essays* (pp. ix–xviii). Aldershot: Ashgate.

Timothy, D.J. and Boyd, S.W. (2006) Heritage tourism in the 21st century: Valued traditions and new perspectives. *Journal of Heritage Tourism* 1(1), 1–16.

Urry, J. (1994) Cultural change and contemporary tourism. *Leisure Studies* 13(4), 233–238.

Waitt, G. (2000) Consuming heritage: Perceived historical authenticity. *Annals of Tourism Research* 27, 835–862.

Wall, G. and Xie, P.F. (2005) Authenticating ethnic tourism: Li dancers' perspectives. *Asia Pacific Journal of Tourism Research* 10, 1–21.

Wang, N. (1999) Rethinking authenticity in tourism experience. *Annals of Tourism Research* 26, 349–370.

Yang, L. and Wall, G. (2009) Authenticity in ethnic tourism: Domestic tourists' perspectives. *Current Issues in Tourism* 12(3), 255–274.

RECOMMENDED WEBSITES

Colonial Williamsburg – http://www.history.org/

Jamestown Settlement – http://www.historyisfun.org/

Japanese American National Museum – http://www.janmonline.org/visit/

Kalevu Cultural Centre and Gecko's Resort – http://www.fijiculturalcentre.com/

Plimouth Plantation – http://www.plimoth.org/

Polynesian Cultural Center – http://polynesia.com/

Step into History – http://www.stepintohistory.com/

Welcome to the Densho Website – http://www.densho.org/

World War II Internment Camps –
http://www.tshaonline.org/handbook/online/articles/WW/quwby.html

CHAPTER 6

TOURISM AND THE POLITICS OF HERITAGE

LEARNING OBJECTIVES

After reading this chapter, you should be able to:

1. Understand how certain elements of the past have been written out of the heritage narrative through societal amnesia.

2. Realize that heritage narratives are often biased and inaccurate, largely by deliberate action.

3. Appreciate that cultural resources and historic locales are among the most hotly contested features of the human environment.

4. Know that history is always told and heritage preserved from the perspective of the people in power.

5. Evaluate how heritage can be manipulated in various ways to achieve political ends.

6. Discover how war and political crises negatively affect cultural resources and their management.

INTRODUCTION

There are few subjects within the realm of tourism that are more political than heritage. Not only is history itself political by nature, the designation of heritage as something to be consumed by the public is in itself a political endeavor, for not all aspects of the past can be documented, interpreted and sold to heritage consumers. Thus, decisions have to be made regarding what will and will not be presented from the past; this decision is nearly always made by people in power, and choices will be made that benefit decision makers best.

Likewise, the past and its tangible remains are constantly the center of struggles between factions, manipulated by ruling classes, targeted during times of conflict and war and forgotten by society or intentionally written out of official history. The use of heritage for tourism is also a controversial and highly politicized action, because choices have to be made regarding what elements of the past will be shown to tourists and which ones will be ignored. This chapter examines the primary current issues in the realm of heritage politics or the ways in which heritage is used and misused for political purposes.

WHAT PAST? SOCIETAL AMNESIA AND THE ERASURE OF THE PAST

One of the most pervasive political manifestations of heritage and heritage tourism is the intentional disregard (or societal amnesia) of certain elements of the past. All heritage relics and products for tourism must be selected from a wide range of heritage resources, which inherently means that some elements and features of the past will not be selected – instead they will be ignored or written out of official history altogether. Thus, some segments of society become 'disinherited' in the process. This happens because a society and its leaders are uncomfortable with certain aspects of patrimony or they are embarrassed by it. In other cases they purposefully exclude parts of the past because they believe they can achieve an ideological goal. In most cases this erasure of the past has racist undertones which endorse the superiority complex of the powerful in society.

Unfortunately, there are too many examples of this in all corners of the globe. The African-American experience with slavery in the USA is an oft-cited example of one of the most inhumane and regrettable periods of human history in that country. Like colonialism in some respects, slavery in the USA (1650s–1860s) was marked by a brutal disregard for human life and individual freedom. Slaves imported from Africa were bought and sold as property; slave owners were free to beat, rape, imprison, separate families, overwork and even kill their slaves as they saw fit. Many slaves were in fact murdered in fits of anger, but few slave owners were ever tried or executed for their actions.

The Native American experience was not much different from that of Africans. Thousands of Native Americans were enslaved by the whites, with most of the slaves being purchased by the British and sent to work on the sugar plantations of the Caribbean. In addition to slavery, American Indians were mistreated in many other ways. In some cases they were torn from their ancestral lands and herded like cattle to far flung reservations that were established by the white-controlled federal government, which knew little about Indian ways of life and connections to nature. In addition, many battles were waged between white American army battalions and Native Americans, who were seen as a threat to the American goal of subduing the continent, and numerous treaties between the US government and the Indians were broken by the USA. Large numbers of American expansionists were slaughtered by the natives for encroaching upon their traditional lands, but a large number of battles resulted in the wanton massacre of Native Americans as well.

Until recently, one of the world's greatest examples of societal amnesia existed, wherein the heritages of African-Americans and Native Americans were hidden from public view, or at least the story was told only from the Anglo perspective. History books revealed the brutality of the Natives, but conveniently left out the cruelty of the Europeans towards the Indians they encountered. Southern history and stories of plantation life focused only on the lives of the white land owners; the only mention of the slaves was in a derogatory context, and only when it was pertinent to laud the power and stellar lives of plantation owners. Given this perspective, much heritage consumed by tourists has been biased for generations. The 21st century audience is now demanding a more accurate portrayal of the past, and efforts to reduce the societal amnesia so commonly associated with the lives and struggles of black American slaves and Native Americans are succeeding (see Plate 6.1). The National Park Service is a key player in trying to make heritage inter-pretation more objective and balanced, although there are many other organizations and agencies with the same objectives.

Today, plantation tours are beginning to interpret the lives of slaves along with those of the slave owners, including the brutality and horrid living conditions the captives endured. Many more prominent African-Americans and their home sites are being commemorated by local governments, and black American museums are cropping up throughout the country, appealing not only to African-Americans but to white Americans and foreign tourists as well. Much of this growth in African-American patrimony has been assisted in

Plate 6.1 A recently-constructed slave cabin at Mount Vernon, Virginia, helps portray a more accurate version of history

recent years by official apologies on the part of state and federal governments. In 2007, the state of Virginia became the first US state to apologize for its maltreatment of African slaves. In 2008 and 2009, the USA government also apologized for its historical part in the slave trade and the discriminatory laws and actions that followed.

Efforts to un-erase some elements of the Native American past and to commemorate the indignity associated with the treatment of Native Americans can be seen, among others, in the enactment of the 1987 law that established the Trail of Tears National Historic Trail under the auspices of the National Park Service. In 1830, the Indian Removal Act became law in the USA and mandated that all Native tribes east of the Mississippi River were to be relocated to lands west of the river. The national historic trail today commemorates and interprets the 1831–1838 forced removal of 15,000–16,000 American Indians of various tribes from south-east USA to Indian Territory (now the state of Oklahoma). The forced relocation was brutal, and estimates suggest that nearly one quarter of all the emigrants died en route or from other consequences of their removal. The Trail of Tears National Historic Trail attempts to illustrate that the US government is taking ownership of the shameful actions of its predecessors and to provide some form of reconciliation. While the state of Virginia in 2007 also expressed regret to the Native American population for its mistreatment, the US government has not yet fully apologized for the country's unkind history against its aboriginal peoples.

The USA is certainly not the only culprit in forgetting the past. White South Africa's treatment and exclusion of its indigenous heritage was equally merciless and paralleled very closely the experiences of African-Americans and Native Americans. The oppressive apartheid policy of the South African government not only repressed native heritage of the distant past, it also attempted, unsuccessfully, to prevent the development of an aboriginal identity. With the collapse of the white-dominated government in 1994, the forgotten past of the native Africans was allowed to flourish. Museums, historic sites, townships and tribal areas were immediately placed on the tourist map of South Africa, and a more balanced view of history is now being told.

Attempts to erase the Nazi past in Germany and the communist past in parts of Eastern Europe are another example of attempts by certain segments of society to hide, suppress or ignore periods of disgraceful history – keeping them away from the public view and from consumption by tourists. Instead of hiding the past, support from Israel and Jewish organizations throughout the world has led to the development of a highly visible network of holocaust museums, monuments and refurbished concentration camps in Germany, Poland, Belgium, Austria and a handful of other countries that were occupied by Germany during the Second World War.

The heritage of colonialism is also a controversial topic in many parts of the world, which some countries have long chosen to ignore. While colonialism resulted in a few positive outcomes, in most regions it created exploitative and dependent relationships that still continue today between the former colonies and their European metropoles, some of which have made the process of economic development much more challenging, causing many countries to remain impoverished.

In the Caribbean, the harmful tenets of colonialism were especially acute, particularly since colonialism was nearly synonymous with slavery. The indigenous Arawaks and Caribs were subjugated and the islands' natural resources were over-exploited. With the arrival of the Spanish, French, British and Dutch between the 15th and 18th centuries, diseases, especially smallpox, also arrived from Europe, wiping out much of the native population of the islands. In addition, early enslavement eradicated many aboriginals, forced relocations displaced people from their homelands and intermarriage diluted the population considerably. Once the enslaved Arawaks and Caribs died and their populations diminished, and with the growing need for slaves to work in the new plantation economies of the Caribbean, Europeans began to import captured slaves from the coasts of Africa in the 1500s and 1600s.

Life for the slaves under British, French and Spanish rule was brutal, to say the least, as it was in all regions where slavery existed. In some areas, death rates exceeded birth rates. Most slaves died of a combination of malnutrition, overwork and lack of medical care, although some were also intentionally killed or tortured until death brought a welcome relief. Most of those who did not die continued a life of imprisonment, misery, abuse and rape. Eventually, with the abolition of slavery in the Caribbean during the 1830s and 1840s, residents of African descent were freed and today remain the primary population of the region.

The European superpowers essentially purloined the islands, exploited the people and their natural resources and established sugar cane plantations, which entailed the enslavement of hundreds of thousands of Africans. Many development scholars today believe that the exploitative treatment of former colonies, the raping of their resources and the subservient master-slave relationship are some of the chief reasons so many countries today remain underdeveloped.

Given this background, it is not surprising that most Caribbean countries have opted to put the colonial past out of sight, or at least not highlight its role in their national history. While the colonial architecture and remnants of the patrimony of slavery in most Caribbean nations has significant tourism potential, most of the islands have not focused on heritage because most physical remnants of the past are colonial in nature, and the colonial period is not remembered with any degree of affection; the public memory of slavery is still fresh. Instead their tourism development has focused on the sun, sea and sand (SSS) product – a resource that the colonialists could not deplete. Nonetheless, a few countries in the region (e.g. the Bahamas, Cayman Islands, Jamaica and the Turks and Caicos) are slowly beginning to realize the potential of heritage to augment the SSS product that already exists.

HERITAGE DISSONANCE AND CONTESTATION

One of the most often noted political aspects of the past is the contested nature of heritage, which can range from disagreements about what heritage means or what it entails, including diverging views about what is or should be marked as heritage, and hostilities over whose heritage belongs to whom. Heritage dissonance refers to dissenting views of the past, including conflicting accounts of 'real', 'authentic' or 'accurate' history and heritage. Many observers now agree that it is virtually impossible to know the true, objective history, because every perception of the past is subject to muffled interpretations, which obviously affects the way it is presented.

Civil and international wars have been waged over differing views of the past and the more ancient the claims, the more cantankerous the conflict tends to be and the more 'disinherited' the view of the 'others' becomes. Likewise, political campaigns have been won or lost based on how the past is interpreted and presented to the public; and generations of children have been taught separate and opposing versions of the same events in official school curricula, depending on which side of a border or ocean they live on. The only consistency about history is its inconsistency, as the account depends on who is telling the story, who is in a position of power to influence the past or who designs the curriculum and therefore which stories or versions of those stories are told. Thus, historic places have not only a story to tell but a multiplicity of stories to tell, and what we do know is that these stories can change with time as new parties come into power. This results in biased views of the past, with other heritages being disinherited – particularly those held in esteem by opponents of the ruling powers.

Contested heritage takes on many forms and is manifested in a variety of ways. One of the most common modes of heritage dissonance is multiple groups claiming the same past and therefore the same heritage places, yet they choose to understand their shared past differently. Each group claims to be the steward of the 'real, objective' truth about what happened at a location of historical significance. In carrying out these claims, other groups are written out of history or their versions of reality dismissed. While there are many examples of this situation, Jerusalem remains one of the most illustrative of these and merits consideration here.

Jerusalem is one of the most hotly-contested spaces in the world today on many levels. It is a holy city for Jews, Muslims and Christians, which alone has led to many conflicts and much bloodshed. Jerusalem, and the entire Holy Land, has been the core of failed attempts at reconciliation between Israel and Palestine. For Israelis and Palestinians, Jerusalem is the unconditional, eternal capital of their nations and recommendations to share sovereignty over it have been rejected by both sides. For Muslims, Jerusalem is the home of ancient prophets and Father Abraham, from whom the Arab nation is believed to have originated. To Jews (and Christians), the land is sacred because it was promised to the Israelites – also the progeny of Abraham.

Timothy and Emmett (forthcoming) reference a few specific cases in Jerusalem that illustrate on a smaller scale the contested nature of place when multiple groups share the same heritage spaces. One of them deserves particular attention here. Although Jerusalem is at the core of the Palestinian-Israeli hostilities, the Temple Mount (*Haram al-Sharif* – the noble sanctuary, in Arabic) is at the very center of the core. This rocky outcrop has for thousands of years been a bone of contention. For Jews, the mount is revered as the location of the Temple of Solomon and is mentioned many times in Jewish and Christian scripture. The Western Wall, which abuts the mount on the west, is the last remaining vestige of Solomon's Temple. The mount and the wall together form the most sacred place in the world for Jews. For Muslims, the Temple Mount is the location where Abraham went to sacrifice his son, Ishmael (Isaac in Judeo-Christian tradition), but was stopped by an angel of God. Likewise, it is the location where the Prophet Mohammed ascended to heaven on a horse and met with ancient prophets and Allah. These events have rendered the *Haram al-Sharif*, with its *al-Aqsa* Mosque and Dome of the Rock, the third holiest site in the world for Muslims. For both Israelis and Palestinians, the mount symbolizes their rightful and divine claims over overlapping spaces and the legitimacy of both a Jewish and a Palestinian state.

Another popular example of this first form is Stonehenge, England, which is a highly visible and contested historic site. The value and meaning associated with Stonehenge varies between several groups, none of which are entirely harmonious. One problem is that the site itself and the territory surrounding it is under multiple ownerships and jurisdictions. The Neolithic monument itself is owned by English Heritage, while the National Trust and the Ministry of Defense own most of the land around it. Various scientific communities also have a claim on Stonehenge as an important laboratory of the Neolithic and Bronze Age eras in southern England. Use of the site, which is claimed as their own heritage and considered sacred by Druids and New Age spiritualists, is contested between the spiritual adherents and the public bodies that oversee it. For many years there have been disagreements between English Heritage, the National Trust, archaeologists and the Druids regarding the site's use, interpretation, management and conservation.

The second form of heritage dissonance is disagreement within a single group, including nationalities or religious orders. In this case, diverging factions within a larger social network have differing views of heritage, each claiming to be the rightful interpreter of the past. From a national perspective, colonialism is a salient culprit of this form of discord. For their administrative ease, the European powers that took possession of Africa, Asia and Latin America carved up the continents and established states without any kind of social or ethnic justification for their chosen boundary delimitations. This has resulted in countries being home to various cultural groups that do not necessarily get along well or see eye to eye on political matters. This haphazard process also separated families, ethnic groups and tribal clans. This pattern of intrusive statehood with its superimposed boundaries has resulted in a longtime struggle to create a unified national identity in many former colonies in Africa and Asia. This in turn has provoked far too many civil wars, ethnic identity crises and intentional erasure of many aspects of the past, thereby disinheriting many citizens.

A much less intense situation, but nonetheless a manifestation of the second form of heritage dissonance, can be seen in the diverging opinions of community members in a small California town, where a women's group desired to commemorate the history of life of gold rush-era prostitutes. Other members of the same community argued that such lascivious behavior should not be celebrated or rewarded with a monument and public recognition ceremony, and the town council voted down the suggestion.

The final perspective on contested pasts relates to more than one history occurring at the same time and in the same place. The unfolding of more than one history results in a parallel set of paradigms, histories, heritages and practices that may or may not have a strong linkage. One of the most common manifestations of this is colonial and indigenous heritages – both happened simultaneously, but are in general terms interpreted and remembered differently. Oftentimes native heritage was ignored or expunged by the ruling colonialists, or at least prevented from flourishing, as was noted earlier under the concept of excluded pasts and societal amnesia.

In many cases, tourism has emphasized the heritage of the colonial elites in places such as Asia, Africa, Latin America, the Pacific and the Caribbean, at the exclusion of indigenous pasts. While the reason for much of this is the Eurocentric view of dominance over the colonized, it is also attributable to the fact that tourism has always focused on the grandiose vestiges of the urban past, such as castles, cathedrals, government buildings, museums and palaces, usually ignoring the everyday cultural landscapes of the peasantry. A similar situation exists in the USA, where Native American heritage as told by Caucasian Americans has long been a Eurocentric view of conquering and taming the land and converting the savages to Christianity. In situations where American troops defended the colonizers on the western frontier during the 1800s by killing large numbers of aboriginal Americans, the accounts are skewed towards a heritage of defending the lands of the white settlers and opening untamed lands for homesteaders. The Native view of the same events, however, is one of malicious and unnecessary slaughter, and the stealing of lands that had been theirs for thousands of years. This dissonance of parallel heritages comes through quite readily at US National Park Service properties that explain Indian wars and at Native American interpretive centers that explain their version of the past. While some of the gaps in these versions of history have been bridged, there is still a considerable amount of work to be done before parallel, or simultaneous, heritages will reveal the same stories.

What pervades all three of these types of disputed heritage is the notion of 'them versus us', the influence of power and a lack of objectivity in all accounts of events and in stories of places.

POLITICAL USES OF TOURISM AND HERITAGE

Heritage and tourism are both manipulated in many contexts as political tools to achieve some nationalistic purpose, ideological goal or security aim. Governments, usually at the national level, use tourism to promote political ideals to their own people, as well as to foreign visitors or via the media to the entire world. In some cases, tourism-related policies are used to punish other governments for non-compliance with the will of their neighbors. Kim *et al.* (2007) and Hall (1994) described several political uses of tourism, which can be extended to examine the heritage dimensions as well.

One of the most significant ways in which tourism is used for political purposes is governments issuing travel alerts, travel warnings or out-and-out travel bans. While in most cases, these warnings are issued to alert citizens to the potential risks (e.g. terrorism, kidnappings, natural disasters, crime, war and general instability) associated with traveling to certain fragile destinations, they are sometimes employed with political undertones to determine where people should travel and to retaliate against or pressure other countries to submit to the will of the state issuing the warning. The US government's relationships with Syria, Lebanon and Iran, and warnings against travel to those countries are a good example. While the Australian government published travel advisories for 167 countries as of July 2010, its list of countries to avoid entirely or to seriously reconsider the necessity of visiting was only 26 (see Table 6.1).

Table 6.1 Countries on the Australian government's travel warning list, 2010

Advisory type	Country	Reasons for the advisory
Avoid entirely	Afghanistan	Terrorism, war, kidnappings
	Burundi	Civil unrest, serious crime
	Central African Rep.	Warring rebels, crime, lawlessness
	Chad	Civil unrest, violence, terrorism
	Guinea	Violence, security risks
	Iraq	Terrorism, war, kidnappings
	Niger	Kidnappings, banditry, rebels
	Somalia	War, terrorism, lawlessness
	Sudan	Armed conflict, terrorism, crime
Avoid unnecessary travel	Algeria	Threat of terrorism, kidnappings
	Angola	Civil unrest, criminal violence

	D.R. Congo	Lawlessness, civil unrest, crime
	Eritrea	Threat of terrorism, civil unrest
	Ethiopia	Threat of terrorism, civil unrest
	Haiti	Lawlessness, crime, instability
	Indonesia	Threat of terrorism, natural disasters
	Kyrgyzstan	Political insecurity, crime, terrorism
	Lebanon	Threat of terrorism, civil unrest
	Liberia	Crime, civil unrest
	Madagascar	Civil unrest, violent demonstrations
	Mauritania	Threat of terrorism, political tensions
	Nigeria	Crime, terrorist threats, civil unrest
	Pakistan	Threat of terrorism, political tensions
	Saudi Arabia	Threat of terrorism
	Yemen	Threat of terrorism, civil unrest
	Zimbabwe	Violence, civil unrest, crime

Source: Government of Australia (2010)

The 167 Australian alerts, and those issued by other countries of the world, significantly affect travel to the countries listed, including mainstream nations such as Argentina (travelers are warned about crime), Belgium (risk of terrorist attacks), Singapore (risk of terrorist attacks) and Thailand (risk of terrorist attacks and political insecurity). Most important, however, are the travel warnings. Several countries, such as Yemen, Ethiopia, Pakistan, Zimbabwe, Lebanon and Indonesia, which are on the severe warning lists of Australia, Canada, the UK, the USA and several European states, are home to extremely momentous heritage sites, including several UNESCO World Heritage Sites, which could have tremendous tourism potential if political conditions were different.

Second, the issuing of visas and changing passport requirements demonstrate another political use of tourism. In some cases there is a reciprocal arrangement between countries regarding visas. For example, the European Union countries do not require a visa for US or Canadian citizens. The US and Canada in turn do not require visas for EU citizens. However, there are other regional differences. Canada does not require visas for citizens of certain Middle Eastern countries, while the USA does. This translates into stricter border controls for people traveling from Canada to its southern neighbor. Likewise, new US passport requirements came into full effect in the summer of 2009. Canadians have never needed a passport to visit the USA and vice versa, Americans visiting Mexico have not needed a passport to return home (although Mexicans have always required a passport and visa), and cruise passengers traveling throughout the Caribbean basin or Mexico have not needed passports on their return trips to US ports. However, passports are now required by everyone entering the US. This includes Canadians and returning US citizens.

Another related political manipulation of tourism is the use of travel bans or embargos. Tourism is often at the center of international embargos, such as the current US government prohibition against travel to Cuba. Many other examples have existed in the past as well, such as restricted travel to the Turkish Republic of Northern Cyprus, South Africa, North Korea and Vietnam – bans that were established to punish these 'rogue states' for their oppressive racist policies, divisive declarations of independence or lack of conformity to the norms of the world community. These sanctions are extremely influential in the potential destinations as prospective markets are dissuaded from visiting. From a heritage perspective, both of these types of government actions, warnings and embargos, draw attention to a heritage of contention that reveals a great deal about relationships between nations of the world.

The fourth political use of heritage and tourism is manifest when states restrict the behavior of tourists and control their travel patterns and itineraries. In most cases, these types of tourism autocracies are linked to strict communist countries or totalitarian states that do whatever they can to prevent contact between their own citizenry and outsiders. One-on-one guides or group tours on strict itineraries were/are used to assure that interaction between locals and visitors was/is kept to a minimum. Among the best examples of this are present-day North Korea and former strict communist countries such as Albania before the 1990s. Restrictions on tourists also included historic sites that could or could not be photographed and visited; anything with strategic importance was generally off limits, such as government buildings, bridges and certain national/war monuments. Certain places that were important domestic heritage sites were entirely written off from the itineraries of foreigners and vice versa.

Authoritarian communist states are not the only ones to regulate tourists in this respect, however. Bhutan, a multiparty constitutional monarchy where nearly all tourism is based on cultural heritage, exhibits some of the same controlling behaviors exercised by communist states. However, rather than being solely for ideological and military reasons, the controls exercised by the government of Bhutan are meant to increase tourism earnings while decreasing the negative impacts of tourism. Tourists in Bhutan are required to purchase a pre-packaged tour wherein all sites are selected and pre-arranged, and which costs a minimum daily tariff of USD $200, although one can pay more for higher-rated accommodations. Foreigners in Bhutan, with the exception of Indians, can only travel with a state-certified guide and driver. Visas are difficult to acquire and must be obtained through a certified travel agent in Bhutan, and tourists must enter or depart the country at least one way by plane on the country's only airline, Druk Air. These economic and political restrictions necessarily weed out independent travelers (i.e. backpackers) and mass tourists, who are seen to be the perpetrators of most social and ecological damage.

A fifth perspective is when tourism and national heritage are used to spread propaganda to foreign tourists. An opium museum in Mongla, Myanmar, near the border of China and the Golden Triangle, where Thailand, Myanmar and Laos meet, extols the virtues of the totalitarian military government of Myanmar in its efforts to eradicate poppy farming for opium (see Plate 6.2). The museum is splashed with displays and slogans that praise the government for all the good it does and venerates the military junta that is so often criticized by the international community for human rights abuses and lack of international goodwill.

In the case of heritage used for propaganda purposes, tour itineraries are overloaded with historic sites that praise a certain political ideology and skew history to be something that it never was. Nationalist monuments, including self-designed statues of great leaders, are an important part of the heritagescape tours and are controlled to debunk foreign

Plate 6.2 An opium propaganda museum in Mongla, Myanmar (Burma)

criticisms of a particular country and its policies, or extol its good qualities. The communist countries of Asia and most of the former communist states of Eastern Europe utilized this approach to propagandize foreign visitors. This continues to occur today. In North Korea, for example, a 'propaganda village' has been erected on the north edge of the North Korea-South Korea demilitarized zone, within view of South Korean onlookers and peacekeepers, to provide a staged environment that demonstrates the high standard of living and idealized *Juche* system in the north and the industriousness of the North Korean farmers and workers. Formerly, in China, Vietnam and other communist countries, tourists were rushed to schools and government offices for similar purposes, to show the high quality of education, the functioning of heritage places and the great success of the communist system.

Another use, closely aligned with the point above, is the manipulation of domestic heritage to build nationalism and patriotism within a country. This is a common use of heritage in all parts of the world, and is not endemic to socialist or communist regimes. Museums, monuments, battlefields, rural landscapes, historic houses and many other heritage attractions can be manipulated to achieve some political ends, such as legitimizing administrations in power, building patriotism or garnering support for an ideal or political movement. Such efforts also come into play with diasporic groups. Diasporic homelands are often idealized or made flawless in the minds of emigrants and their progeny via cultural heritage campaigns and solidarity movements that aim to reinforce traditional ideologies, customs and cultural cohesion in all corners of the world. This use of heritage fosters moral, ethnic and financial support for the homeland abroad.

Tourism and other forms of economic trade can also be used as an enticement to win favor or reinforce support for an international issue or particular policy. The promise of Taiwanese tourists visiting Mainland China for heritage and other reasons and to celebrate their many common cultural values is an important manifestation of this pattern. US support for tourism growth in many Middle Eastern countries (e.g. Qatar, Bahrain and the UAE) is also a form of enticement, which suggests that getting these and other countries on America's good side will enable more collaboration in the fight against terrorism, create more stability in the region and perhaps even gain a modicum of recognition for Israel in the broader Middle East.

Finally, as discussed earlier in the chapter, collective amnesia may also be an intentional use of heritage, when controversial or embarrassing periods of time are written out of the official historical narrative. Until recently in South Africa, for instance, black African heritage was purposefully left out of the tourism circuit, with the exception of some limited visits to black townships, which emphasized white domination over the indigenous race. Thousands of examples of this exist throughout the world where people in power have conveniently left out certain elements of the past, while enhancing and promoting others.

WAR AND ITS IMPACT ON THE PAST

The impacts of physical combat on the built heritage of a place are profound and irreparable. Unfortunately, war, terrorism and civil unrest are rampant in the modern day in nearly all regions of the world. Besides the tragedy of untold lives lost, the torture of innocent people, destruction of infrastructure and ecological damage, war and other political hostilities affect built heritage in myriad ways, damaging or destroying non-renewable resources that nations hold near and dear to their hearts (see Plate 6.3). War, terrorism and other acts of violence influence built heritage in a variety of ways: heritage as intentional target, broken heritage as collateral damage, looting and pillaging and diversion of conservation resources.

Perhaps the most notable outcome of war and terrorism on cultural heritage is when that heritage becomes a deliberate target for destruction. Typically this happens when enemy combatants try to harm or destroy the symbols, emblems and historic places that help define national identity and radiate a sense of native pride. Likewise, sites that epitomize or idealize a cultural/ethnic identity are frequently sought out for destruction. This has been all too evident in recent history, particularly with regard to warring ethnic factions in Rwanda, Yugoslav military aggression against its secessionist states (e.g. Croatia and Bosnia Herzegovina), Muslims destroying Catholic churches and Catholics destroying mosques during the 1990s Bosnian war (see Plate 6.4), the recent civil war in

Plate 6.3 The destroyed Mostar Bridge (a UNESCO site) in Bosnia before its reconstruction

Plate 6.4 This destroyed mosque near Medjugorje, Bosnia Herzegovina, is a casualty of the mid-1990s Yugoslavian wars

Sri Lanka between Tamil rebels and the majority Sinhalese-led government, and even Muslims and Hindus destroying each other's historic places of worship in India.

Another very recent example is the short-lived August 2008 war between Russia and the Republic of Georgia. During this 15-day war, Russia targeted several important natural areas in Georgia, as well as several iconic heritage places that symbolize the Georgian national identity. Near the city of Gori, rockets were fired into the ancient cave city of Uplistsikhe, a rare settlement carved into bedrock, caves and cliffs. Following the war, significant damage was confirmed. In all, more than 340 ancient monuments and historic sites were located within the combat zone, at least 16 of which were damaged.

Another perspective on heritage as calculated target is paramilitary groups, terrorists or malevolent governments destroying ancient artifacts and sites because either they disagree with what the artifacts represent or they do so in a spirit of retaliation. One of the best recent examples was the March 2001 destruction of the ancient Buddhist statues and shrines in the Bamyan Valley of Afghanistan. The despotic Taliban government destroyed the 4th- and 5th-century Buddha statues, the tallest in the world and designated a UNESCO World Heritage Site, using explosives and anti-aircraft artillery. The Taliban's excuse was that the statues were idols to false gods and needed to be destroyed because they ran counter to the teachings of Islam. Critics and international observers, however, argue that the devastation was done to spite the international community for invading

141

Afghanistan and issuing sanctions against the country. A similar attempt at destroying Buddhist statues in northwestern Pakistan occurred in 2007, less successfully, by extremists with a similar motive to that of the Taliban.

In a related vein, the terrorists who masterminded the horrific events in the USA on September 11, 2001, set their sights on three important heritage places in that country – the World Trade Center, which symbolized affluence, freedom, capitalism and western influence throughout the world, all important heritage concepts in the USA; the historic Pentagon building – the headquarters of the US armed forces and symbol of the country's military might; and an unknown location in Washington, DC, most likely the White House or Capitol Building. The destination of the Washington-bound aircraft used in the attack is still unknown, because it crashed in a rural field in Pennsylvania before reaching the capital. Unfortunately, many ancient and modern examples of this sort of determined annihilation of one group's heritage by a hostile faction abound all over the world.

The second way in which remnants of the past are devastated by conflict is when they become innocent casualties or collateral damage. Such was the plight of Angkor Wat, one of humankind's leading icons of the ancient world. The temples and other structures at Angkor were heavily damaged in that country's civil war and subsequent occupation by Khmer Rouge guerillas. Many of the statues' heads and limbs were broken or used for target practice. Rebel soldiers lived within the temple complex, damaging the ancient fabric with fires, wear and tear, landmines and munitions.

Likewise, in November 2008, Pakistani terrorists launched an attack on tourist sites in Mumbai, India, killing 172 people, including Indians and foreigners. The explosions and gunfire associated with the attacks heavily damaged several historic buildings, including the UNESCO-listed Chhatrapati Shivaji Railway Station. Wherever terrorist attacks occur and where grenades or bombs explode in acts of war, collateral damage will occur to historic buildings or other heritage sites.

Looting and pillaging are the third major impact of war on cultural heritage. Regrettably, political instability nourishes the illicit trade in antiquities and therefore looting of cultural artifacts. For example, in the Democratic Republic of the Congo and Somalia, unsalaried and ravenous soldiers do whatever it takes to purchase food, including grave-robbing, ransacking museums and stealing from historic sites. During the 2008 Russia-Georgia war, several ancient churches, including Samtavisi Cathedral, were looted by Russian troops. Likewise, the invasion of Iraq by the USA and its allies in 2003 left museums abandoned or occupied by warring factions, leading to mass pillaging of them by local warlords, gangs and other profit-seekers. Some of the lost items have been recovered, but many will never be found and returned to Iraq.

Plundered artifacts are also commonly sold to fund warfare and terrorism. The September 11, 2001, terror attacks in New York and Washington, for instance, were apparently financed in part by selling stolen artifacts from historic sites in the Middle East. Correspondingly, attacks against Israel by Palestinian revolutionaries are believed to be partially subsidized by selling artifacts stolen from graves and archaeological sites in the West Bank.

Lastly, war stretches already overburdened economies and diverts potential funding away from conservation efforts. Quelling radical militants or enemy armies is an expensive endeavor, leaving very little in national budgets for 'trivial' pursuits like heritage conservation and management. In some cases, the lack of attention to, and funding for, cultural heritage is equally damaging if not more so, in some cases, than the actual conflict. Human resources, too, are usually in short supply during times of political crisis, again restricting a government's ability to staff historic sites and maintain them, and access to cultural sites in need of attention is often restricted or completely obstructed.

SUMMARY AND CONCLUSION

As noted at the outset of this chapter, there are few tourism resources that are as political as heritage. This chapter illustrates clearly the ways in which the past is manipulated for political purposes. One of the most interesting perspectives is collective amnesia, or the intentional forgetting of elements of the past that are deemed unworthy, uncomfortable or unsuitable for preservation. The maltreatment of ethnic minorities and racism, unsavory aspects of local patrimony and the desire to forget difficult periods of history commonly result in official forgetfulness in preserving the past.

In addition, almost every period of history and every historical incident can be told in a multitude of ways. Thus, history is contested and heritage becomes dissonant, as different groups vie for recognition as the truth-tellers and caretakers of the past. This commonly leads to parallel heritages that in some cases hardly resemble one another, despite supposedly being about the same event, person or place.

Finally, war is perhaps the most damaging politically-charged abuse ever to befall the built patrimony of any given society. Cultural icons and heritage places are commonly targeted in an effort to break down the enemy or dissuade them from fighting. Even when heritage is not the main target, it suffers considerable collateral damage, as can be seen from many recent conflicts in the former Yugoslavia, the Republic of Georgia and Iraq. The politics of heritage is one of the most dynamic areas of study among heritage scholars, and as long as there is conflict in the world it will continue to be a rich source of scholarly debate.

REVIEW QUESTIONS

1. The heritage of many racial or ethnic minorities traditionally has been suppressed and excluded from heritage narratives, promotion and conservation. How has this changed in recent years? What might be causing a more accurate portrayal of history to tourists?

2. In what ways has colonialism affected the modern-day heritage tourism product in former colonial territories?

3. Why is heritage so hotly contested between parties? What are three ways in which contested heritage can be viewed?

4. How do governments manipulate heritage and heritage tourism to punish other countries? How common do you think this is?

5. Can you think of additional examples where cultural heritage has been targeted for destruction in times of war or political conflict?

6. How might wartime pillaging of sites of cultural importance be linked to tourism?

RECOMMENDED READING

Allen, G. and Brennan, F. (2004) *Tourism in the New South Africa: Social Responsibility and the Tourist Experience.* London: I.B. Tauris.

Ashworth, G.J. (1991) *War and the City.* London: Routledge.

Ashworth, G.J. (2003) Heritage, identity and places: For tourists and host communities. In S. Singh, D.J. Timothy and R.K. Dowling (eds) *Tourism in Destination Communities* (pp. 79–97). Wallingford, UK: CAB International.

Ashworth, G.J. and Hartmann, R. (2005) *Horror and Human Tragedy Revisited: The Management of Sites of Atrocities for Tourism.* New York: Cognizant.

Boyd, S.W. (2000) Heritage tourism in Northern Ireland: Opportunities under peace. *Current Issues in Tourism* 3(2), 153–174.

Buchholz, D. (2005) Cultural politics or critical public history? Battling on the Little Bighorn. *Journal of Tourism and Cultural Change* 3, 18–35.

Cable, M. (2008) Will the real Dai please stand up: Conflicting displays of identity in ethnic tourism. *Journal of Heritage Tourism* 3(4), 267–276.

Carter, S. (2004) Mobilizing Hrvatsko: Tourism and politics in the Croatian diaspora. In T. Coles and D.J. Timothy (eds) *Tourism, Diasporas and Space* (pp. 188–201). London: Routledge.

Charlesworth, A. (1994) Contesting places of memory: The case of Auschwitz. *Professional Geographer* 51, 91–103.

Cheung, S. (2003) Remembering through space: The politics of heritage in Hong Kong. *International Journal of Heritage Studies* 9, 7–26.

144

Chronis, A. (2005) Coconstructing heritage at the Gettysburg storyscape. *Annals of Tourism Research* 32, 386–406.

Clarke, R. (2000) Self-presentation in a contested city: Palestinian and Israeli political tourism in Hebron. *Anthropology Today* 16(5), 12–18.

Cohen-Hattab, K. (2004) Zionism, tourism and the battle for Palestine: Tourism as a political-propaganda tool. *Israel Studies* 9(1), 61–85.

Darcy, S. and Wearing, S. (2009) Public private partnerships and contested cultural heritage tourism in national parks: A case study of the stakeholder views of the North Head Quarantine Station (Sydney, Australia). *Journal of Heritage Tourism* 4(3), 181–199.

Dearborn, L.M. and Stallmeyer, J.C. (2010) *Inconvenient Heritage: Erasure and Global Tourism in Luang Prabang.* Walnut Creek, CA: Left Coast Press.

Fontein, J. (2006) *The Silence of Great Zimbabwe: Contested Landscapes and the Power of Heritage.* London: UCL Press.

Golden, J. (2004) Targeting heritage: The abuse of symbolic sites in modern conflicts. In Y. Rowan and U. Baram (eds) *Marketing Heritage: Archaeology and the Consumption of the Past* (pp. 183–202). Walnut Creek, CA: AltaMira Press.

Goudie, S.C., Khan, F. and Kilian, D. (1999) Transforming tourism: Black empowerment, heritage and identity beyond apartheid. *South African Geographical Journal* 81, 22–31.

Graham, B. (1996) The contested interpretation of heritage landscapes in Northern Ireland. *International Journal of Heritage Studies* 2(1/2), 19–22.

Grainge, P. (1999) Reclaiming heritage: Colourization, culture wars and the politics of nostalgia. *Cultural Studies* 13(4), 621–638.

Hall, C.M. (1997) The politics of heritage tourism: Place, power and the representation of values in the urban context. In P.E. Murphy (ed.) *Quality Management in Urban Tourism* (pp. 91–101). Chichester: Wiley.

Hall, C.M. (2003) Politics and place: An analysis of power in tourism communities. In S. Singh, D.J. Timothy and R.K. Dowling (eds) *Tourism in Destination Communities* (pp. 99–113). Wallingford, UK: CAB International.

Hall, C.M. and Tucker, H. (2004) *Tourism and Postcolonialism: Contested Discourses, Identities and Representations.* London: Routledge.

Harrison, D. (2004) Introduction: Contested narratives in the domain of World Heritage. *Current Issues in Tourism* 7, 281–290.

Henderson, J.C. (2007) Remembering the Second World War in Singapore: Wartime heritage as a visitor attraction. *Journal of Heritage Tourism* 2(1), 36–52.

145

Hitchcock, M. and Harrison, D. (eds) (2005) *The Politics of World Heritage: Negotiating Tourism and Conservation*. Clevedon: Channel View Publications.

James, J. (2004) Recovering the German nation: Heritage restoration and the search for unity. In Y. Rowan and U. Baram (eds) *Marketing Heritage: Archaeology and the Consumption of the Past* (pp. 143–166). Walnut Creek, CA: AltaMira Press.

Johnson, N.C. (1999) Framing the past: Time, space and the politics of heritage tourism in Ireland. *Political Geography* 18, 187–207.

Kim, S.S., Timothy, D.J. and Han, H.C. (2007) Tourism and political ideologies: A case of tourism in North Korea. *Tourism Management* 28, 1031–1043.

Leong, W.T. (1989) Culture and the state: Manufacturing traditions for tourism. *Critical Studies in Mass Communication* 6, 355–375.

Light, D. (2000) An unwanted past: Contemporary tourism and the heritage of communism in Romania. *International Journal of Heritage Studies* 6, 145–160.

Light, D. (2000) Gazing on communism: Heritage tourism and post-communist identities in Germany, Hungary and Romania. *Tourism Geographies* 2, 157–176.

McLean, F. (1998) Museums and the construction of national identity: A review. *International Journal of Heritage Studies* 3, 244–252.

Metreveli, M. and Timothy, D.J. (2010) Effects of the August 2008 War in Georgia on tourism and its resources. In O. Moufakkir and I. Kelly (eds) *Tourism, Progress and Peace* (pp. 134–147). Wallingford, UK: CABI.

Mitchell, T. (2001) Making the nation: The politics of heritage in Egypt. In N. Alsayyad (ed.) *Consuming Tradition, Manufacturing Heritage: Global Norms and Urban Forms in the Age of Tourism* (pp. 212–239). London: Routledge.

Moore, N. and Whelan, Y. (eds) (2007) *Heritage, Memory and the Politics of Identity: New Perspectives on the Cultural Landscape*. Aldershot, UK: Ashgate.

Mordue, T. (2005) Tourism, performance and social exclusion in 'Olde York'. *Annals of Tourism Research* 32, 179–198.

Norkunas, M.K. (1993) *The Politics of Public Memory: Tourism, History, and Ethnicity in Monterey, California*. Albany, NY: State University of New York Press.

Nyaupane, G.P. and Timothy, D.J. (2010) Power, regionalism and tourism policy in Bhutan. *Annals of Tourism Research* 37 (4), 969–988.

Odermatt, P. (1996) Built heritage and the politics of (re)presentation: Local reactions to the appropriation of the monumental past in Sardinia. *Archaeological Dialogues* 3, 95–119.

Olsen, D.H. and Timothy, D.J. (2002) Contested religious heritage: Differing views of Mormon heritage. *Tourism Recreation Research* 27(2), 7–15.

Poria, Y., Biran, A. and Reichel, A. (2007) Different Jerusalems for different tourists: Capital cities – the management of multi-heritage site cities. *Journal of Travel and Tourism Marketing* 22(3/4), 121–138.

Prodanic, I.J. and Timothy, D.J. (2007) Effects of the Yugoslavian wars on tourism in the Republic of Montenegro. *Journal of Hospitality and Tourism* 5(1), 67–82.

Reddy, M.V. (2009) World Heritage Site selection in sensitive areas: Andoman and Nicobar Islands. *Journal of Heritage Tourism* 4(4), 267–286.

Richter, L.K. (1999) The politics of heritage tourism development: Emerging issues for the new millennium. In D. Pearce and R.W. Butler (eds) *Contemporary Issues in Tourism Development* (pp. 108–126). London: Routledge.

Schofield, J. and Cocroft, W. (2007) *A Fearsome Heritage: Diverse Legacies of the Cold War.* Walnut Creek, CA: Left Coast Press.

Smith, L. (2004) *Archaeological Theory and the Politics of Cultural Heritage.* London: Routledge.

Soper, A.K. (2007) Developing Mauritianness: National identity, cultural heritage values and tourism. *Journal of Heritage Tourism* 2(2), 94–109.

Teo, P. and Yeoh, B. (1997) Remaking local heritage for tourism. *Annals of Tourism Research* 24, 192–213.

Timothy, D.J. (ed.) (2007) *The Political Nature of Cultural Heritage and Tourism: Critical Essays.* Aldershot, UK: Ashgate.

Timothy, D.J. and Boyd, S.W. (2003) *Heritage Tourism.* Harlow: Prentice Hall.

Timothy, D.J. and Daher, R.F. (2009) Heritage tourism in Southwest Asia and North Africa: Contested pasts and veiled realities. In D.J. Timothy and G.P. Nyaupane (eds) *Cultural Heritage and Tourism in the Developing World: A Regional Perspective* (pp. 146–164). London: Routledge.

Timothy, D.J. and Emmett, C.F. (forthcoming) Jerusalem, tourism and the politics of heritage. In M. Adelman and M. Elman (eds) *Jerusalem across Disciplines.* Syracuse, NY: Syracuse University Press.

Timothy, D.J., Prideaux, B. and Kim, S.S. (2004) Tourism at borders of conflict and (de)militarized zones. In T.V. Singh (ed.) *New Horizons in Tourism: Strange Experiences and Stranger Practices* (pp. 83–94). Wallingford, UK: CAB International.

Tunbridge, J.E. and Ashworth, G.J. (1996) *Dissonant Heritage: The Management of the Past as a Resource in Conflict.* Chichester: Wiley.

Waters, A.M. (2006) *Planning the Past: Heritage Tourism and Post-Colonial Politics and Port Royal.* Lanham, MD: Lexington Books.

Winter, T. (2007) *Post-Conflict Heritage, Postcolonial Tourism: Culture, Politics and Development and Angkor.* London: Routledge.

Worden, N. (1996) Contested heritage at the Cape Town Waterfront. *International Journal of Heritage Studies* 1, 59–75.

RECOMMENDED WEBSITES

Apartheid Museum – http://www.apartheidmuseum.org/

Archaeological Institute of America – http://www.archaeological.org/webinfo.php?page=10242

Auschwitz-Birkenau Museum and Memorial – http://en.auschwitz.org.pl/m/

Cold War Museum – http://www.coldwar.org/museum/berlin_wall_exhibit.html

European Heritage Library – http://euroheritage.net/

Evolution of the White Right – http://www.iss.co.za/Pubs/Monographs/No81/Chap2.html

Georgia Civil War Heritage Trails – http://www.gcwht.org/

Museum Haus am Checkpoint Charlie – http://www.mauermuseum.de/english/frame-index-mauer.html

Peres Center for Peace – http://www.peres-center.org/

Slave Heritage Resource Center – http://www.sonofthesouth.net/slavery/

South Carolina Plantations – http://south-carolina-plantations.com/plantation-tours.html

CHAPTER 7

THE NEED TO CONSERVE THE PAST: THE IMPACTS OF TOURISM

LEARNING OBJECTIVES

After reading this chapter, you should be able to:

1. Recognize the negative social and physical impacts of tourism at heritage sites and locales.

2. Understand that tourism can also result in positive social and ecological outcomes.

3. Develop an understanding about the characteristics and patterns of socio-cultural and ecological influences of heritage tourism.

4. Recognize that most positive impacts of mass tourism in areas of cultural importance come in the form of economic benefits.

5. Know that not all economic outcomes of cultural tourism are positive.

INTRODUCTION

All societies have been blessed with rich heritages, which they can use in a variety of ways. Tourism, as already noted, is only one of several uses of the past. The remains of history have been of interest to travelers for millennia, as even the ancient Egyptians, Greeks and Romans traveled throughout the known world of their time to experience renowned places of historical importance. The population of the world is much more mobile now than in ancient days, and increasing numbers of people are visiting ancient monuments and other historic sites. The pressures of increased visitation have taken their toll on many built environments; hundreds (thousands in some cases) of years of human contact with ancient relics have resulted in some places being altered in irreparable ways (see Plate 7.1).

Tourists climbing on or abusing heritage structures in other ways is a direct effect. Likewise, indirect human-induced change also occurs, particularly through the erosive effects of toxins and acids in the air and rain from factories, excessive numbers of automobiles and other sources of pollution. Likewise, pressures from agriculture and urbanization have put many historic places at risk of severe damage or depletion altogether.

Analogously, natural forces have unleashed their own vehemence on archaeological sites and other human-made structures. While it is obvious that different construction

Plate 7.1 This medieval pilgrim graffiti has become a permanent part of a sacred site in the Holy Land

materials have different degrees of resistance to weathering, all are affected in some way by the processes of nature. Deterioration and wear are very important problems in heritage management, and for most heritage managers protecting the past is their primary concern. To provide a background for understanding the need to conserve human heritage, which will be discussed in greater depth in the next two chapters, this chapter examines the impacts of tourism on heritage sites and living culture, the effects of local residents utilizing heritage resources and how natural processes affect cultural resources. The need for conservation is clearly established in this chapter.

HUMAN IMPACTS ON HERITAGE RESOURCES

Heritage tourism falls somewhere on the boundary line of mass tourism and special interest tourism, with mass tourism long being fingered as the primary culprit for the ecological and social damage by tourism so often acknowledged by scholars. On the other hand, special interest travel, many argue, is more ecologically and culturally sensitive, with smaller numbers of better-educated travelers visiting with fewer harmful outcomes. Mass heritage tourism is commonplace – usually manifested in package tours and comprised of the casual heritage tourists mentioned in Chapter 2. Special interest heritage tourism aligns more closely with the notion of serious heritage enthusiasts, who are earnest seekers of the past, whether for personal discovery, general education or to fulfill hobby-related needs. Regardless of this distinction, however, all heritage-based tourism exacts consequences on the socio-cultural, physical and economic environments they visit. Timothy and Boyd (2003) and Timothy and Nyaupane (2009) consider these issues in significant detail.

Social and cultural impacts

Among the most widely cited set of tourism impacts are those of a socio-cultural nature. This is especially important in the context of heritage tourism, since culture, including living culture, is at the center of this worldwide phenomenon. There is a vast and growing line of research that examines communities' perceptions of tourism, including why community residents might want to invite or expand tourism or why they object to it. No matter where the studies are done, there is a consistent set of outcomes, with only a few place-based variations. What communities desire most is jobs, but what they fear most about tourism are the negative social and cultural elements it brings with it. In the sphere of heritage tourism, several major negative effects can be identified:

- conflicting use of social space;
- cultural change;
- cultural commodification;
- cultural theft;
- forced displacement;
- disharmonious resident-tourist or destination-tourism relations.

Conflicting use of social space

Conflicts in the use of social space are manifest in various forms and situations. When thousands of tourists at a time descend upon small towns and villages, or hundreds of visitors at individual historic sites, overcrowding becomes a serious problem. Not only does this have ecological implications, it also deteriorates the social environment within which heritage is located.

Many heritage-rich communities suffer this fate. Historic urban centers and heritage shopping villages are especially prone to traffic and pedestrian congestion. In places such as Niagara-on-the-Lake, Ontario (Canada), and Fredericksburg, Texas (USA), which are both known as important regional heritage shopping villages, weekend and high-season crowds pack the streets and sidewalks. Residents of the two communities have difficulty leaving their garages – often their driveways are blocked by tourists' vehicles. In addition, many cases have been reported of garbage being disposed in people's yards and cars being parked on private property without permission. At peak times, village residents have little access to public spaces, such as supermarkets, laundries, restaurants or post offices because they are crowded out by outsiders. This congestion is not experienced only by residents; the sheer number of visitors in these communities can depreciate their own experiences. The same is true of historic centers in old cities. Füssen, a small town in southern Germany, and Innsbruck, a medium-sized city in Austria, are popular heritage destinations. Their historic cores become overcrowded on weekends, holidays and during the summer months, making navigating the streets, shopping and dining a significant challenge. In some places, such as St Jacobs, Ontario, and Fredericksburg, Texas, there are so many cars and pedestrians they block the views of the heritage buildings and other resources that have made the villages popular, creating frustrated visitors and stressed residents.

One prominent example of the same situation at a specific site is the Vatican Museums and Sistine Chapel in the Vatican City (see Plate 7.2). The chapel is home to magnificent artworks by the hands of masters such as Raphael and Michelangelo. For many people, viewing the works of art is a spiritual or otherwise moving experience. However, during peak season and weekends, throngs numbering hundreds at a time crowd inside the small

Plate 7.2 Large crowds of tourists waiting to enter the Vatican Museums

chapel. Humidity and heat levels run high during the summer months, and the noise can be overbearing at times, detracting from many people's experiences. To subdue the noise, the Vatican Museum employs professional shushers – employees with microphones who silence the audience every minute or two as the crowd grows louder.

Sites of religious significance are especially prone to congestion. The Vatican City is home to another situation that bears similar resemblance. St Peter's Basilica, the largest Catholic church in the world and the center of Roman Catholicism, is considered an extremely sacred place for the world's billion-plus Roman Catholics. It also happens to be one of the most important icons of Rome, and nearly every tour of the 'eternal city' makes a stop at the basilica. During the summer months, visitation is so heavy that prayerful pilgrims have little chance to meditate, pray or feel the spirit of the place as non-pilgrim tourists snap photos with flashes, yell or speak loudly. Similar conditions exist in Shinto shrines in Japan, Buddhist temples in Thailand and the Western Wall in Jerusalem.

Tourists are not known for being the most sensitive people to local cultures and social mores. Much disrespect is shown to local Buddhists in Thailand when western tourists photograph them praying, speak too loudly or refuse to take off their shoes to enter the holy temples.

While religious settings are among the most impacted by crowdedness, religious gatherings also tend to be among the largest tourist gatherings in the world. They are somewhat different from other forms of heritage tourism in the sense that the crowds sometimes enhance the religious experience. Few other types of heritage tourism encourage large crowds, but religious tourism is the exception. The annual *hajj* to Mecca, Saudi Arabia, and the tri-annual *Kumbha Mela* in India draw millions of religionists at the same time and in a relatively small and crowded space.

Cultural change

Cultural change is the second social impact. While many forces exist today that have a bearing on how cultures change (e.g. media, the internet, modernization), tourism is often blamed as one of the biggest culprits. It is suggested that as tourists come to town, bringing their own values and behaviors with them, they influence the values and behaviors of destination residents. Thus, a form of acculturation occurs, wherein the meeting of different groups of people causes changes to occur, including the adoption of tourist behaviors and social mores by the communities the tourists visit. Although not all cultural changes brought about by tourism, or partially by tourism, are bad, many cultural observers suggest that heritage tourism is in fact partly responsible for destination cultures undergoing some permanent changes and cultural modifications. This includes the deterioration of traditional values, a modification of ceremonies and rituals and a decreased appreciation for one's ancestors and indigenous past.

The demonstration effect is one concept that has been aptly applied to this context. It suggests that local people in tourist destinations observe the leisure lifestyles, wealth and materialism of the foreigners and desire to emulate it, because it exemplifies the 'good life'. This translates into people, usually youth, copying the consumption patterns and behaviors of the tourists, which has the potential to result in permanent changes to lifestyle, dress, food, family relations and other elements of culture.

Cultural commodification

A widespread form of cultural change is the commodification of culture. This occurs when tourist demand for tangible and intangible culture (i.e. heritage tourism) drives the production and 'packaging' of heritage for tourist consumption. The problem with this is that in the process of commoditization, the traditional values and meanings associated with music, dance, ceremonies, handicrafts and other artworks are lost as they are performed or assembled as merchandise for mass consumption. Art is manufactured according to tourists' taste rather than customary design. Once a point of pride among skilled people who took great care and delight in maintaining skills and art forms that had been passed down from generation to generation, unskilled and shoddy workmanship dominates the handicraft sector today almost everywhere. This results in the proliferation of 'tourist art', 'tourist kitsch' or 'airport art' – souvenirs that have little original significance and are inexpensive, sloppily made and easy to transport home.

An intangible and tangible example is the *wayang kulit* shadow puppet theater in Indonesia, which originally lasted many hours and sometimes a couple of days during a major celebration. Original *wayang kulit* and *wayang golek* puppets were handcrafted with great care and artistic detail, for they were considered the performers of the royal family, and there was also a spiritual element associated with the shows. Today, however, tourists buy *wayang* puppets that are mass produced and made of cheap materials by people who have little connection with the traditional form. In addition, the puppet shows themselves have been reduced from several hours to one hour or half an hour to fit tourists' itineraries instead of fulfilling the story-telling purpose of the event.

Similarly, many Maori performances for tourists in New Zealand are now done away from their traditional environments. While many of the dances are based on original scores and celebrations, they can now be viewed in strobe-lighted theaters in hotels and resorts, which somehow diminishes their credibility and authenticity. Many researchers have made similar observations regarding dances and other celebratory events in Indonesia, where tooth-filing ceremonies are brought to hotels and resorts and funerary rituals are modified and staged for tourists.

Cultural theft

Cultural theft is another important outcome of tourism. This can be seen from two perspectives: the literal stealing of historic artifacts and the misappropriation of culture from indigenous people by outsiders. History's remnants are stolen every day all over the world. As noted earlier in Chapter 3, the illicit trade in ancient artifacts is now widespread and growing. Recent estimates suggest that antiquities collectors number in the hundreds of millions, feeding a booming multi-billion dollar trade in illegal ancient artifacts and following only drugs and armaments in volume and scale on the global black market.

Several tourism-specific perspectives on the illegal trade in antiquities can be highlighted. In many Mediterranean destinations, such as Turkey, Lebanon, Syria, Egypt and Jordan, tourists are commonly approached by small-scale antiquities sellers who try to convince them to buy something the seller has found or dug illegally. These artifacts are commonplace in tourist markets in Asia, Africa and Latin America. Likewise, some legitimate antiquities dealers also sell clandestine artifacts among their lawful artifacts; they can get away with doing this relatively easily because it is hard for government agents to know which artifacts were obtained legally and which were obtained illegally. Additionally, dealers and brokers are also tourists as they travel to purchase or sell their relics. They frequently travel to their source regions to purchase stock from excavators or middle people, then return home to sell their products. Finally, tourists themselves may find artifacts on the ground or conduct their own digs at historic places.

The misappropriation of living culture is a significant aspect of theft as well. This happens most often in traditional societies, where outsiders come in and 'borrow' aspects of culture without permission – sometimes even with permission but with a loss of control by the natives. Of primary concern here is the loss of power and true ownership over culture by the people whose culture it is. Many indigenous groups have lost ownership over certain elements of their heritage as foreigners and tourism promoters have misused them, usually without acquiescence. Native Americans have been especially prone to this in the past. Traditional aboriginal American dress has long been used by Anglo-Americans for entertainment purposes in movies, games and tourism, much to the chagrin of the natives. Feathered chief headdresses, moccasins and weaponry (tomahawks and spears) have long been stereotypically used by all but Native Americans themselves to portray the lifestyle and patrimony of the indigenes. These, together with miniature teepees (conical shelters made of skins) that were used by the Plains Indians as homes, and other cultural objects, have a long history of being commodified for tourist consumption – far beyond the influence of the Plains Indians to whom this heritage belongs (see Plate 7.3). Today most of these items are mass produced in China, are cheap tourist kitsch and ownership of their cultural significance by Native Americans has been lost.

The use of American Indian icons and concepts in the sports arena has raised some interesting controversies in recent years as well. The Washington Redskins and Kansas City Chiefs football teams and the Cleveland Indians and Atlanta Braves baseball teams have been at the center of debates and are facing pressure from Native American groups to change their names or risk being sued. This is a way the natives are trying to reclaim intellectual ownership of their heritage and prevent what they feel is an insulting use of their heritage.

Plate 7.3 Indian teepee being commodified in Arizona, where teepees never originally existed

In other cases, native symbols have been appropriated by government agencies and private companies as trademarks for their own products. The Maori koru has long been used by Air New Zealand to create a recognizable trademark. Other companies and government agencies have used Maori sacred symbols in their logos as a way of shoring up national sentiment, but also to serve as an impetus for the commercial growth of tourism. According to the Maoris, the tourism industry in New Zealand has long misrepresented and misappropriated Maori culture, including the use of symbols and living culture. The Maoris, today, however, have taken back the intellectual property rights of their cultural symbols, based on earlier treaties and laws, and use of their emblems is now subject to Maori approval.

Forced displacement

Forced displacement occurs when villages and neighborhoods are moved to make way for tourism development. Almost always, residents have little choice in the matter and the compensation offered them is miniscule and hardly compensatory for the trauma of being uprooted from ancestral lands and having to build a new home in an unfamiliar region or

156

area. Unfortunately, forced out-migration occurs more often than we think it does and is especially problematic in the less-developed parts of the globe. There are many instances where villagers have been forced from their homes and ancestral lands to make way for tourism development, including heritage tourism.

In Indonesia, this happened at the Prambanan and Borobudur temple complexes in the 1970s; villages were removed and villagers were threatened and intimidated when they refused to leave or accept the government's insignificant compensation. Bullying, threats, torture, imprisonment and extortion are not uncommon tactics used by oppressive governments to clear the way for the 'protection' of cultural and natural heritage areas. This usually results in the exclusion of native peoples from their own lands. While foreign tourists are welcomed openly, the original inhabitants, who were compelled to leave, are shunned and shut out. Plenty of signs in the less-developed world warn locals against entering a tourism property, national park or heritage zone – areas they and their grand-parents once freely used for fishing, hunting and grazing livestock.

Disharmonious relations between residents and tourists

All of these negative conditions – crowdedness, cultural change, cultural commodifi-cation, cultural theft, forced migration and others (e.g. prostitution, crime, poverty) – combine to create disharmonious resident-tourist and community-tourism relations. Given these conditions it is little wonder that some communities despise the notion of tourism. Sharing their living and built heritage with outsiders becomes a necessary evil for many, because they need jobs and income, while others shun the idea of developing tourism altogether.

Positive social impacts

While the socio-cultural implications of heritage tourism seem grave, they are not all bad. There are in fact several important ways in which tourism can contribute to social and cultural well-being. Perhaps the most notable of these is tourism's role in the revival of lost or declining elements of culture. Dances, certain musical traditions and architectural styles in Asia that were lost or on the verge of being lost have been revived, in part at least by the desire to share traditional culture with tourists. In many instances, tourism has provided the economic rationale for saving historic buildings that might otherwise be demolished.

Societal esteem may also be a result of cultural tourism. It is common in the less-developed world for local residents to wonder what about them and their villages could possibly be of interest to foreign tourists. However, when communities realize their culture is of interest to outsiders it can help incubate a sense of cultural pride, which in turn helps preserve living heritage, clean up the built environment and maintain a greener and cleaner community. Some countries, such as Indonesia, have offered prestigious awards for the cleanest and best kept heritage communities.

Related to societal esteem is the notion of empowerment and control through tourism, especially heritage tourism. Social empowerment enhances a community's solidarity as stakeholders work together for the common good of the entire community. Customarily, tourism development planning has been done in a top-down fashion and imposed upon local people in tourist destinations with little feedback or generation of ideas coming from the community. However, the paradigm is shifting, and indigenous knowledge is now viewed as an important part of finding solutions to more sustainable uses of historical and natural resources. Traditionally, development projects in most parts of the world have caused local residents to choose between tradition and conservation. Now, however, the two are not seen as being on opposing ends of a development spectrum, as local and indigenous knowledge are seen as salient constituent parts of the policy-making process. This approach builds a common identity, community capacity and social capital, and develops the strengths of indigenous knowledge.

Finally, the honor with which many indigenous people and other local residents approach the tourist use of their culture has in some cases resulted in the nurturing of traditional art forms and the creation of new art forms that are high in quality and which do not detract from the traditions of the people. High-quality art forms that accurately depict the lives and customs of the people have an inherent value in preserving the past, illustrating traditions and teaching the past to new indigenous generations and outsiders as well.

Physical impacts

Perhaps even more profound are the impacts of heritage tourists on the physical fabric of the environment. Paradoxically, it is the very presence of the visitors themselves that deteriorates the items they have come to gaze upon.

Wear and tear

Wear and tear is the most obvious. Years of visitation and millions of clambering feet or probing fingers on stone, tile, metal or ceramic surfaces wear away motifs, carvings, designs and other details but also change the form of the base material itself, which is obvious on ancient stairs and walkways. Wherever there are ancient heritage sites, there are examples of wear and tear by excessive tourist traffic. The floors of many churches and cathedrals in Europe are the final resting places of famous priests, government leaders and royalty. Hundreds of years of wear and tear over the embedded grave stones have caused many of them to disappear almost entirely. Canterbury Cathedral in England and the Monastery of Alcobaça in Portugal are examples where numerous grave motifs have seriously deteriorated.

In St Peter's Basilica, in the Vatican City, centuries of time and millions (if not billions) of pilgrims' fingers and lips touching or kissing the feet of the 13th century bronze statue

Plate 7.4 Tourists rubbing the feet of St Peter in the Vatican City

of St Peter Enthroned have almost completely worn away the apostle's toes (see Plate 7.4). Likewise, many of the stairs and paving stones in Jerusalem where Jesus was said to have walked have been worn down by years of use by pilgrims and curiosity seekers. The construction stones of the Pyramids of Giza were also being worn down to the point where the Egyptian government finally erected barricades to prevent visitors from climbing on the stones. Cemeteries are also important heritage resources that struggle with various tourist activities such as 'grave rubbing', where people place paper over tombstone epithets and rub pencils or charcoal over them to trace the gravestone design onto paper. In the eastern USA (e.g. Boston and Philadelphia) this is a problem at the very old graves of famous people, such as Paul Revere and Benjamin Franklin. Some of these stones are hundreds of years old and in a delicate condition. Rubbing hastens the corrosion of the stones, and it can mark them permanently. This problem occurs in Great Britain and mainland Europe as well, wherever very old gravestones are found.

Erosion and soil compaction

A related problem is compaction and erosion associated with people trampling the green space around historic monuments. Walking off prescribed paths and trails is a salient problem at heritage sites, although it is more fixable than the wear and tear exacted on the ancient artifacts themselves. Nonetheless, soil compaction occurs, preventing vegetation from growing and increasing water runoff and erosion. This is a serious problem in national parks and other protected areas. Not only does this do harm to the natural environment, but it can also result in damage to the built environment as mudslides and flooding result.

Vandalism

Vandalism, like wear and tear, usually results in irreparable damage to historic environments. There is something about the human psyche that causes some people to want to leave their mark when they visit interesting and meaningful places. Even more common, however, is the desire to take a piece of a splendid place home with them as a way of proving they have been somewhere important, or simply because they want to own a piece of history. Countless ancient sites are riddled with graffiti, painted and carved (see Plate 7.5). Names, dates and comments about the location are typical types of graffiti. These not only detract from the spirit of place and the esthetic experience, they also ruin

Plate 7.5 Caves in Aruba where ancient Arawak Indian paintings were destroyed by tourist vandals

much of the scientific value of such places. While spray paint is somewhat easier to clean up than carved graffiti, both are extremely destructive – and sometimes the cleaning process can be more damaging than the vandalism itself, depending on the construction material, the nature of the graffiti and the type of method used for restoration (e.g. chemicals, sand blasting or painting over).

The other type of vandalism, collecting, is a significant problem at archaeological sites worldwide. In most places, it is illegal even to pick up pottery shards if found in archaeological parks or other historic areas. Heritage site managers are well aware of the constant threat of breaking, digging or picking up bits and pieces of the past as souvenirs. Many statues in English cathedrals have been victimized by collectors as limbs or other appendages have been broken off by unscrupulous visitors. Tile mosaics in the Middle East, Turkey and Greece are regularly pillaged by tourists, and Native American sites often fall prey to pottery and arrowhead collectors.

Illegal trade in artifacts

As already mentioned, the illicit trade in antiquities is extremely destructive to the past, as relics and precious artifacts are dug and sold on the black market. In addition to the loss of small relics, many ancient tombs and archaeological sites are destroyed in the process. Most grave robbers dig, remove, break and plunder without regard for the archaeological sites or tombs that house the historical objects, destroying them in the process. One of the saddest aspects of this tragic pattern is the loss of scientific knowledge and the history that will remain untold.

Pollution and litter

Litter and pollution are equally injurious to the historic environment. In urban historic zones, there is a particular problem with car emissions. In crowded, ancient cities like Rome, Paris, Florence, Budapest, Prague or Madrid automobile exhausts have blackened white and grey stone structures during the past century. Additionally, the poisonous chemicals in the exhaust are known to eat away at granite, bronze and even cement, thus contributing to the corrosion of statues, monuments and historic buildings. Some of these have to undergo periodic reparation work. During spring and summer 2009 the outer walls of St Peter's Basilica in Rome underwent a major cleansing, which had not been done at such a scale since before the advent of the automobile!

Litter can be a major problem at historical monuments from a number of perspectives, but primarily in that it takes away from the visitor experience and can damage the physical structure of the site. The esthetic appeal diminishes notably as litter increases and places become unsightly. One particular form of garbage derived from heritage tourists is 'ritual litter', which is ordinarily found at sites of spiritual or religious importance. Local religious adherents and religious tourists use flowers, papers, candles, dyes, incense and bottles in

Plate 7.6 Ritual litter in the Ganges River, India, creates health and esthetic problems

their ritual performances, which cause pollution and scar the landscapes where they worship. In some places, such as Varanasi, India, on the Ganges River, this is a very salient problem particularly in relation to public health (see Plate 7.6).

Rubbish strewn about at historic sites, including food, food and drink containers, cigarettes and newspapers can have serious and long-lasting impacts on delicate surfaces. Fried food, candy, gum and spilled soft drinks can ruin some surfaces. Certain types of stones are absorbent and can soak up grease, gum and candy, making them particularly hard to clean.

Positive physical impacts

In common with the cultural realm, not all physical impacts of heritage tourism are negative although most of them are. One positive outcome is the generation of additional income to help preserve heritage places. Most countries in the world face severe budget cuts, and unfortunately built heritage is oftentimes one of the first 'luxuries' to be slashed from public budgets. Conservation is not cheap, so most destinations and site managers welcome visitors for the additional revenue they bring in to help in meeting conservation objectives. Likewise, tourism can act as an impetus for creating public awareness of the need to preserve the built environment. The establishment of national parks, national monuments and other protected areas is often justified by the existence of tourism.

Economic impacts

Like all other forms of tourism, from an economics perspective, heritage tourism's impacts are mostly positive. In fact, in the arena of economic impact, there are few differences between heritage and other forms of tourism. Nevertheless, this section examines some of the issues that apply well to cultural heritage-based tourism.

Job creation

One of the most pressing needs in all destinations is jobs, and tourism is commonly seen as a labor-intensive industry that generates both direct and indirect employment. This is usually cited as the number one reason governments and destination managers target tourists as a vehicle for economic development. Direct employment refers to the jobs that are created directly in tourism – where the workers work face to face with the tourists or in the various sectors of tourism. Examples of direct employment include a museum curator, a historic theme park actor, a cashier at an historic site, a housekeeper at an historic hotel and a warden or park ranger at a national monument (see Table 7.1). These are usually the most desirable and visible jobs, but destination managers should also understand the indirect and induced employment that accrues to an area via a tourism multiplier, which measures the total impact of tourist expenditures in an area including the ripple effects into other sectors. Multipliers tell how much money is actually generated in a region for every dollar spent by outsiders.

Table 7.1 Examples of direct employment jobs in heritage tourism

Establishment type	Job type
Ancient monument/ruins	Groundskeepers, cashiers, ticket vendors, site managers, security guards, interpreters, archaeologists, historians, wardens/rangers
Cultural festivals	Planners and organizers, vendors, cashiers, custodians, performers, set-up and take-down staffers, first-aid personnel, lighting specialists
Museums	Managers, assistant managers, interpreters, custodians, shop managers, museum and shop cashiers, historians, staff scientists
Historic theme parks/folklife museums	Gardeners, groundskeepers, animal caretakers, actors, interpreters, maintenance staffers, managers, cashiers, first aid personnel, security guards
Heritage railways	Train conductors, engineers, ticket agents, food and drink servers, housekeepers, maintenance crew
Religious sites	Custodians, groundskeepers, clergy, donation desk workers, philanthropic organization representatives
Historic hotels	Front desk clerk, housekeepers, cooks, serving staff, groundskeepers, managers, reservation agents, security staff, human resource managers

Indirect employment is an application of the multiplier concept and refers to the additional non-tourism jobs that are created by the spending of people who work directly in tourism. So, for instance, when the cashier at a museum shop takes his grandchildren bowling, the money he spends (which he received from heritage tourism) creates additional income and jobs at the bowling alley. When the manager of an historic hotel spends money at the supermarket, she is helping to create additional indirect jobs. This ripple effect continues throughout the region as jobs are created when the supermarket and bowling alley employees buy gasoline, groceries and new shoes. In this regard, then, tourism, including cultural tourism, is an important consideration for decision makers as they plan the future courses of their communities.

Regional income growth

Regional income is another positive fiscal outcome of heritage tourism and is another of the most important goals of destination planners and marketers. Research shows that heritage tourists tend to be big spenders for a variety of reasons. One reason is that they are more affluent than general tourists and are therefore more able to spend more money while in the destination. Also, people visiting heritage sites often want a piece of the past to take with them so souvenir and handicraft shopping tends to be an important part of the heritage experience as well. There is also a tendency among most heritage tourists to want to take something home for friends and family when they have had a positive cultural experience as a way of sharing the experience with those who were not in attendance.

The importance of increased regional income is that heritage tourism can bring money that was not there before into a province, state, region or country. From the perspective of a country, domestic tourism is very important because it gets money moving about the economy and increases spending and entrepreneurship. However, international tourism has the added benefit of bringing currency, which was not there before, into a country. The same perspective can be taken from any scale: a state in Australia receiving tourists from another state, a city in Thailand receiving tourists from another city or a canton in Switzerland receiving visitors from another canton.

Tax revenue

Tax revenue generation provides another impetus for developing tourism. Tourism generates nearly all forms of taxes, including income, property, sales, tobacco and alcohol, and there are several that are tourism-specific: car rental, lodging and airport fees. There are fewer taxes that derive specifically from heritage tourism, but it is important to consider the general tourism taxes from a heritage perspective and remember that much of the general tourism phenomenon is cultural in nature. Admissions fees at historic sites and monuments often include a government surcharge or sales tax ranging from a few tenths of a percent to several percent of the total entrance fee. In many countries this tax, or much of it, is used to repair or preserve historic properties or to pay for their management and interpretation. In Parks Canada and US National Park Service properties this is generally the case. In most places, however, the money goes to other costs such as road maintenance and education.

Government fees/taxes are also levied on legal antiquities dealers who sell to tourists through licensing and annual registration fees, and the same is true of heritage transport operators. Likewise, airport departure taxes apply to all departing visitors but are more directly linked to heritage tourism in destinations whose primary appeal is remnants of the past or living culture.

Negative economic implications

While tourism is seen overwhelmingly in a positive economic light there are a few negative implications associated with its growth. Inflation is perhaps one of the most notable of these. As tourism grows prices have a tendency to grow as well, making everyday life more expensive not only for visitors but for local residents as well. Over-inflated property value is a related concept. When tourism grows property values also rise, making it difficult for local people to afford to pay their property taxes and for younger people to afford to buy homes or businesses, which can in fact result in more expatriate and foreign ownership of businesses. Among other negatives, this results in heavy leakages of money from local economies into the hands of affluent investors from abroad. Unfortunately, heritage and its conservation contribute to over-inflated property values. When urban neighborhoods, villages or heritage buildings in general are allocated heritage status by some authoritative governing body, prices almost always escalate to unaffordable levels.

Overdependence on tourism or one type of tourism is a problematic situation. When destinations are too dependent on tourism for their economic well-being, it puts them in a highly vulnerable position in relation to world markets and trends. As soon as economic downturns occur in the primary source regions, tourist arrivals plummet. As well, when demographic profiles change (e.g. increased numbers of baby-boomers), or weather-related events transpire (e.g. hurricane season), tourism industries begin to suffer tremendously. Thus, places that are too economically dependent on tourism are at the mercy of external forces that are beyond their control. The key is diversification. Places that have a balance of agriculture, fishing, manufacturing, mining and service sectors such as tourism have a much better chance of weathering the economic storms that will come.

There are many regions and countries that are overly reliant on built and living culture as their primary attraction. The province of Yogyakarta, Indonesia, a region extremely rich in heritage resources, realized this in the 1990s and began efforts to develop alternative forms of tourism, such as beach-based tourism, agritourism and mountain hiking. Bali, too, has had considerable success in emphasizing cultural and beach tourism in its tourism plans. Some islands that have become too dependent on sun, sea and sand tourism have begun to realize the need to diversify and have begun to focus on native and colonial heritage as well, such as the Turks and Caicos Islands and the Bahamas.

SUMMARY AND CONCLUSION

This chapter provided a broad overview of the socio-cultural, physical and economic impacts of heritage tourism on cultural resources and destinations. It has also described many of the impacts exacted on heritage sites by residents and natural processes and has set the tone for the next two chapters on conservation by illustrating the urgent need to preserve the past against the growing threat of tourism.

Tourist activities exact physical impacts on precious heritage in the form of vandalism, wear and tear and pollution, although tourism can also stimulate conservation and help fund it. From a socio-cultural perspective tourism affects cultural resources through changes in forms and functions of traditional artworks, commodification of living culture, crowded conditions and the development of a general ill-will against tourists on the part of community members. Nonetheless, it can also help resurrect lost traditions and preserve endangered ones. On a more positive note, tourism helps create jobs and taxes and stimulates entrepreneurialism in heritage destinations.

Cultural tourism, like other forms of tourism, is not all positive for heritage environments, and contrary to some marketing specialists should not be promoted at all costs. Careful planning and concerted conservation efforts are needed to counteract the destructive forces of large-scale heritage tourism.

REVIEW QUESTIONS

1. Why are religious sites especially prone to discord between tourists and worshippers?

2. Why would native peoples be offended by the tourism establishment adopting emblems of their culture to produce for tourist consumption?

3. In what ways can heritage tourism bring about negative outcomes or accentuate existing problems in a region?

4. What are the primary problems facing heritage site managers from a physical impacts perspective?

5. To what extent do you think the physical impacts of tourism at cultural sites are fixable?

6. Are the positive economic contributions that cultural tourism provides any different from those created by other types of tourism?

RECOMMENDED READING

Alley, K.D. (1998) Images of waste and purification on the banks of the Ganga. *City and Society* 10(1), 167–182.

Brimblecombe, P. (2003) *The Effects of Air Pollution on the Built Environment.* London: Imperial College Press.

Brunt, P. and Courtney, P. (1999) Host perceptions of sociocultural impacts. *Annals of Tourism Research* 26, 493–515.

Cabeza, A. (2001) Evaluating the environmental impact of development projects on the archaeological heritage of Chile. *Conservation and Management of Archaeological Sites* 4(4), 245–247.

Carter, B. and Grimwade, G. (1997) Balancing use and preservation in cultural heritage management. *International Journal of Heritage Studies* 3(1), 45–53.

Cohen, E. (1993) The heterogeneization of a tourist art. *Annals of Tourism Research* 20, 138–163.

Fyall, A. and Garrod, B. (1998) Heritage tourism: At what price? *Managing Leisure* 3(4), 213–228.

Gauri, K.L. and Holdren, G.C. (1981) Pollutant effects on stone monuments. *Environmental Science and Technology* 15, 386–390.

Graburn, N. (1984) The evolution of tourist arts. *Annals of Tourism Research* 11, 393–419.

James, J.A. and Wilde, C.M. (2007) The bigger they are, the harder they fall! Sustainable tourism planning at Naracoorte Caves World Heritage Site, Australia. *Journal of Heritage Tourism* 2(3), 196–210.

Kasim, A. (2006) The need for business environmental and social responsibility in the tourism industry. *International Journal of Hospitality and Tourism Administration* 7(1), 1–22.

Kausar, D.R. and Nishikawa, Y. (2010) Heritage tourism in rural areas: Challenges for improving socio-economic impacts. *Asia Pacific Journal of Tourism Research* 15(2), 195–213.

Kirtsoglu, E. and Theodossopoulos, D. (2004) "They are taking our culture away": Tourism and culture commodification in the Garifuna community of Roatan. *Critique of Anthropology* 24(2), 135–157.

Lafont, M. (2004) *Pillaging Cambodia: The Illicit Traffic in Khmer Art.* Jefferson, NC: McFarland and Co.

Mathieson, A. and Wall, G. (1982) *Tourism: Economic, Physical and Social Impacts.* London: Longman.

Saiz-Jimenez, C. (2004) *Air Pollution and Cultural Heritage.* London: Taylor and Francis.

Setiawan, B. and Timothy, D.J. (2000) Existing urban management frameworks and heritage conservation in Indonesia. *Asia Pacific Journal of Tourism Research* 5(2), 76–79.

Timothy, D.J. (1994) Environmental impacts of heritage tourism: Physical and socio-cultural perspectives. *Manusia dan Lingkungan* 11(4), 37–49.

Turkington, A.V. (ed.) (2005) *Stone Decay in the Architectural Environment.* Boulder, CO: Geological Society of America.

Wall, G. and Mathieson, A. (2007) *Tourism: Changes, Impacts and Opportunities.* London: Prentice Hall.

RECOMMENDED WEBSITES

Fredericksburg, Texas – http://www.fredericksburg-texas.com/

Maori Cultural Performances – http://www.newzealand.com/travel/media/features/maori-culture/kapa-haka-performances_feature.cfm

Niagara-on-the-Lake Chamber of Commerce – http://www.niagaraonthelake.com/

Vatican Museums, Sistine Chapel – http://mv.vatican.va/3_EN/pages/CSN/CSN_Main.html

Wayang Kulit shadow puppets – http://discover-indo.tierranet.com/wayang.html

CHAPTER 8

PROTECTIVE LEGISLATION AND CONSERVATION ORGANIZATIONS

LEARNING OBJECTIVES

After reading this chapter, you should be able to:

1. Learn about national laws that help protect the built environment and living culture in key heritage destination countries.

2. Understand key points in protective legislation throughout the world.

3. Be aware of the vital role of cross-border cooperation in protecting cultural sites and areas.

4. Know the importance of heritage protection at the supranational level.

5. Understand the leadership position of UNESCO, ICOMOS and the World Monuments Fund in protecting the world's heritage.

INTRODUCTION

As the previous chapter indicated, human and natural forces combine to deteriorate the cultural environment in many ways. Because heritage is a non-renewable resource and easily damage or destroyed, it is vital that individual countries and multinational organizations work to achieve goals of sustainability in the realm of heritage, so that valuable and fragile resources will be maintained for the benefit of future generations. At the national level legislation can be ratified to protect the built and living culture within a country. Beyond the nation, however, at the supranational level, laws are virtually impossible to enact because sovereignty lies with each country, not within multinational alliances. Nevertheless, many bilateral and multilateral arrangements have been made by international treaty to encourage, or even obligate, member nations to uphold heritage protection measures.

This chapter examines legislative actions and non-profit organizational endeavors within individual countries that aim to protect elements of the human past, using Australia, Canada, Italy, the USA and the United Kingdom as examples. It then presents the notion of supranationalism, wherein multinational forums and trade alliances are created to deal not only with cross-border trade but conservation treaties as well.

CONSERVATION BODIES: NATIONAL LEGISLATION AND INTERNATIONAL COOPERATION

Since the heritage protection movement began several decades ago, awareness has increased among national governments about the need to protect the past. Many diverse laws, which aim to protect both natural and cultural environments, have been enacted throughout the world in recent years. Unfortunately, many of these have laws were passed too recently with the result that much heritage has been destroyed in the meantime. Nonetheless, these pieces of legislation have been instrumental in facilitating considerable heritage protection endeavors in the post-colonial era. Table 8.1 illustrates a selection of national laws in post-communist Eastern Europe and the Caucasus region that aim to protect, define and manage each country's national heritage. The following sections describe the development of heritage protection legislation in several countries where culture features prominently in the tourism landscape.

Table 8.1 Recent laws protecting the cultural heritage of Eastern Europe and the Caucasus

Country	Law	Purpose
Albania	The Cultural Heritage Act, 2003	This is the most important legal framework for all activities related to preserving, promoting and managing Albania's national heritage.
Azerbaijan	The Law on the Protection of Historical and Cultural Monuments, 1998	This defines the issues and responsibilities of state and local authorities, and lays down principles for the use, study, conservation, restoration, reconstruction, renovation and safety of monuments. It prevents the privatization of artifacts at monuments and in museums, archives and libraries.
Estonia	The Heritage Conservation Act, 2002	The law distinguishes between different types of historical monuments and strictly controls the use of historical monuments. Local governments have the right to impose restrictions on building activities in historically valuable areas.

Georgia	Cultural Heritage Law, 2007	The 2007 law supersedes a 1999 law and defines the terms and general mechanisms for protecting the cultural past from encroachment. It pertains to movable and immovable objects and outlines protection zones throughout the country.
Moldova	Law on Historical Monument Protection, 1993	The current legal framework, together with the Law on Museums (2002), aims to protect monuments through a state register. It includes both movable and immovable cultural elements.
Serbia	Law on Heritage Protection, 1994	This law provides rules regarding how to conduct inventories, categorize heritage and define the duties of archives, libraries and museums.

Source: Based on Compendium (2009)

Australia

Australia has a long indigenous history that remains strong, with the aboriginal people still firmly connected to the lands of their ancestors. European settlement began in the 1700s and established coastal towns and eventually the states and territories that currently make up the Australian state. As the natives of Australia were nomadic hunters and gatherers, not village dwellers, very few physical remains exist of their thousands of years on the continent, with the exception of movable artifacts. The main thrust of aboriginal heritage today is living culture, hunting, music and dance and folkways. The country's built heritage dominates the coastal cities and interior mining and ranching communities.

Australia's first national park (The National Park) was created in 1879, following the example of Yellowstone in the USA. While The National Park was established primarily as a recreation venue for Sydneysiders, rather than as a protected area for nature, it laid the foundation for an eventual widespread network of national parks and other protected areas in Australia (see Plate 8.1). Other national parks were established in the 1890s and early 1900s and have since spread throughout the country.

Various legislative acts were passed in Australia during the 1900s that dealt with specific projects or properties. With an increased concern about the country's growing cities, population pressures and environmental concerns, additional legislation was needed to help protect nature and culture. The Historic Shipwrecks Act of 1976 protects historic wrecks and their related relics that are older than 75 years, although the law enables the Department of Environment, Water, Heritage and the Arts to protect wrecks younger than 75 years if they are deemed to be of significant heritage value. The act protects shipwrecks

Plate 8.1 Instructional sign to help conservation efforts in a national park in Australia

for conservation, recreation, education and scientific purposes. Three more recent laws have particular relevance to nationwide cultural heritage: the Protection of Movable Heritage Act (1986); the Aboriginal and Torres Strait Islander Heritage Protection Act (1984), and the Australian Heritage Council Act (2003). The 1986 decree aims to protect Australia's movable cultural artifacts and supports the protection by foreign states of their own movable cultural objects. The 1984 act protects the places and objects of cultural importance to the indigenous population. Finally, an act of 2003 established the Australian Heritage Council, whose job is: to assess heritage issues under the country's broader environmental protection laws; to advise the environment minister on heritage places being considered for the National Heritage List or Commonwealth Heritage List; to nominate places for these lists; to advise the minister about education, promotion, research training, policies, grants, finances, monitoring, assessing and conserving cultural heritage (Department of Environment, Water, Heritage and the Arts, 2009).

The Australian National Heritage List is a registry of places considered to be of outstanding heritage importance for Australia and currently includes 103 indigenous, colonial and natural heritage areas throughout Australia and its territories (including the Australian Antarctic Territory) under the protection of the Environmental Protection and Biodiversity Conservation Act of 1999. A similar list, the Commonwealth Heritage List was founded in 1999 and is comprised of natural, native and European heritage sites that are owned and operated by the Australian government and reflect the development of Australia as a nation (Department of Environment, Water, Heritage and the Arts, 2009).

Canada

Canada is a multicultural society. Unlike its neighbor to the south, the USA, which has long adopted an assimilationist stance to immigration, Canada encourages immigrants to retain their cultures and contribute to the country's multicultural society. Thus, many immigrant groups (e.g. Ukrainians, Italians, Finns, Greeks and Chinese) have remained relatively intact and a distinct part of the living heritage of Canada. In addition, the indigenous population (First Nations) is varied, representing a wide range of ethno-linguistic groups and social networks. Nonetheless, the Canadian government, in its endeavors to preserve the nation's heritage, has sought to protect and promote Canadian national unity and identity.

Canada has a long tradition of conserving its varied cultural pasts at national, provincial and municipal levels. The Dominion Lands Act was passed by parliament in 1883, putting the management of public lands in the hands of the Minister of the Interior and enabling the federal government to designate public lands as nature preserves. Established in 1885, Banff National Park was the first national park in Canada. In 1930 the National Parks Act was passed, paving the way for additional parks to be established as well as cultural properties under Parks Canada as National Landmarks and National Historic Sites. The National Archives of Canada was founded in 1872 and the National Gallery of Canada in 1880 to preserve works of art and documents of historical importance.

The Historic Sites and Monuments Board was established in 1985 via the Historic Sites and Monuments Act to help Canada preserve its cultural past (see Plate 8.2). In 1990 the Museums Act and in 1995 the Department of Canadian Heritage Act were created to preserve the country's heritage for current and future generations. The Department of Canadian Heritage is charged with promoting Canada's heritage of human rights and multiculturalism. It also directs policies related to matters of the arts, literature, film, national battlefields, sport, state ceremonial symbols, culture in general, national museums, archives and libraries, and oversees the conservation, importation and exportation of cultural property (Canadian Heritage, 2009).

Italy

Italy as we know it today only became a country in 1861 after the unification of several small kingdoms and microstates on the Italian Peninsula, but its rich and varied heritage became a point of discussion in the national assembly as early as 1902 – when legislators

Plate 8.2 A commemorative marker in Saint John, New Brunswick, erected by Canada's Historic Sites and Monuments Board

adopted laws and policies to protect the ancient and nationalist heritages. In the 1920s the Ministry of Popular Culture was created to oversee all aspects of culture, but it soon became unpopular owing to its political underpinnings in a fascist state. During the 1930s several key laws were passed that helped protect the built heritage and cultural landscapes, including the Law on 2% for the Arts in Public Buildings. The Institute for Restoration was also established in the 1930s to administer the policy making and protection of historic artifacts and the built environment.

In 1975, the Ministry of Heritage was formed to oversee activities related to monuments, museums, libraries, book publishing and cultural institutions. The ministry's responsibilities were expanded in 1998 to include the performing arts and cinema and in 2000, under the new name of the Ministry for Heritage and Cultural Activities, to embrace copyright issues as well (Compendium, 2009).

USA

Ioannides and Timothy (2010) identify five distinct themes that dominate the heritage tourism product of the USA: Native American; nationalistic and colonial; immigrant; frontier and westward settlement; and industrial. Given the size and varied history of the USA, there is a vast variety of cultural places and living cultures that have become important visitor attractions both for domestic and foreign tourists.

Perhaps the earliest major milestone in the US conservation movement was the establishment of Yellowstone National Park, which not only started the national parks program in the USA but also initiated the lands protection movement across the globe. In 1906, the Antiquities Act empowered the president to designate additional protected cultural areas as historic landmarks or national monuments. The National Park Service Act of 1916 was especially important in developing the role of the National Park Service and the protection of additional natural and cultural areas. This law established the legal mechanisms by which the government could safeguard the cultural and natural heritage for future generations (see Plate 8.3).

Bills of more recent vintage are also crucial tools in the preservation of America's cultural heritage. Perhaps the most influential with the specific purpose of preserving cultural heritage is the 1966 National Historic Preservation Act. This created the National Register of Historic Places (NRHP), the list of National Historic Landmarks (NHLs) and individual State Historic Preservation Offices. NHLs are recognized by the US government for their national significance. All 2455 NHLs are listed among the 80,000-plus properties on the National Register of Historic Places. The 80,000-plus registry is maintained by the National Park Service and lists sites, buildings, objects, districts and other structures that are considered important enough to preserve.

In 1949, President Truman signed a bill that established the National Trust for Historic Preservation with the aim of providing leadership, education, advocacy and resources to rescue the country's historic places and revitalize communities. The trust itself owns

Plate 8.3 San Juan National Historic Site (US National Park Service), one of Puerto Rico's most significant cultural attractions

29 historic properties, but it also provides technical assistance and direct financial aid to non-profit organizations, communities, individuals, government agencies and for-profit enterprises involved in preservation projects. The trust also assists these parties in searching for additional funding from government and non-government sources, and the agency itself is funded by membership fees, donations and corporate partnerships. Several programs have been directed under the trust's auspices that aim to increase public awareness of the importance of heritage in our daily lives. These include, among others, the Main Street Program, Historic Hotels of America, Endangered Places, Heritage Tourism, Save America's Treasures, Neighborhood Schools, Rural Heritage and Gulf Coast Recovery (National Trust for Historic Preservation, 2009).

As a federal system with several lower-order civil divisions (e.g. states, counties, municipalities), heritage preservation in the USA can take place on many different levels or scales. In addition to the National Park Service (NPS) each state has its own State Historic Preservation Office, which consults with the NPS about potential new listings for the NRHP. Likewise, each state has its own state parks agency that protects not only natural landscapes but also places and buildings of heritage significance at the state or local levels. Kentucky State Parks operates 17 state resort parks, 24 recreation parks and

11 state historic sites. Additionally, ten of Kentucky's recreation and resort parks have a cultural heritage significance.

Many counties in the US also have established county parks of a heritage nature. San Diego County, California, for example, manages eight heritage sites important to the San Diego region. Similarly, most municipal governments have parks and recreation departments, many of which own and operate park properties of an historical nature. In Arizona, for instance, the Phoenix Parks and Recreation Department operates more than 185 parks, playgrounds and recreation areas. The department's holdings include museums, historical sites and historic homes plus Native American ruins and petroglyphs.

United Kingdom

Great Britain's ancient heritage is among the most valued in Europe and the entire world. Its ancient Celtic, Anglo-Saxon, Roman and Viking heritage is among the best in the world, not to mention its rural landscapes and locations of literary, educational and industrial importance. Tourism in the United Kingdom is in fact nearly synonymous with heritage tourism, particularly from the perspective of foreign visitors. The United Kingdom has a longer history of cultural heritage-specific protective legislation at the national level than many other countries.

The 1882 Ancient Monuments Protection Act was particularly important just as the industrial revolution began to make the entire country more accessible to the masses. This law made possible the early preservation of ancient monuments throughout Britain and Ireland. At the time the act was passed, 29 sites in England and Wales, 21 in Scotland and 18 in Ireland were set aside for government protection. The listing and protection of historic buildings began in earnest in the mid-1900s following the brunt of the Second World War with the passing of three Town and Country Planning Acts in 1932, 1944 and 1947. In 1953, the Historic Buildings and Ancient Monuments Act was passed in Parliament. This law has been extremely influential in helping to acquire and preserve buildings of outstanding architectural and historical value. The National Heritage Act of 1980 was fundamental to the funding of British national heritage, and the second National Heritage Act (1983) established boards of trustees of several museums and gardens to transfer ownership of certain properties to these museums and gardens, to establish a Historic Buildings and Monuments Commission for England (now English Heritage) and sundry other details (English Heritage, 2009).

English Heritage's primarily role is caretaker of significant historical and archaeological sites. The public agency plays a crucial role in conservation, registering and protecting the cultural environment and is the government's advisor related to the historic environment. The agency promotes research, provides grants and educational services, identifies and protects buildings and archaeological sites, makes its properties accessible to the public and maintains a public national archive, the National Monuments Record, for England's rich heritage. Currently there are more than 400 properties under the care of English Heritage.

The other component parts of the United Kingdom also have their own government agencies with similar charges as those of English Heritage. Founded in 1984, Cadw is the heritage conservation body of the government of Wales. Like that of English Heritage, Cadw's job is to list, conserve, protect and promote the tangible patrimony of Wales, particularly in partnership with private property owners and other stakeholders. Presently there are 120 sites listed under the guardianship of Cadw. Historic Scotland (created 1991) is the counterpart of Cadw and English Heritage in Scotland. Its job, like its sister organizations, is to represent the interests of the built environment to the Scottish government through listing, conserving and interpreting the tangible past. There are over 360 buildings and monuments listed under the care of Historic Scotland. The agency classifies its properties into several general classification types (see Table 8.2).

Table 8.2 Types of properties operated by Historic Scotland with examples

Property type	Example
Agriculture	New Abbey Corn Mill
Burghs	St Andrews: West Port
Carved stones	Knocknagael Boar Stone
Castles and towerhouses	Kilchurn Castle
Cathedrals, abbeys and churches	Dryburgh Abbey
Early Medieval	Eileach An Naoimh
Gardens	Edzell Castle and Garden
Industry	Bonawe Historic Iron Furnace
Mansions and houses	Duff House
Maritime and lighthouses	Kinnaird Head Castle Lighthouse and Museum
Military fortifications	Edinburgh Castle
Palaces and parks	Scalloway Castle
Prehistoric houses and settlements	Culsh Earth House
Prehistoric ritual and burial	Wideford Hill Chambered Cairn
Roman	Dere Street Roman Road, Soutra
Transport and communications	Stirling: Old Bridge
Viking and Norse	Jarlshof Prehistoric and Norse Settlement

The National Trust, founded in 1895, is a non-profit conservation institution in England, Wales and Northern Ireland, which is not affiliated with English Heritage or Cadw. The National Trust for Scotland is its Scottish counterpart. The goal of the National Trust is to preserve, protect and promote the countryside, coastline and historic buildings of England, Northern Ireland and Wales. The trust is custodian of more than 612,000 acres of countryside, over 700 miles of coastline and in excess of 200 buildings and gardens of historic significance. Most of the organization's properties are open to the public with on-site facilities (National Trust, 2009).

Cross-border and regional cooperation

In addition to national legislation and domestic conservation associations, several international bodies also enact policies on a multilateral scale. Supranational alliances, such as the European Union (EU), the North American Free Trade Agreement (NAFTA), the Association of Southeast Asian Nations (ASEAN), the Southern Common Market (MERCOSUR) in South America, and the South Asian Association for Regional Cooperation (SAARC), among dozens of others, have established cross-border, regional policies related directly to tourism, as well as other factors that touch upon tourism, such as environmental protection, trade, visas and passports and cross-border travel. Some of these have even extended their policy-making and funding reach into the realm of cultural heritage (see Plate 8.4). In addition to these regional trade blocs, other global organizations have developed to help protect the cultural environment, most notably the United Nations Educational, Scientific and Cultural Organization (UNESCO), the International Council on Monuments and Sites (ICOMOS) and the World Monuments Fund (WMF). These are all examined in the sections that follow.

European Union

The European Union (EU) recognizes the importance of tourism as a social and economic force in Europe. Tourism is among the EU's top development priorities, particularly in peripheral and less-developed regions, and many pan-European policies have been endorsed in areas that are closely related to tourism: environmental protection, flow of people, transportation, infrastructure, passports and visas, taxes and culture. In the realm of cultural heritage, The Maastricht Treaty of 1993 made it possible for the EU to address common cultural issues, including protection of heritage and promotion of culture. Most of the European Commission's efforts have been geared toward collaboration between member states in areas of sharing cultures and cross-border collaboration in the area of heritage tourism.

While most cultural protection legislation is still enacted and maintained at the national level within each country, the EU has initiated some programs to help emphasize the common heritage of all of Europe. One of the best examples is the European Capital of

Plate 8.4 A MERCOSUR-funded renovation project at Jesuit Missions World Heritage Site, Paraguay

Culture Programme, which started in 1985 and designates one or more cities in Europe as a cultural capital for one year. The designation provides a considerable amount of publicity for the city throughout Europe, as the community is given a platform upon which it can promote itself all over the world. The positive economic and social outcomes of this title are believed to be extremely significant and are taken into account when the award is granted.

Other policies and initiatives have been passed by the European Commission that deal directly with heritage, including the export of cultural products and the return of cultural artifacts that were illegally removed from a member state. Digitization of cultural heritage is also under way to create electronic inventories of Europe's archives, museums and libraries, making them accessible to the public for leisure, education, work and preservation for future generations.

Association of Southeast Asian Nations

Although not as well established or integrated as the EU, the Association of Southeast Asian Nations (ASEAN) is another supranationalist alliance that has a well-established interest in tourism. It has begun to consider the importance of cultural heritage in the advancement of human welfare and the protection of the past in its regional planning and promotional efforts. In an effort to standardize the recognition of the importance of the past among all member states (Brunei, Cambodia, Indonesia, Laos, Malaysia, Myanmar, the Philippines, Singapore, Thailand and Vietnam), the ASEAN Declaration on Cultural Heritage was signed in July 2000, in Bangkok, Thailand.

Based on the recognition of the importance of culture and its conservation, as well as the rapid loss of tangible and intangible heritage, the declaration established 15 policies and programs to assist in the protection of the past and the recognition of cultural equality throughout the region (ASEAN Secretariat, 2009):

- National and regional protection of ASEAN cultural heritage – Each member nation will identify, delineate, protect, conserve, promote and develop in a sustainable fashion the cultural heritage within its borders. ASEAN-wide and international assistance should be sought wherever possible. While each member nation is a sovereign state, ASEAN acknowledges that the national heritage of each member also constitutes the heritage of Southeast Asia as a whole, over which ASEAN maintains a significant interest and spirit of cooperation. Each nation must guarantee the protection and promotion of its cultural heritage by creating policies, programs and services to enable conservation.
- Protection of national treasures and cultural properties – Cooperation will be a high priority for ASEAN in protecting antiquities, including movable and immovable works of historic significance. Relics of national history, architectural wonders, ancient monuments and sites of scientific and anthropological importance should be declared National Treasures, Protected Buildings or Protected Artifacts. Cultural landscapes, areas of scenic beauty and historic sites need to be identified, recognized and protected. Member states must take all necessary steps to defend the cultural patrimony from natural and human dangers, including armed conflict, military occupation and other civil unrest.
- Sustaining worthy living traditions – All ASEAN members will cooperate to maintain and preserve worthy living traditions and folklife, and recognize people's right to own their own culture. Member states shall cooperate to protect creative living traditions within the policies and development frameworks of each country. To do this, members shall formulate formal and informal educational programs to promote living traditions in cities and rural areas, emphasizing the dignity and wisdom of these cultural traditions. Awards should be given to recognize the living artisans who sustain traditional cultural skills.
- Preservation of past and living scholarly, artistic and intellectual cultural heritage – The magnum opuses of distinguished scholars, writers, artists, philosophers and poets from the past and in the present should be respected as crucibles of

illumination, insight, guidance, direction and wisdom. Their protection, documentation, preservation and promotion must be a high priority.

- Preservation of past and living popular cultural heritage and traditions – Popular modes of expression constitute an important artistic, sociological, intellectual, anthropological and historical foundation for social and cross-cultural understanding. ASEAN will encourage and support the preservation of exceptional 'popular' traditions and heritage.

- Enhancement of cultural education, awareness and literacy – ASEAN members agree to undertake cultural exchanges and programs of cultural awareness-building as a foundational element of cross-border cooperation. The development of regional cultural strengths and resources, especially shared heritage and historical linkages, and a sense of regional identity can be achieved through such programs.

- Affirmation of ASEAN cultural dignity – ASEAN states shall do all they can to balance the growing place of materialism by recognizing and affirming human spirituality, creative imagination and wisdom, social responsibility and ethical dimensions of progress. Members shall help strengthen ASEAN values at the local, national and regional levels, using them to provide direction in human development in the areas of education, media, governance and business.

- Advancement of cultural heritage policy and legislation – All member countries will guarantee the effectiveness of cultural preservation policies and the protection of social/communal intellectual property. Cultures with a global reach must not deprive local, national and regional cultures of their own identity or reduce them to relics of the past. Cultural laws and policies must empower all people to harness their own creativity for human development. Communities need to benefit from the research, creation, performance, recording or dissemination of their cultural heritage.

- Recognition of communal intellectual property rights – Traditional knowledge systems and practices, such as designs, technology and oral literature, should be owned collectively by their community of origin. Communities must have access, protection and rights of ownership of their own patrimony. ASEAN firmly recognizes the rights of indigenous populations as legitimate owners of their own cultural heritage.

- Prevention of the illicit transfer of ownership of cultural property – ASEAN countries will actively strive to protect cultural artifacts from theft, illegal trade, black-market trafficking and illegal transfer. ASEAN states commit to return, seek the return or help facilitate the return of stolen artifacts to their rightful owners. ASEAN members should act to subdue the acquisition of illicit cultural objects by institutions or individuals within their national boundaries, and assist other member states in protecting their cultural relics through effective import and export controls.

- Commercial utilization of cultural heritage and resources – ASEAN commits to strengthening regional cooperation to ensure that the commercial utilization of the past does not impinge upon the integrity, dignity or rights of any particular ASEAN society or community.

- Integration of culture and development – Cultural creativity is a crucial element of development. Cultural development and economic growth have a symbiotic relationship. Thus, member countries will strive to integrate cultural knowledge into their development plans and policies. They shall make cultural policies one of the primary components of their development programs.

- Development of national and regional networks on ASEAN cultural heritage – Cooperation between ASEAN countries is essential to develop and establish national and regional inventories, databases, networks of academic institutions, government agencies, archives, galleries, museums, mass media agencies and other institutions that have an interest in cultural heritage and its preservation and promotion.

- Allocation of resources for cultural heritage activities – Each country should make an extra effort to provide additional resources of heritage protection. ASEAN cultural heritage activities shall be provided with increased resources, and other multilateral associations (e.g. the United Nations) are urged to increase their level of assistance to protect the past in Southeast Asia in terms of money, training, infrastructure development and legislation.

- Development and implementation of an ASEAN program on cultural heritage – ASEAN's Committee on Culture and Information will draw up a work program related to cultural heritage, including the observance of an ASEAN Decade for Cultural Heritage between 2001 and 2010.

UNESCO

While not a political- or trade-based supranational alliance as ASEAN and the EU are, the United Nations Educational, Scientific and Cultural Organization (UNESCO) is probably the best example of global cooperation in the realm of heritage resource conservation. The mandate of UNESCO extends into all aspects of science, culture and education. However, its World Heritage List (WHL) is the most salient responsibility for the present discussion.

UNESCO was formed in 1945 in an effort to assist in rebuilding the world after the Second World War by promoting peace through international collaboration in the areas of education, science and culture. As part of its program to facilitate cooperation in protecting the world's cultural and natural heritage, UNESCO adopted the Convention Concerning the Protection of the World Cultural and Natural Heritage in 1972, which created the World Heritage List (WHL), maintained and managed by the World Heritage Committee. The list and 1972 treaty charged UNESCO with the job of encouraging nations to identify, protect and preserve the world's cultural and natural heritage considered to be of outstanding universal value to humankind. The committee's primary functions are to identify properties, based on the signatory states' recommendations, that should be protected on the list; to make decisions about which sites should be placed on the World Heritage Sites in Danger list; and oversee resources that might be available to help signatory states protect their heritage places.

UNESCO has a very wide-reaching mandate to help protect the past from the dangers of the modern world. Its primary concern is the long-term, inter-generational sustainability of the world's irreplaceable patrimony. Within this broader mandate, the agency's (2009a) World Heritage mission includes several directives:

- encouraging countries to ratify the World Heritage Convention and ensure they will protect their natural and cultural heritage;
- encouraging signatory countries to nominate sites inside their borders for inclusion on the WHL;
- encouraging signatory states to develop management plans and establish reporting systems to evaluate the success of their World Heritage Sites (WHSs);
- assist states in safeguarding WHSs by providing professional training and technical support;
- providing emergency help for WHSs in immediate danger;
- supporting member countries' public awareness-building activities for WHS conservation;
- encouraging local populations to help in the preservation of their cultural and natural heritage;
- promoting international cooperation in World Heritage conservation.

As of April 2011, 187 countries have ratified the World Heritage Convention, and there are currently 911 properties on the WHL, including 704 cultural sites, 180 natural places and 27 mixed natural and cultural locations. The 1980s and 90s were a period of rapid growth in the expansion of the WHL. During the 1980s, 266 sites were added to the list. During the 1990s, 372 properties were listed and in 2009, 13 new sites were added in Switzerland, Cape Verde, China, the United Kingdom, South Korea, Burkina Faso, Peru, Iran, Belgium, Kyrgyzstan, Spain, Italy, Germany and the Netherlands.

Through its field offices and national branches, the commission accepts and evaluates nominations based on the justification and other documentation provided by the state's nominating body. By treaty, only countries that have ratified the World Heritage Convention are able to nominate properties to be inscribed on the WHL. Site nominations must be demonstrable examples of exceptional worldwide (universal) historical importance; the site is required to meet specific criteria that are dictated by the convention, and recommending states must guarantee adequate protection of the sites being nominated. The most problematic of these three requirements for most countries is their ability to ensure their financial, political and technical capability to manage, conserve and provide access to their various sites. States are allowed to request assistance for this requirement, however, via the Heritage Fund to aid them in preparing proposals and plans, in preserving properties and training staff members. While the Heritage Fund operates on a rather meager budget, some money is available for the most vulnerable sites, and loans may also be obtained to reach the needed goals for listing and maintaining WHSs.

Convention signatories are encouraged to submit a Tentative List to the World Heritage Commission. This list provides an inventory that each state party intends to consider for nomination sometime in the near future. The lists should not be exhaustive of all historic sites in a country and they should be devised in collaboration with a wide range of stakeholders, such as government agencies, local residents, site managers and non-governmental organizations. Nominations to the WHL will not be considered unless the property has first been submitted at least one year in advance on the tentative list. As of April 2011, 167 of the 187 member states had submitted a tentative list ranging from one property to 59.

UNESCO classifies the cultural heritage sites on its list into four different types of properties or sites. The first is monuments, which include archaeological structures, works of sculpture and painting, architectural works, inscriptions and cave dwellings. Groups of buildings are the next type of WHS. This category includes groupings of individual or connected buildings that because of their architecture, homogeneity or their position in the landscape are of universal value. Third are sites, which UNESCO defines as human works or a combination of human works and natural processes, including areas and archaeological sites. Fourth, cultural landscapes are manifestations of the interactions between humans and nature. These embody evolutionary and adaptive processes between humans and their environment, and illustrate human settlement and land use over time.

In addition to being of outstanding universal value, heritage places must meet one or more cultural or natural criteria established by the committee to be considered for WHL inscription (see Table 8.3).

Table 8.3 Selection criteria for inscription on the World Heritage List

1. represents a masterpiece of human creative genius
2. exhibits important human values over a period of time or within a cultural area of the world, on developments in architecture or technology, monumental arts, town planning or landscape design
3. illustrates exceptionally a cultural tradition or a civilization that is living or which has disappeared

4. exemplifies a type of building, architectural or technological collection or landscape which illustrates a significant stage in human history

5. represents an outstanding example of a traditional human settlement, land use or sea use that is representative of culture or human interaction with the environment, especially when it has become vulnerable under the impact of irreversible change

6. is directly or tangibly associated with events or living traditions, with ideas or beliefs, with artistic and literary works of outstanding universal significance

7. contains superlative natural phenomena or areas of exceptional natural beauty and aesthetic importance

8. is an outstanding example of major stages in the earth's history, including the record of life, ongoing geological processes, land formation, physiographic features or geomorphological processes

9. exemplifies significant ongoing ecological and biological processes in the evolution and development of terrestrial, water, coastal and marine ecosystems and communities of animals and plants

10. contains the most significant natural habitats for in-situ conservation of biological diversity, including threatened species of outstanding universal value from the view of science or conservation

Source: UNESCO (2009a)

To have a site or several sites on the WHL is an extremely desirable proposition for most countries, but especially for small, less-developed nations (see Plate 8.5). For them, World Heritage designation is a sign of coming of age and lends a degree of prestige on the world stage. It also helps to solidify national ambitions of unity or, at its most basic, a sense of nationhood. There are potential political uses of UNESCO designation as well to legitimize governments in power or to illustrate an administration's ability to accomplish great things. Many countries desire to have their historic properties inscribed on the list owing to the administrative and protective support they can receive. While direct money typically is not something UNESCO is able to grant to individual countries, the organization does have a budget to help states train staff and conserve artifacts.

While some countries have reported seeing an increase in visitor arrivals at heritage properties once they have been listed as WHSs, most often this does not occur and listing certainly is not a guarantee for tourism growth. Many countries' tourism officials are under the misguided assumption that once a heritage place is inscribed on UNESCO's list, the site will, with certainty, be inundated with foreign tourists and the destination's economic ills will be cured. Few studies have been able to show adequately a positive correlation between WHS status and increased tourist arrivals. Instead, it is likely that

Plate 8.5 UNESCO marker in Nepal, a country that strongly values its World Heritage Sites

WHS status will enhance already popular and accessible destinations, while unknown and inaccessible locations will see relatively little, if any, growth in visitor arrivals. Nevertheless, many destinations are busily utilizing the UNESCO label as a marketing tool, which may in fact prove an effective instrument, although before and after studies in a variety of contexts will be needed to affirm the erroneous assumption of automatic tourism growth.

ICOMOS

The International Council on Monuments and Sites (ICOMOS) is a professional association of some 9,500 members worldwide from a wide range of scholarly disciplines – geography, anthropology, history, archaeology, architecture, engineering, tourism studies and planning – working together to solve common conservation challenges. ICOMOS was founded in 1965 with the goal of conserving and protecting important cultural heritage sites of four varieties: historic cities, archaeological sites, cultural landscapes and individual buildings. It plays a crucial role in advising UNESCO on which cultural properties to include on the World Heritage List.

ICOMOS collects scientific data, evaluates conservation policies and techniques and helps implement international conventions on the conservation of cultural heritage. Other mandates include growing the ICOMOS National Committees, defining effective management approaches for cultural properties, developing training programs on an international level, enriching the ICOMOS International Documentation Centre in Paris and establishing a video library dedicated to architectural heritage, counseling UNESCO about the cultural properties to be included on the World Heritage List and reporting on the circumstances regarding conservation of the properties already inscribed on the list (ICOMOS, 2009).

World Monuments Fund

The World Monuments Fund (WMF) was established in 1965 and is currently based in New York. It is a private, not-for-profit organization that is devoted to preserving architectural heritage throughout the world by means of research, grant giving, education, training, advocacy and acting as liaison between public and private stakeholders.

The WMF categorizes its core programs and/or responsibilities into the following classifications: advocacy, education and training, cultural legacy, capacity building and disaster recovery (World Monuments Fund, 2009a). Through its advocacy platform the WMF works to build popular and government awareness of the need to conserve the past. Part of this is raising awareness of ongoing threats to the cultural patrimony of places. Training and education is the second responsibility and includes training craftspeople in lost or disappearing arts, as well as teaching modern approaches to heritage preservation that can help communities, governments and organizations become better prepared to conserve their heritage. The cultural legacy classification refers to saving the world's built wonders from injury and obliteration. Providing monetary and technical support is a critical element of this responsibility. In terms of capacity building, the WMF tries to help communities build their own legal, fiscal and technical abilities to protect and maintain their built heritage by assembling teams of specialists to formulate conservation plans, develop training curricula, conduct feasibility and impact studies and plan for future sustainable use. Finally, disaster recovery involves quick and decisive assistance in both natural and human-induced disasters to assess damage, shore up damaged structures and plan for future recovery efforts.

SUMMARY AND CONCLUSION

It is clear that heritage is a valuable resource, not only for tourism but also for education, social well-being and community esteem. Countries have authority within their own boundaries to enact laws that will protect tangible and intangible heritage. In some countries, subnational governments, such as counties, provinces and municipalities, might also be empowered to created enforceable regulations that aim to defend against the deterioration of the area's patrimony. National-level organizations that are not necessarily associated with government agencies are important players in compelling governments to recognize the importance of the past and protect it. Multinational alliances and non-profit organizations play an extremely important role in international policy making but, perhaps more importantly, they are also critical in building global awareness among public officials, the private sector and the general public about the importance of protecting the human past.

REVIEW QUESTIONS

1. In what ways do you think colonialism prevented the enactment of effective protective legislation for heritage in places such as Africa, Asia and Latin America?

2. How do cultural protection laws in Australia, Canada, the United Kingdom, Italy and the USA compare? What are the similarities and differences?

3. In what ways can supranational treaties and alliances such as the European Union or the North American Free Trade Agreement help further the cause of heritage protection?

4. Do you feel there are any dangers or drawbacks in protecting the past at a supra-national level rather than at a national level?

5. What are the primary goals of UNESCO, ICOMOS and the World Monuments Fund? How do they work together to protect the cultural heritage of humankind?

RECOMMENDED READING

Alexandrowicz, Z., Urgan, J. and Miskiewicz, K. (2009) Geological values of selected Polish properties of the UNESCO World Heritage List. *Geoheritage* 1(1), 43–52.

Burley, D.V. (1994) A never ending story: Historical developments in Canadian archaeology and the quest for federal heritage legislation. *Canadian Journal of Archaeology* 18(3), 77–98.

Di Giovine, M.A. (2009) *The Heritage-Scape: UNESCO, World Heritage and Tourism*. Lanham, MD: Rowman & Littlfield.

Frey, B.S. and Pamini, P. (2009) Making world heritage truly global: The Culture Certificate Scheme. *Oxonomics* 4(2), 1–9.

Gregory, J. (2008) Reconsidering relocated buildings: ICOMOS, authenticity and mass relocation. *International Journal of Heritage Studies* 14(2), 112–130.

Hesmondhalgh, D. and Pratt, A.C. (2005) Cultural industries and cultural policy. *International Journal of Cultural Policy* 11(1), 1–13.

Leask, A. and Fyall, A. (eds) (2006) *Managing World Heritage Sites*. Oxford: Butterworth Heinemann.

Leask, A. and Fyall, A. (2008) Introduction: Managing world heritage. *Journal of Heritage Tourism* 2(3), 131–132.

Littoz-Monnet, A. (2007) *The European Union and Culture: Between Economic Regulation and European Cultural Policy*. Manchester: Manchester University Press.

Petkova, S. (2005) *Cultural Heritage Legislation in the Transition Countries of South-East Europe*. New York: Open Society Institute.

Pickard, R. (2001) *Policy and Law in Heritage Conservation*. London: Spon Press.

Prideaux, B., Timothy, D.J. and Chon, K. (eds) (2008) *Cultural Heritage and Tourism in Asia and the Pacific*. London: Routledge.

Severino, R.C. (2006) *Southeast Asia in Search of an ASEAN Community*. Singapore: Institute of Southeast Asian Studies.

Shyllon, F. (1996) Cultural heritage legislation and management in Nigeria. *International Journal of Cultural Property* 5, 235–268.

Timothy, D.J. and Boyd, S.W. (2006) Heritage tourism in the 21st century: Valued traditions and new perspectives. *Journal of Heritage Tourism* 1(1), 1–16.

UNESCO (2009) *World Heritage Sites: A Complete Guide to 878 UNESCO World Heritage Sites*. Richmond Hill, ON: Firefly Books.

Ward, D. (ed.) (2008) *The European Union and the Culture Industries: Regulation and the Public Interest*. Aldershot: Ashgate.

RECOMMENDED WEBSITES

ASEAN Secretariat – http://www.aseansec.org/

Cultural Policies and Trends in Europe – http://www.culturalpolicies.net/web/

English Heritage – www.english-heritage.org.uk

European Commission – http://ec.europa.eu/

Friends of World Heritage – http://www.friendsofworldheritage.org/

Historic Scotland – http://www.historic-scotland.gov.uk/

Hong Kong Antiquities and Monuments Office – http://www.amo.gov.hk/en/main.php

International Council on Monuments and Sites – http://www.icomos.org

National Trust – http://www.nationaltrust.org.uk/main/

National Trust for Historic Preservation – http://www.preservationnation.org/

Parks Canada – http://www.parkscanada.ca/

UNESCO World Heritage Center – http://whc.unesco.org/

US National Park Service – http://www.nps.gov/

World Monuments Fund – http://www.wmf.org/

CHAPTER 9

PROTECTING THE PAST FOR TODAY: HERITAGE CONSERVATION AND TOURISM

LEARNING OBJECTIVES

After reading this chapter, you should be able to:

1. Recognize the extreme importance of protecting the world's cultural heritage.

2. Be familiar with the reasons built and living heritage is and should be protected.

3. Know the various management approaches to conservation used by site and destination managers.

4. Comprehend the human-induced and natural barriers to successful heritage conservation.

5. Reflect on actions that could be taken to help further the global cause of cultural preservation.

6. Underscore the salience of heritage conservation as a key principle of sustainable development.

INTRODUCTION

Heritage tourism is often looked upon as an environmentally and socially-friendly form of tourism, but as Chapter 7 made abundantly clear this is not always the case. It is a type of special interest tourism, but heritage visits are also a critical part of mass tourism, which has for centuries taken its toll on living and built culture. According to the tenets of sustainable tourism resources must be protected, but tourists must also be allowed to enjoy them. Thus, a delicate balance between use and conservation needs to be developed. This chapter examines the importance of heritage conservation, including the reasons why the past needs to be preserved for the future. It also examines the most common approaches to conservation problems and highlights the most salient political, social and economic challenges to protecting the past.

THE IMPORTANCE OF CONSERVATION

Given the gravity of the impacts that heritage tourism triggers, it is especially important that planners, elected officials, property managers and destination managers understand the importance of conserving the past. The built environment is a non-renewable resource. Unlike forests and grasslands, heritage cannot regenerate organically – once it is gone, it is gone forever. As the allusions in Chapter 7 attest, heritage is changing rather quickly under human-induced pressures (e.g. tourism, agriculture and modernization). Thus, there is a sense of urgency in the heritage field to arrest decay and prevent the further deterioration of historically valuable locations.

The notion of preserving the past has been around for a few hundred years. Eighteenth and 19th century writers and environmentalists noted the importance of protecting wilderness areas and natural landscapes. With the onslaught of the industrial revolution and rapid urbanization in the 1800s, safeguarding nature became an especially prominent discussion point in books, newspapers and art. This movement, together with a growing tourism sector, helped bring about the establishment of the global national park movement, with Yellowstone National Park (USA) being the first national park in the world in 1872. During the past century, this overarching concern for conservation has spilled into the cultural arena. Realizing the importance of natural heritage, cultural heritage was next on the conservation agenda. National monuments were established in the USA as early as 1906, with the enactment of the Antiquities Act of Congress, which authorized the government to declare prehistoric structures, historic landmarks, historic structures and other relics of historic or scientific interest as national monuments.

Today the past has a much higher profile than ever before and is protected for a variety of reasons: scientific and educative importance, environmental diversity, artistic merit, economic value, nostalgia, nationalism and utilitarian functions.

Scientific and educational value

The first of these is the scientific and educative value of heritage. Historic buildings, ruins, ancient monuments and intangible cultural traditions have the potential to reveal a lot about civilizations and their traditions in earlier periods. Some ruins and archaeological sites have provided a wealth of knowledge not only about lifestyles, social structures and human relations with nature, but some have also been instrumental in bringing to light historical data about health problems, pestilences, poverty, conflict and battles, gender roles, funerary practices and food production and consumption in ancient days. People's coping mechanisms and adaptations to changing functional environments have also been discovered largely through archaeological research at excavation locales (see Plate 9.1). Through dendrochronology and carbon dating even the very construction materials (e.g. logs/wood) can reveal much about environmental conditions at various periods of time, such as floods, fires, droughts or cooling and heating trends.

Plate 9.1 Archaeological digs at Historic Jamestowne, USA, provide information about American colonial life

Linked particularly well to the scientific importance is the educational role of heritage. Heritage places are important resources for both formal and informal education. Formal education refers to the role of heritage as part of the official curriculum. School field trips and site visits, as well as college and university programs that deal directly with heritage, are important in this regard. Museum management and curatorship programs, park and recreation training programs and travel and tourism degrees are examples of official post-secondary educational curricula that all focus on patrimony as a critical component of the learning experience. Informal education refers to the unofficial learning that takes place among visitors to historic sites. Interpretive media and the way a site is managed are an important part of this experience and can help facts and meanings sink in to the visitors' minds.

One important aspect of the informal educative role of sites is to remind the public about negative events and times in history that should not be forgotten. Slavery-related sites, holocaust museums and markers, Second World War Japanese-American Internment Camps in the USA and sites of terrorist-induced disasters all serve to remind the world of the injustices of the past and help assure public awareness so that atrocities such as these will not happen again.

Environmental diversity

As already noted, the built environment is a non-renewable resource that cannot be regenerated. Certain heritages have been covered up or destroyed in the past in favor of other heritages. This is unfortunate as the past is an amalgamation of many different pasts, each one with an important story to tell and lessons to be learned. Conservation can help end wanton destruction of the historic environment and has some potential to make the past more realistic in terms of eliminating some of the biases that exist in the protection and interpretation of heritage. Through conservation efforts on a regional scale, colonial and indigenous pasts can be exposed in equal portion or at least with fair representation. A diversity of protected pasts makes a destination more interesting and expands its resource base far beyond the monotonous, one-sided and inaccurate portrayals endemic to heritage milieus everywhere.

Artistic merit

Many heritage places are important simply by virtue of their esthetic qualities or because they have a 'scarcity value', meaning they are old and old is disappearing. Built patrimony represents yesteryear, a time when construction and design were an art, when buildings possessed a soul, and great care was taken to perfect a masterpiece. Antithetical to this is

Plate 9.2 Batalha Monastery, Portugal, is an example of Late Gothic architecture worth preserving

196

the mass production of many nondescript edifices we see today that lack individuality, meaning, pride in artisanship and harmony with place and time.

Historic buildings and ancient monuments are unmistakable exemplars of celebrated architectural styles. The 14th–16th century Batalha Monastery in Portugal is a notable example of a Late Gothic style of architecture (see Plate 9.2). It is a UNESCO World Heritage Site and an important heritage attraction in Portugal. The Pantheon and Coliseum are two of the best holistic representations of ancient Roman architecture, while the Taj Mahal in India is illustrative of Indo-Islamic design (see Plate 9.3). Old structures throughout the world have an architectural story behind them. Many are renowned as products of enormous creative genius; these are the ones that become the most popular tourist attractions.

Plate 9.3 The Taj Mahal is among the most valued historic buildings for its esthetic design

Revenue generation

As contended in Chapter 7, the economic implications of heritage tourism are enormous. With the widespread popularity of heritage places and events as tourist attractions, destination planners and government agencies have realized the potential financial benefits of developing their heritage resources for tourism. This commonly leads to heritage conservation being motivated by the need for revenue. Simply stated, conserving the past is good for business and can contribute to a region's economic growth and stability. While many observers frown on this motive, even profit-driven protection of patrimony is better than no protection at all.

Although idealistically it would behoove places to preserve their pasts simply for altruistic reasons, the reality is that in most developed and developing countries the built past would be largely ignored without an economic justification. Almost everywhere, funding for heritage protection is in short supply. As a result, many historic properties are required to seek their own means of remaining viable. While many heritage custodians detest the idea of preserving for profit, they realize that the deep public coffers of the 20th century have now become shallow – a characteristic reality of the 21st century.

Nostalgia

The wave of historic preservation that swept the western world from the 1960s to the 2000s was spurred in part by rapid modernization and the industrialization of the 20th century. Change, especially rapid change, is uncomfortable for everyone. In an era of rapid change, protecting remnants and symbols of a simpler and less worrisome past has driven much of the recent boom in historic preservation. Many observers believe that protecting the past is modern society's way of coping with the unstable present – artifacts and edifices from the past provide stability in an unstable world. It provides comfort, reality and a sense of social identity.

Many modern societies, such as those in Japan, the USA, Canada and the United Kingdom, tend to look upon the fakery of city life with a touch of disdain, but they see rural heritage and the peasant landscapes of everyday life as more wholesome, safer and grounded in a more authentic past. The Japanese sense of national identity is grounded very much in rural Japan and many city dwellers fear for the loss of Japanese rural heritage, including the buildings, agricultural landscapes and living traditions. This has resulted in the resurgence of rural folk museums, model agricultural villages and village museums – all of which draw most of their visitors from the country's bustling metropolises.

This bittersweet sense of 'collective nostalgia' drives many people to experience heritage places as a way of getting back to their roots. They often pay a visit to historic sites with their children as a way of holding on to elements of the past that they remember from their own childhoods or which were shared with them verbally by parents and grandparents. In Israel, urbanites taking their children to self-pick farms or spending a day working on a kibbutz is representative of an intergenerational yearning for a more place-bound social identity.

Nationalism

Much heritage is actively protected by regimes in power as a way of building national solidarity with a homeland or a government in power, or nurturing a sentiment of patriotism and loyalty. Diasporic groups are avid protectors of the idyllic notion of the motherland, the old country or the homeland. Sometimes perceptions of place transform as the homeland becomes more virtuous the longer a group is away. Celebrations of faith, culture, music and food in the new country help extol the virtues of the homeland, thereby building solidarity among members of the diaspora. Croatian-Americans, Ukrainian-Canadians, Czech-Americans, Greek-Australians, Turkish-Germans, Samoan-New Zealanders and worldwide Jews are all illustrative of diasporic groups that have managed to retain strong ties to the motherland by preserving language, religion and other elements of culture in their new country of residence. This sentiment is composed of efforts from within the diaspora community itself, via propaganda from the homeland or a combination of both.

Many autocratic governments maintain their version of heritage by conserving places and artifacts that best represent their ideological viewpoints. The pre-1994 apartheid government of South Africa exalted the role of the white colonizers in establishing the great Republic, while marginalizing and untelling the thousands of years of history of the aboriginal population. In this they garnered support for an oppressive regime among the white people, and undermined any sense of indigenous pride among the natives.

Domestic tourism in the Democratic People's Republic of Korea focuses almost entirely on indoctrinating North Koreans about the virtues of *Juche* communism, the uprightness of their leaders and the malevolence of the outside world. Monuments and battlefields attest to the North Korean victory against South Korea, the USA and their allies. Homes and villages associated with the lives of esteemed political figures provide the backdrops for nationalist parades and museum displays.

Functional use of heritage resources

The functional utility of historic buildings is another important impetus for conserving them. Oftentimes it is more cost-effective to raze an old edifice and rebuild a new one in its stead. However, for people who appreciate the worth of protecting the past, refurbishing old structures in lieu of tearing them down adds value and appeal to urban or rural landscapes and contributes to a community's sense of well-being. The wanton destruction of historic houses and industrial heritage of the 1960s–1980s in favor of new construction has slowed considerably since the 1990s. An increased appreciation for aged buildings, largely a result of the societal nostalgia mentioned above, has stimulated a remarkable preservation movement wherein historic properties are renovated and used for alternative purposes from their original functions (see Plate 9.4).

Many examples exist of old factories and barns being renovated into very expensive and swanky homes. In St Jacobs, Ontario, barns and grain silos have become souvenir and handicraft shops. In Vermont, several old covered bridges have been enclosed and now function as handicraft stores. The Youth Hostel Långholmen in Stockholm, Sweden, is located in an old jail. The historical museum in Scone, New South Wales, Australia, is housed in an old jail. There are hundreds of examples in North America and Europe of old trains being used today as restaurants and tourist lodging.

Until its demise, the Soviet Union was home to thousands of large factories. With the breakup of the USSR in the early 1990s, however, many of the factories sat derelict and began to deteriorate. Several of these have been remodeled in recent years and now have alternative functions. A new nightclub is located in the remodeled rooms of an old Soviet-era factory. A power plant in Riga, Latvia, is currently being proposed as the new

Plate 9.4 This 1880s hospital in Fredericksburg, Texas, is now a tourist shop and restaurant

location for the Contemporary Art Museum of Latvia. Factories in and near Moscow now function as shopping malls.

APPROACHES TO HERITAGE AND CULTURAL CONSERVATION

In some societies, conservation efforts are held in high regard. In others, conservation is either frowned upon or viewed as an unnecessary luxury. Conservation is expensive, time-consuming and requires a great deal of coordination between government agencies, property owners and public-sector supporters. Thus, it is not always an easy choice but what most observers acknowledge is that it is a worthwhile choice. Heritage places continue to disappear year after year, so decision makers have to face difficult choices about how best to approach conservation. Several approaches (or non-approaches) to protecting historic places and heritage structures must be acknowledged. Wall (1989) alluded to a few of these (preservation, restoration and renovation), but additional per-spectives are highlighted here as well. The decision about which of these approaches to use will depend upon the location, the nature of the patrimony being protected, the goals about why such a place should be protected and the expectation of the potential users.

Doing nothing

The first of these is ignoring the problem, which Ashworth and Tunbridge (2000) describe as heritage euthanasia as it generally entails doing nothing to protect the past and essentially allows it to continue deteriorating. There are thousands of places today where the physical elements are rapidly deteriorating, which could be arrested by a conscious choice to conserve in one form or another. The primary obstacles to conservation will be discussed later in this chapter, but there are many root causes of this such as budget shortfalls, political agendas and lack of interest in the public arena.

Preservation

According to this concept, buildings and other artifacts are maintained in their current condition; thus, they are not rebuilt or refurbished in any way. A great deal of effort, planning and good management are required for such an endeavor, to prevent the place or object from deteriorating beyond its present form. Ruins and other archaeological sites are a prime example of historic places that are often kept in a state of perpetual ruin, although some efforts often have to be made to keep the site from deteriorating further (see Plate 9.5). Sometimes reconstructing buildings is too expensive, or site owners feel that rebuilding a ruined structure might compromise the authenticity of the place. Similarly, there are instances where ruined villages or individual buildings are more scientifically worthwhile and revealing than re-constructed buildings would be. In this case the present condition of the site itself has value, perhaps in understanding a society's demise or how they might have lived or died. The city of Pompeii, Italy, which was

Plate 9.5 Efforts to retard deterioration at Paquimé (Casas Grandes) World Heritage Site, Mexico

destroyed by the eruption of the volcano Mount Vesuvius in 79AD, is still in ruins and partially buried by volcanic material. Because the ancient city remains in a ruinous state it has not only become a major tourist destination, it is also a priceless scientific resource which has helped scientists develop a better understanding of the catastrophic potential of volcanic eruptions and how communities might better prepare for such an event.

Ghost towns exist all over the world where villages, towns or cities have been abandoned because a natural resource that the community has depended on has been depleted, because a natural disaster or unhealthy conditions pushed out the local population or because a new highway or railroad bypassed the community. In Australia, Canada and the USA there are hundreds of ghost towns that are important tourist attractions. Ravenswood (Queensland, Australia), Cossack (Western Australia), Bodie (California, USA) and Barkerville (British Columbia, Canada) have all become popular tourism-oriented ghost towns. These, too, are best preserved in their current conditions. What makes ghost towns appealing to visitors is their sense of abandonment and dereliction. Repairing and refurbishing a ghost town would diminish its fascination for visitors and would be a senseless endeavor if the village is meant to become a heritage attraction.

Renovation

This form of adaptation involves making some changes to the built environment while maintaining some part of its historical composition. Such additions as facades, extra rooms, an extended porch or loft or the addition of a new fireplace are examples of renovations (see Plate 9.6). In some locations, local conservation laws require the exteriors of buildings to remain as original as possible – even though interiors can be modified for commercial or residential uses. Examples of common renovation projects include constructing an additional room to use as office space at an historic building or rebuilding a crumbling wall.

Unfortunately, many renovation jobs have either destroyed the historical integrity of buildings or caused irreparable damage to them because of substandard and inappropriate work. Jonathan Taylor (2009) somewhat cheekily suggests 10 ways to ruin an historic building:

- hire consultants and builders who do not specialize in historic buildings;
- do not perform any essential maintenance work;
- use cement instead of lime for mortars and other traditional materials;
- paint over surfaces that were originally left natural;

Plate 9.6 Example of a medieval house in the Netherlands with visible renovations

- expand or modify the structure in a way that conflicts with its style;
- introduce mix-and-match 'period style' details;
- replace original components unnecessarily;
- position modern service equipment intrusively (e.g. satellite dishes);
- use cleaning methods that damage original surfaces;
- overload an existing structure.

By doing the opposite of these, obviously, heritage sites can be better protected from deterioration and decay.

Restoration

As the name indicates, restoration involves restoring, or bringing back, an object or site to some original form. This can entail removing parts that have been added in the intervening years since the structure was built, as well as restoring parts that are missing (see Plate 9.7). To be a true restoration effort all original materials need to be used, although many restoration projects have not had the luxury of having all original parts to work with. In this case a conservation project is more a reconstruction effort than a restoration effort.

Plate 9.7 Vianden Castle, Luxembourg, was restored from ruins to its 14th century form in the 1970s

Some critics have argued that true restoration is impossible, as some non-original elements must be used, and nobody knows for certain exactly how most ancient buildings looked except in general terms. Wall (1989) contends that most historic structures have undergone many adaptations through time, and so a decision has to be made about which period or appearance will be returned. This itself can be a highly political process, as people in positions of power will almost always want restoration outcomes to reflect their own ideologies or what they perceive the authentic past to be.

Urban renewal

In the developed portions of the world, mass urbanization began with the Industrial Revolution in the early and mid-1800s. This process, whereby masses of people began moving from rural areas and small villages to cities in search of work in emerging factories and services, created crowded conditions in terms of both people and the built environment. Many urban geographers have modeled the spatial development of cities and suggested varying morphologies depending on the purpose of the city, its location and physical features, its location in relation to other urban areas and the existence or not of natural resources such as water. Most of these models illustrate the spatial extent of urban cores, industrial zones, service areas and residential districts. While some cities now have multiple cores, or nuclei, the original centers usually represent the area of earliest settlement and the area of intense commerce.

Most large and medium cities grew and developed in post-industrialization because of commerce, trade and/or transportation. Some of the more ancient cities were established because of their strategic location from a military standpoint. Regardless of origin and reasons for spread in the modern era, cities are densely populated areas where commerce, trade and governance occur on an everyday basis. Through time, the oldest and most heavily industrialized portions of first-world cities have become dilapidated, with many urban nuclei in a ramshackle state of decay and dereliction. Industrial complexes have shut their doors or been removed to other parts of the city and the more affluent residents have moved to the suburban districts or rural areas nearby. Areas that were once vibrant centers of trade and manufacturing, and desirable places to live for the middle and upper classes, are either now abandoned or inhabited by some of the poorest segments of society. Conditions are somewhat different in less-developed parts of the world, however, such as in Latin America and the Caribbean, where many urban cores are still the most vibrant parts of the city, albeit still dilapidated, with the outskirts having become home to squatter settlements and the urban poor.

Since the 1960s and 1970s there has been an earnest effort to reverse the trend toward urban deterioration. In most cases urban revitalization involves a combination of selective demolition, reconstruction, renovation and commercial development. Recreation and tourism are an important part of the impetus for these efforts.

Urban gentrification is one important approach to renewal, although it has a good share of critics. Gentrification refers to older, run-down neighborhoods being bought out by investors and turned into luxury living, recreational space and commercial establishments. Proponents argue this is good for cities and draws consumers to older inner-city and downtown areas. Opponents contend that it does little to close the gap between the rich and the poor. When the rich acquire the poor neighborhoods, it displaces the underprivileged to other difficult areas in the city or pushes them to the periphery. Nonetheless, many urban planners and developers see gentrification and other models of urban renewal as opportunities to revitalize an important heritage complex and improve local economies via tourism, recreation and local retail. Regardless of the approach, the notion of urban rejuvenation in the modern day entails community networks, resident participation, economic development and the restoration of a heritage milieu.

Brownfield redevelopment is another controversial urban renewal approach. Brownfields are abandoned, formerly industrial, lands that are believed or shown to be contaminated by low levels of contamination or pollution, such as solvents, pesticides, heavy metals, lead, asbestos or hydrocarbon leakage. Their potential hazardous conditions have led to their being ignored traditionally in urban redevelopment plans, although this is beginning to change. Some cities in the USA have started cleaning up their brownfields of waste, toxins and even underground storage tanks. Pittsburgh, Pennsylvania, has found considerable success in developing several of its derelict, and potential hazardous, industrial parks into shopping centers, recreational properties, office buildings and parks. Atlanta, Georgia, has done the same in undertaking one of the USA's largest brownfields redevelopment projects, which includes shopping, parks, residences, cafes and offices.

Several conservation programs have developed over the years to address urban decline and revival. In 1974, the US Congress passed the Housing and Community Development Act, which promotes the refurbishing and revitalization of urban neighborhoods and buildings rather than tear them apart. In 1980 the National Trust for Historic Preservation in the USA initiated its Main Street Program, which aims to help towns and cities revitalize their traditional commercial districts. Most states in the USA (40 of 50 states) have developed Main Street Programs under the auspices of the National Trust with many of their communities utilizing the trust's support and training to help curtail urban decay and revitalize local economies. Other countries have similar programs that try to build public awareness of the importance of conserving historic city centers and encourage investment in them.

Several urban renewal projects in Yogyakarta, Indonesia, and the nearby city of Solo, have helped preserve much of the historic ambience of the cities and have given local people the momentum to help preserve their homes, many of which have become guest houses for tourists. As early as the late 1960s, the Mexican federal government established its border region development initiative, part of which called for the greening and cleaning of city cores near the US border. This was seen in large part as a way of evading the popular American view of Mexican border towns as unsafe, dirty and shabby. Historic buildings were renovated or restored, sidewalks were poured, parks were planted, curbsides were painted and welcome archways were erected in an effort to revitalize the urban environment, not only for the well-being of Mexicans but also to be more inviting to their American visitors.

Waterfront development is another important form of urban renewal. Although this often requires some demolition of old buildings and construction of new, non-original structures, it is becoming a popular form of heritage 'preservation' (really redevelopment) for recreation and tourism purposes. Craig-Smith (1995: 34) suggested some important guidelines for waterfront developments, which will help in the long-term success of such endeavors:

- The wider array of uses for the development, the better the community will be. Tourism should not be considered the only use for new waterfronts. Services and activities for locals should also be planned.
- Nonetheless, tourism and recreation are very important and should be a key goal in undertaking such a project.
- Location is vital. Locations near central business districts are much more inclined to succeed than those in marginal areas.
- Local residents must be involved in the planning and decision-making of port and harborfront development to help alleviate discontent and promote a sense of community ownership.
- Inasmuch as possible, historic buildings should be reused instead of torn down.
- Large projects should not be undertaken too quickly, and positive results should not be expected right away.
- Large-scale development is often the only solution to some significant urban problems, such as abandonment and decay.
- Finally, to achieve renewal successfully, governments need to be involved as development agents and/or financiers.

Waterfronts have long been important features of coastal urban life, and deep ports have been a determining factor in where and how coastal cities have developed. The industrial economies of many countries were based on seafront cities. However, with the transition from an extractive (e.g. mining and fishing) and manufacturing-based economy (Fordism) to one grounded largely in services (post-Fordism) during the 20th century, the industrial landscapes that so well paralleled waterfront areas began to decline in their social and economic role. As a result, many harbors, ports and wharfs around the world sat in a state of disuse and abandonment; they became breeding grounds for mischief and crime, including illicit drugs and prostitution.

As part of the broader movement to rejuvenate old city centers, waterfront development began to appear in the mid-1900s as a way of conserving and reusing the industrial past, promoting environmental health and providing alternative economies such as tourism, retailing and recreation. One of the best and most often-cited examples of this

Plate 9.8 Darling Harbor, Sydney, Australia, exemplifies waterfront redevelopment for tourism and recreation

phenomenon is Baltimore, Maryland, and its Inner Harbor, which had been an important US harbor since the 18th century. During the 1950s efforts were made to try to clean up the harbor area, and during the next quarter century grassy parklands were planted and old piers were torn out. The 1970s were crucial for the area with more amendments being made during that time, and Harborplace, the festival marketplace, was opened up in 1980. Aquariums, museums, hotels, cafes and many other recreational amenities have since been added to create one of Baltimore's most important tourist zones.

The Toronto Harbourfront, Wellington Waterfront, the London Docklands, Darling Harbour (Sydney) and the Royal Naval Dockyard (Bermuda) are examples of large-scale waterfront developments (see Plate 9.8). Even smaller cities, such as Toledo, Ohio and Windsor, Ontario, have jumped on the redevelopment wagon to redesign and renovate their urban shorelines. All of these have an important tourism and heritage conservation function in their respective cities. The Barcelona Waterfront was developed largely in preparation for the 1992 Olympic Games. Other cities have initiated similar projects for the purpose of presenting themselves to the world during mega-events.

CHALLENGES TO CONSERVING THE PAST

Although conserving the world's patrimony is a laudable and necessary endeavor, it is not easy. There are many social, economic, political and ecological constraints to conserving the cultural past, some of which are more noticeable in the less-developed portions of the world. This mix of limitations manifests in many important heritage locations being endangered for a variety of reasons. Each year UNESCO publishes a list of World Heritage Sites in Danger (see Table 9.1 for cultural sites in danger in 2010). This danger list aims to inform the global community about conditions threatening the distinctive traits that originally qualified the property for the WHL, and it serves as a call to action to arrest the deteriorative effects of disaster, war, pollution and other natural and human-induced pressures.

Table 9.1 UNESCO Cultural World Heritage Sites in Danger, 2010

Country	Site	Year listed in danger	Threats against the site
Afghanistan	Bamiyan Valley	2003	Abandonment, military action, dynamite explosions, looting, illicit excavations, anti-personnel mines
Afghanistan	Remains of Jam	2002	Earthquakes, lack of protection, illegal digging, looting
Chile	Humberstone and Santa Laura Saltpeter Works	2005	Lack of maintenance, looting, vandalism, natural deterioration
Egypt	Abu Mena	2001	Agricultural development, structural collapse, harsh environmental conditions
Georgia	Historic Monuments of Mtskheta	2009	Lack of preservation, deterioration of the sites
Iran	Bam and its Cultural Landscape	2004	Earthquake, natural deterioration
Iraq	Ancient city of Ashur	2003	Lack of protection, possible flood threat with construction of a new dam
Iraq	Samarra Archaeological City	2007	War, bombings, insurgent attacks
Israel/Palestine	Old City of Jerusalem and its Walls	1982	Urban development, lack of maintenance, impacts of tourism
Pakistan	Fort and Shalamar Gardens in Lahore	2000	Destruction to make way for urban infrastructure, natural site deterioration
Peru	Chan Chan Archaeological Zone	1986	Natural erosion, lack of protection

Philippines	Rice Terraces of the Philippine Cordilleras	2001	Abandonment of agriculture by younger generation, deforestation, climate change
Serbia/Kosovo	Medieval Monuments in Kosovo	2006	Political instability, lack of conservation management
Tanzania	Ruins of Kilwa Kisiwani and Songo Mnara	2004	Danger of building collapses due to natural erosion, climate change, vegetation pressures
Venezuela	Coro and its Port	2005	Natural erosion, inappropriate construction of walls, new construction
Yemen	Historic Town of Zabid	2000	Lack of conservation, deterioration, new construction replacing old buildings

Source: UNESCO (2009b)

The dangers defined by UNESCO are viewed as 'ascertained' (a proven, pending threat) or a 'potential threat', when a site is facing threats that could in the near future jeopardize its heritage values. Inscription on the List of World Heritage Sites in Danger is not a sanction but a call for action to save places on the verge of imminent damage or destruction. This list allows the committee to allocate aid from the World Heritage Fund to protect the threatened property. Inscription on this list necessitates the World Heritage Committee developing and adopting a program for corrective measures and monitoring of the site. Every effort must be made to restore the site's original values to enable it to be removed as soon as possible from the danger list (UNESCO, 2009b).

If the problems cannot be resolved, a property faces the possibility of being delisted from the WHL altogether. Because human-induced pressures were too great to restore their original World Heritage character, two sites were recently delisted: the Dresden Elbe Valley, Germany (delisted in 2009), and the Arabian Oryx Sanctuary in Oman (delisted in 2007). The Dresden Elbe Valley was original listed as an important cultural landscape along the Elbe River. However, the construction of Waldschlösschen Bridge across the river, which began in 2007, was seen by UNESCO as diminishing the integrity of the cultural landscape to the point where the area no longer deserved to be on the list. As a result of extensive illegal hunting and habitat destruction, the oryx population in the Arabian Oryx Sanctuary was profoundly degraded to an extent that, when the preserve was delisted, there were only four breeding pairs left in the sanctuary. In addition, UNESCO was pressured by the government of Oman to delist the property so it could be used for oil exploration.

The World Monuments Fund (WMF) also labels heritage sites in danger with its bi-annual Watch List, which highlights 100 historic properties that are threatened by disaster, overdevelopment, armed conflict, neglect or intentional demolition (see Table 9.2). The aim of WMF's Watch List is to raise public awareness of, and funding for, conservation problems, encouraging local participation, forward innovation and help in finding effective solutions (World Monuments Fund, 2009b). While the WMF and UNESCO are not official partners in their salvation efforts, several endangered sites are on both organizations' lists.

Table 9.2 A selection of sites on the World Monuments Fund's Watch List for 2010

Country	Site	Location of site
Afghanistan	Old City of Herat	Heart
Armenia	Aghjots Monastery	Garni
Austria	Weiner Werkbundseidlung	Vienna
Bahrain	Suq al-Qaysariya	Muharraq
Bhutan	Phajoding	Thimphu
Comoros	Ujumbe Palace	Mutsamudu
Ecuador	Todos Santos Complex	Cuenca
Guatemala	Kaminaljuyu	Guatemala City
Haiti	Gingerbread Houses	Port-au-Prince
India	Chiktan Castle	Kargil
Italy	Ponte Lucano	Tivoli
Mexico	Las Pozas	Xilitla
Panama	Corozal Cemetery	Panama City
Peru	Tambo Colorado	Humay
Philippines	San Sebastian Basilica	Manila
Spain	Historic Landscape of Toledo	Toledo
Uganda	Wamala King's Tombs	Nansana
United Kingdom	St John the Evangelist Parish Church	Shobdon
USA	Taliesin West	Scottsdale (Arizona)
Venezuela	Parque del Este	Caracas

Source: World Monuments Fund (2009b)

As is evident from the WMF and UNESCO lists of endangered heritage, there are many constraints to the successful conservation of the built and living past. The following sections describe several limitations to heritage protection that are evident in both developing and developed world contexts. They all fit within a broader classification of financial and human resource constraints, human pressures, political history and natural processes.

Financial and human resource constraints

Budgetary limitations

Perhaps the most paramount of all conservation constraints everywhere is a lack of funding. With budget cutbacks facing many public agencies throughout the world during the past quarter century, heritage managers have had to stretch their operating budgets, reduce services and find alternative ways of earning revenue to support their goals of conserving and educating. In some extreme cases, heritage places have to shut their doors to visits and even basic maintenance and scientific exploration. A perfect example of this tragedy is currently happening (2009–2011) in Arizona, USA, where the state legislature has reduced funding for Arizona State Parks so severely that the agency plans to close a good number of its park properties, including those housing ancient Native American ruins, 17th century Spanish mission buildings and other historic structures and sites. There are many public fears about the economic repercussions of such drastic measures for the rural communities where most of these sites are located, as well as the potential for vandalism and deterioration at locations that will not be staffed or regularly monitored. There are also looming threats of additional budget cuts in 2010–2011 that could spell the demise of Arizona State Parks entirely, 'which could make Arizona the first state in the nation to close its entire parks system' (Newton, 2010: B6).

Utility services, repair materials, mechanical equipment, human resources, conservation techniques, expert assistance, landscaping materials, interpretive media and other necessities are expensive but crucial elements of the management of heritage resources. In the absence of adequate funding, many historic places have not been well maintained; some very important properties have been left entirely to the forces of nature and human impact. When budgets are reduced, site managers must decide on the most appropriate use of scarce resources. Unfortunately, these are too commonly utilized for short-term solutions, such as cosmetic maintenance or tourism promotion, rather than for deeper preservation and personnel training, which in the long term would be more beneficial.

Inadequate funding leads to favoritism, wherein sites deemed more important by some public officials are funded while other equally important, though not as personally connected, sites are fully subsidized. There are many instances of properties in the hometowns of influential politicians and social elites receiving disproportionately more financial support than areas that might be in even more need of it.

Money problems also lead to inappropriate conservation methods, such as using cheaper materials and labor. Less experienced staff are also less expensive, so the people hired to protect and maintain valuable sites are sometimes unqualified to do so and may do more harm than good in their efforts to protect the past.

As already noted, in light of fiscal shortfalls, property managers have had to become creative in concocting ways to finance conservation. Admission fees, sponsorships and hosting special events (e.g. art shows, wedding receptions and family reunions) are now commonplace in many historic areas as a way of adding much-needed cash to dwindling coffers. People's outcries about having to pay to visit their own heritage are not uncommon and while many site managers and strict heritage enthusiasts decry the commoditization of the cultural environment for rent or sale, this has become an economic reality wherever patrimony is being preserved.

Inappropriate preservation tactics

The lack of money noted above is an endemic problem in the realm of heritage protection. Unfortunately, this leads to improper conservation. This is particularly problematic in less-developed countries where efforts to conserve are often disguised in cosmetic cover-ups instead of more resilient structural recuperation that will survive through decades of human-induced or natural deterioration. Much preservation work is shoddy and haphazard which, while an effort to improve a site, can in fact deteriorate it further. Incompatible materials and substandard restoration techniques are a common problem at ancient sites. In Pagan, Myanmar, for instance, hundreds of ancient temples have been reconstructed with brightly-colored bricks and cement stems, items that were never originally used. In addition, new temples have been constructed out of other non-local materials atop crumbling ancient foundations. Similar problems can be found all over the world including at Angkor Wat, Cambodia, where early conservationists used non-original and incompatible materials that have not only covered up ancient reliefs, but have also stained and tarnished antique facades beyond repair.

There's just too much heritage to save

In countries that have a long and ancient record of human habitation, archaeological sites and historic buildings abound far beyond the nation's ability to excavate, list and preserve them. In countries such as Israel, Italy and Greece, which have experienced a multitude of successive empires and civilizations, built and re-built upon one another, almost every public works project can expect a delay because an ancient site is discovered. Likewise, enormous countries with massive populations and large cities, such as China, India and Indonesia, are overwhelmed with hundreds if not thousands of historic buildings, ancient artifacts and a plethora of cultural landscapes – all of which could not possibly be protected even if money and personnel were more abundant. In most cases, the need for modern comforts such as roads, sewerage systems and power lines, as well as a lack of funds and personnel, prevents even a fraction of many countries' patrimony being delineated and protected. In some cities, such as Delhi, India or Beijing, China, there are thousands of historic homes, palaces, religious sites, schools, administrative edifices and other buildings that merit conservation attention, but social, political and economic priorities cannot realistically encompass them all.

Human pressures

Tourist pressures

As noted already in Chapter 7, tourists and local visitors are one of the biggest threats to the preservation of historic relics, buildings and archaeological sites. The wear and tear resulting from thousands of feet and hands each year is a glaring problem at many precious places. Vandalism in the form of graffiti, collecting or breakage damages antiquities forever, as clean up costs and methods are prohibitively expensive and sometimes even more damaging than the defacement itself. Stolen bits and pieces of statues, paintings or mosaics can never be replaced. In addition, increased tourism begets increased vehicular traffic. Thousands of examples exist of historic places that are tarnished by the exhaust fumes of cars, motorcoaches, taxis and scooters as these become more commonplace with the growth of tourism. Acids and toxins in the air deteriorate delicate carvings and mosaics, and ancient buildings become discolored.

This problem is so apparent in some locations that tourism is the primary threat to ancient monuments. The Old City of Jerusalem, which was listed as a UNESCO World Heritage Site in 1981, was included on the List of World Heritage in Danger in 1982 owing in large part to the pressures of mass tourism in one of the holiest cities on earth. Graffiti, broken monuments and structures, wear and tear, litter and pollution are among the tourism-specific threats associated with Jerusalem (see Plate 9.9).

Human habitation

People living inside historic properties create an additional layer of concern for heritage conservationists. In many less-developed parts of the world, villages have grown intermingled with remnants of ancient civilizations. In these situations, residents oftentimes use ruins as foundations for their present homes. They utilize miscellaneous relics as tools and farm equipment, and they may even carry pieces off to sell or use in constructing other buildings. Cows, goats, horses and chickens are allowed to wander freely, often breaking or wearing down delicate surfaces and artifacts. Sometimes the damage done by local people is more severe than that of tourists.

Historic cities face many preservation challenges, not least of which is the local population inhabiting heritage quarters. Their cars, school buses, bicycles, pets, garbage and sewage contribute to the degradation of historic urban centers. The installation of satellite dishes, air conditioners, balconies and other modern amenities often reduces the

Plate 9.9 The Old City of Jerusalem suffers severe pressures from masses of tourists

authenticity of historic cities and calls into question the integrity of urban areas that have been deemed worthy of protection. While historic-city dwellers have rights and are entitled to the comforts of modern living, urban planners and policy makers must use caution and prudence in allowing any kind of restructuring, and unrestrained growth must never take place.

On a more specific level, antiquated houses all over the world are inhabited by families, some of which have been living in the home for many generations. Unfortunately, most families cannot afford to maintain the homes in traditional form, and it is not uncommon for renovations to be done that are incongruent with original forms and functions. Most governments are loathe to grant public funds for private home maintenance and restoration, so more and more historic homes continue to dilapidate.

Urbanization and modernization

The spread of cities is one of the most salient problems facing heritage in urban and rural contexts. Urban encroachment prevails when population pressures cause cities to grow rapidly and unofficial squatter settlements develop on the periphery or in the city center. Overdevelopment in terms of planned suburbs also affects exurban areas as roads are

215

built and suburban neighborhoods are constructed near cultural sites, power lines are installed, shopping malls erected and factories built to service new growth areas.

Urbanization is directly connected to modernization, which refers to an evolutionary process wherein traditional elements of socio-economic life and technology are replaced with new innovations and lifestyles. Technological growth and socio-economic development are important ingredients in this process. Unfortunately, historic buildings and ancient traditions are among the most obvious casualties of modernization, as development pressure pushes governments and communities to opt for demolition and new construction before the benefits of preservation are considered. In most cases, the costs and benefits associated with conserving old buildings or constructing new ones are weighed only in economic terms, whereas ideally the aesthetic and historical value should also be evaluated. In developed countries, where a sense of societal nostalgia permeates the air, there is now a trend to keep historic structures, renovating them for modern-day uses. In the developing world, however, old buildings are more often knocked down and replaced by newer edifices that have little connection to place. The prevailing attitude is that preservation is incompatible with development – development is synonymous with change, while keeping traditional buildings and historic areas is antithetical to progress.

Agricultural land use

Population pressures have also increased agricultural pressures. The encroachment of farmland into areas adjacent to parks and heritage preserves has created some contentious situations where both natural and cultural heritage are concerned. Forests, grasslands and even archaeological areas have given way to agriculture land uses, which are harmful in several ways. One is the physical intrusion of agricultural land into rural areas or suburban areas, which sometimes entails the destruction of historic buildings and archaeological sites in favor of farmland. A second problem is the proliferation of pesticides and fertilizers, which leach into the soil and water drainage systems. The toxins are then carried by water to various delicate ecosystems, including rain forests and coral reefs. Research in Australia has demonstrated that agriculture has in fact become one of the biggest threats to the Great Barrier Reef World Heritage Site, contributing to that natural wonder's demise.

Pollution

Alongside industrialization has come pollution in various forms: air, water and soil. With the proliferation of factories and other components of heavy industry during the 1800s and 1900s, the built environment has deteriorated significantly in large cities and rural areas nearby manufacturing plants. Likewise, the popularization of the private automobile had the same effect. Millions of vehicles on the world's streets and highways have more than a slight impact on air quality and hence the physical integrity of the built environment. Most industrial and vehicular pollutants are toxic not only to humans and animals, but also to the natural and built environments.

The damaging effects of acid rain and other toxic air particles (e.g. calcium sulfate and sodium sulfate) can be seen in nearly all parts of the world. The Taj Mahal in India, for instance, suffered considerable damage to its delicate stone surface after many years of industrial output in the Delhi-Agra region to the point where the Indian government took action and had most of the nearby factories removed. The Leshan Giant Buddha, a World Heritage Site, has suffered significant consequences of acid rain from heavy industrialization in Sichuan Province, China. In addition to heavy soot from factories and power plants, which has discolored the ancient cliff carving, acid rain has begun to weaken and deteriorate the stone surface. Many thousands of examples of this exist everywhere, as the damage continues to accelerate with the burning of fossil fuels and continued heavy industrial development.

Illicit trade in antiquities

As noted earlier, the illicit trade in ancient artifacts fuels the growing trend in grave-robbing, illegal digs at important archaeological sites and a flourishing black market for relics that have been removed from their original location. Tourists are often enticed into buying small artifacts from vendors or diggers who approach them. What most tourists fail to realize is that purchasing and possessing these small artifacts is, in most countries, highly illegal, punishable by severe fines and jail sentences. Many innocent tourists have been detained for trying to 'smuggle' ancient artifacts that they thought were legitimately for sale. In addition, on occasion licensed dealers might sell illegal relics in their shops. In most cases this is not permitted. Severe fines and confiscation of licenses (possibly even jail time), for example, can occur in Israel if a shopkeeper, who is licensed to sell antiquities, is found to possess illegal or inauthentic articles. Often it is the tourists themselves that find pieces of pottery, glass, coins, tiles or other relicts at ancient sites. This is very illegal and extremely risky, as in some places even picking up a piece of the past, not just keeping it, can result in fines and legal action.

Politics and political history

Colonialism

While many aspects of colonialism were negative, one of the most abhorrent from the perspective of heritage resources was the suppression of indigenous cultures and traditions by European metropoles. The assimilationist approaches of the French, Portuguese, Spanish, Dutch and British colonialists (some more assimilationist than others) had the effect of replacing many aspects of indigenous culture with European cultural norms (e.g. religion, language, social network, governance), which in the thoughts of some cultural observers has created a real sense of cultural loss, low social esteem and a lack of self-determination. Most traditional pasts were replaced with ones that reflected wealth, elitism and racial superiority. Thus, today there tends to be an imbalance in the heritage resources of the less-developed world, where cultural landscapes reveal much more about the colonizers than they do about pre-colonial history.

The low priority that colonial powers placed on the conservation of indigenous heritage can be seen in the lateness of cultural conservation legislation. In many cases preservation laws were only enacted once countries became independent. In Togo, for instance, protection laws were only put into place in the 1990s. In Ghana they were established in the late 1950s, and in Ecuador in the late 1970s. It could be argued that much irreplaceable heritage was lost in the interim period before such laws were passed.

An additional problem that all colonial powers caused was to plunder the ancient artifacts of their colonies for the purpose of building up royal family or museum collections at home. Many of the national museums throughout the capitals of Europe house artifacts and ancient relics that were brought by explorers, overseas governors, traveling administrators and politicians, royal family members themselves or other colonial tourists back to the homeland for display and to enhance the collections of the privileged.

War and conflict

Chapter 6 focused on the politics of heritage, including the devastation of war on rural and urban landscapes, causing irreparable damage to heritage. Natural areas are also destroyed and while many of these can regenerate organically, the built environment cannot. War targets emblems that demarcate the national identity of the opponents – cities, monuments, government buildings, villages, cemeteries, historic structures and museums. It also affects the cultural landscape when it becomes an innocent bystander (see Plate 9.10).

Psychologically, political conflict not only destroys the material culture of people, it also persuades them to seek vengeance on others, which in itself is damaging to heritage preservation. This is particularly the case in countries where more than one ethnic group exists and which have been at odds sometime in the past. Minority (or majority) groups and their heritage sometimes become the targets of revenge for past injustices or political tensions that existed in recent history or even many generations earlier.

Inharmonious planning and lack of cooperation

Collaboration between government agencies (e.g. Ministry of Tourism and Ministry of Public Works), the public and private sectors (e.g. national tourism organizations and hotel associations), different levels of government within a state (e.g. county, state, province, municipality), private-sector organizations (e.g. airlines and car-rental companies) and cross-border entities that share common resources (e.g. nature preserves that overlap borders or cultural areas that lie adjacent to one another on opposite sides of a border) are all important in upholding the principles of sustainable tourism. This is particularly the

Plate 9.10 New roofs in Dubrovnik have replaced many of those destroyed in the mid-1990s Yugoslavian wars

case in the area of heritage, for as a non-renewable resource the built environment must have extra care and attention.

Too often plans are made that exclude certain important stakeholders, such as tourism services. Utility installation is notorious for destroying archaeology and historic buildings, which in many cases is entirely unnecessary and could be prevented better with more integrated, cross-sectoral cooperation. Unfortunately, some government agencies within the same country are unaware of what the others are doing. Similarly, it is not at all uncommon for public agencies to carry out development or restoration projects without input from various stakeholders, including the private sector, which stand to gain or lose a great deal if tourism or conservation plans are done well or poorly.

Cross-border cooperation is extremely important in areas where natural or cultural heritage overlaps political lines. Important resources such as Iguazu Falls (Argentina/ Brazil) and Victoria Falls (Zambia/Zimbabwe), and the interesting historic towns of Rivera (Uruguay)/Santana do Livramento (Brazil) and Valka, Latvia/Valga, Estonia, are bisected by an international boundary but require a great deal of transnational cooperation to protect their unique features. Traditionally, political boundaries at international and subnational levels have formed salient barriers to cooperation because each entity is concerned only with its own affairs. In the case of international cooperation, borders have always functioned as barriers to communication and collaboration because of state sovereignty, protective barriers (e.g. tariffs) and an isolationist mentality. Today, while regional alliances are growing and becoming stronger, there are still relatively few true cross-boundary networks to help conserve heritage areas. Without adequate cross-border collaborative networks, it is virtually impossible for equitable relationships to exist and for cultural resources to be managed holistically, particularly as conservation rules and policies change from country to country.

Lack of social determination

There is a tendency in traditional societies, particularly those in the developing portions of the world, to view conservation with an eye of skepticism. The prevailing attitude suggests that preserving the old is incongruous with progress and modern life. Traditional lifestyles and old buildings are often equated with backwardness. Many of the less-affluent of the world wonder why their heritage should be conserved at all, since it is a sign of poverty and old-fashioned living. These attitudes are often harnessed by developers to justify the demolition of historic homes and other buildings, to make way for new developments which promise the world's poor a brighter (and shinier) future in a modern society.

Along these same lines, there is a pervasive feeling that heritage should not be saved unless there is a profit-oriented motive driving conservation. In the developed countries of the world, as noted earlier, conservation is carried out for a variety of reasons, including education, science and esthetic and architectural value. In most parts of the world, however, these are insufficient rationales for the protection of the built environment. Again, this unfortunately often results in the demolition of historic buildings and historic urban zones to make way for more profitable developments, such as apartments, hotels or business suites.

Lack of political support

Public agencies frequently place heritage on the back burner in terms of both funding and policy development. Preserving the past is seen in many places and at many times as an unaffordable luxury, when public works, education, social welfare and health care are vying for scarce tax capital. This has led to the deterioration of heritage sites but also the widespread control of nations' heritage by outside interests. International funding agencies sometimes take control of a country's heritage, fund its planning and preservation and operate it from outside. While this is laudable and an important intervention to saving pasts that are on the verge of disappearing, it creates conditions whereby governments become complacent and adopt an 'others will take care of it' attitude.

There are numerous examples of government corruption manifesting itself in the realm of heritage. Economic and political favors are commonly exchanged for turning a blind eye to a negative situation. This has happened on a number of occasions in cultural areas, where government officials were paid off to allow film crews to alter cultural landscapes for the purpose of producing motion pictures. Perhaps even more damaging is when police and other public officials receive some sort of compensation for turning their backs to the plundering of historic buildings and pillaging of archaeological sites. Unfortunately this happens in many parts of the world, more often than we are able to ascertain.

Natural processes

Natural deterioration

One of the biggest threats to tangible heritage is not directly human-induced at all. The natural elements and their erosive processes are one of the most lethal forces affecting the built environment (see Plate 9.11). Historic sites in extreme climates and harsh environments are the most prone to these conditions. In the coldest climates, the process of freezing and thawing can be a significant problem as stones and concrete crack and expand, eventually breaking apart, as has happened at historic sites in Arctic and Antarctic regions. The natural wear associated with wind and waves in coastal areas also poses a hazard to the built heritage, including the undermining of the soils and bedrock that support it. Martello towers, or small defensive forts, built on coastlines around the world are an example of built heritage that is especially prone to these forces. Heat, wind and sand erosion is a salient concern in desert environments as well – something heritage managers and policy makers in North Africa and the Middle East have had to deal with for years. The desertification process has been especially difficult in historic places such as Timbuktu, Mali, where not only have erosive effects of wind and sand taken their toll, but occasional excessive rains wear away delicate mud buildings. This is a common problem in desert environments, where much of the traditional built environment was constructed of mud and clay. While rain is infrequent, when it falls, it falls in torrents, causing adobe and mud walls to corrode and eventually collapse. Such has been the fate of many ancient Native American sites in the southwestern USA.

SUMMARY AND CONCLUSION

Protecting cultural heritage is an extremely important endeavor given the effects of tourism's growth, pressures exacted by local populations and natural processes of erosion. Conservation efforts today reflect a set of values and purposes that realize the economic, social, political and scientific merits of the built environment and that it is worthy of protection. Most efforts today take the form of renovation, restoration or preservation, or all of them combined into urban renewal or rural development projects. Despite valiant efforts on the part of most cities, towns, countries and other regions to preserve their past today, too much of it has already been lost owing to political conflicts, a lack of political will, financial constraints, modernization efforts that preceded conservation legislation, a lack of well-trained staff, pollution and the vagaries of nature, to name but a few forces.

221

Plate 9.11 Christ the Redeemer statue (Brazil) undergoing reinforcement and cleaning to mitigate the effects of erosion

Fortunately, there is a growing and already widespread conservation ethos in the public and private realms regarding the built and living past. Not all places, however, are adequately armed with protective laws and sufficient human resources to enforce them. In places that are at greatest risk of losing their heritage, mostly in the less-developed world, there is an even greater need to overcome the human and natural challenges to establish sound conservation practices that will help carry the past far into the future.

222

REVIEW QUESTIONS

1. How did early environmental thinking help develop the modern notion of heritage conservation?

2. Of the several reasons discussed in this chapter on why cultural conservation is undertaken, are some more important than others, or does it matter why it is done as long as it is done?

3. Why does collective nostalgia cause societies to desire heritage preservation?

4. To what degree is conservation through modern-day use of historic buildings a viable option?

5. How do preservation, restoration and renovation differ in their goals and approaches to heritage protection? How are they similar?

6. How is gentrification a benefit for older cities, from a tourism perspective?

7. Can you think of at least three harbor cities where waterfront redevelopment has provided an economic boost and helped build social capital? How does it accomplish this?

8. How do the constraints to heritage protection differ between the developed and developing worlds?

RECOMMENDED READING

Barthel, D. (1996) *Historic Preservation: Collective Memory and Historical Identity.* New Brunswick, NJ: Rutgers University Press.

Batra, N.L. (1996) *Heritage Conservation: Preservation and Restoration of Monuments.* Noida, India: Aryan Books.

Carter, F.W. (1982) Historic cities in Eastern Europe: Problems of industrialization, pollution and conservation. *Mazingira* 6(3), 62–76.

Cheng, E.W. and Ma, S.Y. (2009) Heritage conservation through private donation: The case of Dragon Garden in Hong Kong. *International Journal of Heritage Studies* 15(6), 511–528.

Delafons, J. (1997) Conservation of the historic heritage. *Town & Country Planning* 66(5), 136–137.

Fawcett, J. (ed.) (1976) *The Future of the Past: Attitudes to Conservation*, 1174–1974. London: Thames and Hudson.

Feilden, B.M. (2003) *Conservation of Historic Buildings.* Oxford: Architectural Press.

223

Ferreira, S. and Visser, G. (2007) Creating an African Riviera: Revisiting the impact of the Victoria and Alfred Waterfront Development in Cape Town. *Urban Forum* 18(3), 227–246.

Galán, E. and Zezza, F. (eds) (2002) *Protection and Conservation of the Cultural Heritage of the Mediterranean Cities*. Lisse, Netherlands: Swets & Zeitlinger.

Garrod, G.D., Willis, K.G., Bjarnadottir, H. and Cockbain, P. (1996) The non-priced benefits of renovating historic buildings: A case study of Newcastle's Grainger Town. *Cities* 13(6), 423–430.

Gordon, D.L.A. (1996) Planning, design and managing change in urban waterfront redevelopment. *Town Planning Review* 67(3), 261–290.

Hall, C.M. and McArthur, S. (eds) (1993) *Heritage Management in New Zealand and Australia: Visitor Management, Interpretation, and Marketing*. Auckland: Oxford University Press.

Haskell, G.H. (ed.) (1993) *Caring for Our Built Heritage: Conservation in Practice*. London: E & FN Spon.

Henderson, J.C. (2008) Managing urban ethnic heritage: Little India in Singapore. *International Journal of Heritage Studies* 14(4), 332–346.

Hoyle, B. (2001) Lamu: Waterfront revitalization in an east African port-city. *Cities* 18, 297–313.

Isar, Y.R. (ed.) (1986) *The Challenge to Our Cultural Heritage: Why Preserve the Past*. Washington, DC: Smithsonian Institute.

Jones, G.A. and Bromley, R.D.F. (1996) The relationship between urban conservation programmes and property renovation: Evidence from Quito, Ecuador. *Cities* 13(6), 373–375.

Kreps, C.F. (2003) *Liberating Culture: Cross-Cultural Perspectives on Museums, Curation and Heritage Preservation*. London: Routledge.

Larkham, P.J. (1996) *Conservation and the City*. London: Routledge.

Lee, A.J. (ed.) (1992) *Past Meets Future: Saving America's Historic Environments*. Washington, DC: Preservation Press.

Lloyd, K. and Morgan, C. (2008) Murky waters: Tourism, heritage and the development of the ecomuseum in Ha Long Bay, Vietnam. *Journal of Heritage Tourism* 3(1), 1–17.

Lowenthal, D. (1979) Environmental perception: Preserving the past. *Progress in Human Geography* 3(4), 549–559.

Lu, T.L.D. (2009) Heritage conservation in post-colonial Hong Kong. *International Journal of Heritage Studies* 15(2/3), 258–272.

Magness-Gardiner, B. (2004) International conventions and cultural heritage protection. In Y. Rowan and U. Baram (eds) *Marketing Heritage: Archaeology and the Consumption of the Past* (pp. 27–40). Walnut Creek, CA: AltaMira Press.

Marks, R. (1996) Conservation and community: The contradictions and ambiguities of tourism in the stone town of Zanzibar. *Habitat International* 20(2), 265–278.

Mason, R. (2008) Be interested and beware: Joining economic valuation and heritage conservation. *International Journal of Heritage Studies* 14(4), 303–318.

Mayer, C.C. and Wallace, G.N. (2007) Appropriate levels of restoration and development at Copán Archaeological Park: Setting attributes affecting the visitor experience. *Journal of Ecotourism* 6(2), 91–110.

McCarthy, J. (2004) Tourism-related waterfront development in historic cities: Malta's Cottonera Project. *International Planning Studies* 9(1), 43–64.

McCaskey, T.G. (1975) Conservation of historic areas: Management techniques for tourism in the USA. In A.J. Burkart and S. Medlik (eds) *The Management of Tourism* (pp. 151–159). London: Heinemann.

Mohit, R.S. and Kammeier, H.D. (1996) The fort: Opportunities for an effective urban conservation strategy in Bombay. *Cities* 13(6), 387–398.

Morosi, J., Amarilla, B., Conti, A. and Contín, M. (2008) *Estancias* of Buenos Aires Province, Argentina: Rural heritage, sustainable development and tourism. *International Journal of Heritage Studies* 14(6), 589–594.

Munasinghe, H. (2005) The politics of the past: Constructing a national identity through heritage conservation. *International Journal of Heritage Studies* 11(3), 251–260.

Orbaşli, A. (2000) *Tourists in Historic Towns: Urban Conservation and Heritage Management.* London: E & FN Spon.

Rghei, A.S. and Nelson, J.G. (1994) The conservation and use of the walled city of Tripoli. *Geographical Journal* 160, 143–158.

Rogers, M. (1996) Beyond authenticity: Conservation, tourism, and the politics of representation in the Ecuadorian Amazon. *Identities* 3(1/2), 73–125.

Rossides, N. (1995) The conservation of the cultural heritage in Cyprus: A planner's perspective. *Regional Development Dialogue* 16(1), 110–125.

Sable, K.A. and Kling, R.W. (2001) The Double Public Good: A conceptual framework for 'shared experience' values associated with heritage conservation. *Journal of Cultural Economics* 25(2), 77–89.

Slater, T.R. (1984) Preservation, conservation and planning in historic towns. *The Geographical Journal* 150(3), 322–334.

Stabler, M. (1998) The economic evaluation of the role of conservation and tourism in the regeneration of historic urban destinations. In E. Laws, B. Faulkner and G. Moscardo (eds) *Embracing and Managing Change in Tourism: International Case Studies* (pp. 235–263). London: Routledge.

Talley, M.K. (1995) The old road and the mind's internal heaven: Preservation of the cultural heritage in times of armed conflict. *Museum Management and Curatorship* 14(1), 57–64.

Teo, P. and Huang, S. (1995) Tourism and heritage conservation in Singapore. *Annals of Tourism Research* 22, 589–615.

Tiesdell, S., Oc, T. and Heath, T. (1996) *Revitalizing Historic Urban Quarters*. Oxford: Architectural Press.

Timmons, S. (ed.) (1976) *Preservation and Conservation: Principles and Practices*. Washington, DC: National Trust for Historic Preservation.

Timothy, D.J. (1999) Built heritage, tourism and conservation in developing countries: Challenges and opportunities. *Journal of Tourism* 4, 5–17.

Timothy, D.J. and Boyd, S.W. (2003) *Heritage Tourism*. Harlow: Prentice Hall.

Timothy, D.J. and Nyaupane, G.P. (2009) *Cultural Heritage and Tourism in the Developing World: A Regional Perspective*. London: Routledge.

Tunbridge, J. (1984) Whose heritage to conserve? Cross-cultural reflections upon political dominance and urban heritage conservation. *Canadian Geographer* 28, 171–180.

Tunbridge, J.E. (2002) Large heritage waterfronts on small tourist islands: The case of the Royal Naval Dockyard, Bermuda. *International Journal of Heritage Studies* 8(1), 41–51.

Varotsos, C., Tzanis, C. and Cracknell, A. (2009) The enhanced deterioration of the cultural heritage monuments due to air pollution. *Environmental Science and Pollution Research* 16(5), 590–592.

Weiner, L.W. (1980) Cultural resources: An old asset – a new market for tourism. *Journal of Cultural Economics* 4(1), 1–7.

Willson, G.B. and McIntosh, A.J. (2007) Heritage buildings and tourism: An experiential view. *Journal of Heritage Tourism* 2(2), 75–93.

Worden, N. (1994) Unwrapping history at the Cape Town Waterfront. *The Public Historian* 16(2), 33–50.

Zetter, R. (ed.) (1982) *Conservation of Buildings in Developing Countries*. Oxford: Oxford Polytechnic, Department of Town Planning.

Ziegler, A.P. and Kidney, W.C. (1980) *Historic Preservation in Small Towns: A Manual of Practice*. Nashville: American Association for State and Local History.

RECOMMENDED WEBSITES

American Institute for Conservation of Historic and Artistic Works – http://www.conservation-us.org/

Assorestauro – http://www.assorestauro.org/

Baltimore Inner Harbor – http://www.baltimore.to/baltimore.html

Building Conservation Directory – http://www.buildingconservation.com/articles/ten/tenways.htm

Darling Harbour – http://www.darlingharbour.com/

Heritage Conservation Network – http://www.heritageconservation.net/

Institute of Conservation – http://www.icon.org.uk/

Institute of Historic Building Conservation – http://www.ihbc.org.uk/

International Centre for the Study of the Preservation and Restoration of Cultural Property – http://www.iccrom.org

International Council of African Museums – http://www.africom.museum/

Toronto's Harbourfront Centre – http://en.wikipedia.org/wiki/Harbourfront_Centre

World Heritage Sites in Danger – http://whc.unesco.org/en/danger

CHAPTER 10

TELLING THE STORY: INTERPRETING THE PAST FOR VISITORS

LEARNING OBJECTIVES

After reading this chapter, you should be able to:

1. Identify the purposes and benefits of heritage interpretation.

2. Comprehend the critical character of education and entertainment in interpretation.

3. Be familiar with the most common and most effective interpretive methods.

4. Recognize the characteristics of each approach to heritage interpretation.

5. Understand effective interpretation in light of social and global diversity in demand for heritage places.

6. Learn about the interpretive planning process and its components.

INTRODUCTION

As we already know, people visit cultural places in large part for the opportunity to learn something new, to be edified or to spend quality time enjoying someone else's company. Interpretation forms an important part of that experience. Interpretation refers to the act of revealing the significance of a place, person, artifact or event. It is telling the story in such a way that people will want to learn and perhaps return again and again. Heritage scholars also point out that high-quality interpretation can add value to an attraction, giving it a competitive advantage over other cultural offerings in an area.

Timothy and Boyd (2003: 196–197) provide an overview of the origins of interpretation. Interpretation in one form or another likely began with ancient storytelling among hunters, fishers and traders. In later centuries Greek and Roman philosophers began to interpret the universe, supernatural happenings and various natural phenomena for their students and the general public. Travel during the medieval period embodied pilgrimage and educational travel among the gentry of Western Europe, who undertook cultural and education trips such as the Grand Tour and pilgrimages to the Holy Land. These two forms of travel at the time involved heavy doses of interpretation in the form of historical analysis, lectures, museum visits, prayer and meditation, learning literature and visits with artistic masters.

While ancient travelers undertook various forms of interpretation, the genesis of modern interpretation started with nature guiding in the western world in the early 20th century. With the spread of the nature preservation movement in North America, Europe, Australia and New Zealand, principles of sound interpretation were developed and disseminated throughout the world. Later in the 20th century, the same concepts and principles were applied to cultural environments so that historic sites and museums became the new venues for interpretive planning and management.

This chapter examines the main principles of effective interpretation and describes the main benefits that derive from it, including education, entertainment, conservation, visitor management and income. The chapter also looks briefly at several interpretive methods, such as guides, audio tours and contemporary high-tech media, and finally it considers the interpretive planning process and its importance for cultural site managers.

INTERPRETATION AS A MANAGEMENT MECHANISM: BENEFITS AND PURPOSES

Interpretation is a valuable management tool. It can help all cultural heritage sites manage crowds, conserve the past and educate the public, to name only a few uses. Interpretation aims to educate people with the ultimate goal of creating awareness of the need to conserve. It also creates an enjoyable, even fun, environment that helps guests remember their experiences. Freeman Tilden (1883–1980) was one of the first people to pioneer the processes, procedures and theories of interpretation in the context of cultural and natural heritage and how these are used in the management context. His guiding principles, most fully established in his 1957 book, *Interpreting Our Heritage*, are still used to train conservationists and curators and continue to maintain their validity into the 21st century. Tilden (1957) established six chief principles of interpretation that have guided interpretive planning, programming and media all over the globe (see Table 10.1).

Table 10.1 Freeman Tilden's Six Principles of Interpretation

1. Interpretation needs to relate the visited place to something within the personality or the experience of the visitor will be sterile.
2. Information, as such, is not interpretation. Interpretation is revelation based upon information.
3. Interpretation is an art or many arts, whether the materials presented are scientific, historical or architectural. Any art is to some degree teachable.
4. The primary aim of interpretation is not instruction but provocation.

5. Interpretation should present a whole rather than a part and must address itself to the whole person rather than any single phase or part.

6. Interpretation addressed to children should not be a diluted version of the presentation to adults. Instead it should follow a fundamentally different approach and program.

Source: Tilden (1957)

The first of Tilden's principles is that interpretation must play to each visitor's own life experience and personality. Failing to relate the historic place, object, person or event directly to people's own experiences and life meanings will stir little interest in the visitor and thereby fall short of the goal of educating guests and creating a sense of urgency about conservation within them. He argued that history and its places must be meaningful to each individual visitor.

Second, simply spewing out information should not be mistaken for interpretation. Instead, interpretation is revelation based on information and must effectively inspire people by disseminating something new. In common with the first principle, this one suggests that people have different experiences and that the interpretive experience must be made meaningful through the revelation of knowledge, not just facts and figures.

Third, Tilden viewed interpretation as an art or set of arts and skills. Good communication skills, people skills, creativity and imagination are a large part of this concept. These aptitudes are critical in creating an enjoyable setting and environment that is conducive to learning, pondering and relating personally to the place being visited.

Fourth, the main purpose of interpretation is not to lecture or regurgitate facts but to trigger positive action on the part of visitors. By bringing the past alive and drawing out personal meaning, visitors can develop relationships between themselves and the place being visited. An important goal of interpretive programs should be to provoke people to action in conserving, learning, volunteering or perpetuating a love of heritage to future generations.

The fifth principle, holistic experiences, suggests that interpretation needs to be holistic, painting bigger pictures and telling complete stories rather than simply presenting bits and pieces of the past. While this may be a difficult expectation, it should be done as much as possible. The principle also suggests that the whole person must be stimulated via many sensory and cognitive experiences.

Lastly, while Tilden used children as an example, the notion should be broadened to consider all varieties of different visitor groups. Thus, different visitor cohorts need different approaches to interpretation. Interpretive planning must consider the needs of children, adults, foreign visitors and school groups, for example. Each of these has varying levels of understanding or cognitive skills and should be considered in planning interpretive programs.

These are all important concepts that are used today in many interpretation contexts. The US National Park Service, for instance, still uses Tilden's guiding principles for much of its own interpretive programming. Tilden's work and that of many others elucidates the important functions of interpretation, including education, entertainment, preservation, crowd management and financial gain in an era of decreasing budgets. While there are other potential benefits of interpretation, these five will be the focus of this section.

Education

Education is the most important overarching role of interpretation in the cultural heritage setting with the aim of getting visitors to understand and appreciate the location or site they are visiting. This increased appreciation, it is believed, will translate into less physical damage by visitors and increase the public's awareness of the need to conserve. The learning process at heritage sites can occur as informal or formal education (Light, 1995; Prentice, 1995). The formal educative role refers to visits to historic sites and museums that are part of a formal school or university curriculum, where in essence learning is required for a passing grade. Informal education refers to guests learning something new by virtue of participating in an interpretive program or viewing interpretive media. Thus, it is not part of a formalized school activity but all visitors nonetheless can learn something from their visits.

Many schools include visits to museums and historic sites in their formal curriculum (see Plate 10.1). Historic buildings, living heritage villages, archaeological sites and museums are important teaching tools in history, geography, literature, art, music and archaeology. Experiential learning through hands-on and field interpretation is extremely effective in helping people retain what they have learned by extending the experiences beyond textbooks and classrooms to personalized experience that goes far beyond facts and figures. School children studying literature in England receive remarkable benefits from visiting Stratford-Upon-Avon, the birthplace of William Shakespeare. Visits to Hadrian's Wall or Viking sites in the UK provide a hands-on approach to learning and seeing the history of the British Isles and Europe. Field trips to Maori places in New Zealand help European (*Pākehā*) New Zealanders appreciate the culture, music and language of their country's natives. Likewise, field excursions to Salzburg, Austria, will help music students appreciate the remarkable life of Wolfgang Amadeus Mozart, one of the world's great classical composers. In short, there really is no replacement for formal education-based field experiences.

From a pragmatic management viewpoint, school field trips provide a justification for public funding for heritage places, and managers see such visits as opportunities to educate an upcoming generation of visitors who will remember their experiences, share them with others and eventually bring their own children to experience the patrimony on show. This contributes to the overall mission of interpretation to educate the public so that they will have a desire to help conserve their past.

Plate 10.1 Elementary school field trip to Harper's Ferry National Historical Park, USA

Informal education refers to the learning undertaken (consciously or unconsciously) by general visitors to heritage sites and occurs outside the formalized educational curriculum. Almost all visitors to heritage places glean knowledge about the site being visited by utilizing interpretive media and seeing the artifacts on display. Some people's visits to heritage places are motivated by a desire to learn, while others simply want a leisure experience away from home. Mindful visitors, or those who pay attention and are attentive to the signage or guides, are much more inclined to learn than less attentive guests, who are more passive and do not participate in discussions.

For many museum and heritage site visitors, learning is the most important motivation for their visit. For others it is of secondary importance, but important nonetheless. In a study by Poria, Reichel and Biran (2006) of visitor outcomes and future visit intentions at Anne Frank House in Amsterdam, the top six motives for a future visit were found to be related to learning and education (see Table 10.2), perhaps with some overlap. These included visitors desiring to pass the Anne Frank story on to their children, contribute to one's education, learn more about the history of the site, understand better the historical background and enrich their knowledge about Anne's historic house.

Table 10.2 Motives for a future visit to Anne Frank House, Amsterdam

Motive for visit	Mean (0 = disagree, 5 = agree)
To pass on the Anne Frank story to your children	3.66
It is important for your children to visit the site	3.64
Visiting the site will contribute to your education	3.51
You want to learn about the history of the site	3.51
You want to learn of its historical background	3.49
You want to enrich your knowledge of the site	3.44
It is a famous tourist attraction	3.16
You feel you should visit the site	3.05
You want to feel emotionally involved	2.34
You have read *The Diary of Anne Frank*	2.29

Source: After Poria *et al.* (2006: 322)

Another study conducted at the Discover Queensland exhibition, which explains the history and geography of the state at the Queensland Museum in Brisbane, Australia, aimed to find out about the museum experiences of individual visitors and those who visited with a companion (Packer & Ballantyne, 2005). The results of the learning category of the study are quite insightful (see Table 10.3). The majority of individuals did in fact learn something new or remember something they once knew. This was slightly higher among people visiting in pairs, presumably because they were able to discuss the contents of the exhibits and other interpretive media together, thereby gaining additional insight. The heritage visit also aroused emotions in more than half of the participants, although only slightly more than a quarter of visitors changed their way of thinking or feeling about Queensland based on their experience at the exhibition.

Table 10.3 Individual and shared learning experiences at the Discover Queensland exhibit

	Individual % yes	Pairs % yes
Did you learn anything new during your visit?	83	88
Were you reminded of anything you already knew?	83	88
Did anything arouse any emotions within you?	63	60
Did your visit help change the way you think or feel about anything?	28	26

Source: After Packer and Ballantyne (2005)

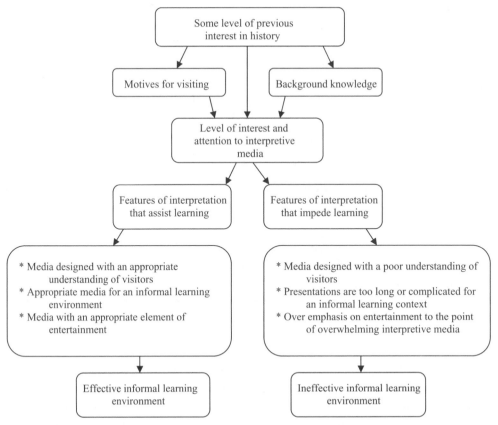

Figure 10.1 Influential factors in informal education at heritage sites

Source: After Light (1995)

Among museum studies specialists, heritage scholars and heritage site managers, it is a foregone conclusion that most people who visit historic sites or museums learn something new, whether they intend to or not. Light (1995) contends that tourists' background knowledge, motives for visiting, use of interpretive media and personal interest in the site being visited will affect their level of learning but that, at the very least, some learning will take place. Figure 10.1 summarizes Light's perspectives on the forces that influence informal learning at museums and historic sites.

Entertainment

The second benefit or purpose of heritage interpretation is entertainment. Today, curators and site managers are beginning to acknowledge that even the most entertaining interpretive approaches have an educational value, and learning can indeed be fun. At the outset, it should be noted that site managers should never allow the entertainment element to overshadow the importance of portraying the past as accurately as possible

234

and providing a solid learning environment. Nonetheless, recent research shows that entertainment can be an effective medium for educating visitors at historic places. This so-called 'edutainment' can be a useful tool in getting and keeping visitors' attention. It can also help plant a seed of inquiry within less-inquisitive guests that might someday blossom into a stronger desire to visit historic sites and appreciate them.

The entertainment element of interpretation has the potential to add public appeal to historic sites, thereby adding a competitive advantage over other leisure options – something which is especially important in difficult economic times when museums and historic monuments are competing for scarce public and private funds. It is important for site managers to remember that visits to museums and heritage places are primarily recreational in nature, so the experience should be enjoyable not boring. Enjoyable interpretive programs should be a recognized part of the attraction of an historic environment. Simple, dry facts and figures no longer suffice in the modern world of hyper-sensory stimulation. Contrary to many approaches of traditional interpretation, entertainment and education are not dichotomous concepts but rather complementary, symbiotic approaches that can help achieve the tripartite goals of education, conservation and funding.

Some of the most effective contemporary ways of providing a pleasurable and learning environment include humor, high-tech media and re-enactments (see Plate 10.2). Good humor in exhibit explanation can grab and keep people's interest. It also affects visitors' interest in returning to the attraction more than once. Technology in interpretation is critical today. Interactive, computer-based media is especially appealing to younger visitors and their parents. The creative value and expanse of technologically-advanced learning tools is almost limitless. Re-enactments of famous people and events has frequently been shown to be an effective tool in getting guests to remember the characters, dates and incidents associated with specific places and events. This is particularly the case when visitors themselves are encouraged to participate.

Preservation/Conservation

As noted earlier, interpretation theory posits that the more educated visitors are about the historic building, ancient monument, museum artifacts or historic environment they visit, the more they will appreciate its historical significance and have a desire to help protect it, or at least refrain from causing it harm. Effective interpretation heightens the value of sites in the minds and hearts of visitors, stimulating a sense of ownership and care. The sustainability view of heritage tourism is that people who have positive experiences at museums and historic sites in their formative years, will wish to share those same experiences with their children and grandchildren.

Crowd management

While not the most obvious outcome of sound interpretation programming, crowd management is certainly an important benefit of interpretation. Almost all explanatory

Plate 10.2 A Benjamin Franklin re-enactor lends humor to a visit to historic Philadelphia

media can be used to direct tourists away from the most sensitive sites in a heritage complex or conversely to the most resilient areas that can withstand higher flows of traffic. Personal guides, brochures, audio and video presentations and signs (including warning signs) are especially salient means for dispersing crowds or getting them to funnel through less sensitive sections (see Plate 10.3). Alternative routes can also be suggested, and explanations why certain areas are more delicate than others go a long way not only in educating people about the environment but also in letting them know why certain areas might be off limits.

Plate 10.3 Signage to help direct tourists away from a sensitive historic artifact

Income earner

Interpretive media can bring in additional funds to cash-strapped museums and historic sites. Sales of guidebooks, audio tours or guided tours at some locations have found success in adding money to management budgets. Even at some publicly-owned sights, such as US National Park properties, tourists can hire guides who will accompany them in their own vehicles to explain battlefield events or other historical happenings.

Perhaps the most important aspect of fundraising via interpretation, however, is the positive economic impact it can have on the destination community when it becomes part of the attractive appeal of the destination. Well-known and high-quality interpretive programs that add value to heritage sites work with other aspects of tourism to get travelers to stay longer in the destination and spend more money on accommodation, meals and other recreational activities, including visiting other museums and historic sites. Interpreters might play a key role in disseminating information about local places to stay, eat or visit, contributing to the local economy and supporting local businesses. Rather than just being a series of individual, unrelated businesses, tourism is a system, whose component parts are interdependent for their success as a whole. Thus, historic environments and museums are dependent on other tourism services, and vice versa. Unfortunately, many heritage stewards have by tradition been reluctant to accept the fact their establishments are part of tourism, because this carries a negative connotation. For their own economic success and

237

that of their local communities, however, it is vital that site and museum managers begin to recognize more fully their important role in tourism and the interdependent relationships between heritage and other tourism services to the same degree these relationships are already accepted by tourism planners and destination management organizations.

MODERN INTERPRETIVE TOOLS

Heritage interpretation has a long history, with guide 'books' and signs being used by travelers more than a thousand years ago. In the modern world there is a variety of personal and non-personal media available to choose from in developing an interpretive program, and with the age of technology and globalization the array of possibilities has grown even larger.

Tour guides

There are several approaches to personal interpretation in the heritage context. What they all have in common is the use of a live person as the information source. One of the most common and popular media is a tour guide. Guides usually work for the agency or

Plate 10.4 A guide interprets the past for tourists at Casa Grande Ruins National Monument, USA

organization that operates the heritage place being visited. Some, however, might be individually contracted or hired by a tour operator. Regardless of who their boss is, guides are an important source of information for visitors and can help make or break the visitor experience depending on the person's personality, depth of knowledge and previous experience. Guided tours through museums and other historic sites are an important tool for disseminating a lot of information to groups of visitors (see Plate 10.4). For large groups, this approach is usually seen as being more effective than herding them through display areas where they are unable to see printed placards or watch a video presentation because of crowd and time constraints.

Actors/Role players

One of the most popular personal modes of interpretation is actors at living history museums. These living characters don period dress and are charged with providing information about life in the past, and in some settings they are not allowed to step out of character. They answer questions visitors might have and demonstrate various activities of everyday life during the period of time they are portraying. This often includes making baskets, gardening, shoeing a horse, weaving cloth, baking and cooking, working as a blacksmith or carding wool (see Plate 10.5). Most actors in these setups are not drama-

Plate 10.5 Actors at Mount Vernon (George Washington's home) demonstrate historic crafts

tizing any particular person. Others, however, might be involved in role-playing, or portraying the life of a well-known individual in an historic setting. Yet other actors are involved in re-enactments, such as war battles or cultural ceremonies. These methods of live interpretation provide a comfortable setting in which visitors can relax, ask questions and interact on a more personal level with the interpreter.

Attendants

Information attendants are an important part of an interpretive program as well. They are typically stationed in a specific location, such as near a doorway or at an information booth. Visitors can get directions and information from attendants, and they usually work in conjunction with guides to help direct visitors from place to place within a museum or other historic site. Attendants can also be trained to function as security staff as they scan the crowd and observe people's behavior.

Printed material and signage

Non-personal media include written materials and audio and video apparatuses. The most common interpretive media at heritage places worldwide is the written form, such as placards, posters, brochures, guidebooks, signs and other displays (see Plate 10.6).

Plate 10.6 This placard tells the story of Mission Espada, part of Texas' Spanish colonial heritage

Plate 10.7 This scale model of the Vatican City helps tourists appreciate the layout of the tiny microstate

Brochures are sometimes given to visitors as part of admission fees, while at some places they are sold separately as souvenirs. Interpretive signs are important tools that provide information along trails or at displays in a museum. In historic city centers, and even along long-distance trails, signs guiding tourists between sites or interpretive stations are very important. Placards at archaeological sites and in museums provide in-depth information about the display being viewed, and scale models have become popular media in historic towns, ancient cities and archaeological parks, allowing tourists to get a holistic overview of heritage areas (see Plate 10.7).

Hands-on displays

Hands-on and experiential media have gained importance during the past 25 years. Whereas earlier interpretive planners saw hands-on approaches as being antithetical to the purposes of museums and sites (i.e. protection), tangible experiences are now seen more as an effective way of providing information and allowing the information to sink in to the minds of visitors. Science museums have become especially innovative in this regard, allowing visitors to touch skeletons, meteorites, animals/insects and rocks, or be engulfed in a virtual thunderstorm. Even some cultural heritage museums have started promoting a hands-on approach where visitors can use historical farm equipment, handle bits and pieces of ancient pottery and touch other antique accoutrements (see Plate 10.8).

241

Plate 10.8 This interpretive display invites visitors to touch and handle cultural artifacts

Individual audio tours

Self-guided audio tours, usually purchased at the information desk or ticket counter, or sometimes included in the entrance fee, are important media, especially for foreign-language visitors (see Plate 10.9). Objects, sites and displays are numbered, and the numbers in the audio recording correspond with the numbers of the sites. With audio mechanisms, scenes and objects can be described in considerable detail. Among the most important advantages of audio tours is that they allow users to progress through a display at their own pace and re-listen to the information as much as they need.

Modern technological devices

New technologies continue to provide innovative ways of telling stories and revealing the past to heritage visitors. Computer-based interpretation is the most popular trend today. Interactive computer displays at stations in museums or heritage areas are taking front stage as images depict what relics or archaeological sites might have looked like in the primordial past (see Plate 10.10). These are becoming more popular because they allow visitors to control the types of information they receive and offer several sensory experiences. Electronic media are beginning to replace personal guides in some historical buildings and museums, but it is critical for managers to prevent the medium from

Plate 10.9 This vendor is renting multilingual self-guided audio tours of the Alamo in Texas

overshadowing the artifacts for which observers came to the museum or site to see in the first place.

Other computer-aided issues must also be mentioned. Satellite imagery can now be acquired via geo-spatial technologies, including global positioning systems (GPS) and geographic information systems (GIS). The technology now exists for visitors to a heritage area to wander about at their own pace, receiving live-feed information and data about specific locations along a trail, in an archaeological zone or in a museum setting via mobile phones or other portable media players. In addition, the now widespread use of 'volunteered geographic information' via online tools and social media such as Google Earth, Flickr, WikiMapia, Wikipedia, Twitter and YouTube allows people to begin their journeys at home before their actual departure to a destination. Videos, photographs, information, commentaries and customer ratings are available about heritage sites throughout the world, which many people use as a data source in making their travel decisions and in beginning to 'interpret' cultural sites before even arriving in the destination. The use of various travel-related social media while actually traveling is becoming more commonplace and currently plays an important role in travel planning and site interpretation. It will be interesting in the future to watch the interpretive trends

243

Plate 10.10 This young visitor utilizes interactive, computer-based interpretation at an archaeological site

associated with the internet, satellite imagery and volunteer contributions to see their potential role in interpretation and site management.

VISITOR DIVERSITY AND INTERPRETIVE PROGRAMS

The diversity of the world's population is becoming more accepted than it was even a couple of generations ago. Attraction managers and destination planners realize that providing for the needs of a diverse audience is good business, because visitors to museums, historic and archaeological sites, living folklife museums, cultural performances, industrial areas and historic buildings are no longer seen as a homogeneous, undifferentiated group of people seeking the same heritage experience. Catering to individual needs and interests through effective interpretive programs is a hallmark of good heritage management in the 21st century.

People with physical disabilities, for instance, are no longer seen as a passive audience, but instead are rightfully viewed as an active market with the means to travel and participate in heritage and cultural activities. Likewise, with the process of globalization

244

and all it entails there has been an increase in migration throughout the world, and there are few places today that are inaccessible to tourists. Similarly, there are very few countries in the modern world from which people are restricted from traveling to other parts of the world. These modern conditions mean that truly homogeneous populations are few and far between. Even some of the more conservative countries of Europe, in terms of immigration laws, such as Finland and Denmark, by virtue of their membership in the European Union have become more racially and ethnically diverse with increased immigration from Eastern Europe, Africa and Asia.

There are many aspects of diversity with policy considerations: ethnicity, race, sexual orientation, gender, physical or learning disabilities and military veteran status, to name but a few. Some elements of diversity are more directly applicable to interpretive planning than others. This section focuses on the most pressing issues facing interpretation managers today as regards diverse markets and special-needs populations.

Given the rapid growth of international tourism during the past half century, and its particular salience in the 21st century, there is an ever-increasing need for interpretation that addresses the needs of foreign tourists. Perhaps the most significant of these is multilingual interpretation methods (see Plate 10.11). While multilingual interpretation is

Plate 10.11 Non-English speaking tourists visiting Bingham Canyon Copper Mine, USA, can hear the story in several languages

among the most critical elements of heritage site management today, it is one of the least understood and researched. Only a few scholars have examined the role of bilingual or multilingual methods at cultural attractions, arguing that multilingual media enhance the foreign visitor's experience and provide a user-friendly environment.

Some multilingual countries, including some of those that have more than one official language (e.g. Canada, Finland, Israel, South Africa, Switzerland, Belgium, Singapore), have a long tradition of providing heritage site interpretation in two or more languages (see Plate 10.12). In Canada, for example, all national government-operated sites (e.g. Parks Canada) are required to provide both French and English interpretation options. Other multilingual societies do the same, which is an important part of providing for the needs of domestic visitors. In countries where a multitude of languages are spoken (e.g. India, Ghana, Nigeria, China), interpretive signs are usually printed in one or two official languages or in the primary lingua franca – the common language(s) of commerce and trade.

International travelers, however, are an important focus of heritage site managers as well. China, for instance, is known as a heritage and cultural destination among most

Plate 10.12 Many interpretive signs in Israel are printed in the country's two official languages, Hebrew and Arabic, as well as in English

foreign visitors. Thus, providing interpretive signs and other media in the languages of the country's primary visitors (e.g. English, Japanese, Korean) would be beneficial for tourists and managers alike. Some countries, such as the USA, Australia and England, tend to be very Anglo-centric (i.e. English only) at the majority of their heritage sites. Many foreign visitors to important sites in both countries have commented on their inability to understand the English-language media and therefore have not had a very satisfactory experience. In the southwestern USA, Spanish-language media are often employed owing to the large population of immigrants from Latin America, but few other languages are commonplace. This situation is changing, however, as even though signage might be only in English or English and Spanish, brochures, maps and audio tours are now commonly offered in Japanese, German, French, Italian, Korean and Dutch – the languages of most international tourists in the USA. At most National Park Service properties, interpretation is done in English and occasionally Spanish. However, at the most widely acclaimed NPS properties, which draw millions of international visitors each year, multilingual warning/hazard signs are becoming more common, such as at the Grand Canyon, in conjunction with foreign-language brochures.

Chinese outbound travel has received considerable attention by scholars in recent years. Until fairly recently, the Chinese were limited on the number of countries their own government would allow them to visit as vacation travelers. Since the 1990s, however, China has developed a list of countries with 'approved destination status' (ADS), which means the countries are eligible to receive Chinese tour groups and are permitted to advertise in China. More than 130 countries are now on the list, with Canada being one of the most recent major additions. The coveted ADS is seen as an opportunity to grow the tourism economy as wealthy and middle-class Chinese expand their travel potential and increase their expenditures abroad. In the near future hundreds of millions of Chinese citizens will have the capability to travel overseas on package tours that include many heritage sites and cultural events. As one of the new up-and-coming markets for heritage experience throughout the world, it would behoove ADS countries to begin considering Mandarin Chinese interpretive programs at their most visited historic sites.

In areas where there is a minority language, including it in interpretive signage and other media can add appeal to a site and increase its level of authenticity in the minds of outsiders. Light (1992) studied several heritage places in Wales and found that even though only less than 2% of visitors at some sites were Welsh speakers, having Welsh text alongside English script increased the enjoyment and authenticity among non-Welsh speaking visitors and enhanced the cultural experience of being in Wales.

Site managers are responsible for accommodating the special needs of certain population cohorts, including the elderly, families with small children and people with learning or physical disabilities. This includes interpretation. For people with intellectual disabilities, interpretation should be done in such a way that is not intimidating but rather relates to their own needs. Story telling and other media devices that allow for extensive learning opportunities for visitors with learning disabilities should be adopted.

People who are wheelchair-bound need adequate floor space to pass from one display to another. Smooth and even surfaces are also important, and it is vital for placards, signs, displays and other tools to be readable from a wheelchair's distance away. Visitors with visual impediments appreciate extra lighting, large print and Braille. For guests with special hearing requirements, there are devices that can help magnify what is being spoken – and adequate print literature is a necessity. For the elderly, display areas should have places to sit and rest, and supports to lean on while reading or listening to an interpretive message.

In addition to the physical media and mechanisms, it is important for interpretive staff to be sensitive to the needs, feelings and emotions of all visitors. Using terms such as 'over here we have ...' rather than 'as you can see ...'. Likewise, sight-impaired guests usually have vivid imaginations and can benefit from rich descriptions of people, places and events. Cox (1994) suggested that to make scripts more effective for visitors with visual disabilities they should be written by someone who has visual disabilities.

Most developed countries now have legislation that requires public agencies and businesses to accommodate the needs of people with physical disabilities. The 1992 Americans with Disabilities Act (ADA), for instance, provides a legal framework for meeting the needs of people with disabilities. Heritage sites and their interpretation are affected by this law. For example, interpretive programs for people with disabilities must be equal to those for people without disabilities. Interpretation must occur within the most integrated context as possible. Interpreters must use techniques that do not highlight the differences between people with or without disabilities. Historic properties and museums must provide supporting media to facilitate visits by all people (Knudson *et al.*, 1995).

For small children, creative interpretative media are required. Buttons, lights and music might be an important part of keeping children's attention so that they will have opportunities to learn. Verbal communication should be done in such as way that understandable words and phrases are used rather than scientific jargon. At science museums, using all the senses is an important part of the learning experience. Using media that allow visitors to feel, smell, see, hear and even taste can contribute significantly to the sensory, and therefore learning, experience of children and their families.

Cultural sensitivity is an important heritage management principle. What is acceptable in terms of both story and medium for one group might not be for others. Objectivity and neutrality are especially important in this regard. According to Upitis (1989), interpretation must recognize human dignity and the right of others to have different views from those of site managers. It is crucial to view different cultures as equally important and vital and to accept difference with interest and fascination rather than debasement.

Finally, empathy, respect and equity must prevail in attitudes towards people of other cultural backgrounds.

The interpretation of indigenous heritage by non-indigenous people has been extremely problematic in this regard for many years. Today, however, more input from, or control over, indigenous pasts and how the stories are told has remedied much of the problem (see Plate 10.13). Nonetheless, interpretation managers still must provide relevant and truthful information while being culturally sensitive to dissenting views. Even certain interpretive media themselves might be considered insulting or degrading for some cultures, so that alternatives should be sought that are acceptable to all stakeholders.

While political correctness has evolved to an unfortunate extreme in some cases, there are some basic concepts that must be kept in mind in designing interpretive displays that go a long way in maintaining an agency's public credibility in the modern world. One such principle is gender-neutral language. Gender-neutral language is an important issue in today's intellectual circles, which includes users of museums and historic sites. Instead of using terms such as man or mankind to refer to human beings, 'humankind' is considered more appropriate now. Police officer and fire fighter are now more politically correct than policeman or fireman. Despite one's own views on political correctness, it is important to remain up to date in the socio-political world and to avoid causing any offense to guests. This could have major bearings on community relations, guest satisfaction, educational effectiveness and ultimately funding.

INTERPRETIVE PLANNING

Planning is an important part of managing any tourism destination or tourist attraction. Planning can be viewed broadly as a way of manipulating the future to achieve one or more desired outcomes. Just as individuals plan their days to be able to achieve the optimum level of productivity, heritage attractions should undertake careful planning to ensure that their goals are met. One important perspective in this regard is interpretive planning, or the process of organizing interpretive programs to achieve a desired out-come. Sound planning will help establish goals and objectives, identify financial and time constraints, understand the supply and demand for interpretation and assist in developing policies that can be supported better through an adequate interpretive program.

Interpretive planning should be guided by several principles, including safety of visitors and employees. This is paramount in today's litigious and security environment. Likewise, interpretation approaches and individual media must be realistic and user friendly. Interpretive media should be selected and designed to maximize the visitor experience and allow visitors to progress at their own pace. Efficiency in design is also crucial so that attractions and areas can be serviced and maintained efficiently. Lastly, interpretation and its media should not have any negative impacts on the natural or cultural environment.

Plate 10.13 This native Guarani guide at Iguazu Falls, Argentina, contributes to the indigenous narrative of the region's heritage

Construction and signage should be congruent with environmental conditions, and the media selected should dissuade visitors from doing harm to the local environment.

Like all forms of planning, interpretive planning is done in a series of steps that help managers formulate plans and make better policy decisions. Procedural planning (see Figure 10.2) is comprised of at least six phases that build on the previous phase. While each circumstance is unique, the planning process includes some common elements regardless of context or situation.

The first step, setting goals and objectives, is vital because it sets the tone for the entire plan and functioning of the interpretive program. Goals and objectives guide the planning process, as all subsequent steps reflect back on the purpose of the plan. Planning goals are typically stated in general terms, while objectives are more specific and describe ways in which the goals might be met. One possible goal for a museum's interpretive program might be to develop closer relationships with local schools and become a more salient

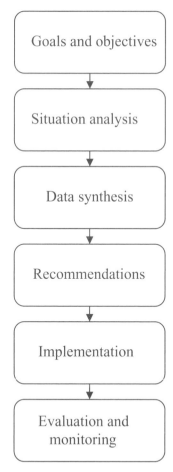

Figure 10.2 The procedural planning process

player in a region's formal education/curriculum. Objectives to help meet this goal could include offering special events that involve schools and school children, or allowing teachers to become involved as actors and interpreters.

To meet the stated goals and objectives, a situation analysis needs to be done so that managers can know where they currently are in relation to interpretation. The situation analysis clarifies past and present trends, which is vital in making decisions about future directions. This entails a thorough analysis of existing interpretive media, cultural resources and infrastructure. Analyzing the effectiveness of interpretive setups is also critical in maintaining an educational, informative and enjoyable heritage environment. And, a market analysis might need to be done to understand the audience or potential audience for heritage places and their needs and expectations. Checklists, systematic observations and visitor surveys are among the most commonly utilized data-collection tools in this phase of the planning process.

The third step is analyzing and synthesizing the data collected in the situation analysis. Here the information is collected, assembled and analyzed to create a big picture of the effectiveness of the program and where changes might need to be made and corrective actions taken. Visitation patterns also emerge in this synthesis, which assist managers in making decisions about future plans regarding visitor use, impacts and education. From the situation analysis new interpretive themes might reveal themselves, or new resources, such as extant features in the cultural landscape or recent acquisitions which become obvious and need to be worked into the program.

Based on the situation analysis and data synthesis, recommendations are made, either by outside consultants who have conducted the survey on behalf of site managers or internally. Perhaps an old-fashioned interpretive medium is found to be ineffective or somehow less than satisfactory for a new type of art museum. Or maybe new attractions have been added through excavations or additions to collections. These will need to be worked into the existing interpretive program.

Implementation is the fifth step in the planning process. It involves putting into practice the actual recommendations made by the managers or consultants. As noted in the previous chapter, there are several challenges that might prevent the successful implementation of the recommendations. A lack of funds or human resources would be a good example of two major constraints. Purchasing a new computer system for visitor use, buying lower quality artifacts that can be handled by tourists or hiring more staff to assist as guides or information attendants can be an expensive endeavor for a museum that is funded almost entirely by donations, or a public agency-operated ancient monument during times of government cutbacks. Alternatives are important to consider as part of the recommendation step that can come to bear in obvious ways during the implementation phase.

Finally, the continuous process of monitoring and evaluation is a long-term management commitment. Evaluating and monitoring are not a one-time process but instead require years of visiting and revisiting interpretive programs. Revisions to the program and media might have to be made as new acquisitions arrive, as new areas are excavated or as modernization requires more technical approaches to telling the important story of the place. Continuous monitoring assures adaptability, efficiency and flexibility in management responsibilities, and allows visitors to express concerns, provides feedback about successes and failures and provides a mechanism to appraise staff effectiveness and training.

SUMMARY AND CONCLUSION

Interpretation is one of the most vital elements of sustainable management at heritage properties. It assists heritage stewards in disseminating information to the visiting public in an effort to educate them and provide enjoyable experiences that will make an impact and help them realize the need to conserve. It is also key in providing fiscal resources for protection and maintenance and is a useful management tool for crowd control. Because of its relevance and salience in protecting the past and raising revenue, effectual interpretative planning is essential.

There are many traditional methods of telling the story, including placards, brochures, videos, guides, hands-on exhibits and audio tours. These are time-tested, effective interpretive tools, but today's sophisticated public is demanding a broader range of media they can relate to better. Interactive computer displays and hand-held satellite-based devices now assist visitors in navigating cultural destinations and heritage attractions with live feed information. While it is unlikely that these tools will replace traditional media entirely in the very near future, they will nonetheless become more commonplace, functioning parallel to the more traditional means of revealing the significance of place, person or event.

REVIEW QUESTIONS

1. Can you explain how an effective interpretation program helps develop a sense of stewardship over cultural resources?

2. How do Freeman Tilden's principles of interpretation help guide site managers in carrying out their duties?

3. Can education and entertainment work together to add appeal to an historic monument, or are they incompatible concepts?

4. In what ways can interpretive media be used for crowd control?

5. What benefits derive from having live interpreters (e.g. actors and tour guides) versus print material and signs?

6. How might hands-on displays, where visitors can handle historic artifacts or replicas, help alleviate some physical pressures?

7. How is new technology contributing to more effective ways of telling the story at cultural heritage locales?

8. What are some ways heritage managers can cater to the needs of an increasingly globalized marketplace? How important is it to facilitate the needs of population cohorts who might need extra care or who have accessibility concerns?

RECOMMENDED READING

Ablett, P.G. and Dyer, P.K. (2009) Heritage and hermeneutics: Towards a broader interpretation of interpretation. *Current Issues in Tourism* 12(3), 209–233.

Alderson, W.T. and Low, S.P. (1996) *Interpretation of Historic Sites.* Lanham, MD: AltaMira Press.

Austin, N.K. (2002) Managing heritage attractions: Marketing challenges at sensitive historical sites. *International Journal of Tourism Research* 4(6), 447–457.

Bagnell, G. (2003) Performance and performativity at heritage sites. *Museum and Society* 1(2), 87–103.

Ballantyne, R., Packer, J. and Hug, K. (2008) Environmental awareness, interests and motives of botanic gardens visitors: Implications for interpretive practice. *Tourism Management* 29, 439–444.

Banz, R. (2008) Self-directed learning: implications for museums. *Journal of Museum Education* 33(1), 43–54.

Barnard, W.A. and Loomis, R.J. (1994) The museum exhibit as a visual learning medium. *Visitor Behavior* 9(2), 14–17.

Barrow, G. (1994) Interpretive planning: More to it than meets the eye. *Environmental Interpretation* 9(2), 5–7.

Beck, L. and Cable, T. (1998) *Interpretation for the 21st Century: Fifteen Guiding Principles for Interpreting Nature and Culture.* Champaign, IL: Sagamore.

Boyd, S.W. (2002) Cultural and heritage tourism in Canada: Opportunities, principles and challenges. *International Journal of Tourism and Hospitality Research* 3(3), 211–233.

Boyd, S.W. and Timothy, D.J. (2001) Developing partnerships: Tools for interpretation and management of World Heritage Sites. *Tourism Recreation Research* 26(1), 47–53.

Bramwell, B. and Lane, B. (1993) Interpretation and sustainable tourism: The potential and the pitfalls. *Journal of Sustainable Tourism* 1(2), 71–80.

Buzinde, C.N. and Santos, C.A. (2009) Interpreting slavery tourism. *Annals of Tourism Research* 36, 439–458.

Caffyn, A. and Lutz, J. (1999) Developing the heritage tourism product in multi-ethnic cities. *Tourism Management* 20, 213–221.

Carver, A.D., Basman, C.M. and Lee, J.G. (2003) Assessing the non-market value of heritage interpretation. *Journal of Interpretation Research* 8(1), 83–92.

Chidester, R.C. (2009) Critical landscape analysis as a tool for public interpretation: Reassessing slavery at a western Maryland plantation. *CRM: The Journal of Heritage Stewardship* 6(1), 34–54.

Falk, J.H. and Dierking, L.D. (2000) *Learning from Museums: Visitor Experiences and the Making of Meaning.* Lanham, MD: AltaMira Press.

Foxlee, J. (2007) Cultural landscape interpretation: The case of the sorry rock story at Uluru-Kata Tjuta National Park. *Tourism Recreation Research* 32(3), 49–56.

Frost, W. (2005) Making an edgier interpretation of the gold rushes: Contrasting perspectives from Australia and New Zealand. *International Journal of Heritage Studies* 11(3), 235–250.

Frost, W. (2006) Braveheart-ed Ned Kelly: Historic films, heritage tourism and destination image. *Tourism Management* 27, 247–254.

Gross, M.P. and Zimmerman, R. (2002) Park and museum interpretation: Helping visitors find meaning. *Curator: The Museum Journal* 45(4), 265–276.

Hale, A. (2001) Representing the Cornish: Contesting heritage interpretation in Cornwall. *Tourist Studies* 1(2), 185–196.

Ham, S. and Weiler, B. (2004) Diffusion and adoption of thematic interpretation at an interpretive historic site. *Annals of Leisure Research* 7, 1–18.

Hartley, E. (1995) Disabled people and museums: The case for partnership and collaboration. In E. Hooper-Greenhill (ed.) *Museum, Media, Message* (pp. 151–155). London: Routledge.

Hein, G.E. (1998) *Learning in the Museum.* London: Routledge.

Hems, A. and Blockley, M. (eds) (2006) *Heritage Interpretation.* London: Routledge.

Herbert, D.T. (1989) Does interpretation help? In D.T. Herbert, R.C. Prentice and C.J. Thomas (eds) *Heritage Sites: Strategies for Marketing and Development* (pp. 191–230). Aldershot: Avebury.

Hetherington, K. (2000) Museums and the visually impaired: The spatial politics of access. *The Sociological Review* 48(3), 444–463.

Hill, S. and Cable, T.T. (2006) The concept of authenticity: Implications for interpretation. *Journal of Interpretation Research* 11(1), 55–65.

Hooper-Greenhill, E. (ed.) (1999) *The Educational Role of the Museum* (2nd edn). London: Routledge.

Hooper-Greenhill, E. (2000) *Museums and the Interpretation of Visual Culture*. London: Routledge.

King, E.M. (2008) Buffalo soldiers, Apaches, and cultural heritage education. *Heritage Management* 1(2), 219–242.

Knudson, D.M., Cable, T.T. and Beck, L. (1995) *Interpretation of Cultural and Natural Resources*. State College, PA: Venture.

Lehr, J.C. and Katz, Y. (2003) Heritage interpretation and politics in Kfar Etzion, Israel. *International Journal of Heritage Studies* 9(3), 215–228.

Lennon, J.J. and Foley, M. (1999) Interpretation of the unimaginable: the U.S. Holocaust Memorial Museum, Washington, D.C., and "dark tourism". *Journal of Travel Research* 38, 46–50.

Lepouras, G. and Vassilakis, C. (2004) Virtual museums for all: Employing game technology for edutainment. *Virtual Reality* 8(2), 215–228.

Light, D. (1991) The development of heritage interpretation in Britain. *Swansea Geographer* 28, 1–13.

Littlefair, C. and Buckley, R. (2008) Interpretation reduces ecological impacts of visitors to World Heritage site. *Ambio* 37(5), 338–341.

Machlis, G.E. and Field, D.R. (eds) (1984) *On Interpretation: Sociology for Interpreters of Natural and Cultural History*. Corvallis: Oregon State University Press.

Mintz, A. (1994) That's edutainment. *Museum News* 73(6), 32–36.

Moscardo, G. (1999) *Making Visitors Mindful*. Champaign, IL: Sagamore.

Nuryanti, W. (1996) Heritage and postmodern tourism. *Annals of Tourism Research* 23, 249–260.

Orams, M. (1996) Using interpretation to manage nature-based tourism. *Journal of Sustainable Tourism* 4(2), 81–94.

Pardue, D. (2004) Ellis Island Immigration Museum. *Museum International* 56(3), 22–28.

Poria, Y., Biran, A. and Reichel, A. (2009) Visitors' preferences for interpretation at heritage sites. *Journal of Travel Research* 48(1), 92–105.

Prentice, R.C., Guerin, S. and McGugan, S. (1998) Visitor learning at a heritage attraction: A case study of Discovery as a media product. *Tourism Management* 19, 5–23.

Puczkó, L. (2006) Interpretation in cultural tourism. In M. Smith and M. Robinson (eds) *Cultural Tourism in a Changing World: Politics, Participation and (Re)presentation* (pp. 227–243). Clevedon: Channel View Publications.

Putney, A.D. and Wagar, J.A. (1973) Objectives and evaluation in interpretive planning. *Journal of Environmental Education* 5(1), 43–44.

Risk, P. (1994) People-based interpretation. In R. Harrison (ed.) *Manual of Heritage Management* (pp. 320–330). Oxford: Butterworth Heinemann.

Saipradist, A. and Staiff, R. (2007) Crossing the cultural divide: Western visitors and interpretation at Ayutthaya World Heritage Site, Thailand. *Journal of Heritage Tourism* 2(3), 211–224.

Serota, N. (1997) *Experience or Interpretation: The Dilemma of Museums of Modern Art*. New York: Thames and Hudson.

Sharpe, G.W. (ed.) (1982) *Interpreting the Environment*. New York: Wiley.

Silverman, L.H. and Masberg, B.A. (2001) Through their eyes: The meaning of heritage site experiences to visitors who are blind or visually impaired. *Journal of Interpretation Research* 6(1), 31–47.

Spirek, J.D. and Scott-Ireton, D.A. (2003) *Submerged Cultural Resource Management: Preserving and Interpreting Our Sunken Maritime Heritage*. New York: Kluwer.

Stewart, E.J., Hayward, B.M., Devlin, P.J. and Kirby, V.G. (1998) The 'place' of interpretation: A new approach to the evaluation of interpretation. *Tourism Management* 19, 257–266.

Tilden, F. (1977) *Interpreting Our Heritage*. Chapel Hill: University of North Carolina.

Touloupa, S. (2010) Casting identity in the cultural tourism industry: Greek tourist guides in a 'mission' of heritage interpretation. *Public Archaeology* 9(1), 4–33.

Uzzell, D.L. (1985) Management issues in the provision of countryside interpretation. *Leisure Studies* 4, 159–174.

Uzzell, D.L. (ed.) (1989) *Heritage Interpretation, Volume 1: The Natural and Built Environment*. London: Belhaven.

Uzzell, D.L. and Ballantyne, R. (eds) (1998) *Contemporary Issues in Heritage and Environmental Interpretation*. London: The Stationery Office.

van Dijk, P. and Weiler, B. (2009) An assessment of the outcomes of a Chinese-language interpretive tour experience at a heritage tourism attraction. *Tourism Analysis* 14(1), 49–63.

Wilks, C. and Kelly, C. (2008) Fact, fiction and nostalgia: An assessment of heritage interpretation at living museums. *International Journal of Intangible Heritage* 3, 128–140.

RECOMMENDED WEBSITES

American Association of Museums – http://www.aam-us.org/

Association for Heritage Interpretation – http://www.ahi.org.uk/

European Network for Heritage Interpretation –
http://www.geographie.uni-freiburg.de/ipg/forschung/ap6/interpret-europe/

ICOMOS International Scientific Committee on Interpretation and Presentation of Cultural Heritage Sites – http://icip.icomos.org/ENG/home.html

Interpretation Australia – http://www.interpretationaustralia.asn.au/

Interpretation Canada – http://www.interpcan.ca/new/

Interpretation Network New Zealand – http://www.innz.net.nz/

Journal of Interpretation Research – http://www.interpnet.com/JIR/

Museums Galleries Scotland –
http://www.museumsgalleriesscotland.org.uk/what-we-do/collections-development/
interpreting-collections/

National Association for Interpretation – http://www.interpnet.com/

CHAPTER 11

PLANNING PRINCIPLES AND CULTURAL HERITAGE DESTINATIONS

LEARNING OBJECTIVES

After reading this chapter, you should be able to:

1. Learn about design principles associated with cultural heritage sites and areas.

2. Understand how effective planning can alleviate environmental and social pressures.

3. Appreciate the differences between physical planning and regional planning principles in the heritage context.

4. Comprehend the relationship between cultural tourism and sustainable development.

5. Be familiar with principles of participatory, incremental and cooperative planning.

INTRODUCTION

Every individual and every organization plans. Planning refers to the act of organizing the future to meet a specified goal or set of objectives. Tourism planning is an increasingly important part of tourism, and planning specialists who work in destination and attraction development are in demand at various levels of government and in the private sector. Recent and current scholarly work on tourism and sustainable development illuminates how important careful, appropriate planning is for tourist destinations to help mitigate tourism's negative social and environmental impacts and to enhance its positive aspects. Unfortunately, decades of unmitigated tourism growth in various locations has rendered them undesirable for many tourists, and many places are struggling to maintain an environment that supports tourism growth and an economy that supports job creation. Sound planning, based on principles of sustainable development, has become synonymous with improving the longevity and success of tourist destinations. This chapter looks at two primary traditions in tourism planning, namely physical or land-use planning, which is important in developing individual attractions, and regional planning, which focuses more on the sustainable growth of heritage tourism in a cultural destination as a whole.

PHYSICAL PLANNING AND HERITAGE DESTINATIONS

Traditionally the main type of planning in heritage destinations and at heritage sites has been physical, or land-use, planning. This typically involves all elements of a site or location, including landscape design, architectural layout, garden esthetic, site restoration, shops and other ancillary services, traffic flow, utility connections and other elements of the physical infrastructure. Architects, landscape architects and urban planners have characteristically been the most involved in physical planning.

The primary goals of physical planning are to optimize space, improve traffic and visitor flows, protect the heritage and at the same time design areas in such a way as to maximize tourism earnings. Physical plans for cultural attractions must be designed in harmony with existing urban, rural or regional plans; they should, in fact, support one another, and all recommended changes or additions must be done in accordance with local laws and zoning regulations. Site plans usually call for areal zoning, so that boundaries are delineated around a site. Within those boundaries, in non-built up areas, zones are identified as management spaces to help preserve the artifacts/structures while at the same time managing visitor flows and providing an esthetically pleasing environment. The locations of ticket booths, entrance gates, souvenir shops, toilets and parking areas, in relation to the primary attraction, traffic access, wilderness extent and other existing structures, are assessed and plotted.

Most tourist-historic cities are crowded with buildings and people and are therefore not as flexible for zoning purposes as exurban sites are. Nevertheless, zoning and planning are still important elements of urban heritage tourism planning. Jansen-Verbeke and Lievois (1999) asserted that planning in heritage cities should focus more on pedestrian traffic than vehicular traffic; pedestrian-only access enhances the heritage ambience of historic centers, creates more user-friendly leisure spaces and is more ecologically sensitive to the built environment. In the busy historic cities of Europe and North America, pedestrian-only zones are becoming more commonplace and enhance the heritage milieu (see Plate 11.1).

Important locational elements must be considered in created physical design. For example, what approach do most visitors use when they come to the site from the nearest city? Are there major highways nearby? Will a swampy area support an interpretive center or would it be better to locate it further away but on more stable ground? Do local laws require access to all areas for people with physical disabilities? Would it be best to locate the ticket booth at the entrance gate or at the visitor center? Should there be more than one toilet and refreshment area, and if so, why and where? Will the location of the café obstruct the view of the monument? These are illustrative of the spatial issues that must be carefully considered when planning the environs of historic places. Once these and other questions have been answered via an environmental and situation analysis, a site plan is designed and goals are set regarding how best to implement the physical development plan.

Plate 11.1 This pedestrian zone in Warsaw, Poland, contributes to the city's historic ambience

REGIONAL PLANNING CONCEPTS AND PROCEDURES

For many decades planning specialists have highlighted a normative, or procedural, planning process by which communities or regions could be planned in an effective manner to enhance the built and ecological environment of places. Planning has long focused almost exclusively on the physical organization of space (land-use planning), as noted above, including transportation, urban esthetics, mitigating urban decay, gentrification or renewal and suburban growth. Incremental growth was promoted by development specialists, suggesting that physical development needs to be done incrementally and in a heavily monitored fashion so that changes in the plan can be made if obstacles are encountered.

Against a background of mixed failures and successes in top-down procedural planning, specialists began to promote the idea of participatory planning in the mid- and late-1900s which extended beyond mere physical planning to include intangible environments (i.e. social, cultural and economic). The notion caught on quickly with the realization that the people most affected by growth, development and planning ought to have a voice in how their future is programmed. This change in perspective, particularly in the 1980s and 1990s, corresponded with the growing awareness of the need for communities to grow and develop in sustainable ways – ways that optimize economic and social benefits to the community and its people, while minimizing the negatives of development, such as pollution, deforestation, public discontent and social inequality. Toward the end of the 20th century, planning specialists went even further by promoting the idea of collaborative development, wherein community members have a bigger voice in planning and all stakeholders are seen as important in the planning process.

Despite the growing importance in academic and practitioner circles of new, more sustainable approaches to planning cities and regions, the fact remains that development planning is a process, made up of procedural steps that help achieve goals and enable planners to design an effective plan. The basic procedure includes the same steps highlighted under interpretive planning in Chapter 10: goal and objective formulation, situation analysis, data analysis, recommendations, implementation and monitoring. Differing scales and types of planning, however, require some degree of adaptation of this normative approach to meet specific goals and objectives, with some steps being more substantial than others, additional steps being added or others being left out.

Sustainability in the context of tourism

In response to widespread concern about the depletion of natural resources and the human environment, the United Nations convened a World Commission on Environment and Development (WCED, also known as the Brundtland Commission) to discuss critical issues about the natural and human environments. In 1987 the commission published its report, *Our Common Future* (WCED, 1987), which has since become one of the most cited and implemented documents in modern history. The document outlines the committee's desire to see the countries of the world cooperate to achieve the goal of sustainable development, which was defined as 'development that meets the needs of the present without compromising the ability of future generations to meet their own needs'.

Owing to the reputation of mass tourism as a catalyst for ecological and social degradation, the concept of sustainable development was adopted quickly in the realm of tourism by scholars, government officials and some business leaders. Right away, 'alternative tourism' became a focus of academic debate and research, suggesting that there must be alternatives to mass tourism that are less damaging to the destination and which could be studied, and indeed promoted, for their altruistic and sustainability-promoting characteristics. This gave rise to notions such as ecotourism, special-interest tourism or sustainable tourism. Some have included heritage and cultural tourism as a sustainable alternative, although critics argue that even heritage tourism and ecotourism have become mass consumer-driven to the point where many places suffer from 'mass ecotourism' or 'mass heritage tourism', subverting yet again the goals of sustainable development.

Nevertheless, the principles of sustainable development have been well integrated into tourism in both concept and practice, although Butler (1999) noted salient differences between sustainable tourism and tourism development within the context of sustainable growth. Sustainability principles such as integrity, balance, harmony, holism and equity in both natural and socio-cultural realms are now driving the tourism development debate, and many travel sectors are now adopting codes of ethics and best practices guidelines that will help assure a sustainable future both for the industry itself and for the communities where tourism takes place.

To meet the objectives of sustainable growth, tourism planners must approach development from a perspective that is far different from the long global tradition of boosterism, whereby destinations are promoted and marketed blindly without regard for the negative social, environmental and economic consequences. The goal of this uncontrolled form of development is simply to increase tourist arrivals and expenditures. It glorifies the almighty dollar (or euro or pound) and is extremely short-sighted, albeit still the dominant development tactic throughout the world.

Participatory, incremental and collaborative development

Based on knowledge of the preceding discussion, Timothy and Tosun (2003) proposed a three-part framework for undertaking systematic and sustainable planning in tourist destinations (see Figure 11.1). Such an approach is especially suitable for heritage destinations owing to the need to involve community members in preserving and selling their past, as well as an especially vivid need to develop a collaborative approach to

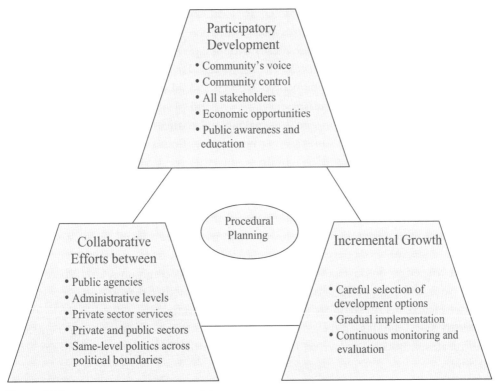

Figure 11.1 The PIC planning model

Source: Adapted from Timothy and Tosun (2003)

tourism. The model, known as the PIC Model, provides a sustainability framework within which the normative planning approach, including steps in the planning process, as outlined earlier, can take place within the guiding principles of participation/community empowerment, incremental development and collaborative development. Each of these is examined below in the context of heritage tourism.

Participatory development

In developing sustainable forms of heritage tourism it is crucial to remember that destination residents are an important part of the cultural product and their concerns, desires and interests must be considered seriously. Planning projects that are entirely top-down, with little or no contribution from the grassroots destination community, have seen only limited success. Many have failed because of public opposition to policies and practices deemed unfair or inequitable, favoring elites and government agencies over lay people and local businesses. This has given rise to an approach known as community-based tourism, which emphasizes the special qualities of places and empowers community members to take control of their own tourism futures. This approach sees the need to develop heritage tourism harmoniously, according to the needs and desires of the host community. It must be done according to local social mores and local aspirations. Participatory development recognizes that destination residents, business people, local government representatives and advocacy groups are all interdependent stakeholders, who must have a voice in the development process. This includes traditionally marginalized groups, such as indigenous people, women and ethnic minorities.

Resident participation in tourism development and planning may be seen from two perspectives: empowerment in decision making and participation in the economic and social benefits of tourism. From the first perspective, flourishing tourism derives from community-based principles that allow residents to have a voice in the development process. This has traditionally meant that influential outsiders, such as ministry of tourism or department of transportation officials, bring their plans to the destination and seek public input via town hall meetings, household surveys or focus groups, comprised of various interested stakeholders. This public input has proved valuable in alleviating many residents' concerns about development in their communities. However, in the developing world it has led to unsatisfactory levels of control by the community itself, because the ideas, plans and power still derive from the top elites rather than the grassroots community. Hence, recent scholarship advocates even more ownership of development problems and solutions at the community level, to the point that development ideas and initiatives should originate with stakeholders in the destination where tourism will take place.

Timothy (2007) outlined several degrees of empowerment in tourist destination communities, each one reaching a higher level of empowerment, from lack of control altogether to absolute control of development from the bottom up. These might also be seen as steps in development efforts as a country or destination region continues to mature. While not really a form of empowerment at all, the first degree is 'imposed development'. In this regard, ideas are incubated and plans made from the outside, usually by government elites, brought into the destination community and imposed with no public input. National politicians often make deals with foreign investors that will bring wealth and prosperity to themselves and which may or may not assist in bringing about greater levels of development for the community. The second degree is 'tokenistic involvement'. This suggests that some development initiatives conceived by outsiders are brought into the community for a public hearing. Stakeholder feedback is sought, but this often occurs only to satisfy the letter of the law rather than to seek true and meaningful participation. 'Meaningful participation' is the third approach. At this stage, consequential participation begins as public agencies have a sincere interest in involving residents, business people and other stakeholders in decision-making and allowing them opportunities to benefit from tourism. While this is a step in the right direction, ownership of development still rests in the hands of outsiders and thus full empowerment has not yet been achieved. Finally, true empowerment occurs when community members and other stakeholders initiate their own goals, programs and projects. Clearly this does not preclude encouragement or assistance from government officials at national and regional levels, but any outsider involvement is limited to a facilitator and consultant rather than decision-maker and driver. In this regard, communities take full responsibility for the successes and failures of tourism development and have ownership of problems and opportunities.

Full control signifies that destination communities are empowered politically, socially, economically and psychologically. Social cohesiveness and community pride for heritage and culture develop. Indigenous knowledge about culture, heritage and nature is valued more highly as a crucial element of the development process, and social pride grows to the point where community members value their own past and what it can offer to visitors. When destinations are psychologically empowered, communities acquire a sense of ownership which often leads to firm stewardship over cultural resources.

One often-cited example of empowered people who own their own cultural property rights are the Maori of New Zealand. The indigenous people of New Zealand are one of the most empowered native groups in the world from a heritage tourism perspective. They have won the right to own their own culture and regulate how the tourism industry uses its symbolisms and trademarks. Some other groups are beginning to find similar success.

The second perspective on resident participation is the enabling of locals to benefit both financially and socially from tourism development. While this sounds logical from a western perspective, it is not as widespread or obvious in many parts of the world as one might think. Community-based tourism planning must also create opportunities for social advancement and economic gain. Heritage tourism, like other forms of tourism, is labor-intensive, sometimes more so, because cultural performances and living museums require large numbers of well-trained staff. Education, or training, is one social advantage. Community members, particularly those who work directly with tourists in a heritage setting, need to understand the history and heritage of their towns, villages or regions.

In addition, heritage tourism should be utilized to stimulate entrepreneurial activity, such as opening inns and bed and breakfasts. These boutique types of accommodations are especially appealing to most heritage tourists and can become an important part of the tourism economy of a destination. Tour companies, souvenir production enterprises and lodging are among the most common locally-owned ventures that bode well in popular cultural tourism destinations. While brand-name multinational companies will almost always creep into burgeoning tourist destinations, efforts should be made to encourage locally-owned and operated shops and other establishments. Small scale typically means that more of the money spent by visitors will remain in the local economy.

Another perspective related to the benefits of tourism is the education of residents and awareness building so that they will know better what to expect from a tourism economy that is based largely on their own cultural heritage. Indigenous knowledge can be shared with outsiders, but residents also should be trained on how best to serve the needs of visitors and how to avoid damaging behavior such as the dumping of waste on or near heritage sites. Because the community being visited is in fact an important part of the cultural tourism product, opportunities must be afforded for local residents to assist in interpreting the heritage of place to outside visitors (Boyd, 2002). This is essential in upholding many principles of sustainability and in assuring ownership of culture and empowerment of host communities.

Incremental development

The incremental aspect of PIC planning is best suited to physical, or land-use planning, but has application for all types of tourism development. The primary thought underlying incrementalism is that once plans have been formulated and actions initiated, progress must be monitored continually to see whether or not any changes are required. Traditional planning controlled by central governments without regard to local conditions was inflexible and encouraged rapid development with big projects. This became problematic if mistakes were made or if events not foreseen happened to affect the success of a development project. Incremental growth allows for new directions to be taken, changes to be made to the initial plan and objectives to be altered if needed.

This approach allows for continuous monitoring and helps to uphold principles of sustainability such as cultural and ecological integrity, holistic development, balance and efficiency. One of its main features is that time is not wasted on projects that might fail or become inefficient; instead planning is done bit by bit to achieve more specific goals and objectives.

266

In the realm of heritage tourism, this is especially important as infrastructure is designed and built. Archaeological sites, for instance, can be positively affected by incremental processes. In the course of restoration or reconstruction, the approach will allow for new scientific evidence to be integrated into the physical plan if new information is discovered during restoration. Likewise, the physical plant associated with ancient ruins, including ticket booths, car parks, souvenir shops, cafes, toilets, sidewalks and trails and interpretive centers, has the potential to distract from the historical importance of a site or contribute to its demise during construction. There are far too many examples of rapid physical development projects, including roads and car parks, which have destroyed or covered up important archaeological sites because care was not taken to assure that a proper cultural impact assessment was completed. Incremental processes allow more time and flexibility for such imperative assessments to be done. Master plans that are comprised of smaller sub-plans that deal with specific projects are most effective in this regard and will allow development to occur as finances and successes permit.

Collaboration

Collaborative, or cooperative, planning is an important approach to sustainable development and helps uphold principles such as holism, equity, conservation, efficiency and balance. There are several different types of collaboration in relation to tourism, which are all very important in the heritage context. The first is cooperation between public agencies. This form of collaboration is crucial as various government bureaus have authority to act over their own domains. These domains often create territorial conflicts that lead to misunderstandings, inefficient and overlapping objectives and other forms of conflict. In some countries where ancient monuments have been developed into major attractions, the spatial and functional jurisdiction among public agencies is so complicated that it becomes difficult to understand which organization manages which element of the destination, even for the government itself.

For instance, at some sites of international importance, different agencies are charged with developing different elements of the attraction: roads and parking lots, fee booths, landscaping and grounds maintenance and the archaeological relics themselves. These elements of the site are all required to make it function, and in many cases each one is managed by a different agency, including ministries of culture, departments of tourism, departments of the environment, archaeology agencies and ministries of public works. Two such examples are Borobudur and Prambanan World Heritage Sites in Indonesia where the monuments and their various components, as well as their development efforts, were operated by different government offices. This is a common situation, particularly in the less-developed world, and it takes serous coordination efforts for such important sites to succeed in attracting visitors and meeting their needs.

The most important matter is that each agency must give up some of its control in order to cooperate with other agencies in such a way that their mandates are not in opposition to one another. Unfortunately, harmonious relations between public agencies do not always exist and many loathe sharing their power, which sometimes leads to development failures and even to physical deterioration of the structures and grounds. This is not easy as agencies must battle each other for scarce funding, each one believing its agenda is most important. Nonetheless, inter-agency cooperation has the potential to save considerable sums of money, create efficient management systems and provide satisfying experiences for visitors.

The second type of collaboration takes place between different levels of administration. Cooperation between different government levels (e.g. national, state/province, county, municipal) is extremely critical in preserving the past and encouraging tourism development. Plans initiated at the national legislature need the cooperation of lower-order civil divisions to be able to connect with stakeholders on the ground and to achieve public support. Likewise, lower-order governments often rely on higher-level governments for legislative frameworks, protocols and funding. For example, in the USA, state governments, through their state parks or other conservation agencies, have traditionally provided grants for cities and towns to erect historic monuments and heritage markers at places deemed worth conserving. Funding to restore old homes, community centers, schools, churches, jails or other heritage structures is commonly given by state governments to municipal governments to enhance their communities' image or commemorate an important event, person or place. These dependency relationships exist everywhere and between all levels of governance.

Third, public and private cooperation refers to efforts to work together between government agencies and private organizations (see Plate 11.2). Tourism is often fueled by the private sector, but collaboration with the public sector is vital in the development of infrastructure and the enforcement of building regulations. Likewise, most national governments throughout the world rely on private investors and multinational corporations to invest in and spur the growth of tourist destinations. In the heritage arena, this relationship is common as public lands are managed by government agencies, but many visitor services are contracted out to private companies. In many US national parks, for instance, catering and lodging services are managed by private enterprises, even though the parklands themselves are owned by the federal government.

Similarly, adjacent lands may be owned by private individuals, corporate landholders, non-profit organizations, local governments or national governments. Careful coordination in land-use planning and environmental controls is essential to protect the cultural landscapes involved. Stonehenge in England provides a good example. The megalithic structure itself is owned by the government and overseen by English Heritage, a public agency. English Heritage provides car parks, toilets, admission tickets, refreshments and a souvenir shop. The land immediately around the stone circle is also under the care of English Heritage, but surrounding land, including that where the parking lots and shops

Plate 11.2 Reflecting public-private cooperation, at this highway rest stop, public services are provided by private businesses

are located, is owned by the National Trust, a non-profit organization that aims to protect historic buildings, archaeological sites, gardens, parks and natural areas. English Heritage charges an entrance fee and National Trust members are admitted free. Given the spatial arrangement of land and the parallel business arrangements at Stonehenge, a great deal of cooperation exists between the public sector and the private/non-profit sector. Perhaps the crowning achievement of their collaborative efforts was the designation of the site and its surrounding landscape as a UNESCO World Heritage Site in 1986.

The fourth type of collaboration exists between private-sector services. These are especially important in product development and service provision. Heritage tours are one of the best examples of this view as lodging, transportation and catering work together to provide satisfying visitor experiences. In terms of place promotion, this form of collaboration is important in not only creating bigger and better products but also in eliminating inefficient overlap. By working with airlines, rental car companies and hotel chains can sell more rentals and beds for the night. Despite the obvious symbiotic relationship between travel service providers, these inter-private sector relationships have not had a long history in tourism.

Cooperation across political boundaries between polities is the fifth and final form of collaborative planning. This form of cross-border planning is vital in areas where natural or cultural heritage resources lie adjacent to or across political boundaries. Political boundaries, both international and subnational, have erected firm barriers between polities on either side. Territoriality ensued and every meter of national space was jealously guarded. This prevented all but a minimal degree of trans-frontier cooperation, but today cross-border cooperation is becoming more commonplace as countries and states realize that symbiotic relationships can be created across political divides to encourage a more balanced use of resources and a more standardized conservation system. Thus, holistic development and equitable relations have the potential to result from these endeavors.

Cross-border cooperation can occur at many levels. Two adjacent communities offering similar heritage products can cooperate in their promotional efforts to market themselves as a single destination. This not only saves budgets but can increase visitation by creating a larger and more intense destination. Countries sharing a border can better assure their common resources are used in responsible ways. There are many examples throughout the world of cultural regions, even individual ruins and heritage sites, being bisected by international boundaries. More and more of the countries that share common resources are beginning to see the value of collaborating on conservation, marketing and

Plate 11.3 This billboard in Nicosia, Cyprus, illustrates the desire of both parts of the island to collaborate for heritage planning

management for the common greater good. Even the opposing sides of Nicosia, Cyprus (the Turkish north and Greek south), which have been separated by war and barbed wire since 1974, have begun to see the value in working together to preserve their shared historic city and its potential tourism dividends (see Plate 11.3).

SUMMARY AND CONCLUSION

Much of the world has utilized boosterist approaches to tourism development – blind promotion without regard for mass tourism's negative implications. Luckily planners in the developed world noticed this problem as tourism began to grow in the post-Second World War era and worked to develop principles and practices to halt the negative outcomes of tourism. Physical planning, wherein all elements of a site are evaluated and understood as part of a system, resulted with many heritage cities and historic sites developing master plans between the 1970s and 1990s. While this was a good start, additional principles became important to assure that entire regions would develop in socially and ecologically sensible ways. Thus, sustainable development became the normative framework for tourism's growth, encompassing social equity, environmental resilience and preservation, visitor education and edification and economic impact. Good heritage tourism has now evolved to encompass principles of sustainable growth at regional and site-specific levels through physical planning and processes that encompass participatory democracy, incremental development and stakeholder collaboration.

REVIEW QUESTIONS

1. What important role do landscape architects and urban planners play in developing cultural destinations?

2. How do the concepts of 'sustainable tourism' and 'tourism within the context of sustainability' differ from one another?

3. How does the PIC model of tourism planning view heritage destinations more holistically?

4. Why is participatory development an especially critical sustainability principle when we talk about living and built culture?

5. What are the dangers of not developing heritage sites in an incremental fashion?

6. Explain the notion of boosterism in tourism growth and why it is dangerous.

7. Why is collaboration an especially poignant necessity in situations where cultural areas are located on two sides of an international border?

RECOMMENDED READING

Aas, C., Ladkin, A. and Fletcher, J. (2005) Stakeholder collaboration and heritage management. *Annals of Tourism Research* 32, 28–48.

Altman, J.C. and Finlayson, J. (1993) Aborigines, tourism and sustainable development. *Journal of Tourism Studies* 4(1), 38–50.

Arthur, S.N.A. and Mensah, J.V. (2006) Urban management and heritage tourism for sustainable development: The case of Elmina Cultural Heritage and Management Programme in Ghana. *Management of Environmental Quality* 17(3), 299–312.

Ashworth, G.J. (1991) *Heritage Planning: Conservation as the Management of Urban Change.* Groningen, Netherlands: Geopers.

Ashworth, G.J. and Howard, P. (1999) *European Heritage Planning and Management.* Exeter: Intellect.

Ashworth, G.J. and Tunbridge, J.E. (1990) *The Tourist-Historic City.* London: Belhaven.

Ashworth, G.J. and Tunbridge, J.E. (1999) Old cities, new pasts: Heritage planning in selected cities of Central Europe. *GeoJournal* 49, 105–116.

Boyd, S.W. and Timothy, D.J. (2001) Developing partnerships: Tools for interpretation and management of World Heritage Sites. *Tourism Recreation Research* 26(1), 47–53.

Coccossis, H. and Nijkamp, P. (eds) (1995) *Planning for Our Cultural Heritage.* Aldershot: Avebury.

Drost, A. (1996) Developing sustainable tourism for World Heritage Sites. *Annals of Tourism Research* 23, 479–484.

du Cros, H. (2001) A new model to assist in planning for sustainable cultural heritage tourism. *International Journal of Tourism Research* 3, 165–170.

Garrod, B. (2007) A snapshot into the past: The utility of volunteer-employed photography in planning and managing heritage tourism. *Journal of Heritage Tourism* 2(1), 14–35.

Hall, C.M. (2008) *Tourism Planning: Policies, Processes and Relationships.* Harlow: Prentice Hall.

Henderson, J.C. (2008) Managing urban ethnic heritage: Little India in Singapore. *International Journal of Heritage Studies* 14, 332–346.

Jamal, T.B. and Getz, D. (1995) Collaboration theory and community tourism planning. *Annals of Tourism Research* 22, 186–204.

Kim, S.S., Lee, H. and Timothy, D.J. (2006) Perspectives on inter-Korean cooperation in tourism. *Tourism Analysis* 11(1), 13–23.

Landorf, C. (2009) Managing for sustainable tourism: A review of six cultural World Heritage Sites. *Journal of Sustainable Tourism* 17, 53–70.

Leask, A. and Fyall, A. (eds) (2006) *Managing World Heritage Sites.* Oxford: Butterworth Heinemann.

Mason, P. (2003) *Tourism Impacts, Planning and Management.* Oxford: Butterworth Heinemann.

McGrath, G. (2004) Including the outsiders: The contribution of guides to integrated heritage tourism management in Cusco, southern Peru. *Current Issues in Tourism* 7(4/5), 426–432.

Okech, R.N. (2007) Local communities and management of heritage sites: Case study of Lamu Old Town. *Anatolia* 18(2), 189–202.

Pearson, M. and Sullivan, S. (1995) *Looking after Heritage Places: The Basics of Heritage Planning for Managers, Landowners and Administrators.* Carlton: Melbourne University Press.

Reed, M.G. (1997) Power relations and community-based tourism planning. *Annals of Tourism Research* 24, 566–591.

Ruhanen, L. (2009) Stakeholder participation in tourism destination planning: Another case of missing the point? *Tourism Recreation Research* 34(3), 283–294.

Russo, A.P. and van der Borg, J. (2002) Planning considerations for cultural tourism: A case study of four European cities. *Tourism Management* 23, 631–637.

Sautter, E.T. and Leisen, B. (1999) Managing stakeholders: A tourism planning model. *Annals of Tourism Research* 26, 312–328.

Setiawan, B. and Timothy, D.J. (2000) Existing urban management frameworks and heritage conservation in Indonesia. *Asia Pacific Journal of Tourism Research* 5(2), 76–79.

Timothy, D.J. (1998) Cooperative tourism planning in a developing destination. *Journal of Sustainable Tourism* 6(1), 52–68.

Timothy, D.J. (1998) Incremental tourism planning in Yogyakarta, Indonesia. *Tourism Recreation Research* 23(2), 72–74.

Timothy, D.J. (1999) Cross-border partnership in tourism resource management: International parks along the US-Canada border. *Journal of Sustainable Tourism* 7(3/4), 182–205.

Timothy, D.J. (1999) Participatory planning: A view of tourism in Indonesia. *Annals of Tourism Research* 26(2), 371–391.

Timothy, D.J. (2000) Building community awareness of tourism in a developing country destination. *Tourism Recreation Research* 25(2), 111–116.

Timothy, D.J. (2002) Tourism and community development issues. In R. Sharpley and D.J. Telfer (eds) *Tourism and Development: Concepts and Issues* (pp. 149–164). Clevedon: Channel View Publications.

Timothy, D.J. and White, K. (1999) Community-based ecotourism development on the periphery of Belize. *Current Issues in Tourism* 2(2/3), 226–242.

Tosun, C. and Timothy, D.J. (2003) Arguments for community participation in the tourism development process. *Journal of Tourism Studies* 14(2), 2–15.

Tosun, C., Timothy, D.J. and Öztürk, Y. (2003) Tourism growth, national development and regional inequality in Turkey. *Journal of Sustainable Tourism* 11(2), 31–49.

Tosun, C., Timothy, D.J., Parpairis, A., and McDonald, D. (2005) Cross-border cooperation in tourism marketing growth strategies. *Journal of Travel and Tourism Marketing* 18(1), 5–23.

RECOMMENDED WEBSITES

Angkor Wat Devata Inventory –
http://www.devata.org/2010/02/angkor-wat-devata-inventory/

Community Tourism Planning and Design – http://www.community-tourism.net/

Guidelines for Land-Use Planning –
http://www.fao.org/docrep/t0715e/t0715e00.HTM

Heritage Site Plan for Places Ghandi Visited –
http://www.gandhitopia.org/group/mgnd/forum/topics/heritage-site-plan-for-places

Nigeria Tourism Development Master Plan –
http://www.nacd.gov.ng/Tourism%20Master%20Plan.pdf

Park County Heritage Site Planning Project – http://www.parkcountyheritage.com/about-our-heritage/preservation-projects/ongoing-preservation-projects

Stonehenge World Heritage Site Management Plan –
http://www.stonehengeconsultation.org/Stonehenge_WHS_Management_Plan.pdf

Tanzania Tourism Master Plan – http://www.tzonline.org/pdf/tourismmasterplan.pdf

CHAPTER 12

MARKETING THE PAST FOR TODAY

LEARNING OBJECTIVES

After reading this chapter, you should be able to:

1. Recognize the difference between marketing an individual attraction and an entire destination.

2. Appreciate marketing's role in sustainable tourism development.

3. Understand how heritage and its brands are used as promotional tools for destinations.

4. Know about the unique product mix of cultural heritage tourism.

5. Learn about the marketing planning process for cultural tourism.

6. Be aware of the use of de-marketing as a management mechanism at heritage sites.

7. See how authenticity is commonly used as a promotional tool.

INTRODUCTION

Marketing has a very long history and has been alluded to in ancient texts and more recent historical accounts. It refers to the act of matching supply with demand, or providing products and services that fulfill people's needs and wants. Marketing's aim is to provide quality products, services and experiences for consumers to create value and build solid customer relations and customer loyalty, and in return capture value (i.e. profit) from satisfied costumers. Perhaps the most important element of marketing is understanding the wants and needs of select consumer groups, known as target markets, and providing them with opportunities that satisfy their necessities and desires.

This chapter examines these and other marketing concepts in the realm of heritage tourism. First, attention is drawn to destination marketing, particularly using cultural heritage as a regional branding mechanism, and heritage symbolisms as tourism promotional emblems. Efforts to market individual attractions are next analyzed, including the tools used to do so. The chapter also examines the marketing planning process that will help destinations and sites achieve management goals, and it offers recommendations for heritage marketing in a sustainable manner.

MARKETING HERITAGE TOURISM

Marketing is an extremely important aspect of management, in some cases the most important depending on the context and the service or product being sold. In the case of heritage tourism, marketing focuses on two primary scales: heritage tourism in a destination and individual heritage attractions.

Destination marketing and heritage tourism

From the first perspective, heritage tourism in destination marketing, historic sites and museums are seen as a major player in the product mix. Some destinations rely almost entirely on the historic built environment for their tourism economies, while in other places heritage plays a secondary role to nature, beaches and resorts, gambling or sport tourism. In either case, heritage forms an important component of tourism in most of the world's destinations. In promoting their places, destination governments, ministries of tourism and management organizations have traditionally used heritage as a competitive advantage over other similar destinations. For instance, in locations dominated by beaches and beach resorts, heritage adds an important secondary appeal that can sway travelers' decision making.

One prevailing marketing concept of the modern era is place branding, place promotion or destination branding. This tactic of tourism marketing sees countries, provinces, regions, cities/towns or rural areas as holistic destinations that can be promoted to tourists, investors or potential new residents. It is a public relations approach that requires more than simply changing a promotional slogan (e.g. What happens in Vegas, stays in Vegas); it requires a complete image overhaul and focuses on the characteristics of place that make a destination special and unique, as well as efforts to strengthen positive images or correct negative images of a destination. Place branding also entails the coordination of service quality, infrastructure, product mix and policies to create a desirable destination brand identity.

Akin to this is the notion of geotourism which, rather than being a type of tourism, like sport tourism, religious tourism or nature-based tourism, is an approach to tourism growth and development. The term geotourism, coined in the late 1990s, is used in two divergent ways: geology-based tourism and sense of place-enhancing tourism. For our purposes the second meaning is most relevant and refers to tourism forms that enhance the physical and human geographical characteristics of a place, including culture, art, cuisine, built heritage, natural environment and welfare of local residents. It is a holistic approach to planning, managing and marketing tourist destinations that is founded on a sense of place and empowerment.

As part of their place-branding efforts, tourist destinations often use heritage resources as symbols of their product. The German National Tourism Board, Tourism Australia, the Tourism Authority of Thailand, the Brazilian Ministry of Tourism, the Jordan

276

Tourism Board, the Jamaica Tourist Board, South African Tourism and the Canadian Tourism Commission are only a few of the dozens of national tourism organizations that currently use or have used cultural heritage as iconic representations of tourism in their countries, either as logos, front page material in brochures or on their main websites. The Nepal Tourism Board's 'Send Home a Friend' ad campaign depicts traditional Nepalese architecture against the backdrop of the Himalayas. The Hong Kong Tourism Board insignia features a Chinese sailboat. India's Ministry of Tourism's 'Incredible India' website highlights many elements of the country's cultural heritage, as does the Ghana Tourism website and hundreds of other national, state, provincial and local promotional websites.

There is also a perpetuation of stereotyped images of place associated with mega-heritage attractions. Even though national governments do not necessarily utilize these intentionally in logos or websites, certain monuments have become nearly synonymous with certain destinations (see Plate 12.1). Tourism in Peru, for instance, is Machu Picchu. Tourism in Egypt is the Great Pyramids and the Valley of the Kings. Tourism in Cambodia is synonymous with Angkor Wat. Such important mega sites have brought considerable visibility to these countries and do in fact form the foundations of tourism.

UNESCO World Heritage Sites are also often used by countries as marketing tools. In their attempts at branding themselves, many countries, particularly in the less-developed

Plate 12.1 For some tourists, these iconic views of Venice epitomize the city and the romanticism of Italy

world, use World Heritage listing as a brand upon which they can develop tourism. While there is no widespread evidence to suggest that UNESCO listing does increase arrivals, there is some initial data that suggest it may increase visitation for sites that are already popular and easily accessible. Nonetheless, countries willingly capitalize on the UNESCO brand in their promotional campaigns, utilizing their world-class heritage places as a competitive advantage over similar destinations.

Similarly, media-induced tourism is an important draw for many destinations. When places, whether small (e.g. villages) or large (e.g. countries), are featured in popular movies or television series, they often become iconic centers of tourist attention as well. People like to visit locations where motion pictures or TV shows are filmed, places that are mentioned in films or areas where movie-related events were said to have taken place. Film heritage has become an extremely salient promotional instrument for a number of places. *Lord of the Rings* sites in New Zealand have become salient attractions for Tolkien fans, with multitudinous tours and use in official promotional efforts nationwide (see Plate 12.2). Australia saw a tourism windfall after the 1980s releases of *The Man from Snowy River* and *Crocodile Dundee*. The television series *Cheers* has been an important heritage draw for Boston and *Seinfeld* tours are still fashionable in New York City. The places featured in

Plate 12.2 The Hobbiton movie set is part of the *Lord of the Rings* appeal of New Zealand

these films and TV shows, whether real or make-believe, have become an important part of the cultural heritagescape of these destinations.

Marketing individual attractions

There are several reasons why museums and other heritage attractions are interested in marketing themselves. Perhaps the most urgent in today's economic and political climate is fundraising. Marketing can be used as a tool for increasing visitation by local residents and tourists. While increasing admission fees often has the effect of deterring people, inviting additional attendees through promotional campaigns that target local people and their families, as well as out of town visitors, can increase fee-based revenues without having to raise prices. Historic sites, museums, heritage houses, parks and other heritage properties realize that they are competing with other leisure service providers for the public's time and money, so marketing has become even more important in light of this fact. While heritage managers have traditionally despised the notion of increasing visitation for financial reasons, they are beginning to realize that they have few alternatives.

Second is building public awareness of the establishment's role in the cultural life of a community and promoting good public relations. Marketing can help a heritage property promote its conservation, educational and non-profit values to the broader community. This can help increase community pride in its own heritage and heritage resources, thereby stimulating a desire among community members to become more conservation-minded. It also creates goodwill with other sectors and citizens, resulting in more support for a heritage property.

Third, like the second point, marketing programs and promotional efforts have the ability to 'set the record straight', or debunk misconceptions about the role of heritage places and museums in a community's social life. Marketing and public relations efforts can replace old misdirected attitudes about historic sites being boring places with information about exciting new interpretive media, recent artifact acquisitions, the discovery of a new archaeological area, an exceptional new cultural festival or the addition of a new attraction at a historic theme park.

Finally, marketing publicly-operated sites or events might be an effort to allow the public to see what their tax dollars are being used for. Some government funding sources require public access to the public's own heritage in order for funding to continue. Heritage properties can take advantage of promotional campaigns and broader marketing efforts to remain visible and viable to the public and funding agencies.

Many marketing scholars have argued that in the heritage context, marketing efforts have to be adapted to individual circumstances, because each site is unique in terms of its offerings and its market. There is in fact no blanket approach to marketing heritage sites in general. However, one thing is certain: heritage is very political and highly emotional, so marketing the past is a delicate matter that must be done in a way that is not offensive to any one group. This is especially important at sites of disaster or human suffering, such as Holocaust concentration camps, the National September 11 Memorial and Museum at the World Trade Center and the slave trade forts on the coast of Ghana.

Marketing heritage sites is usually done through public relations building, advertising and direct sales and promotions. Since most museums are non-profit organizations, surviving on donations, grants and sponsorships, they have fairly modest promotional budgets. Likewise, publicly-owned historic sites are government funded and therefore money is also in short supply. Therefore, efforts should be made to use the most effective means of advertising for the lowest cost. Many studies have shown that word of mouth is the most effective promotional tool available. One of the most important marketing strategies heritage managers can use is to provide high-quality experiences by understanding their market(s), providing high-quality and 'edutaining' interpretive programs and making an otherwise good impression. This will result in the best return on investment as visitors recommend the heritage place to other potential visitors. Many studies show that some 50% of all visitors, or more, receive their information about museums and historic sites from friends and relatives. Brochures are still important for mailing or passing out to visitors, but the internet has, like word of mouth, become one of the most salient promotional tools of all. Once an official website is designed, it does not take a great deal of effort or expense to update it, and, as part of the world wide web, it reaches the highest number of information seekers than any other advertising device.

Other mechanisms are important, however. A study by Prideaux and Kininmont (1999) found that many people decided to visit a historical museum because they saw it while driving by. Road signs, therefore, can be an extremely important advertising medium for people passing by. Prideaux and Kininmont suggested that museums should begin advertising long distances away from the site on major highways to get motorists thinking about a stop ahead of time. Leaving promotional materials at gas stations and rest stops along the way is also important. Near the sites, directional signs should be posted in highly visible locations with clear directions. Large entrance signs with additional information should also be considered, together with leaving brochures at local hotels, restaurants, libraries and other establishments that might have a connection to the community's tourism sector.

MARKETING PLANNING

Marketing planning is an important part of management planning overall. It involves understanding the current situation (i.e. where are we now?), a desired future (i.e. where do we want to be?) and the methods involved in getting there.

Situation analysis

Like interpretive planning, marketing planning involves a situation analysis (sometimes known as an audit) – an evaluation of the current situation, or where are we now. This involves an understanding about who the current and potential markets are. Part of this exercise is segmenting the market, which was discussed in Chapter 2 under the concept of demand. Segmenting the market is important in understanding different groups and their needs and desires, so that products and services can be developed specifically for them. In the heritage context, in understanding the markets for tourism, there are opportunities for different sites to be promoted, packaged and developed for different types of tourists based on their motives and expectations, demographic characteristics or geographic origins.

Competitor analyses are also sometimes included as part of the situation analysis, for these reveal who the primary competitors are and what kinds of advantages they might have over other heritage sites and museums. This analysis examines the strengths and weaknesses of an attraction compared to the attraction conducting the investigation. What makes other museums appealing, how do other historic buildings cater to the needs of their visitors and how does an archaeological park or outdoor living museum maintain its sense of authenticity are all examples of important questions that might be answered through a competitor analysis. This exercise can be an important tool for an establishment in learning about its own strengths and weaknesses in relation to other sites. Such an analysis is useful in understanding what areas can be improved upon and how, the success of marketing strategies, operation costs and maintenance, accessibility for the public (including special needs markets), quality of facilities and services and the effectiveness of extant interpretive programs.

Marketing goals and strategies

A second step in marketing planning is setting goals and formulating strategies. After the current situation is understood, heritage managers can establish goals and objectives, as well as strategies for achieving the goals they have set. Goals can include a wide array of issues, needs and hopes. Examples include improving interpreter training and language skills for increasing demand from abroad or hiring several new cashiers, interpreters and curators, even in light of budgetary problems or a multitude of other aspirations. All goals and objectives must be achievable; strategies need to be feasible within the current political and budgetary climate. A strategy to accomplish the hiring goal, for instance, might be to raise the necessary funds by increasing visitation through advertising in travel magazines, offering special deals or by getting a property inscribed on a national list (e.g. Register of Historic Places) or an international list (e.g. UNESCO World Heritage List), which has the potential to increase a site's visibility, which might translate into increased donations, visitor entrance fees and sponsorships.

A common part of the marketing strategy is 'target marketing', or the selection of certain market segments or niches that can be pursued as potential new or repeat visitors. In identifying target markets, heritage managers have to decide how many market segments will be targeted, develop a clear market profile for each segment and develop a campaign that is appropriate for the heritage property in question and the chosen market segments (Hall & McArthur, 1993). Decisions about how best to market a heritage place can be made from a range of approaches. The first is a 'shotgun' approach, or undifferentiated marketing. This reaches a wider array of audiences, but is often seen as wasteful since much money and effort are spent on reaching people who have no interest or ability to visit the attraction or travel to the destination. A more specific approach is the single-segment method, wherein a specific target market is selected for promotional efforts. Heritage managers often prefer this approach, since they know their efforts will be spent on people who at least have an interest in heritage tourism. Between differentiated and undifferentiated marketing are other options, wherein managers can target several market segments with some of their efforts falling on the disinterested, but with many interested people being included.

Marketing activity

Another step in marketing planning is the actual marketing activities. Once the marketing strategy has been developed, managers must consider the 'marketing mix' or the variables that can be manipulated to achieve the stated goals. This will allow the site to compete more effectively with the selected target markets. While there are different ways of classifying these variables, such as the original four Ps (product, price, place and promotion), there is now a fairly standard seven-P approach to achieving the best marketing mix. The seven Ps include: product, price, promotion, place, packaging, people and positioning.

Product in the heritage context refers to the range of offerings that visitors can choose from at the destination level or the objects and activities available at a particular site. This includes the relics, interpretive programs and media, the staff members, the image of the place and the support services (e.g. shops, cafes). In short, the product is the heritage experience and the components of a site or museum that contribute to the visitor experience. In developing their marketing plan, managers must ask important questions related to the appropriateness of the product. Is it relevant today? Does it match what visitors expect from their visits? Is the current interpretive program helping us achieve our goals?

Price is an important element of the marketing mix because it pertains to all financial aspects of a cultural site. The earnings from concessions and other services are an important part of this element and help make possible many of the conservation goals of heritage managers. Admission costs, special discounts and methods of payment are all part of the price consideration. Monetary access is important in this regard. If entrance fees are set too high, it will necessarily limit the number of people who can attend an event or visit a museum. The dual pricing system discussed previously is an important consideration in establishing a pricing policy. One of the most important, albeit often overlooked, aspects of pricing is value for money. In addition to raw price, it is important for managers to consider the value for price. Are heritage visitors getting their money's worth out of their experience? Is the price too low for the excellent experience they are having? Willingness to pay studies are becoming more common as administrators desire to see how effective their pricing policies are. In some cases, visitors might be willing to pay more for their experience, depending on the value they place on the opportunity to visit and the quality of their experience.

Promotion entails specific efforts to market, including advertising, promotional media and direct marketing activities. It involves managers and destinations constantly thinking of ways to spread the word about their attraction or destination. In short, promotion is the sum of all the ways in which site and destination managers tell the world about their product. Managers have to make decisions about which media they will use to promote their sites and develop an image or brand. The most salient advertising tool today is the internet. It is substantially cheaper to reach a wider audience on the internet than ever before by using only brochures and paid advertisements in magazines. Today the most common ways of promoting cultural heritage attractions from an undifferentiated marketing approach are the internet, in the travel sections of major newspapers, in airline and other travel magazines and via mail-order brochures and destination guides. Differentiated promotional efforts include specific websites, online discussion groups, heritage- and culture-oriented hobby magazines and brochures and printed guides. All of these are effective methods of reaching wide audiences both for destinations and particular historic sites and museums.

Place traditionally has meant the actual location of the event or attraction, as well as the distribution of the product. Geographers refer to this as 'absolute location', which entails the physical position of a destination or individual attractions. New concepts are coming into play in the realm of marketing, however, as marketers are beginning to realize that places are more than just easily-delineated locations. Place must be seen as something more than absolute location; what geographers call 'relative location' is extremely important in marketing heritage. Relative location means the site or situation of something in relation to other factors. For example, even though the absolute location of the ruins of Great Zimbabwe is in south-central Zimbabwe, the relative location is near the town of Masvingo, not very close to a major road or motorway and in an African country that is presently experiencing economic and political turmoil. The notion of relative location requires that the 'place' of heritage sites and destinations be put into proper context. Thus, relative location is more important in being able to promote Great Zimbabwe as an important World Heritage Site than absolute location.

People are another salient part of the marketing mix and one category that many marketing specialists have only recently begun to acknowledge. The people element should be comprised of three parts: the service providers, the consumers and the middle people. In the heritage case, we are referring to site managers and staff members, visitors or heritage tourists and other intermediaries, such as travel agents, ticket brokers or transportation/lodging suppliers. It is critical for heritage managers to hire and retain good-quality workers – people who work well with visitors and other staffers, and who are reliable, skilled and knowledgeable. These are the frontline employees who help create heritage environments and satisfactory visitor encounters. Thus, the actors, staff members, curators, interpreters, security people, ticket sellers and concessionaires are part of the cultural heritage product and must be a constant consideration for managers. Intermediaries, while typically not seen as a particular part of the heritage experience, are part of the broader travel experience and can help make or break the experience, or at least set the mood before or after the museum or archaeological site visit. Care should be taken in selecting middle people to work with or in building marketing networks so that trustworthiness, integrity and good business sense are paramount. Finally, the tourists or other heritage consumers are the consumers in search of heritage or cultural experiences. Their needs must be met, and their satisfaction determines whether or not they will visit again, refer others or even ever visit another historic site again. All of these people elements are crucial.

Packaging refers to the way in which a product is presented to the consumer. The visual appeal of a cultural environment or the way the components of a historic city feature together are part of the packaging of a heritage product. First impressions are very important in tourism. The cleanliness or orderliness of a historic community or living folklife museum, or the design of a museum and its interpretive media and displays, are important in creating satisfied visitors. The visitor experience is heavily influenced by the staff, how they dress and speak and if they are helpful and friendly. As well, the user-friendliness of the media and layout of the place or attraction are important. Clustering, routing and linking are salient aspects of packaging as well. Heritage trails are linearly linked sites and locations that are underscored by a common theme. Texas' Independence Trail links communities and places closely associated with the Republic's independence from Mexico in 1838. Likewise, the Iron Curtain Heritage Trail through Europe traverses along the former border between Eastern and Western Europe. Likewise, in the city of Berlin, the Berlin Wall Trail is a popular tourist attraction that marks the communist heritage of East Germany and the divided past of Berlin.

Positioning entails thinking and decision making about how a property is positioned in the minds of existing and potential visitors. People's perceptions are very significant in this regard, as word of mouth is one of the most relevant marketing tools there is. Positioning necessitates understanding not only what tourists and other visitors think about a museum, heritage site, cultural event or historic house but how the property is positioned in relation to other comparable attractions. What is the competitive advantage over other sites? Why would visitors in Sweden choose heritage destination A over destination B? The notions of branding and place promotion noted earlier are especially applicable in this regard.

Marketing management and evaluation

After marketing plans and promotional campaigns have been initiated, heritage managers need to ensure that target markets are reached and appropriate strategies are adopted.

Sufficient budgets and staff are especially important. A plan of action is needed for each action required in the marketing strategy, to establish timelines, costs, staff duties and set priorities.

Constant evaluation is a crucial part of marketing management. Ineffective strategies and action plans can be corrected if care is taken to evaluate promotional campaigns frequently and thoroughly. Sometimes, some goals will be fulfilled while others will not. Evaluation is important in all aspects of management, as it helps to establish accountability, provide information for future marketing efforts, provide data that can be utilized to understand successes and failures, improve quality and effectiveness and see whether or not goals and objectives are being fulfilled. Visitor satisfaction studies, importance-performance analyses and market segmentation studies are among the most popular evaluative tools in understanding the market for heritage sites and the effectiveness of the marketing approaches selected.

SUSTAINABLE MARKETING

Beach-based tourism and visits to historic sites have long formed the foundations of mass tourism, which has traditionally been cited as the biggest culprit of the negative social and ecological impacts of tourism. Unfortunately, this is true. Mass tourism grew rapidly after the Second World War as destinations began mass promoting themselves to tourists. This boosterist approach was the norm for many years and still is in some places, wherein tourism was promoted blindly in order to increase visitation and bring in spending without regard for the long-term negative implications of such behavior. As a result, 'alternative' forms of tourism began to arise, such as ecotourism, which aimed to appeal more to special interest groups rather than the masses of millions. In response, new planning paradigms have developed and reached the realm of marketing too.

A new trend is sustainable marketing. While many people narrowly see this as marketing environmentally-friendly products, it is much more. In the context of heritage tourism, it includes marketing green products and services but also marketing cultural destinations and sites in a way that assures their long-term viability, as well as that of visitation levels. Boosterism was very short-term oriented, bringing financial gains but exacting social and ecological costs. Sustainable marketing is antithetical to boosterism, as it attempts to draw in people who are truly interested and will be willing to contribute to conservation or at least not hinder it – and it requires the implementation of long-term goals and objectives and the involvement of the community to grow public pride in their heritage and promote it themselves as they become part of the product.

While the long-term viability of places and resources is better assured when marketing is done in line with principles of sustainability, this is often not enough to get everyone on board. This is especially the case with privately-owned heritage attractions or privately-owned services that accompany other types of historic sites and museums, whose main purposes are education and profit making. They have learned, as all for-profit enterprises have in recent years, that green business equals good business. As the public becomes more environmentally conscious, including regarding heritage resources, new demand is created for products, experiences and places that are 'sustainable'. Unfortunately this has resulted in countless heritage tour operators and other service providers using 'green' or 'sustainable' as a marketing gimmick, even when they do not practice ecologically-sensitive marketing and management tactics. Nonetheless, it is now a 'brand' that sells.

Sometimes the most sustainable approach to marketing is no marketing at all. Even more aggressive is de-marketing – the practice of discouraging visitors. This is especially important today at heritage locations in light of the environmental damage brought about by unbridled mass tourism and the growth in global tourism. At individual locations de-marketing can help direct tourists away from delicate areas, or at a cultural destination level can prevent increased arrivals if carrying capacity thresholds are beginning to reach their saturation points. A nice example of de-marketing is Uluru (Ayer's Rock), Australia. Uluru has extremely deep and salient cultural and religious value for native Australians, but it is also an important tourist attraction where more than 150,000 people climb the rock each year, much to the chagrin of the aboriginal peoples. Park managers are actively de-marketing Uluru as a climbing venue not only because of the physical damage to the rock, but because of the irreverence with which tourists treat a place that is considered sacrosanct by so many Australians (McKercher *et al.*, 2008).

Finally, partnership is an important concept in sustainable marketing. Efficiency, equity, holism and other sustainability principles can be better upheld if businesses co-operate together to market what they have to offer. Heritage destinations that market themselves holistically, rather than as a single attraction or collection of individual attractions, will find greater success and efficiency. Likewise, heritage sites in a given area can capitalize on a common product to increase efficiency and equity.

Deepak Chhabra (2009) developed a similar model to that of the PIC model noted in Chapter 11 as it pertains to marketing museums and heritage sites in a more sustainable fashion (see Figure 12.1). This model encompasses many of the principles and practices of sustainability noted above and in Chapter 11 and suggests that heritage sites should work toward meeting their goals and objectives from a marketing perspective (see the center circle of the figure) but that these should also be guided by a set of practices that will better support the principles of sustainability and the ideals of research and conservation. Practices such as partnerships, involvement of local communities, environment analysis and conservation must underscore the marketing efforts of heritage sites as they continue in their efforts to educate, entertain and preserve.

AUTHENTICITY AS A MARKETING TOOL

Authenticity has become one of the trendiest marketing buzzwords in the world. It is in fact one of the chicest marketing gimmicks in leisure and tourism settings today. Many destinations, individual attractions, handicraft guilds and entrepreneurs have adopted

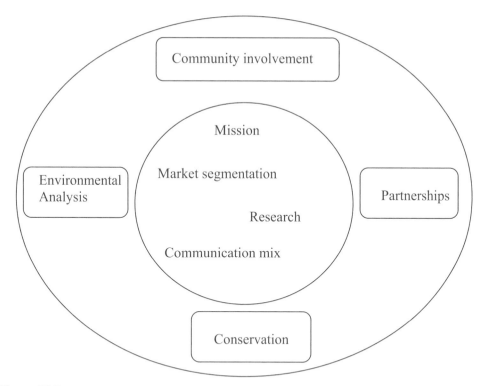

Figure 12.1 A sustainable marketing model

Source: Modified after Chhabra (2009)

'authenticity' to mean whatever they want it to mean as a channel for drawing a clientele. A scan through the internet for tourism-related businesses and attractions reveals thousands that claim some degree of authenticity in one way or another. Whether or not a place is truly authentic by anyone's standards is not important. What is important from the marketing perspective is consumers' perceptions of authenticity.

Visitors can take an 'authentic' African bush safari in the desert of Arizona. According to Out of Africa Wildlife Park's (2010) website:

> On the 45-minute African Bush Safari, you will experience the heart of Africa in the heart of Arizona. This is an authentic African photo safari with expert park guides narrating throughout your tour. While riding in a safari vehicle, you can expect a personal encounter with giraffe, zebra, ostrich and more. We provide treats so that you can feed the animals and maybe receive a gentle kiss from a giraffe. On nearby hills, prides of lions or other big cats overlook their domain, you, and the prey animals in the Safari. It's like Africa, only closer!

Visitors can also hold pythons, boas and anacondas; feed lions and tigers; and watch 'tiger splash', a show of tigers doing tricks in a swimming pool. While much of this safari experience would not be 'authentic' in the Serengeti (e.g. giraffe kisses and feeding the animals), for Arizonans and tourists visiting Arizona, such an experience might provide a cheaper alternative to an actual trip to East Africa. In this sense, 'substitute authenticity' becomes an important part of creating a product that satisfies the needs of visitors. The giraffes, lions and zebras are authentic giraffes, lions and zebras, but the setting, circumstances and activities are staged for an African wilderness experience in the US Southwest.

Holland is a popular Dutch settlement in western Michigan. Like the wildlife park example above, Nelis' Dutch Village in Holland, Michigan, provides its visitors with an authentic environment reminiscent of the Netherlands of a century ago. In the village managers' own words:

> Our theme park is a step back into the Netherlands of over 100 years ago, complete with authentic Dutch architecture, flowering gardens, canals and windmills. The history and culture of the Dutch come to life as our associates, dressed in native costumes including wooden shoes, demonstrate the crafts and life in those olden days. (Nelis' Dutch Village, 2010)

At Nelis' Dutch Village tourists can see the carving of wooden shoes, buy Delft ceramics, eat Dutch cuisine, purchase tulips and bulbs, see cheese being made and slide down a giant wooden shoe slide. Visitors can also step onto a 200-year-old witch scale to see if they are guilty of witchcraft and visit the costume museum and doll exhibit, which houses more than 150 different costumes from Holland.

Authenticity is not used only to market places but goods as well, including handicrafts. In one Navajo gift shop in Arizona, the author saw a selection of small blankets labeled 'authentic Indian blankets'. True enough, when the author turned one over to examine the label, it was made in India! So in fact, it really was an 'authentic Indian blanket' – just not the 'Indian' tourists would expect in Navajo country. Cedar Mesa Pottery, based in Blanding, Utah, and one of the most widespread marketers of Native American arts, labels its pieces 'authentic Native American art'. With each purchase of a Cedar Mesa Pottery piece, collectors are given a 'Certificate of Native American Authenticity' which guarantees that the art is signed or trademarked by Native American artists (see Plate 12.3). In countries such as Indonesia and Thailand, masks, rattan handbags, carvings, clothes, silk ties and bamboo products are often marketed as 'authentic' Thai or Indonesian art, even if they are made in the Philippines or China. Many of the handicrafts are made locally while others are imported but, regardless of origin, the operative concept is authenticity because it appeals to tourists' desire to own a genuine piece of Asia.

Restaurants use authenticity in their marketing efforts as well. 'Authentic Chinese food' on a restaurant window or 'authentic Mexican cuisine' on a menu is common all over the world. However, it is doubtful that the Chinese or Mexican food being offered would resemble the original cuisine of China or Mexico, as tastes and flavors differ significantly from culture to culture. If these restaurants truly offered Chinese food as served in China

Plate 12.3 Authenticity of Native American art is important in marketing indigenous heritage

or Mexican food as served in Mexico, many Finns, Canadians, Germans, Irish, Israelis, Jordanians, New Zealanders and Ghanaians would have little interest in eating it, just as many Chinese or Mexicans might turn up their noses at Finnish, Canadian, Irish or Ghanaian food. Ethnic cooking is almost always adapted to local tastes when prepared abroad. Nevertheless, heritage cuisines are commonly marketed as authentic or genuine as a way of drawing in customers. In short, heritage and tourism managers have learned that authenticity sells and genuineness is good business and, since authenticity cannot be defined objectively, anything can be considered authentic to someone.

SUMMARY AND CONCLUSION

Cultural resources can and should be marketed for tourism. Despite a history of not wanting to play into this capitalist notion, heritage managers now realize that scarce funds are requiring it. Heritage has long been used as a marketing mechanism for destination regions and individual sites, and will likely continue to be used far into the future. Likewise, the concept of authenticity is commonly used as a promotional mechanism to boost the image of a place or historic artifact. To be an authentic place is a significant competitive advantage over destinations that are not.

Unfortunately, decades of mass marketing, without regard for the consequences of large-scale, uncontrolled tourism, has resulted in many negative consequences. Careful marketing planning is needed for the best and most sustainable results to occur in cultural destinations. This is part of the growing notion of sustainable marketing, which entails place and product promotion in such as way that it does not diminish their historical or physical integrity. It involves stakeholder collaboration and community-based planning so that resources will continue to be resources far into the future.

REVIEW QUESTIONS

1. In what ways does cultural heritage play a role in the marketing mix of tourist destinations?

2. Have countries been successful in using the UNESCO heritage brand in their tourism promotional efforts? What evidence is there to this effect?

3. How does the popular media (e.g. TV and movies) provide free exposure for heritage destinations to a worldwide audience?

4. In what ways is heritage destination marketing unique to the needs of other destinations?

5. What characteristics of the seven Ps of marketing for heritage attractions differ from those in other contexts?

6. What are the key principles of sustainable marketing that debunk the notion of boosterism and assist in promoting the longevity of heritage attractions and destinations?

7. How can authenticity, as described in Chapter 5, be used as an effective marketing device?

RECOMMENDED READING

Austin, N.K. (2002) Managing heritage attractions: Marketing challenges at sensitive historical sites. *International Journal of Tourism Research* 4(6), 447–457.

Beeton, S. and Benfield, R. (2002) Demand control: The case for demarketing as a visitor and environmental management tool. *Journal of Sustainable Tourism* 10, 497–513.

Boyd, S.W. (2003) Marketing challenges and opportunities for heritage tourism. In A. Fyall, B. Garrod, and A. Leask (eds) *Managing Visitor Attractions: New Directions* (pp. 189–202). Oxford: Butterworth Heinemann.

Boyd, S.W. and Timothy, D.J. (2001) Developing partnerships: Tools for interpretation and management of World Heritage Sites. *Tourism Recreation Research* 26(1), 47–53.

Boyd, S.W. and Timothy, D.J. (2006) Marketing issues and World Heritage Sites. In A. Leask and A. Fyall (eds) *Managing World Heritage Sites* (pp. 55–68). Oxford: Butterworth Heinemann.

Che, D. (2006) Select Michigan: Local food production, food safety, culinary heritage, and branding in Michigan agritourism. *Tourism Review International* 9(4), 349–363.

Chhabra, D. (2010) *Sustainable Marketing of Cultural and Heritage Tourism.* London: Routledge.

Collins-Kreiner, N. and Olsen, D.H. (2004) Selling diaspora: Producing and segmenting the Jewish diaspora tourism market. In T. Coles and D.J. Timothy (eds) *Tourism, Diasporas and Space* (pp. 279–290). London: Routledge.

Collison, F.M. and Spears, D.L. (2010) Marketing cultural and heritage tourism: The Marshall Islands. *International Journal of Culture, Tourism and Hospitality Research* 4(2), 130–142.

Freire, J.R. (2005) Geo-branding, are we talking nonsense? A theoretical reflection on brands applied to places. *Place Branding* 1(4), 347–362.

Freire, J.R. (2009) 'Local people': A critical dimension for place brands. *Journal of Brand Management* 16, 420–438.

Friedman, M.T. and Silk, M.L. (2005) Expressing Fenway: Managing and marketing heritage within the global sports marketplace. *International Journal of Sport Management and Marketing* 1(1/2), 37–55.

Fyall, A. and Garrod, B. (2005) *Tourism Marketing: A Collaborative Approach*. Clevedon: Channel View Publications.

Geissler, G.L, Rucks, C.T. and Edison, S.W. (2006) Understanding the role of service convenience in art museum marketing: An exploratory study. *Journal of Hospitality and Leisure Marketing* 14(4), 69–87.

Genoways, H.H. and Ireland, L.M. (2003) *Museum Administration: An Introduction*. Walnut Creek, CA: AltaMira Press.

Gibson, C. and Davidson, D. (2004) Tamworth, Australia's 'country music capital': Place marketing, rurality, and resident reactions. *Journal of Rural Studies* 20(4), 387–404.

Hall, C.M. and McArthur, S. (1996) The marketing of heritage. In C.M. Hall and S. McArthur (eds) *Heritage Management in Australia and New Zealand: The Human Dimension* (pp. 74–97). Melbourne: Oxford University Press.

Hall, C.M. and McArthur, S. (1998) *Integrated Heritage Management: Principles and Practice*. London: The Stationery Office.

Hall, C.M., Mitchell, I. and Keelan, N. (1993) The implications of Maori perspectives for the management and promotion of heritage tourism in New Zealand. *GeoJournal* 29, 315–322.

Halls, S. (1994) Marketing heritage. *Leisure Manager* 12(4/5), 32–33.

Hausman, A. (2007) Cultural tourism: Marketing challenges and opportunities for German cultural heritage. *International Journal of Heritage Studies* 13(2), 170–184.

Herbert, D.T., Prentice, R. and Thomas, C.J. (eds) (1989) *Heritage Sites: Strategies for Marketing and Development*. Aldershot, UK: Ashgate.

Héroux, L. and Csipak, J. (2008) Marketing strategies of museums in Quebec and north-eastern United States. *Téoros: Revue de Recherche en Tourisme* 27(3), 35–42.

Kantanen, T. and Tikkanen, I. (2006) Advertising in low and high involvement cultural tourism attractions: Four cases. *Tourism and Hospitality Research* 6(2), 99–110.

Kolar, T. and Zabkar, V. (2010) A consumer-based model of authenticity: An oxymoron or the foundation of cultural heritage marketing? *Tourism Management* 31, 652–664.

Kolb, B.M. (2006) *Tourism Marketing for Cities and Towns: Using Branding and Events to Attract Tourists*. Oxford: Butterworth Heinemann.

Kotler, P., Bowen, J.T. and Makens, J.C. (2009) *Marketing for Hospitality and Tourism* (5th edn). New York: Prentice Hall.

Kozak, M. and Andreu, L. (eds) (2006) *Progress in Tourism Marketing*. Amsterdam: Elsevier.

Light, D. and Prentice, R.C. (1994) Market-based product development in heritage tourism. *Tourism Management* 15, 27–36.

Mattsson, J. and Praesto, A. (2005) The creation of a Swedish heritage destination: An insider's view of entrepreneurial marketing. *Scandinavian Journal of Hospitality and Tourism* 5(2), 152–166.

McArthur, S. and Hall, C.M. (1993) *Heritage Management in New Zealand and Australia: Visitor Management, Interpretation and Marketing*. Auckland: Oxford University Press.

McDonnell, I. and Burton, C. (2005) The marketing of Australian cultural tourist attractions: A case study from Sydney. In M. Sigala and D. Leslie (eds) *International Cultural Tourism: Management, Implications, and Cases* (pp. 16–25). Oxford: Butterworth Heinemann.

McLean, F.C. (1993) Marketing in museums: a contextual analysis. *Museum Management and Curatorship* 12(1), 11–27.

McLean, F.C. (1994) Services marketing: The case of museums. *Service Industries Journal* 14(2), 190–203.

McLean, F.C. (1997) *Marketing the Museum*. London: Routledge.

Mikulić, D. (2009) Marketing valorization of the city of Split as a cultural tourism destination. *Acta Turistica* 21(1), 95–122.

Misiura, S. (2006) *Heritage Marketing*. Oxford: Butterworth Heinemann.

Moresan, A. and Smith, K.A. (1998) Dracula's castle in Transylvania: Conflicting heritage marketing strategies. *International Journal of Heritage Studies* 4(2), 73–85.

Morgan, N., Pritchard, A. and Pride, R. (eds) (2004) *Destination Branding: Creating the Unique Destination Proposition*. Oxford: Butterworth Heinemann.

Pritchard, A. and Morgan, N. (2001) Culture, identity and tourism representation: Marketing Cymru or Wales? *Tourism Management* 22, 167–179.

Richards, G. (2000) Cultural tourism: Challenges for management and marketing. In W.C. Gartner and D.W. Lime (eds) *Trends in Outdoor Recreation, Leisure and Tourism* (pp. 187–195). Wallingford: CAB International.

Rowan, Y. and Baram, U. (eds) (2004) *Marketing Heritage: Archaeology and the Consumption of the Past*. Walnut Creek, CA: AltaMira Press.

Runyard, S. and French, Y. (1999) *The Marketing and Public Relations Handbook for Museums, Galleries and Heritage Attractions*. Walnut Creek, CA: AltaMira Press.

Seaton, A.V. and Bennett, M.M. (1996) *The Marketing of Tourism Products: Concepts, Issues, Cases*. London: Thomson.

Silberberg, T. (1995) Cultural tourism and business opportunities for museums and heritage sites. *Tourism Management* 16, 361–365.

Thompson, K., Schofield, P., Palmer, N. and Bakieva, G. (2006) Kyrgyzstan's Manas epos millennium celebrations: Post-colonial resurgence of Turkic culture and the marketing of cultural tourism. In D. Picard and M. Robinson (eds) *Festivals, Tourism and Social Change: Remaking Worlds* (pp. 172–190). Clevedon: Channel View.

Thorburn, A. (1986) Marketing cultural heritage: Does it work within Europe? *Travel and Tourism Analyst* 6, 39–48.

Thornley, L. and Waa, A. (2009) *Increasing Public Engagement with Historic Heritage: A Social Marketing Approach*. Wellington, New Zealand: Department of Conservation.

Wang, Y.J., Wu, C.K., and Yuan, J.X. (2009) The role of integrated marketing communications (IMC) on heritage destination visitations. *Journal of Quality Assurance in Hospitality and Tourism* 10(3), 218–231.

Wheeler, F., Reeves, K., Laing, J. and Frost, W. (2009) Niche strategies for small regional cities: A case study of the Bendigo Chinese Heritage Precinct Plan. *Tourism Recreation Research* 34(3), 295–306.

Wigle, R. (1994) Making history seem tempting: Marketing an historic site as a visitor attraction. *Journal of Travel and Tourism Marketing* 3(2), 95–101.

Wilkinson, P.F. (2003) Ecological integrity, visitor use, and marketing of Canada's national parks. *Journal of Park and Recreation Administration* 21(2), 63–83.

Yorke, D.A. and Jones, R.R. (1984) Marketing and museums. *European Journal of Marketing* 18(2), 90–99.

Zeppel, H. (1998) "Come share our culture": Marketing aboriginal tourism in Australia. *Pacific Tourism Review* 2(1), 67–81.

RECOMMENDED WEBSITES

American Association of Museums – http://www.aam-us.org/pubs/mn/MN_JA99_EffectiveMarketingPlan.cfm

Heritage Marketing – http://www.heritagemarketing.net/

Museum Marketing Blog – http://www.museummarketing.co.uk/

Sustainable Marketing – http://www.sustainablemarketing.com/

CHAPTER 13

RAISING REVENUE AND MANAGING VISITORS

LEARNING OBJECTIVES

After reading this chapter, you should be able to:

1. Identify the different types of ownership sectors involved in cultural heritage attractions.

2. Understand the financial problems facing heritage site managers today.

3. Be familiar with the most common revenue-generating approaches used by heritage site managers.

4. Know about the most common techniques used by heritage managers to affect visitor behavior.

5. Identify ways to enhance the heritage visitor experience.

6. Comprehend the role of pricing policies in visitor management.

7. Understand how managers can affect visitor flows and access to sensitive areas.

INTRODUCTION

One important way of mitigating the negative impacts of tourism is to manage visitors and their behavior. Heritage consumers should not be allowed to roam freely at sensitive cultural sites or in delicate ecosystems. Tourists have a tendency to make their mark, and many have a desire to depart from prescribed pathways. Without restricting access to certain areas or artifacts, many would also be inclined to touch and possibly break the relics and structures on display. Another key management concern these days is funding; heritage stewards have had to devise creative ways to carry out their mandates to protect the past and educate the public. Certain means have been used for many years to raise funds, but others are of a more recent vintage.

This chapter aims to address two of the premier closely-connected management problems in the realm of cultural heritage: funding and visitor use. The chapter first describes the three sectors involved in owning and/or operating cultural attractions, namely private, public and non-profit agencies, and the differences between them in terms of their ownership structure. It continues by examining the need for historic properties to raise their own funding given today's lean public coffers and the public's own need to cope with the economic downturn. Finally the chapter highlights some of the mechanisms available to heritage managers to help them handle and control visitors and minimize their potentially destructive behavior.

OWNERSHIP OF HERITAGE PLACES

In the domain of tourism and recreation services, we often speak of different types of ownership: private, public and non-profit sectors. Agencies, organizations and corporations in each of the three ownership sectors own and operate heritage attractions, although each one tends to have different management models, goals, financial situations and approaches to visitor involvement. Heritage sites in the private realm include but are not limited to outdoor folklife museums, galleries, industrial heritage places, museums, wineries and other agriculture-based attractions. The primary motive for such places is profit, although providing education and community well-being might be a secondary motive.

Publicly-owned and operated heritage sites often include ancient monuments and archaeological sites, national or local museums, archives and libraries, national or state/provincial parks and historic homes. The primary motives of public sites are conservation and education, although important secondary objectives include fundraising, access by the public to their own heritage and the stimulation of jobs and regional earnings through tourism.

Public-sector historic sites are operated on many scales. National parks, for example, are found in most countries of the world. At this level, policies are developed, and in most cases management agencies operate, at the national level. One exception to this is Australia, where although national park policies and laws are enacted in Canberra for the entire country, the park properties themselves are managed by state and territory governments. In countries such as Canada and the USA, national parks are administered directly by the federal governments through Parks Canada and the US National Park Service, the latter being located within the US Department of the Interior. State parks in the US and provincial parks in Canada are managed by those levels of government, as are county and municipal parks, many of which have a cultural heritage focus. In almost all cases, the most momentous sites and the majority of sites are owned and operated by public agencies.

Pearce (1997) noted several reasons why the public sector is so heavily involved in owning heritage places. Among the most salient is funding. Simple supply and demand principles are inadequate to assure sufficient funding to maintain and protect heritage places. Public funding is usually needed to supplement the mostly non-self sustaining heritage sector. Likewise, most heritage is the patrimony of society at large rather than simply belonging to one group. Thus, there is an inherent public interest in preserving the past. Third, many historic buildings are/were public buildings so they continue to be state-owned. Fourth, as noted already in this book, heritage places often commemorate significant places, events and people in the history and nation-building of a country or state/province and should be protected by the state. Finally, governments always have an interest in creating jobs and increasing regional income. As a result, they are active in preserving the past as a visitor resource that has potential to bring in income and improve local standards of living.

Finally, many agencies and organizations in the not-for-profit, or voluntary, sector own museums, historic buildings, heritage centers, cemeteries and archives. Like that of the public sector, the volunteer sector's main goals are to conserve and to earn enough money to support its sites, with secondary motives being public education, entertainment and community quality of life. Non-profit organizations that operate sites rely on both visitor-spent fees, such as entrance fees and sales in cafes or shops, and donations from philanthropic organizations and individuals. Government grants, sponsorships and other related revenue sources are also important for the non-profit heritage sector. The National Trust in the UK and the National Trust for Historic Preservation in the USA are two examples on the national scale, but there are many more at the community level that operate local museums or aim to protect landscapes, buildings, railways, schools, churches and public buildings that are important elements of the communities' past.

FUNDING THE PAST

Regardless of what agency or organization operates a heritage attraction, funding is of paramount concern. There are many variables that determine the importance of the role of fundraising for heritage protection, but three of the most salient are economic uncertainties, demand shifters and power.

In the past, during affluent times, museums and other heritage properties commonly had the luxury of being able to focus on their main goal of preservation and inter-pretation, rather than fundraising, because subsidies were forthcoming from private and public sources. Government grants for non-profit and privately-owned properties were commonplace. Line items in national and local government budgets were adequate, and in some cases generous. With worldwide economic recessions during the early 1980s, 1990s and into the 21st century, many government budgets dried up, or were severely reduced, for 'non-essential' activities such as cultural heritage protection. Intertwined with this are economic demand shifters, such as unemployment rates, that corresponded with the recessions noted above. During times of recession, more people are unemployed and businesses go bankrupt. This, too, was influential in the heritage sector, as fewer people felt they could afford the 'frivolous' luxury of visiting places of patrimonial importance. Thus, user fee-based income also dried up. Other social changes have occurred in recent

Table 13.1 Common revenue sources for cultural attractions

• Admission fees	• Interpretation
• Donations	• Hosting special events
• Retail sales	• Sponsorships
• Food and accommodations	• Grants

years as well, with certain populations growing or declining, many of which have a keener interest in visiting historic places.

Finally, politics and power underscore many elements of the budgetary crises and demand shifters noted above. Budgets depend very much on who is in power. Certain political parties are more inclined to value culture, arts and heritage conservation than others. Thus, rapid partisan turnover in some places has challenged the need for funding for publicly-owned museums, galleries, monuments, parks and other heritage attractions. The power-based interpretation of cultural importance is exacerbated by government budgetary deficits. In balancing budgets, funding for cultural activities and sites is among the first to be cut, because they are not considered as important as health care, social welfare, education or energy.

Preserving the past is very expensive and, given the situation noted above, heritage managers have had to be creative in devising ways to increase revenue. Besides cutting their budgets significantly, which most managers have done, there are other sources of revenue that many heritage stewards are adopting as a way of supplementing diminishing revenue sources (see Table 13.1).

Admission fees

User fees are among the most important revenue sources. There is considerable debate going on in academic and management circles, though, related to this so-called 'user pays' issue. Admission fees have long been part of the fiscal policy at most museums and heritage sites. People who argue in favor of charging admission fees, or even increasing them, suggest that given fiscal constraints, it is vital for visitors to pay entrance fees to subsidize heritage budgets. In most cases this is not a problem, as most heritage visitors are more affluent than the average population and admission fees are a normal part of the history of heritage visitation. On the other side of the aisle, however, is a smaller contingent of observers who argue that people should not have to pay to see their own heritage, for in fact it is 'their heritage'. This perspective embraces the idea of free access to the people whose heritage is on display.

Fyall and Garrod (1998) suggest that entrance fees are a good thing because when visitors are required to pay, they will likely be less destructive and will appreciate the site more. Likewise, they suggest that because visitors are the ones causing damage to sites

Plate 13.1 Admission prices for foreigners at this museum in Bhutan are ten times higher than for Bhutanese

they should pay for its prevention or repair. Fees can also help reduce traffic at critical periods of time and in sensitive areas.

This debate, together with pressing economic conditions, has led many heritage site managers in the developing world to enact dual-pricing policies. In dual systems everyone pays to enter heritage attractions, but for the people to whom the heritage belongs (i.e. locals or people from neighboring countries) entrance fees are minimal. This parallel pricing system can be seen throughout Asia, Africa and other less-developed regions of the world. In some cases, the difference between the price for residents and that for foreigners can be 10 or 20 times (see Plate 13.1). Although this is seen as a fair way of providing access for local people to their heritage, while still earning money from more affluent foreign tourists, it is an extremely unpopular policy among many foreign visitors, who see this as yet another way to 'rip-off' the tourist.

Donations

Admission fees can be in the form of donations. Some historic places do not charge a set fee, but instead provide a drop box where donations can be made to support the efforts of the property (see Plate 13.2). This is sometimes in lieu of admittance costs, and each individual can donate whatever he or she wishes. Some sites recommend a minimum

Plate 13.2 A typical donation box at a heritage site

amount. Donation boxes might be placed near exits or other locations to elicit additional donations beyond the cost of admission.

The most substantial form of donation, though, is large gifts from individual philanthropists, corporations or other organizations with either an altruistic or business motive or a mix of both. In some countries, such as the USA, donating large sums of money to non-profit trusts, including museums and other heritage places, has several tax benefits. Some companies donate as a way of building public relations and creating a good public image.

Retail sales

Most retail sales come from souvenir vending. Tourists love to spend, and many would not feel a vacation trip was complete without buying a souvenir. Several studies have shown that heritage tourists are bigger spenders than other types of travelers, and shopping is among the most popular non-heritage activities undertaken by heritage enthusiasts.

Almost all museums have some form of retail point, ranging from a desk where postcards are sold to elaborate shops where visitors can buy everything from replicas to food items (see Plate 13.3). Miniature figurines or replicas, models, books and magazines, salt and pepper shakers, mugs and shot glasses, T-shirts, carvings and handicrafts are

Plate 13.3 A museum store at the Smithsonian, Washington, DC

among the most common souvenirs sold at heritage sites. Souvenirs that are significant representations of the place visited and are made locally are the most appealing for cultural tourists, so many managers have begun commissioning local craftspeople to supply such artifacts for sale. Museums are not the only heritage properties to offer merchandise to visitors. Even ancient churches in Europe are known for selling postcards, candles and books to supplement their maintenance budgets.

Besides official shops, it is common to find vendors (licensed and unlicensed) at important heritage locations (see Plate 13.4). Sometimes these are encouraged to add appeal to the site and because they are required to pay a fee or commission to the property manager. To observe artists on site is appealing for many heritage tourists; the artists also pay vendors' fees and assist in keeping consumers longer so that they might spend more money.

Care must be taken not to allow merchandising efforts to overshadow the primary purpose of the site – conservation – even though it is important. Vendors should be organized and not allowed to gather so densely that they block views of the monument or deteriorate the built environment. Likewise, they must be trained not to harass visitors, for this decreases visitors' satisfaction with their experiences and can damage a site's good reputation.

Plate 13.4 Formal souvenir vendors at Lumbini, Nepal, the birthplace of Buddha

Accommodations and food services

Heritage communities, and even some heritage sites, have begun offering places for tourists to sleep and eat. In historic cities, old homes or other buildings are often converted to bed and breakfast lodging which, if managed correctly, can enhance the overall heritage experience and create more satisfied visitors and therefore increase spending. Some heritage attractions provide accommodations on site. Religious sites are especially adept at offering tourist lodging because of the high number of pilgrims that desire to stay on site. The New Valamo Monastery in Heinävesi, Finland, for example, is a popular destination for Finns belonging to the Orthodox Church, but also for cultural tourists interested in cultural and political history.

Food services are regularly offered at museums in coffee shops or restaurants. These serve a dual purpose: they bring in additional revenue and cater to the refreshment needs of visitors. These are particularly important in large museums, exhibitions and archaeological sites, where visitors might spend several hours wandering about. Meals, drinks and refreshments are a welcome respite that also lend allure to heritage attractions. Sometimes foods are adapted to period forms or ethnic types, but in most cases visitors can eat varying forms of fast food, sit-down meals or snacks (see Plate 13.5).

Plate 13.5 This cafe sells Native American traditional food at the National Museum of the American Indian in Washington, DC

Interpretation

While many interpretive media are included in the entrance fee or are fixed at exhibit locations, interpretation can in some cases also be used to increase revenue flows. Even if displays are well marked and explained, audio tours are popular options and can be rented for an additional fee at some attractions. Selling (or renting out) guidebooks and maps to help visitors navigate their way through a museum or around an archaeological area is a popular option, and some places charge a small fee for group tours.

Special events

As a way of offsetting low demand during low season, many seasonal tourist attractions, such as ski resorts, provide alternatives to the main product that will help maintain income levels. The same can be done at heritage sites. Whether during low or high season, events can attract visitors and increase earnings. Vendors, such as publishers or travel agents, pay a fee to participate in events. Museums are an excellent venue for art shows or stamp and coin fairs. Historic houses often rent out rooms and gardens for wedding receptions or banquets, and theatrical performances can be done at outdoor areas, such as archaeological sites (see Plate 13.6).

Plate 13.6 Extra income is earned at the ruins of Caesarea, Israel, by hosting a wedding reception

Sponsorship

Unlike donations, which are essentially gifts, sponsorship is a funding source that requires an in-kind payment of some sort. Naming a historic theater after an airline or hotel company in exchange for a considerable 'gift' to the theater is a good example. Including a corporation's logo on a museum's guidebooks is another example. Some heritage properties go so far as to offer unashamed advertising space at ticket booths, entrances, restrooms, cafeterias and even on interpretive displays. While traditionally this would have been considered repugnant by heritage custodians, it is becoming more of a reality in today's economic and political climate.

Grants

Public, non-profit and even private heritage attractions can apply for government or philanthropic grants. Some public agencies have a limited amount of money set aside to bestow as one-time gifts to private or volunteer organizations such as museums. Most grants are extremely competitive and involve a demonstration of many principles of sustainable development, including cooperation, cultural integrity, green marketing and effective visitor management. Supranational alliances, such as the North American Free Trade Agreement and the European Union, sometimes have grant competitions through various structural funds to support community-drive heritage conservation and tourism development projects. Establishing community museums, securing higher levels of training for park staff or cross-border collaboration on an archaeological dig or con-servation project are illustrations of acceptable projects for this type of funding.

VISITOR MANAGEMENT

Historically, heritage managers have looked upon tourists as a 'necessary evil', a means of supporting the true goals of the institution — conservation and education. While that is still the mindset of many curators and custodians, visitors are now more commonly being accepted as an important part of the management and functioning of heritage places. As a result, managers are looking at ways to improve the visitor experience, which is not only the altruistic thing to do — it can also result in additional funding through repeat visitation, positive word of mouth and donations, as well as an increased public appreciation for the past which, according to interpretation specialists, can cause people to be more respectful of the built patrimony and work for its conservation.

Managing visitors is a complex task for it involves skillful employees, effective inter-pretation, solid conservation methods and good marketing approaches. The goals of heritage management include educating visitors and providing enjoyable experiences for them. More importantly for this chapter, visitor management specifically includes, among other efforts, implementing mechanisms that help reduce the negative social and ecological impacts, such as overcrowding and wear and tear. In doing this, visitation at important attractions becomes more sustainable and visitors' experiences will be more enjoyable and educational.

There is a large assortment of techniques often utilized by heritage managers to affect visitors' behavior. These range from tools that help the spatial flow of crowds to those that help de-market sensitive places (e.g. pricing controls) and those that influence people's behavior through education and awareness-building.

Restricting access to relics

This is one of the most common ways of mitigating the many negative physical impacts of tourism and is frequently used to keep visitors from touching, walking on or otherwise damaging the built environment. Specific devices have proven to be effective in keeping consumers from touching sensitive surfaces and handling artifacts.

Blocking off displays or sensitive artifacts is an everyday practice at museums, archaeological sites and historic homes (see Plate 13.7). Chains or ropes are used to block entrance to exhibits where people might otherwise sit on an old, delicate chair, touch antique kitchen accoutrements, touch artworks or handle vintage toys. Another device is covering objects with glass or plastic (see Plate 13.8). This keeps people from touching fragile items, and locks on cabinets assure that nobody but authorized staff members have access to the relics. It is incumbent upon curators to assure that the tools used to restrict access do not obstruct visitors' views of the objects on display.

Plate 13.7 Railings keep tourists from touching ancient Native American petroglyphs

Plate 13.8 Ancient artifacts in a museum covered to prevent contact with visitors

Trails, pathways and boardwalks in sensitive areas are another essential management apparatus. This 'hardening', as it is known, establishes corridors that lead people from place to place within a heritage area, exacting only minimal impact on the physical environment (see Plate 13.9). While some space must obviously be sacrificed for paving trails or building a boardwalk, the concept suggests that some linear impact is better than visitors wandering everywhere, eroding the soil, bedrock and cultural structures in the process. Parking lots are another type of hardening. Car parks are necessary for visitation to flourish, but they should be far enough away from the site to assure that they do not distract from the heritage resource(s) on display and have no physical impact on historic structures. Likewise, the materials used to harden areas must suit the environmental esthetic of the place and correspond with the local heritage character of the place.

Another way of restricting access to buildings and artifacts is through intimidation via video cameras and security guards. While this might sound harsh, it is a simple and commonplace practice wherein visitors are made aware that their actions are being watched. This can effectively dissuade those who might intentionally do harm to an object from acting on their impulses. Breaking, chipping, carving and spray painting are avoidable if people's behavior is being monitored. In addition to discouraging vandalism, video

Plate 13.9 This trail through a heritage landscape in New Brunswick, Canada, is well 'hardened'

evidence can help prosecute those who cause damage. Guards provide verbal warnings and help monitor people's actions and movements through an exhibit.

Most tourists want to bring something home from their travels; many also want to leave something of their own to mark a place as having been visited by them. This has resulted in many instances of collectors breaking pieces of statues or mosaics, as well as leaving signs of themselves, such as graffiti or engraved surfaces. Souvenir shops can help satisfy the need to take home a memento. Some visitor management specialists have suggested that if visitors are provided with a surface where they can 'leave their mark' they will be less prone to damage buildings and other artifacts. Guest books are one option, which allow visitors to express their feelings and frustrations. Some observers have recommended 'graffiti walls' where youngsters can scribble their names, but this has the potential to encourage scribbling in areas where it should not be done.

Controlling visitor flows

Congestion is damaging from two perspectives: it can ruin visitors' heritage experiences and it has the potential to exacerbate physical impacts on the site itself. At the busiest heritage properties, visitor numbers can amount to hundreds, or even thousands, per hour during high season. In this case, efforts must be made to mitigate visitor use and crowding. There are several ways of controlling traffic at heavily visited heritage attractions. One of the most common is signage. Interpretative signs are useful in directing people away from sensitive areas and in warning people against touching or leaning against delicate surfaces. Even audio tours and brochures can be used as communication devices to ease crowding by encouraging alternate routes or areas.

Another effective tool is limiting group sizes and visitation hours. For example, visits by large groups (e.g. school or church groups and tour groups) can be assigned to times when museums or monuments are less congested, such as a Thursday morning or Monday afternoon. Likewise, size restrictions can be placed on large groups so that they are divided into smaller parties that enter in succession. Making appointments for large groups is another approach now being considered by some site managers.

Although considered an extreme measure, visitor quotas might be helpful in some instances in keeping crowds at manageable levels. Some compact, historic cities (e.g. Venice and Rothenburg ob der Tauber) have considered implementing visitor quotas, but of course this can only be done in geographical situations where there are easily-defined entrance and exit points. This is also a controversial option because of limitations it puts on local merchants and service providers, as well as on tourists' opportunities to visit when they are free to travel.

Related to visitor quotas is the idea of congestion pricing in urban areas. Some cities have adopted policies that charge car owners, sometimes including motor coaches and taxis, to use the most crowded portions of historic centers or downtowns any time during the day. Other policies charge vehicle operators a fee for using city centers only during the busiest times of the day. Singapore was the first to succeed in its congestion pricing scheme. Vehicles entering a seven square-kilometer zone in the city's historic central business district ('restricted zone') are required to pay a user fee. Vehicle activity is monitored and charged electronically. This system, which was established in the 1970s, has reduced traffic in the historic city center and increased the use of public transportation. Given the success of Singapore, other historic cities have followed suit, including London with its Congestion Charge Zones, Milan, Stockholm, Rome, Durham (England), Riga (Latvia) and Valletta (Malta). This mechanism is seen as having a dual benefit: reducing crowdedness during peak periods and cutting the environmental costs associated with dense vehicular traffic, which includes historic buildings, gardens and parks. Similarly, park-and-ride facilities and marketing campaigns to encourage the public to use mass transit help alleviate many of the ecological and social pressures associated with historic cities.

De-marketing efforts can discourage people from visiting the most sensitive and crowded parts of a town or archaeological complex, but efforts also have to be made to encourage visits to less susceptible areas. Planning and marketing heritage areas and historic communities in a holistic fashion, rather than highlighting specific sites or buildings, provides the best chance for this approach to succeed.

Pricing policies

Entrance fees can be manipulated to control visitor numbers if needed. Pricing has long been an important management mechanism, one that 'prices out' less desirable population cohorts. Many research studies have shown that the more educated and more affluent a person is, he or she is less inclined to do intentional damage to a heritage property. Thus, a common generalization is that the blue-collar classes are mass tourists, the most damaging sort, or are involved more often in vandalism. The white-collar classes, on the other hand, are presumed to be better-educated, special-interest travelers, who exact less damage on the built environment. Although this seems to be a harsh practice and is highly controversial as being an elitist and prejudicial policy, it is still used widely as a way of reducing demand. Care must be taken, however, to achieve a delicate balance between pricing and demand, for intervening opportunities (i.e. other, less-expensive museums and sites) might draw some visitors away. This is more common at sites that have experienced exceedingly high numbers of visitors and visible impacts have begun to occur. Fees can help lessen the effects of seasonality as well. During the busiest times of year, prices go up, increasing earnings and easing congestion, while during seasons of low demand, prices can be reduced to attract more guests.

Most economic impact and pricing studies illustrate that heritage tourism is less elastic than other types of tourism. This means that increased prices will deter heritage visitors less often than they would in other tourism circumstances. As prices increase demand for cultural heritage remains fairly constant.

Managing the visitor experience

According to Moscardo (1996), mindful visitors are people who are receptive to learning and who pay more attention to learning and activity programs than mindless visitors. They are the people who enjoy heritage sites most and appreciate what is being preserved and interpreted. Moscardo maintains that mindfulness within visitors can be encouraged by staff, who connect with the visitors, involve them in the experience, relate good stories that make sense, provide a variety of experience and try to know and respect the needs and desires of visitors.

This is an important part of providing high-quality experiences. Good customer service is just as important at public, private and non-profit heritage centers as it is in other private-sector services. Friendly service, pleasant attitudes and plentiful, accurate information will translate into people enjoying their visit more, leading to more respect for the place and potentially positive word of mouth promotion and return visits. Pearson and Sullivan (1995: 284) argue that 'A pleasant, helpful reception is a good insurance against direct damage'. Likewise, interpretation that provides information and grabs the interest of people of all ages helps stimulate mindfulness and may contribute to more satisfactory visits.

Other mundane details, such as clean toilets, adequate baby-changing facilities, short queues and plentiful waiting space (e.g. benches or chairs), also contribute to a hassle-free experience. A particularly important management issue is those requirements associated with visitors with special needs. These valued guests include young families with small children, the elderly, people with physical or learning disabilities and foreign tourists who might not understand the language of the destination. Feeding and changing facilities for babies is essential in museums and heritage sites whose market segments include families and/or children. Likewise, shorter toilets and drinking fountains should be provided and baby carriages can be available for rent. For the elderly, frequent rest areas with seats and water are a good idea. Wheelchairs or scooters (where feasible) can also be provided for the elderly as part of the admission charges or rented out for a small fee, and it is important to design display areas with minimal slopes and textured floor surfaces. Adapted interpretive programs for people with learning or physical disabilities (see Chapter 10) are vital and required by law in most western countries. And, for international visitors, staff members who are able to communicate in the languages of the primary markets are invaluable in building bridges, generating mindfulness and creating overall satisfactory guest experiences.

SUMMARY AND CONCLUSION

This chapter addressed two of the most pressing concerns for cultural attraction administrators, namely funding and visitor management. Without doubt these are two of the most important management matters in the heritage context. Without adequate funding and proper visitor controls, heritage resources cannot be administered in a sustainable manner. There are many fundraising approaches available to site managers, not least of which include admission fees, grants, donations and hosting special events. Some approaches of more recent vintage (e.g. souvenir shops, cafes, special events) are viewed with disdain by many site managers, who are more traditional in their approach to conservation. Nonetheless, they do realize the need to fund their own mandate to protect and educate. With public funding dwindling, they have little choice but to seek alternative sources of revenue.

Monitoring and regulating visitors is another issue of paramount concern. Minimizing human contact with historic artifacts and buildings, controlling crowds and creating mindful, or appreciative, guests are only a few of the most common methods for managing heritage tourists and protecting a non-renewable past.

REVIEW QUESTIONS

1. What are the types of cultural attractions most commonly owned and operated by the public, private and non-profit sectors?

2. How have heritage managers' attitudes toward visitors/tourists changed in recent years and why?

3. Why have heritage sites been facing monumental fiscal setbacks in recent years?

4. What are the most successful methods used by cultural attraction managers to supplement their funding?

5. How can visitor access to artifacts and sites be restricted most effectively? Why is this important?

6. How is de-marketing a potentially useful tool in directing visitor crowds?

7. In what ways do pricing policies help alleviate congestion at museums and historic sites?

RECOMMENDED READING

Aas, C., Ladkin, A. and Fletcher, J. (2005) Stakeholder collaboration and heritage management. *Annals of Tourism Research* 32, 28–48.

Ashworth, G.J. and Howard, P. (1999) *European Heritage Planning and Management.* Exeter: Intellect.

Biran, A., Poria, Y. and Reichel, A. (2006) Heritage site management: The link between visitors' pre-visit perceptions, motivations and expectations. *Anatolia* 17(2), 279–304.

Blandford, C. (2006) Management plans for UK World Heritage Sites: Evolution, lessons and good practice. *Landscape Research* 31(4), 355–362.

Boniface, P. (1995) *Managing Quality Cultural Tourism.* London: Routledge.

Butcher-Younghans, S. (1993) *Historic House Museums: A Practical Handbook for their Care, Preservation and Management.* New York: Oxford University Press.

Corsane, G. (ed.) (2005) *Heritage, Museums and Galleries: An Introductory Reader.* London: Routledge.

Drummond, S. and Yeoman, I. (eds) (2001) *Quality Issues in Heritage Visitor Attractions.* Oxford: Butterworth Heinemann.

du Cros, H. (2007) Too much of a good thing? Visitor congestion management issues for popular World Heritage tourist attractions. *Journal of Heritage Tourism* 2(3), 225–238.

du Cros, H. and Lee, Y.F. (2007) *Cultural Heritage Management in China: Preserving the Cities of the Pearl River Delta.* London: Routledge.

Garrod, B. (2007) A snapshot into the past: The utility of volunteer-employed photography in planning and managing heritage tourism. *Journal of Heritage Tourism* 2(1), 14–35.

Goulty, S.M. (1993) *Heritage Gardens: Care, Conservation and Management.* London: Routledge.

Hall, C.M. and McArthur, S. (eds) (1996) *Heritage Management in Australia and New Zealand: The Human Dimension.* Melbourne: Oxford University Press.

Hall, C.M. and McArthur, S. (1998) *Integrated Heritage Management: Principles and Practice.* London: The Stationery Office.

Hang, L.K.P. and Kong, C. (2001) Heritage management and control: The case of Egypt. *Journal of Quality Assurance in Hospitality and Tourism* 2(1/2), 105–117.

Harrison, R. (1994) *Manual of Heritage Management.* Oxford: Butterworth Heinemann.

Ho, P. and McKercher, B. (2004) Managing heritage resources as tourism products. *Asia Pacific Journal of Tourism Research* 9(3), 255–266.

Hoffman, B.T. (ed.) (2006) *Art and Cultural Heritage: Law, Policy and Practice.* Cambridge: Cambridge University Press.

Howard, P. (2003) *Heritage: Management, Interpretation Identity.* London: Continuum.

Landorf, C. (2009) A framework for sustainable heritage management: A study of UK industrial heritage sites. *International Journal of Heritage Studies* 15(6), 494–510.

Leask, A. and Fyall, A. (eds) (2006) *Managing World Heritage Sites.* Oxford: Butterworth Heinemann.

Leask, A. and Fyall, A. (2007) Managing World Heritage. *Journal of Heritage Tourism* 2(3), 131–132.

Leask, A. and Yeoman, I. (eds) (1999) *Heritage Visitor Attractions: An Operations Management Perspective.* London: Thomson.

Lord, G.D. and Lord, B. (2009) *The Manual of Museum Management* (2nd edn). Lanham, MD: AltaMira.

Lyon, S.W. (2007) Balancing values of outstanding universality with conservation and management at three United Kingdom cultural world heritage sites. *Journal of Heritage Tourism* 2(1), 53–63.

McArthur, S. and Hall, C.M. (1993) *Heritage Management in New Zealand and Australia: Visitor Management, Interpretation and Marketing.* Auckland: Oxford University Press.

McKercher, B. and du Cros, H. (2002) *Cultural Tourism: The Partnership between Tourism and Cultural Heritage Management.* New York: Haworth.

McKercher, B., Ho, P.S.Y. and du Cros, H. (2005) Relationship between tourism and cultural heritage management: Evidence from Hong Kong. *Tourism Management* 26, 539–548.

McManamon, F.P., Stout, A. and Barnes, J.A. (2008) *Managing Archaeological Resources: Global Context, National Programs, Local Actions*. Walnut Creek, CA: Left Coast Press.

Merriman, N. (1991) *Beyond the Glass Case: The Past, the Heritage and the Public*. Walnut Creek, CA: Left Coast Press.

Millar, S. (1989) Heritage management for heritage tourism. *Tourism Management* 10, 9–14.

Moore, K. (ed.) (1994) *Museum Management*. London: Routledge.

Poria, Y., Reichel, A. and Biran, A. (2006) Heritage site management: Motivations and expectations. *Annals of Tourism Research* 33, 162–178.

Prideaux, B., Timothy, D.J. and Chon, K.S. (eds) (2008) *Cultural and Heritage Tourism in Asia and the Pacific*. London: Routledge.

Shackley, M. (1998) *Visitor Management: Case Studies from World Heritage Sites*. Oxford: Butterworth Heinemann.

Shackley, M. (2001) Sacred World Heritage Sites: Balancing meaning with management. *Tourism Recreation Research* 26(1), 5–10.

Sigala, M. and Leslie, D. (eds) (2005) *International Cultural Tourism: Management, Implications, and Cases*. Oxford: Butterworth Heinemann.

Swarbrooke, J. (1995) *The Development and Management of Visitor Attractions*. Oxford: Butterworth Heinemann.

Watkins, J. and Wright, T. (eds) (2007) *The Management and Maintenance of Historic Parks, Gardens and Landscapes*. London: English Heritage.

Willis, K.G. (2009) Assessing visitor preferences in the management of archaeological and heritage attractions: A case study of Hadrian's Roman Wall. *International Journal of Tourism Research* 11, 487–505.

RECOMMENDED WEBSITES

Cultural Heritage Search Engine – http://www.culturalheritage.net/

Europa Nostra – http://www.europanostra.org/

European Network of Cultural Centres-Historic Monuments – http://www.accr-europe.org/Default.aspx?AspxAutoDetectCookieSupport=1

European Network of Regional Culinary Heritage –
http://www.culinary-heritage.com/

Heritage Organizations in Europe – http://www.heritage-organisations.eu/page?page=-home2&lng=2

International Council of Museums – http://icom.museum/

International Council on Monuments and Sites –
http://www.international.icomos.org/home.htm

National Register of Historic Places –
http://www.nps.gov/history/nr/travel/index.htm

Oasis Project – http://oasis.ac.uk/

SECTION 2

CHAPTER 14

MUSEUMS: KEEPERS OF THE PAST

LEARNING OBJECTIVES

After reading this chapter, you should be able to:

1. Be aware of the wide array of different types of museums.

2. Understand the locational advantages and disadvantages of museums.

3. Appreciate the most common challenges facing museums and their managers today.

4. Know how museums help create social capital in broader society.

5. Discover recent trends in demand focus and product delivery in museums.

6. Learn about technology's role in interpreting and marketing museums.

INTRODUCTION

The forerunners to today's museums were personal collections of the social elites in Europe and elsewhere. Their compilations of art and antiquities (often supplemented by acquisitions brought back from overseas by explorers and traders) were housed in their private residences, where the privileged in society were permitted to visit the collections at the owner's discretion, sometimes for a fee. Museums became popularized, open to the public, during the 17th century with the earliest being in England, Switzerland and France. The Royal Armouries in the Tower of London opened in 1660. The Amerbach Cabinet opened to the public in Basel, Switzerland, in 1671. The Musée des Beaux-Arts et d'archéologie de Besançon in France was established in 1694. Other famous museums, such as the Louvre, were opened in the 18th century. Museums in North America, Australia, New Zealand and other non-European locales eventually became established in the 19th and 20th centuries.

Museums may be defined as institutions where collections of artifacts are housed and protected for their historical, artistic or scientific significance. The collections are open for public observation and may be permanent or temporary (Alexander & Alexander, 2008). There are literally tens of thousands of museums all over the world. In addition to world-famous museums that draw people from far away, there are countless small, local museums that concentrate on a very specific topic – the location's history or an influential

Plate 14.1 A local fort museum in Khasab, Oman

individual are the most numerous. The local museum movement sprang to life between the 1970s and the 1990s, and nearly every village, rural district, town and city in the world now has its own historical or heritage museum (see Plate 14.1). In most cases the smaller museums were developed in recent years as a way of commemorating important people and events, revitalizing rural communities, empowering the people and creating jobs.

The focus of this chapter is current and future trends and issues facing museum directors and curators everywhere. The chapter first examines museums as visitor resources, followed by a discussion of conceptual matters that significantly impact museum management today: visitors' time constraints, criticisms of living museums, developing social capital, democratizing museums, political correctness and more accurate heritage, ecomuseum development and internet-based marketing.

MUSEUMS AS VISITOR RESOURCES

Given the definition of museums described above, there is a wide assortment of different types of museums. Terrisse (2007) outlined four primary categories of museums based upon their form, function and management style:

- 'nineteenth century types' which take a simply esthetic approach to their collections without considering popular tastes;
- cultural centers, which provide ancillary services such as displays, cultural performances, libraries and restaurants;
- museums that function as tools for regional development;
- heritage centers, which can be viewed as half museum and half theme park.

While there is considerable overlap between these types of museums, it is a useful attempt to conceptualize the museum form. Additional types of museums could also include visitor centers, which include offices, interpretive areas, gift shops and ticket booths usually located at park entrances or near historic homes and archaeological sites.

The most common way of seeing museum types, however, is based upon the artifacts they accommodate. The following is a broad-based way of categorizing various museum types based upon their resources or their primary focal theme.

- Art museums house collections of artworks of various sorts. Many are geared around the works of famous artists from history, such as Rembrandt, Monet and Picasso. Others focus on modern art by contemporary artists, while there are many that include a combination of both. Sculpture, pottery, woodwork and clothing museums are examples of other art museums.
- War/military museums recount military history and commemorate one specific war or wars in general. They include artifacts related to battlefronts, such as cannons, tanks, ammunition, uniforms and military medals. War museums typically don a highly nationalist perspective and usually tell the story of war from their own nation's perspective.
- Industrial museums in most cases are located in former industrial complexes, such as factories, warehouses or dockyards. Their collections include samples of the resources extracted or produced in the industrial works, such as gold, copper or automobiles and tell the story of the industry's development and possible decline.
- Science museums celebrate technological advances and scientific breakthroughs. They typically include interactive programs, demonstrations and displays of technology. Some common themes include transportation history, computer technology, aerospace engineering, geology, inventions, ecology and animal life.
- Natural history museums are similar to science centers in many respects, as they focus on the natural realm. Natural processes (e.g. fluvial morphology, volcanism and glaciation), paleontological finds, outer space and ecosystems are important themes.
- Archaeological museums house collections of ancient artifacts. Some of them are located on site, in places of archaeological significance. Others are located in cities, with the relics being brought from other places. Period or regional themes are common, such as Roman, Byzantine, Egyptian or Greek periods and locations (see Plate 14.2).
- Maritime museums are geared around coastal areas and oceans and seas as human and wildlife habitats. Ship-building, fishing, shipwrecks and naval history are salient elements of this type of museum, which often also preserve elements of the natural world, such as coral and fish varieties.
- Folk museums and cultural centers are part of the museum experience as well. These living history museums depict life as it was lived at some particular point in

Plate 14.2 This archaeological museum in Thessaloniki houses artifacts from all over northern Greece

history or among a specific ethnic group. Costumed actors, period furnishings and dwellings illustrate some elements of everyday life in the past. Ethnic villages or cultural centers are extremely popular in Asia and the Pacific Islands and they have many counterparts in Europe and North America.

- Local historical museums are small-scale establishments that depict history in a specific location. Most local collections do not have a subject theme but rather focus on the history of the place, with a mixed variety of artifacts and stories from many eras of the past and including many different themes. They often have specific rooms set aside for different time periods or themes.
- In addition to these commonplace museums there are thousands of establishments that spotlight very specific interests or issues. These can be found in all parts of the world and include museums whose entire subject matter hinges on sports, music, stamps, coins, railroads, toys, illicit drugs, prostitution, books, postcards, buttons, farm equipment, law enforcement, religion, food, criminals, spies or murder. These are only a few examples – there are museums devoted to almost every element of personal, work, educational and family life (see Plate 14.3).

Plate 14.3 This tiny brick border museum lies just a few inches inside the Netherlands and is popular among border enthusiasts

As already noted, scale has a lot to do with the nature of a museum and its location. Museums of a grand scale can draw tourists from all over the world specifically to experience them (see Table 14.1). The Louvre is visited by almost 9 million people each year and is probably the most famous museum in the world. These associations house large collections of famous artworks and ancient artifacts, and are 'anchor attractions' in their respective locations – people arrive specifically to see them. A trip to Paris would not be complete without a visit to the Louvre, and an excursion to at least one of the Smithsonian Institute's museums is a crucial part of any visit to America's capital (see Plate 14.4).

Table 14.1 Some of the best-known museums that attract millions of visitors each year

Museum	Location
The Louvre	Paris, France
The British Museum	London, UK

Metropolitan Museum of Art	New York, USA
The Smithsonian Institute Museums	Washington, DC, USA
Hermitage Museum	St Petersburg, Russia
Guggenheim Museum	Bilboa, Spain
The Vatican Museums	Vatican City
Hagia Sophia	Istanbul, Turkey
Kyoto National Museum	Kyoto, Japan
National Gallery of Canada	Ottawa, Canada

There are more regional and local museums than those attracting millions of visitors on their own. In France alone there are approximately 1000 rural heritage museums, many of which play a salient role in the rural economy. Immigration museums dot the landscape of areas of heavy migration. Agriculture museums are common in rural areas and tell the

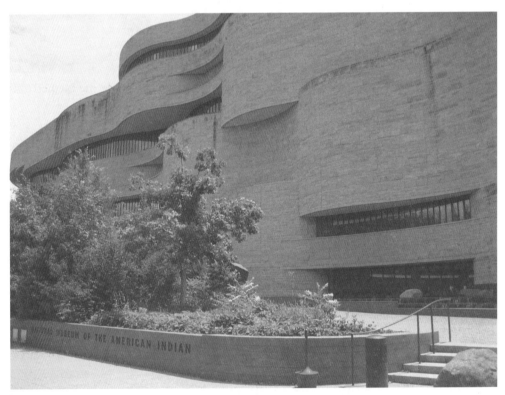

Plate 14.4 The Smithsonian's National Museum of the American Indian is an important attraction in Washington, DC

Plate 14.5 This small mining museum attracts few tourists but is part of the outback landscape of Australia

story of farming. Local mining museums are part of the peasant landscape that now appeals to tourists (see Plate 14.5).

Several studies have shown that 60–70% of visitors at average museums are domestic and foreign tourists, while the remaining guests are locals. It is likely that the percentage of out-of-town tourists is even higher among the biggest and most reputable museums, while for small-scale local establishments, the opposite is true. Nevertheless, all museums form an important part of a destination's tourism resource base that can be used to create civic pride and improve the local standard of living.

TRENDS WORTH WATCHING

Museums in all their forms face many of the same challenges that other cultural attractions have to deal with: interpretation, visitor management, human resources and budget shortfalls. These are not covered here, as they have been discussed in other parts of the book, but there are several contemporary concepts that are especially pertinent in the realm of museum management.

Time limitations

Something that many commentators have acknowledged is the fact that museums must compete with other activities and attractions for people's leisure time. In the past this was not such a significant problem. In modern societies, though, there is a real 'time squeeze' as people over-commit themselves with work, school and family duties, leaving little time for leisure pursuits. Even the recreational activities undertaken in today's fast-paced world are fast-paced endeavors, so that people have little time for slower pursuits like museums. Even when they do have a little extra time, they usually spend it on the internet or watching movies. Museums have in many cases slipped down the scale of priorities for leisure.

Museum visitors can also be looked at as agents of their own time. Some people spend hours in museums visiting every exhibit and absorbing as much information as possible. They are likely to be 'serious museum enthusiasts' whose hobbies include history, archaeology, art, sport, science or other themes found in various museums. Other customers may rush through a museum looking only at the displays that are of most interest to them while ignoring others. There is a range of possibilities for this behavior. Perhaps they are running short of time, or maybe their interests are limited to one or a few displays. For many visitors stepping into the museum and looking around briefly is simply a symbolic act; being in Paris 'requires' a visit to the Louvre, even if one is not interested in art. It is just a part of being in Paris. Limited leisure time and the de-prioritizing of museums in favor of other pursuits is a vital concern to museum managers today.

Criticisms of living museums

Of all the different types of museums, folklife museums receive the most criticism. Cultural purists point out the inauthentic nature of these outdoor centers, suggesting that they exude fakery and misrepresent history. Critics argue that such places are not dynamic; they remain frozen in time while the world around them evolves, and they cannot possible be truly authentic because nobody knows what the details of life were like centuries ago. In addition, some people suggest that using non-original building materials, mowing grass with gas-powered lawnmowers, putting in flushing toilets, working with electric lights or installing fire alarms or fire hydrants contribute to an unreal setting. In their minds, accurate representations of the distant past would not include modern conveniences. All of this combines to create a past that never existed and, according to opponents like Oliver (2001), site managers have ruined as much cultural heritage as they have preserved.

Supporters argue that the sites are not meant to be authentic in the strictest sense but rather representative and entertaining, and that visitors care little about whether or not original nails were used in building construction or whether the grass being fed to the cows is indigenous to the area. These cultural or heritage centers allow visitors to get away from their everyday cares and relax in an enjoyable and educational environment.

Certainly visitors are grateful for flushing toilets and air-conditioned cottages! As well, as noted in Chapter 5, what is an authentic experience to one person may not be to another. Of this type of situation, Herbert (1995: 45) contends:

> If visitors seek an experience from their visit which is meaningful to them ... should we be concerned whether that experience draws upon fact or reality, or whether or not the two can be distinguished? The answer to that question is 'probably not'. If the experience is authentic to the visitor, that is sufficient.

Developing social capital

Social capital is a term that originated in the early 1900s but which has gained widespread popularity during the 1990s and early 2000s. It refers to social connections or networks that have an innate value, not necessarily a monetary value but some kind of shared esteem for humankind. Social cohesion and community support for a cause, as well as one's personal investment in a community, are all manifestations of social capital.

Museum studies scholars often view museums as venues for building social capital. Market demand research finds that invariably people prefer to visit museums with other people. This builds relationships and extends people's social networks by having common experiences with people they know.

The rising popularity of volunteering indicates a desire to pursue leisured work experiences with like-minded people. Museum volunteers create social capital by helping to embed the establishment into the surrounding community, at the same time improving society's quality of life which returns to building support for the museum. This is in stark contrast to the elitist tendencies of museums in the past that set themselves above the community rather than being embedded within it. Social capital is created when educational facilities are created for locals, civic pride is enhanced and standards of living improved.

Democratization of museums: Visitor-oriented management

Museum management styles and techniques have changed dramatically in recent years, from decades ago when museums were seen as the caretakers of patrimony but rather inhospitable to visitors. Changing socio-economic climates have caused heritage managers to re-think their role in society. Because of this reconceptualization process, museums are for the most part now more visitor-oriented rather than simply artifact-oriented as their antecedents were (and some still are). In the words of one pair of commentators, '... museums have evolved from buildings devoted primarily to educational and cultural presentations into public spaces where the visitor reigns' (van Aalst & Boogaarts, 2002: 195). This 'democratization' of museums has several manifestations.

Part of the new culture of museum management deals with allowing the market to determine, to some degree at least, the artifacts that will be shown and the methods

327

used to show them. Interpretive planning is becoming more participatory than before. Museums in Europe are beginning to specialize in preservation and interpretation according to the preferences of visitors rather than simply what curators believe to be most important. Even in places with historically limited democratic environments, such as China, museums are becoming more democratized, more 'market-oriented institutes of representation' rather than an 'ideological state apparatus' (Ku, 2003: 13).

Some of this change has come about because museums have started losing their appeal for some market segments, particularly the internet-bound younger generations. In essence museums have become boring, largely owing to curators viewing themselves as educators who treat their consumers as inert receivers. Museum managers have realized the need to alter their viewpoint somewhat to compete with the internet, video games and television. Cynics point out that this new mode of museum is indicative of the broader process of McDisneyfication, wherein places become predictable, calculable and controlled (Kirchberg, 2000), whereas others believe it to be opposite, suggesting that the former approach was more predictable and controlled.

Another expression of this change is the personalization of experiences. Many museums now see themselves as identity creators or authenticators. Many establishments now aim to cause visitors to reflect on their own lives compared to the lives of others, to appreciate what they have and, in the case of human atrocity (e.g. the Holocaust), to discourage it from happening again. Rather than being just a sterile environment, some museums reinforce national pride and patriotism through exhibitions or interpretive methods. Many scholars accept that individuals' perceptions of heritage places and the cultural baggage they bring with them help to determine their level of satisfaction and the degree to which they learn something from their visit.

Political correctness and more accurate pasts

The social movement toward political correctness during the past 20 years has determined the need for interpretive displays to be balanced, non-biased and inclusive. Museums now are being faced with issues of sensitivity to protected populations and are required to adapt in several ways. One positive outcome of this has been more truth in history as museums erect more realistic images of past events, places and people. Outdoor living museums, which have long been seen as celebrating white rural life, are finally integrating indigenous experiences in their idealized pasts. Plimoth Plantation, Massachusetts, one of America's best-known outdoor living museums, has integrated a Native American village within its premises with true indigenous interpreters demonstrating some elements of traditional life. At Plimoth, a more balanced story is told beyond the 'whitewashed' traditions of American history. Similar trends can be seen at plantations and historical museums in the southern US states, where for years only the white people's heritage was exhibited. African-Americans were written out of most heritage scripts, but if they were included, most of the time, stories were told by white interpreters. The situation has improved considerably with more staff at historical museums and other heritage places now being staffed by African-American interpreters and researchers.

Ecomuseums

Another manifestation of the democratization of heritage is the now-commonplace ecomuseum. The term *écomusée* originated in France in 1971 and refers to a more holistic approach to interpreting regional cultures and nature. It arose as a response to the traditional museum that is spatially limited, usually to one building or set of buildings, and which focuses on interpreting a selection of objects, most of which are brought to the museum from their authentic locations. Ecomuseums, on the other hand, are defined areas or regions with a distinct heritage identity, and their purposes include conserving the past and improving the well-being, in socio-economic terms, of the local communities. Unlike the common public perception of traditional museums as egotistical and elitist organizations, ecomuseums are community-oriented and require the involvement of community members. In addition, it is the community itself that defines what elements of nature and culture are important to share with outsiders. Ecomuseums encompass living and built culture in small villages, towns and cities together with rural areas – in short, all parts of a region that share a similar cultural heritage identity. In essence ecomuseums can be defined by what they do (community empowerment, improved livelihoods and conservation) just as much as by what they are (Corsane *et al.*, 2007).

Approximately 300 ecomuseums operate in various parts of the world, with the majority being in Europe. Table 14.2 shows a sampling of ecomuseums in various countries. Many of these areas are already important cultural destinations. The ecomuseum brand simply allows the broader destination to emphasize its sense of place and link rural areas, villages and towns together in a themed cultural product.

Table 14.2 A selection of ecomuseums around the world

Ecomuseum	Location
Écomusée d'Alsace	Alsace region of France
Søhøjlandets Økomuseum	Central Denmark
Ecomuseu do Matadouro	In and around Santa Cruz, Brazil
Ekomuseum Bergslagen	Central Sweden
Ecomuseo del Casentino	Central Italy
Kalyna Country Ecomuseum	Alberta, Canada
Suojia Miao Ecomuseum	Guizhou Province, southern China

Toten Økomuseum	South-central Norway
Living Museum of the West	Melbourne, Australia
Ecomusée Creusot-Montceau	Burgundy, France

While the notion of ecomuseums is catching on as regions begin to see the value of declaring themselves ecomuseums, there are unfortunate examples where economic growth supersedes and compromises the other goals of conservation and empowerment.

Internet marketing

In the past, museums have been loath to attract more visitors, seeing themselves as caretakers of the past rather than tourist attractions. Today, however, museum managers realize the need to increase revenue and justify their existence to a skeptical public. The internet has proved to be an effective instrument for promoting museums and increasing visitation. The speed with which museums and other historic sites are embracing new technology is increasing, with interesting outcomes.

Internet-based marketing is now more commonplace than ever before, and several uses have been identified for promoting museums via the internet. Poria and Gvili's (2006) study found three main types of content that visitors expect to find in museum websites. First is functional information, which includes opening hours, entrance fees, directions, maps and other utilitarian facts. The second type of content is educational information, such as historical facts, archaeological information, display data and inter-pretation. The final sort is emotional information that creates a personal interest in visiting. Life history narratives about people's struggles to survive or the effects of war or other tragedies on individuals' lives are two cases in point. This and other online content can be adapted easily with web-based technology to the needs, interests and desires of target markets.

Another important promotional use of the internet is virtual tours. We know very little about their impact and how they might be best designed to meet marketing objectives. Web technology has been adopted by many museums to involve at-home consumers in taking virtual tours through virtual exhibits. The Toyota Automobile Museum in Tokyo has a fascinating virtual tour that allows users to observe the large variety of cars in the museum by clicking on different sections of the floor plan. The United States Holocaust Memorial Museum provides a complete online inventory of its various exhibitions with photographs and interactive maps. Some museums have live-feed webcams, while others allow web surfers to navigate corridors and exhibition halls in proxy as though they were there.

Opponents of these advances lament that such freedoms might keep people from visiting because they either replace real experiences with virtual ones or they create even more immobile 'couch potatoes', who will not likely visit museums anyway. Supporters contend that simulated visits can help sustain museums through sponsorships. Virtual tours might also whet people's appetites so that they want to visit in person, plus they provide important educational experiences without having to bear the burden of over-visitation.

SUMMARY AND CONCLUSION

Museums are some of the most visited tourist attractions in the world. They range from large-scale, globally-recognized establishments to the smallest village cottage in the smallest village. While a small number draw millions of visitors each year, millions of museums draw small numbers of visitors but are important in other ways, such as building social capital and enhancing civic pride and community solidarity. There are many types of museums catering to a multitude of market segments – hobbyists, cultural enthusiasts, school children and families, to name but a few.

While museums have always been an important part of community life, at least since the 17th century, their role is changing as socio-economic and cultural environments also transform. Directors and curators now must deal with modern realities in the world of museums, encompassing temporal constraints, public skepticism, popularization of once-elitist resources, interpretive revamping to reflect special interests and more truthful history, non-traditional museum formats and technology-based marketing.

REVIEW QUESTIONS

1. Based on what criteria are most museum types identified? What is the role of theming in their designation?

2. What is the difference between 'anchor' museums and other, less popular museums in terms of scale of appeal?

3. Museums are having to compete with other attractions and activities for people's leisure time. What do you think museums could do to be more competitive?

4. What are some of the main criticisms levied against living folklife museums, and are these criticisms justified?

5. What is social capital and how do museums contribute to it in destination communities?

6. How are ecomuseums different from more traditional museums? Are they even museums at all?

7. What role does the internet play in marketing museums?

RECOMMENDED READING

Bailey, S.J. and Falconer, P. (1998) Charging for admission to museums and galleries: A framework for analysing the impact on access. *Journal of Cultural Economics* 22(2/3), 167–177.

Basso, A. and Funari, S. (2004) A quantitative approach to evaluate the relative efficiency of museums. *Journal of Cultural Economics* 28(3), 195–216.

Chhabra, D. (2008) Positioning museums on an authenticity continuum. *Annals of Tourism Research* 35(2), 427–447.

Corsane, G. (ed.) (2005) *Heritage, Museums and Galleries: An Introductory Reader.* London: Routledge.

Corsane, G. (2006) Using ecomuseum indicators to evaluate the Robben Island Museum and World Heritage Site. *Landscape Research* 31(4), 399–418.

Davis, P. (2004) Ecomuseums and the democratization of cultural tourism. *Tourism Culture and Communication* 5(1), 45–58.

de Rojas, C. and Camarero, C. (2008) Visitors' experience, mood and satisfaction in a heritage context: Evidence from an interpretation center. *Tourism Management* 29(3), 525–537.

Edwards, D. (2005) It's mostly about me: Reasons why volunteers contribute their time to museums and art museums. *Tourism Review International* 9(1), 21–31.

Frochot, I. (2004) An investigation into the influence of the benefits sought by visitors on their evaluation of historic houses' service provision. *Journal of Vacation Marketing* 10(3), 223–237.

Geissler, G.L., Rucks, C.T. and Edison, S.W. (2006) Understanding the role of service convenience in art museum marketing: An exploratory study. *Journal of Hospitality and Leisure Marketing* 14(4), 69–87.

Gurt, G.A. and Torres, J.M.R. (2007) People who don't go to museums. *International Journal of Heritage Studies* 13(6), 521–523.

Harrison, J. (1997) Museums and touristic expectations. *Annals of Tourism Research* 24(1), 23–40.

Holmes, K. and Edwards, D. (2007) Volunteers as hosts and guests in museums. In K.D. Lyons and S. Wearing (eds) *Journeys of Discovery in Volunteer Tourism: International Case Study Perspectives* (pp. 155–165). Wallingford: CAB International.

Johanson, L.B. and Olsen, K. (2010) Alta Museum as a tourist attraction: The importance of location. *Journal of Heritage Tourism* 5(1), 1–16.

Johnson, P. and Thomas, B. (1998) The economics of museums: A research perspective. *Journal of Cultural Economics* 22(2/3), 75–85.

Kinghorn, N. and Willis, K. (2008) Measuring museum visitor preferences towards opportunities for developing social capital: An application of a choice experiment to the Discovery Museum. *International Journal of Heritage Studies* 14(6), 555–572.

Kirshenblatt-Gimblett, B. (1998) *Destination Culture: Tourism, Museums and Heritage.* Berkeley: University of California Press.

Lennon, J.J. and Graham, M. (2001) Commercial development and competitive environments: The museum sector in Scotland. *International Journal of Tourism Research* 3(4), 265–281.

Lloyd, K. and Morgan, C. (2008) Murky waters: Tourism, heritage and the development of the ecomuseum in Ha Long Bay, Vietnam. *Journal of Heritage Tourism* 3(1), 1–17.

Lord, G.D. and Lord, B. (2009) *The Manual of Museum Management* (2nd edn). Lanham, MD: AltaMira Press.

Markwell, S., Bennett, M. and Ravenscroft, N. (1997) The changing market for heritage tourism: A case study of visits to historic houses in England. *International Journal of Heritage Studies* 3(2), 95–108.

McCarthy, J. and Ciolfi, L. (2008) Place as dialogue: Understanding and supporting the museum experience. *International Journal of Heritage Studies* 14(3), 247–267.

McIntyre, C. (2009) Museum and art gallery experience space characteristics: An entertaining show or a contemplative bathe? *International Journal of Tourism Research* 11(2), 155–170.

McLean, F. (1997) *Marketing the Museum.* London: Routledge.

McLean, F. (1997) Museums and the construction of national identity: A review. *International Journal of Heritage Studies* 3(4), 244–252.

Minghetti, V., Moretti, A. and Micelli, S. (2002) Reengineering the museum's role in the tourism value chain: Towards an IT business model. *Information Technology and Tourism* 4(2), 131–143.

Mitchell, S. (1996) *Object Lessons: The Role of Museums in Education.* London: HMSO.

Momchedjikova, B. (2002) My heart's in the small lands: Touring the miniature city in the museum. *Tourist Studies* 2(3), 267–281.

Moore, K. (1994) *Museum Management.* London: Routledge.

Mylonakis, J. and Kendristakis, E. (2006) Evaluation of museum service quality: A research study of museums and galleries visitors' satisfaction. *Tourism and Hospitality Management* 12(2), 37–54.

Newman, A. and McLean, F. (2006) The impact of museums upon identity. *International Journal of Heritage Studies* 12(1), 49–68.

Orr, N. (2006) Museum volunteering: Heritage as 'serious leisure'. *International Journal of Heritage Studies* 12(2), 194–210.

Prideaux, B. and Kininmont, L.J. (1999) Tourism and heritage are not strangers: A study of opportunities for rural heritage museums to maximize tourism visitation. *Journal of Travel Research* 37(3), 299–303.

Rátz, T. (2006) Interpretation in the house of terror, Budapest. In M. Smith and M. Robinson (eds) *Cultural Tourism in a Changing World: Politics, Participation and (Re)presentation* (pp. 244–256). Clevedon: Channel View Publications.

Reussner, E.M. (2003) Strategic management for visitor-oriented museums. *International Journal of Cultural Policy* 9(1), 95–108.

Rowley, J. (1999) Measuring total customer experience in museums. *International Journal of Contemporary Hospitality Management* 11(6), 303–308.

Soren, B.J. (2009) Museum experiences that change visitors. *Museum Management and Curatorship* 24(3), 233–251.

Srinivasan, R., Enote, J., Becvar, K.M. and Boast, R. (2009) Critical and reflective uses of new media technologies in tribal museums. *Museum Management and Curatorship* 24(2), 161–181.

Stamer, D., Lerdall, K. and Guo, C. (2008) Managing heritage volunteers: An exploratory study of volunteer programmes in art museums worldwide. *Journal of Heritage Tourism* 3(3), 203–214.

Timothy, D.J. and Boyd, S.W. (2003) *Heritage Tourism*. London: Prentice Hall.

Tufts, S. and Milne, S. (1999) Museums: A supply-side perspective. *Annals of Tourism Research* 26(3), 613–631.

Walters, D. (2009) Approaches in museums towards disability in the United Kingdom and the United States. *Museum Management and Curatorship* 24(1), 29–46.

Williams, P. (2007) *Memorial Museums: the Global Rush to Commemorate Atrocities*. Oxford: Berg.

Xie, F.F.P. (2006) Developing industrial heritage tourism: A case study of the proposed Jeep Museum in Toledo, Ohio. *Tourism Management* 27(6), 1321–1330.

Young, L. (2006) Villages that never were: The museum village as a heritage genre. *International Journal of Heritage Studies* 12(4), 321–338.

RECOMMENDED WEBSITES

American Association of Museums – http://www.aam-us.org/

Association of Art Museum Directors – http://www.aamd.org/

Association of Science-Technology Centers – http://www.astc.org/

Canadian Museums Association –
http://www.museums.ca/en/info_resources/canadas_museums/

Euromuse.net – http://www.euromuse.net/en/resources

Fédération des écomusées et des musées de société –
http://fems.asso.fr/index2.html

Irish Museums Association – http://www.irishmuseums.org/

Museum Net – http://www.museums.co.uk/

Museums Aotearoa – http://www.museums-aotearoa.org.nz/

Museums Association – http://www.museumsassociation.org/home

Museums Australia – http://www.museumsaustralia.org.au/site/index.php

National Museums Association – http://icom.museum/nat_as_mus.html

Outlook on Ecomuseums –
http://www.osservatorioecomusei.net/start.php?mf=home&lng=en

Small Museum Association – http://www.smallmuseum.org/

Smithsonian Institution – http://www.si.edu/

The British Museum – http://www.britishmuseum.org/

The Japan Association of Art Museums –
http://event.yomiuri.co.jp/jaam/m_birenkyou_en.cfm#seg01

CHAPTER 15

ARCHAEOLOGICAL SITES AND ANCIENT MONUMENTS

LEARNING OBJECTIVES

After reading this chapter, you should be able to:

1. Understand the prominence of ruins and ancient monuments as heritage tourist attractions around the world.

2. Be familiar with the crossover between volunteer tourism and archaeological sites.

3. Recognize the spatial planning principles associated with ancient heritage sites.

4. Evaluate the needs of restoration, renovation and preservation of archaeological locations.

5. Consider the role of the Seven Wonders of the World as tourism icons.

INTRODUCTION

Prehistoric ruins, ancient monuments, antiquated buildings and archaeological sites are among the most popular resources upon which heritage tourism is based. They are also among the most prized elements of the past for scientific and educational purposes, and they form much of the foundation of tourism in areas where there were indigenous pasts, colonial pasts or both. This category of historic site includes a wide array of buildings and sites, perhaps one of the largest, including castles, cathedrals, ruins, archaeological digs, ancient monuments, old buildings, walls and gates, antiquated harbors and historic monasteries. Certain destinations have become synonymous with international icons. For instance, the mystique associated with visiting Egypt, Peru, China and Mexico derives largely from those countries' archaeological patrimony.

In most parts of the western world there is a dichotomous history of native peoples and colonists who settled in new territories, displacing the natives or assimilating them. Many countries have dual or parallel built heritages that many times do not overlap or coincide. Pre-colonial architecture and living culture was often supplanted by colonial buildings and European cultures. Thus, in many places, indigenous built and living culture is either non-existent, in fragile condition or in need of emergency care and legislation for their protection. Colonial heritage came later, but is also an important part of many nations' heritage.

This chapter looks at several issues that are most pertinent to ancient buildings, ruins and archaeological sites. From a management perspective, it reiterates the economic crisis and visitor issues that all managers must concern themselves with. It then touches on the crossover between heritage tourism and volunteer tourism to create unique volunteer travel opportunities for people interested in archaeology and heritage preservation, followed by an examination of the use of archaeological symbolisms as national and marketing icons.

HERITAGE ECONOMICS AND ARCHAEOLOGICAL SITES

As noted earlier in the book, funding is a hot topic in the area of heritage these days. Archaeological sites are no exception to this important discussion. Traditionally, historic sites were funded in large part by public monies, but with severe budget cutbacks in recent years, and shrinking public coffers even before that, sites have had to devise ways to become more self-sufficient. Archaeologists need funding just as museum and historic site managers do, and with increasingly reduced budgets many sites are now required to fund themselves through entrance fees and volunteer labor.

Like historic homes and other heritage places, archaeological areas must compete for scarce consumer spending. One way of doing this, which has become more normative in recent years, is to host special events and rent out heritage spaces for public gatherings of various sorts. Some heritage managers in Greece, Italy and other parts of Europe rent space amid the ruins for weddings and concerts after regular open hours. The Coliseum and Parthenon are good examples. Roman and Greek theaters in other parts of the Mediterranean double as modern theaters and venues for special events (see Plate 15.1). In regions where there are many heritage places, each one has to be competitive – not just as a tourist attraction but for broader social functions as well.

Additionally, site managers, who have in the past loathed the notion of tourism because of its negative connotations in relation to heritage conservation, now realize the need not only to fund the sites themselves but the broader economic role that archaeological areas can play in local economies. As noted already, some destinations rely entirely on the ancient past for their economic livelihood. Thus, more and more historic sites and ruins are becoming more integrated into local economies because they are now seen as a viable economic engine for destination communities; no longer are they viewed as simply government 'protectorates' or agency-funded projects.

VISITOR ISSUES

A number of studies have shed light on the motives of people visiting ancient sites. Among the most significant are to experience culture, to learn about the past and to seek an authentic experience. In some cases, a site's inclusion on UNESCO's World Heritage

Plate 15.1 This ancient amphitheater in Caesarea, Israel, doubles as a venue for modern performances

List adds extra appeal as some visitors see this as a seal of affirmation of the site's authenticity and universal cultural value. The notion of authenticity as described earlier in the book is a salient heritage motive and one that can determine whether or not visitors have a positive experience. At Native American ruins in the USA visitors often note their interest in meeting indigenous people, experiencing native culture and learning about native customs. According to a study by Budruk, White, Wodrich and Riper (2008), the preservation of archaeological resources, learning about customs and values, meeting local people and visiting ruins with a native guide contributed most to their perception of an authentic heritage experience. This goes hand in hand with the idea of empowerment in tourism development. Even if an indigenous site is not located on native lands, the heritage being visited is still indigenous heritage, and indigenous populations should have a voice in how it is portrayed and managed for tourism.

Willingness to pay is an important area of research today in the realm of site management. It is especially crucial at sites of antiquity, owing to the special importance of visitor satisfaction and return visits. The quality of the visitor experience can be determined by many factors, including crowdedness, esthetic appeal (e.g. not blocking views with signage) and a sense of authenticity. Even archaeological sites can have competitors, all trying to capture tourist spending. Pricing is an important part of this, and understanding how much people are willing to pay for a heritage experience can help a site understand its unique selling points and its competitive advantage over other areas. In areas where there are less expensive monuments that have a similar history, chances are that people will be less willing to pay a higher price for similar experiences.

Accessibility is another pressing concern these days for archaeological site managers. While this is a concern for all heritage managers, ruins and ancient monuments are especially prone to problems of physical access given the sensitivity and agedness of the structures being visited. Legislation in some countries even requires archaeological sites to offer accessible options to people with physical or mental disabilities. This is a tricky prospect and requires well-trained personnel who are sensitive to visitor needs and conservation of the built past. It is important for such attractions to adopt policies of access while simultaneously making the site entertaining and informational, as well as preserving the endangered past.

VOLUNTEER TOURISM AND ARCHAEOLOGY

An interesting crossover between two sub-sectors of tourism, which has become an important issue in recent years, is volunteer tourism and heritage. Volunteer tourism, sometimes referred to as voluntourism or volunteer vacations, refers to people traveling to assist in unpaid charity efforts. There are many different types of volunteer travel experiences, including building houses and digging wells in third-world villages, planting trees and fixing fences in national parks, educating children in schools, cleaning up after a natural disaster, teaching women to read, instructing villagers how to plant certain disease-resistant vegetables, nurses and physicians traveling to offer free health care in less-developed regions, short-term missionaries sharing a religious message or short-term volunteer positions in national or state parks. These are only a few of the multitudes of volunteer experiences undertaken by tens of millions of people every year. In most cases, people are motivated by altruistic purposes – to help improve the conditions of the earth or humankind. They typically pay their own way, or have sponsors, and donate their vacation time to a worthy cause. In addition to altruism, some volunteer tourists participate as a way of building their resumes, gaining international experience, learning a language or meeting interesting people.

There is also a growing trend in this realm related to scientific research and exploration. One manifestation of this is people traveling to volunteer in archaeological digs. While other aspects of volunteer tourism might include some elements of heritage (e.g. living culture), the relationship is perhaps best manifested in volunteer archaeology. In some countries there are plentiful opportunities to undertake this unique holiday experience. It is popular as a domestic activity in the USA at Civil War sites, in mining towns and at Native American sites. Many Europeans, Australians and North Americans prefer an international experience at digs in various parts of Africa, Asia or Latin America. Most amateur archaeology volunteers undergo training exercises where they are instructed on appropriate extraction and cleaning methods and are well supervised by professionals (see Plate 15.2). The educational element, self discovery, meeting like-minded people, as well as the ability to help bring history to life, are cited as among the most important motives for people who participate in these types of activities.

Intermediaries, such as tour agencies, play on these desires in getting people to purchase archaeology-based holidays. For instance, one operator tempts potential volunteers by saying 'Don't just read about history. Help make a difference – feel it, discover it, and make it a part of you' (Archaeological Digs, 2010).

Some archaeological sites are heavily dependent on volunteer travelers to meet their scientific and budget goals. Like all volunteering in the heritage arena, there is a monetary value associated with archaeological volunteers. With volunteer labor, scarce excavation, cleaning and presentation budgets can be stretched further and more work accomplished. Every year, managers and scientists associated with hundreds of ruins and other historic

Plate 15.2 Volunteer archaeologists catalogue colonial-era glass shards in Philadelphia, USA

sites call for volunteers, including student groups, to assist in meeting their excavating objectives. Much of the world's knowledge of the human past has come to light through the labors of amateur archaeology tourists.

There are agencies and websites that help people find volunteer opportunities in various parts of the world. Many specialize in youth experiences, although most cater to a general market. Earthwatch Institute, for instance, sells a variety of archaeology volunteer trips that can be purchased for a sizable 'contribution' (see Table 15.1). The trips include dig sites in North America, the Pacific Islands (Easter Island), Asia and Europe, with activities ranging from excavation and recording to developing computer models of cultural landscapes with Geographic Information Systems.

Table 15.1 Examples of Earthwatch archaeological volunteer trips, 2010

Destination	Name of trip	Type of experience	Duration of trip
Easter Island	Easter Island (Rapa Nui) Culture	Conduct surface surveys of house sites and test pits in gardens	14 days
England	Romans on the Tyne	Excavating, cleaning and recording finds	7–14 days
England	Romans on the Tyne – Short	Washing, marking and recording	3 days
England	Romans on the Tyne – Family	Excavating, cleaning and recording finds with more supervision	5 days
England	Romans on the Tyne – Teens	Excavating, cleaning and processing finds	14 days
Italy	Discovering Italy's Ancient Roman Coast	Excavate a coastal Roman settlement	6–13 days
Italy	Discovering Italy's Ancient Roman Coast – Teens	Excavate, clean and document artifacts at a coastal Roman settlement	8 days
Mongolia	Archaeology of the Mongolian Steppe	Identify and document cultural sites in a nature reserve	14 days
Thailand	Origins of Angkor	Excavating a Thai village	7 or 14 days
United States	Mammoth Graveyard	Excavate, preserve and record bone fragments	15 days
United States	Cultural Landscapes of the Yakima Nation	Compile records of place names and resource use, document cultural places and build models with GIS	8 days

Source: Earthwatch (2010)

The importance of this form of heritage tourism cannot be overstated. As the public continues to become more sophisticated in taste and better educated, they seek more educational and fulfilling experiences beyond the seeming mindlessness associated with traditional sun, sea and sand-based excursions. The growing popularity of archaeology volunteer tours attests to a more demanding clientele that seeks more personal experiences with considerable intellectual growth potential.

RESTORATION AND PRESERVATION ISSUES

Preservation and/or restoration are important principles and practices at all heritage sites, but they are particularly vital at locations of ancient monuments and archaeological areas owing to the delicate condition of the historic structures. The following sections shed light on several contemporary preservation issues facing heritage managers today.

Physical planning and zoning

One of the most pressing issues at archaeological sites is physical, or land-use, planning. This addresses the preservation or restoration of ruins, as well as facilitates the modern-day visitor use of the sites in ways that do the least amount of damage. By surveying the archaeological area and taking a comprehensive inventory of cultural resources, precise boundaries are determined within which conservation practices and policies are established to protect the resources in question. Physical planning also helps direct vehicular and pedestrian traffic away from sensitive areas.

Zoning is one of the main principles of physical planning at ruins and archaeological sites and refers to the physical development or protection of sites in various zones of contact or distance from the resource (see Figure 15.1). Buffer zones need to be established and managed as part of the heritage site. The purpose of buffer zones is to provide an ecological cushion between the 'outside' world and the protected precinct or site. They often provide a shield against land clearing for agriculture, urbanization and industrial development. Buffer zones take the form of forests, grassland areas or gardens and well landscaped grounds plus the ruins themselves.

Many sites also have an amenity zone (sometimes part of a buffer zone), where parking, toilets, ticket booths and souvenir shops are located separately from the built resource. Zoning allows certain amenities and visitor services to be present without detracting from the ambience of the historic structure itself and is a useful tool for managing visitor impacts. Many studies have shown a much higher level of satisfaction among visitors who said they were unable to see the modern amenities because they were tucked away from the view of the ruins. There are many approaches to land-use planning and zoning at historic monuments; each site has its own unique needs and environmental concerns. Some sites have only one or two zones while others are known to have several zones, each with its own protective mandates and management needs.

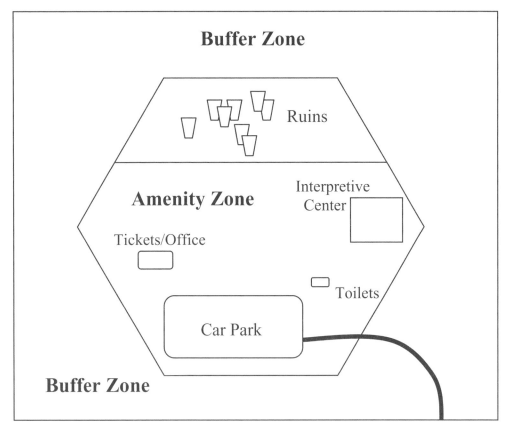

Figure 15.1 A hypothetical archaeological site with planning zones

People living in archaeological sites

Another significant preservation issue, as noted earlier in Chapter 9, is people inhabiting historic sites; this is particularly poignant in the context of ancient archaeology. There is a long and widespread history of squatter settlements developing inside ancient sites. They are ideal locations owing to pre-existing shelters, building materials, such as stone and wood, and they are often viewed simply as abandoned places of no particular importance. Coming to terms with this phenomenon has been a difficult challenge for preservationists, as modern inhabitants often deteriorate the structures and destroy artifacts.

While this is in fact a major concern for public agencies charged with the care of cultural monuments, the handling of such populations, many of which might have lived among the ruins for many generations, has an equally negative track record. Forced displacement disconnects people from their traditional lands and habitations, creates animosity not only between residents and governments but also between residents and tourists, and creates hardships for already disadvantaged population cohorts. Even when compensation is offered, it usually falls short of the attachment to place that is severed.

Many examples of this exist throughout the world. The Bidul nomads in Jordan were forcefully displaced from ancient Petra because Jordan's government felt they were a menace to tourists, and their herding activities were hazardous to the ruins. This is an example of heritage tourism causing people to become separated from their own personal past and has resulted in a deteriorated pride in their culture and negative social consequences, particularly in relation to tourism.

Ratu Boko, an ancient palace and temple complex in Indonesia, was inhabited for many generations by local villagers, who were eventually relocated to other areas of Java because the government felt they were damaging too much of the archaeological site. More violent still were the earlier relocations of villagers away from the Prambanan temple complex in Java near Ratu Boko in the 1970s and 1980s. These are not isolated instances. While it is true that much human habitation in archaeological sites can, and does, cause irreparable damage, governments need to realize the impact of forced migrations from traditional lands, and compensation needs to be commensurate with the social and personal trauma associated with uprooting from one's ancestral home.

Sindhudurg Fort, India, is an example of a 17th century fortress ruin that is inhabited by some 35 villagers. Rather than remove them, the local government has learned to utilize them as caretakers for the site, tour guides and providers of other services. In turn, the community knows its role in relation to the fort structure and must act in ways that do not damage it (Chakravarty, 2008).

To preserve or restore

The differences between renovation, restoration and preservation were discussed early in this book. When it comes to archaeological sites, there is considerable pressure on archaeologists and site managers to reconstruct ruined edifices for scientific, educational and touristic purposes. However, there are many benefits of preserving ruined sites in a state of disrepair, such as keeping the originality of place and not disturbing fragile artifacts. There are also benefits associated with restoring ancient structures for esthetic and scientific reasons.

From a tourism perspective both perspectives are important. Some visitors would prefer to see ancient buildings and villages in a ruined state, as this adds an element of genuineness, antiquity or authenticity to the heritage place. Others, however, would prefer to see ancient monuments re-built, so that the public can see what the buildings once looked like and their prominence in the cultural landscape. Several research studies of archaeological site visitors have concluded that most heritage visitors would prefer a mix of restored monuments and those remaining in a state of disrepair. In the majority of cases throughout the world there is a mix of elements that have been restored and those that have been preserved in a condition of being over-run by the forces of nature.

At ancient Prambanan (Indonesia), for instance, several of the main Hindu temples have been restored to their ancient form. Scattered amid the temples are stones and debris of other temples in the complex that have yet to be restored. Likewise, at Tikal (Guatemala) there are dozens of unexcavated mounds surrounding the pyramids and ancient city courtyards (see Plate 15.3). This mix of unexcavated, un-restored and restored elements of an ancient landscape adds appeal for most tourists, as it provides the advantages of esthetics and originality that so many people seek. Decisions to excavate

Plate 15.3 This overgrown ruin at Tikal, Guatemala, has yet to be excavated

and reconstruct some archaeological elements, while leaving others in ruin, is usually a strategic decision, but it is also an economic decision since few archaeological projects have sufficient money to be able to complete the restoration of all buildings on site. Some countries simply have too much archaeology from a financial perspective. They cannot afford the money or personnel to excavate hundreds or thousands of sites; instead priority must be given to the most endangered places and sites that might draw the most public interest.

ICONIC SYMBOLS OF NATIONALISM AND HERITAGE

Ancient and medieval monuments of human ingenuity in many parts of the world have become important iconic symbols with international acclaim and recognition. Some countries use these ancient resources as national symbols, such as Angkor Wat on Cambodian currency, the Great Wall of China on Chinese currency and the ruins of Baalbek on Lebanese currency (see Plate 15.4). In addition, some countries' coats of arms depict symbols of ancient buildings and historic sites that help affirm national identity.

In the same manner, archaeological sites and ancient monuments are used frequently by the tourism industry of various countries as symbols of importance on the global marketplace. This occurs in tourism logos and symbols, as well as in major advertising

Plate 15.4 The temple of Bacchus in Baalbek, Lebanon, is one of the best preserved Roman temples in the world

campaigns, such as in many of the successful 'Incredible India' television ads produced by India's Ministry of Tourism. Palaces, temples and other ancient buildings, including the Taj Mahal, feature prominently together with living culture and natural heritage as representations of what India is about and what a holiday in India can do for potential visitors.

One aspect of the importance of ancient monuments in national symbolism is a series of successive efforts to declare various 'Seven Wonders of the World'. The original ancient wonders of the world were cultural in nature and focused on the Mediterranean, since it was the ancient Greeks who originated the idea of the seven wonders. Today the only remaining wonder on the original list is the Pyramids of Giza in Egypt. Since that time there have been other interesting campaigns to designate various seven wonders of the world, including Seven Wonders of the Medieval World, Seven Wonders of the Industrial World, Seven Wonders of the Modern World and Seven Natural Wonders of the World. There is no universal body that can 'officially' designate wonders of the world; most of these efforts have been led by private companies, famous entrepreneurs or non-profit organizations.

Perhaps the most widely publicized campaign was the 2001–2007 New Seven Wonders of the World movement undertaken by the New7Wonders Foundation to bring up to date the list that was started in ancient times. Based on the results of more than 100 million votes from around the world, seven well-known historical monuments were chosen as the world's new seven wonders (see Table 15.2). Of the new designees, five can be considered ancient monuments because of their age; a few of them are also archaeological sites (e.g. Machu Picchu, Petra, and the Colosseum). Christ the Redeemer was built in the early 1900s and has become highly symbolic for the city of Rio de Janeiro. The Taj Mahal was constructed in the 17th century and is also emblematic of India. As the only remaining ancient wonder, the Pyramids of Giza were inscribed as an honorary member of the seven wonders.

Many national governments, private individuals, companies and non-profit organizations sunk millions of dollars into efforts to get certain ancient sites nominated. Ministries of tourism initiated advertising campaigns to get people to vote their sites onto the list of

Table 15.2 The Seven New Wonders of the World

Site	Location	Site	Location
Chichen Itza	Mexico	Machu Picchu	Peru
Christ the Redeemer	Brazil	Petra	Jordan
Colosseum	Italy	Taj Mahal	India
Great Wall of China	China		

seven. Other finalists included Alhambra, Spain; Angkor Wat, Cambodia; Kiyomizu Temple, Japan; Neuschwanstein Castle, Germany; Easter Island Statues, Chile; Stonehenge, UK; Sydney Opera House, Australia; the Acropolis, Greece; the Eiffel Tower, France; the Hagia Sofia, Turkey; the Kremlin and Red Square, Russia; the Pyramids of Giza, Egypt; the Statue of Liberty, USA; and the ancient city of Timbuktu, Mali. This list of 14 finalists also reflects the importance of ancient monuments and archaeological sites in the global image of place and in the promotional efforts of destination countries.

SUMMARY AND CONCLUSION

This chapter focused on historic buildings, ancient monuments and archaeological sites. All of these are found in rural and urban contexts and are extremely important components of the heritagescapes of many destination regions. In fact many places are branded and marketed with archaeological symbols, and their mega-sites become synonymous with their national tourism identities.

Managers of these kinds of visitor sites must concern themselves with pressing fiscal constraints, and they must be creative in finding ways to generate revenue without compromising the authentic and fragile nature of the places under their stewardship. This is not an easy task, and balancing the unique needs of visitors at places that are particularly sensitive to structural changes and visitor impacts, as well as addressing other conservation issues, makes managers' jobs very challenging. One way of accomplishing several goals is to employ volunteers and provide volunteer opportunities for tourists to donate their vacation time and resources to assist in preservation projects and archaeological digs. Ancient sites and structures are one of the most salient and beloved elements of cultural tourism. They are a non-renewable resource that must be protected at all costs, and it is up to managers, community members and visitors themselves to assure their sustainable use in the future.

REVIEW QUESTIONS

1. How does the notion of 'willingness to pay' play out in the context of archaeological sites?

2. In what way does the sustainability principle of participatory development and indigenous control come into play in the heritage environment discussed in this chapter?

3. How and to what extent are ancient monuments utilized by countries and regions as iconic marketing mechanisms to attract tourists and tourism investment?

4. Can you identify three or more ancient buildings or archaeological sites that help distinguish your country or community as a world-class destination?

5. Do you think the Seven New Wonders of the World movement is linked to cultural tourism? How so?

6. What are the main global issues and challenges facing archaeological site and ancient monument managers today?

RECOMMENDED READING

Adams, J.L. (2010) Interrogating the equity principle: The rhetoric and reality of management planning for sustainable archaeological heritage tourism. *Journal of Heritage Tourism* 5(2), 103–123.

Alexandros, A. and Jaffry, S. (2005) Stated preferences for two Cretan heritage attractions. *Annals of Tourism Research* 32(4), 985–1005.

Beltrán, E. and Rojas, M. (1996) Diversified funding methods in Mexican archaeology. *Annals of Tourism Research* 23(2), 463–478.

Bender, B. and Edmonds, M. (1992) Stonehenge: Whose past? What past? *Tourism Management* 13(2), 355–357.

Cossons, N. (1989) Heritage tourism: Trends and tribulations. *Tourism Management* 10(3), 192–194.

Found, W.C. (2004) Historic sites, material culture and tourism in the Caribbean islands. In D.T. Duval (ed.) *Tourism in the Caribbean: Trends, Development, Prospects* (pp. 136–151). London: Routledge.

Gillespie, J. (2009) Protecting World Heritage: Regulating ownership and land use at Angkor Archaeological Park, Cambodia. *International Journal of Heritage Studies* 15(4), 338–354.

Helmy, E. and Cooper, C. (2002) An assessment of sustainable tourism planning for the archaeological heritage: The case of Egypt. *Journal of Sustainable Tourism* 10(6), 514–535.

Jones, T. (1986) Archaeology in a natural area: The case at Landels-Hill Big Creek Reserve. *Natural Areas Journal* 6(4), 13–19.

Kan, Y.P., Li, J. and Li, M. (2000) Study on the strategy in Xinjiang's tourism resource of cultural ruins. *Arid Land Geography* 23(2), 149–154.

Krakover, S. and Cohen, R. (2001) Visitors and non-visitors to archaeological heritage attractions: The cases of Massada and Avedat, Israel. *Tourism Recreation Research* 26(1), 27–33.

Mason, P. and Kuo, I.L. (2008) Visitor attitudes to Stonehenge: International icon or national disgrace? *Journal of Heritage Tourism* 2(3), 168–183.

Mayer, C.C. and Wallace, G.N. (2007) Appropriate levels of restoration and development at Copan Archaeological Park: Setting attributes affecting the visitor experience. *Journal of Ecotourism* 6(2), 91–110.

McGrath, G. (2004) Including the outsiders: The contribution of guides to integrated heritage tourism management in Cusco, southern Peru. *Current Issues in Tourism* 7(4/5), 426–432.

Medina, L.K. (2003) Commoditizing culture: Tourism and Maya identity. *Annals of Tourism Research* 30(2), 353–368.

Mosler, S. (2009) Aspects of archaeological heritage in the cultural landscape of Western Anatolia. *International Journal of Heritage Studies* 15(1), 24–43.

Polyzos, S., Arabatzis, G. and Tsiantikoudis, S. (2007) The attractiveness of archaeological sites in Greece: A spatial analysis. *International Journal of Tourism Policy* 1(3), 246–266.

Prideaux, B., Timothy, D.J. and Chon, K. (eds) (2008) *Cultural and Heritage Tourism in Asia and the Pacific*. London: Routledge.

Ramsey, D. and Everitt, J. (2008) If you dig it, they will come! Archaeology heritage sites and tourism development in Belize, Central America. *Tourism Management* 29(5), 909–916.

Riganti, P. and Willis, K.G. (2002) Component and temporal value reliability in cultural goods: The case of Roman Imperial remains near Naples. In S. Navrud and R.C. Ready (eds) *Valuing Cultural Heritage: Applying Environmental Valuation Techniques to Historic Buildings, Monuments and Artifacts* (pp. 142–158). Cheltenham: Edward Elgar.

Rossides, N. (1995) The conservation of the cultural heritage in Cyprus: A planner's perspective. *Regional Development Dialogue* 16(1), 110–125.

Saipradist, A. and Staiff, R. (2007) Crossing the cultural divide: Western visitors and interpretation at Ayutthaya World Heritage Site, Thailand. *Journal of Heritage Tourism* 2(3), 211–224.

Shetawy, A. and El-Khateeb, S.M. (2009) The pyramids plateau: A dream searching for survival. *Tourism Management* 30(6), 819–827.

Wager, J. (1995) Developing a strategy for the Angkor World Heritage Site. *Tourism Management* 16(7), 515–523.

Wager, J. (1995) Environmental planning for a World Heritage Site: Case study of Angkor, Cambodia. *Journal of Environmental Planning and Management* 38(3), 419–434.

Willis, K.G. (2009) Assessing visitor preferences in the management of archaeological and heritage attractions: A case study of Hadrian's Roman Wall. *International Journal of Tourism Research* 11(5), 487–505.

Winter, T. (2006) Ruining the dream? The challenge of tourism at Angkor, Cambodia. In K. Meethan, A. Anderson and S. Miles (eds) *Tourism Consumption and Representation: Narratives of Place and Self* (pp. 46–66). Wallingford, UK: CAB International.

RECOMMENDED WEBSITES

Archaeological Digs – http://www.archaeologydigs.blogspot.com/

Earthwatch Institute – http://www.earthwatch.org/exped/camilli.html

New7Wonders Foundation – http://www.new7wonders.com/en/

Volunteer Dig Sites – http://www.ubarchaeologist.com/Volunteer-Digs.html

CHAPTER 16

LANDSCAPES OF THE ELITE AND THE ORDINARY

LEARNING OBJECTIVES

After reading this chapter, you should be able to:

1. Learn about the change in demand from elitist heritage to the heritage of the everyday.

2. Understand the components of the elitist landscape that have long attracted most tourist attention.

3. Identify elements of the everyday heritage that are now beginning to be the focus of tourist attention.

4. Be aware of the place of rural landscapes, agro-heritage and heritage cuisines and foodways in the tourism mix.

INTRODUCTION

Most heritage tourism of the past was based upon landscapes and edifices of the powerful players in society: the wealthy, royalty, the church, the colonialists and other symbols of high stature and control. Hundreds of millions of people visit stately homes, mansions, castles, palaces, fortresses, cathedrals and massive temples every year. These are the bedrocks of mass tourism. Fewer in number are the people who visit elements of the landscape of everyday living. During the past few decades, however, heritage consumers have begun to realize that the elitist artifacts are not true or holistic representations of past society – only parts of it. Modern cultural tourists are beginning to demand more accurate, authentic and balanced representations of the past, including the peasant past or historic sites and buildings that embody the everyday life of common folk. Barns and pastures, agricultural landscapes, farming hamlets, cuisine and foodways, seaports and fishing villages, cemeteries, schools, country churches and many other symbols of what life was like for the majority of the population in days gone by have become the focus of much heritage tourism today.

This chapter highlights some of the patterns and resources traditionally associated with elitist heritage and the more commonplace elements of the past that now appeal to the masses. In particular, it describes rural landscapes and villages, agricultural traditions, and cuisine and foodways as important elements of the modern-day heritage product.

THE PRIVILEGED PAST

As already noted, most heritage sites and development projects have focused over-whelmingly on the heritage of nobility and aristocracy. Castles, cathedrals, country estates, monasteries, palaces, grand government edifices, graves of famous people, fortresses and colossal monuments are among the most pervasive and have traditionally received the largest public expenditures for preservation and promotion. The seven wonders of the ancient world were comprised of some of the most privileged cultural artifacts in the world. Most of The Seven New Wonders of the World are in the same genre as in ancient days. Likewise, the majority of UNESCO's World Heritage List includes sites of monu-mental proportions, primarily because of the organization's mandate to list the most noteworthy elements of universal heritage.

Castles and palaces have become iconic for some destinations and are extremely captivating tourist attractions, as they are usually associated with revered royalty, well-known historical figures or infamous events. Famous castles such as Bran Castle (Dracula's Castle) in Romania, the Blarney Castle in Ireland, Neuschwanstein and Neuschwangau castles in Germany and Windsor Castle in England are examples of castles that have been well marketed as tourist attractions and feature prominently in those countries' promotional materials (see Plate 16.1). Castles and palaces are most

Plate 16.1 Neuschwanstein Castle in Germany is one of the country's most recognizable elitist icons

353

pervasive in Europe and feature prominently on package tours, as well as individual travel itineraries.

Cathedrals, churches and temples are another prominent element of tours in Europe and elsewhere. Such edifices attract more than just religious devotees; for most tourists they are simply historic buildings that mark religious traditions and form a part of a place's socio-cultural past. Some cathedrals are important heritage sites known throughout the world, such as St Peter's Basilica in the Vatican City or Canterbury Cathedral in England. The Mormon temple in Salt Lake City is a prominent attraction in the American west, and the massive Buddhist temples of Thailand are an important part of that country's heritage appeal.

Government buildings are another elitist landscape feature that exude an appeal unlike many others. For people whose national heritage includes certain government buildings, visits can be a strongly emotional, even patriotic, experience. American visitors to the Capitol building in Washington, DC, or the White House, might feel a sense of patriotism but also a sense of national pride and excitement because of their exposure to such places in the media since childhood (see Plate 16.2).

Plate 16.2 The Capitol Building in Washington, DC, is an important symbol of the American nation

Another important component of the aristocratic landscape is paradors, or historic hotels in Spain and Portugal. Paradors are essentially grandiose palaces, mansions, monasteries and other such structures that have been redeveloped into tourist accommodation. Similar to paradors are the country palaces and castles of the British Isles and Italy that can be rented for weddings or used for high-class tourist accommodations (see Plate 16.3). Such ostentatious edifices stand in stark contrast to humble bed and breakfasts, country inns and even roadside motels, which are more commonplace and geared toward everyday people. In Spain alone there are nearly 100 paradors made from hospitals, convents, castles, fortresses, manner houses and gothic palaces. For their elitist heritage value, as well as world-class service, these are an important part of heritage tourism and an appealing lodging alternative to four- and five-star resorts. Their use as tourist accommodation facilities is seen as a means of preserving their historical integrity through funding and conservation legislation.

Finally, graves of famous artists, poets, actors, politicians and scientists have a long history of drawing fans and other spectators. These monuments dedicated to the lives of people who have made salient contributions to the world are often visited as part of a 'secular pilgrimage', out of curiosity, or out of dedication to the deceased's music, artistry or politics.

Plate 16.3 This castle in Northern Ireland can be rented for special events and exemplifies the elitist heritage of the British Isles

THE EVERYDAY PAST

The everyday past includes elements of heritage that illustrate the life of the everyday person, rather than the more commonly preserved and promoted aristocratic landscapes as noted above. As people in the western world have become increasingly dissatisfied with the grandiose and over-publicized, over-promoted and even over-propagandized majestic elements of patrimony, they have sought to experience more mundane markers of past civilizations and livelihoods. In most cases, members of modern society realize that they are not a part of the gentry classes of yesteryear, but instead originated ancestrally in the farm fields, villages and factories of the world. This closer personal connection to the past leads many people to seek out the ordinary and simpler elements of life in the past. Several of these are examined in the sections below.

Rural landscapes

By their very nature, rural landscapes create an added appeal to tourist destinations. In some cases, they are the primary draw as people desire to escape the chaos of urban life. Agricultural landscapes, the countryside esthetic, barns, sheds, farm houses and peasant

Plate 16.4 These colorful rice terraces in southern China are an important tourist attraction

and agrarian lifestyles are important elements of the rural heritage of places that satisfy even the most discerning heritage tourists. Living culture, too, is important in this regard. Recent studies have shown that rural landscapes actually have an economic value for tourists, which means that a substantial portion of rural tourists' expenditures can be attributed simply to the appeal of the countryside.

The rice terraces of Luzon Island and Bali are popular attractions in the Philippines and Indonesia. The rice terraces of Ifugao, Philippines, have been inscribed on UNESCO's World Heritage List because of their economic, social, religious and environmental importance in the heritage of Luzon Island and as a critical example of terraced farming in other parts of the world (see Plate 16.4). For approximately two millennia, the rice fields have been worked and knowledge transferred from one generation to another, and they 'represent an enduring illustration of an ancient civilization that surpassed various challenges and setbacks posed by modernization' (UNESCO, 2010a).

Farm fields, and their accompanying farm houses and fences, are an important part of the rural landscape everywhere (see Plate 16.5). This is an important part of the

Plate 16.5 This farmland scene adds to Austria's cultural appeal

commoner heritage in rural regions and is considered extremely attractive to many tourists. Stone farmhouses set against lush, green fields in Great Britain epitomize the rural appeal of England, Wales and Scotland. In the USA, there is a national psyche associated with the countryside wherein rural living and agriculture are symbolic of wholesome living and an innocent, idyllic landscape that is more American than the cities.

Barns and other farm structures are a salient part of the rural idyll. There are many efforts now to preserve old sheds, barns, grain elevators and even outhouses (outdoor toilets) as an important part of the agrarian heritage landscape (see Plate 16.6). According to the 2007 USDA Census of Agriculture, there are approximately 664, 264 historic barns built before 1960 on farms in the USA. In recognition of this immense heritage resource, the National Trust for Historic Preservation established a project, known as the BARN AGAIN! Program, to help farmers preserve historic barns and other farm buildings as heritage places and useful components of a modern, operational farm. The aims of the program are as follows (National Trust, 2010):

- To promote the preservation and use of old barns for active farm needs.
- To provide practical information and technical assistance to barn owners.

Plate 16.6 These grain elevators in Manitoba, Canada, are important symbols of the prairie agricultural heritage

- To present annual awards to farmers who exemplify barn rehabilitation and farm/ranch preservation.
- To convince farmers and ranchers that rehabilitating sturdy older farm buildings can be more cost-effective than tearing them down and building new structures.
- To assist local groups in planning and organizing BARN AGAIN! training sessions and workshops.
- To work with farmland owners to use their older outbuildings more effectively.
- To lobby local, state and federal governments for funding to help preserve barns and other farm buildings.
- To function as a national resource for all citizens concerned with the maintenance of America's rural heritage.

The National Trust believes that such a program will help preserve this important component of the rural heritage landscape, especially for farmers and ranchers who believe in the principles of sustainability. The program emphasizes how barn preservation can meet the salient economic, marketing and functional needs of the modern-day farmer.

Villages not only provide a scenic view for passersby; in some cases they also become centers of tourism, particularly day trips from nearby cities (see Plate 16.7). As they

Plate 16.7 This village in Bhutan forms part of an appealing cultural landscape in the Himalayas

capitalize on their unique ethic or agricultural patrimony, some villages become salient destinations in their own right as shopping villages and cultural centers. Thousands of agricultural, mining or ethnic villages throughout the world have chosen to emphasize their distinctive heritages to draw in tourists who want to see an alternative past to the castles, cathedrals and national monuments included on so many tour circuits.

Also part of the rural setting, living culture provides insight into times past and is an extremely important heritage attraction. In Pennsylvania (USA), the cultural landscape of the Amish draws hundreds of thousands of onlookers each year. The conservative dress, horses and buggies, tidy farms, neatly-kept schools and churches, farmers markets and roadside stands selling honey and blankets are an important part of the rural heritage environment of Pennsylvania. The living culture of Native Americans, Maori of New Zealand, the Incas of Peru and the Ashanti of Ghana are considered by many tourists to be the highlights of their travels. Living cultural museums add another dimension to the mix, as they provide a peek into what life might have been like at some particular time in the colonial past. Such living outdoor museums thrive throughout North America, Europe and Asia.

Agritourism

Tourist activities based on farming or agricultural places, products and processes are known as agritourism or agrotourism. This sort of attraction is another important element of heritage, as it reflects the land-use patterns and agrarian traditions of places that have traditionally relied upon farming for their livelihoods. Plantation tours, visiting fruit and vegetable processing plants, watching a harvest, staying on a farm, assisting in herding cattle and u-pick farms, where visitors can harvest their own produce, are all examples of agritourism activities. May people undertake these activities because of their need to escape the rush of modern urban life and get back to the countryside. For some people this might be a highly nostalgic experience if they or their parents were raised on a farm, while for other urbanites such activities and destinations might provide a simple getaway or educational experience.

Cuisine and foodways

Closely related to agritourism is the notion of food-based tourism, which in most cases can also be seen as a form of heritage tourism. Cuisine and foodways are heritage because they reflect:

- cultural norms and values;
- struggles with the natural realm;
- realities of geography and place;
- refinement through history;
- inter-generational traditions;
- imprints on other heritage realms.

National cuisines originate and develop based on environmental conditions, soil types, social mores, religious practices and many other variables, and have become an important heritage product for many tourist destinations. Traditional foods and ancient foodways have become an important part of many nations' image and appeal.

Cuisine can be seen as cultural heritage from several different perspectives. First, cuisine is reflective of indigenous people and traditional societies. Whatever foods native peoples were able to glean from the land as hunters and gatherers, or agrarian farmers, was used to develop ancient foodways and gastronomical customs. In Australia, the aboriginal peoples often share 'bush food' demonstrations with guests at cultural centers. Seeds, grubs and other insects, berries and roots formed much of the traditional aboriginal diet in Australia; demonstrations of these items are a sought-after cultural experience Down Under (see Plate 16.8).

Second, cuisines are indicative of a peasant past. They provide insight into the tastes, living conditions, celebratory milestones, interpersonal relationships and even social power relations of the everyday man and woman in the distant and recent past. The third perspective is the recipes and preparation methods themselves. These are typically handed

Plate 16.8 This native Australian demonstrates traditional 'bush tucker' to tourists at an aboriginal cultural center

down from generation to generation from parents to children. Familial and regional recipes are an important part of some people's personal past but also lend variety to national cuisines. Fourth, certain foods and ingredients become connected with certain regions and help those regions form a heritage identity. For instance, cheese and chocolate in Switzerland are an important part of that country's heritage milieu. Paprika in Hungary, meatballs in Sweden, pasta in Italy, dumplings in China, nutmeg in Grenada, hot chilies in Thailand and fish in Iceland are additional examples of primary ingredients that have become almost synonymous with native gastronomy.

Well-known drinks also contribute to the heritage product of places. Wine in countries such as France and Portugal play a very long and salient role in those countries' socio-economic development. Many wine routes have been developed in the US, Canada, South Africa, France, Portugal and other wine-producing countries that not only emphasize wine tasting but also the wine-making process and the viticultural landscapes from which the drink derives (see Plate 16.9). Tequila, Mexico, is home to the world-famous agave-based spirit, Tequila, that is served not only in Mexico but around the entire world. Scotch whiskey and its associated history is a unique selling point for Scotland, which has also

Plate 16.9 Wine routes link viticulture heritage sites together in British Columbia, Canada

developed several scotch whiskey trails that take visitors to sites of production, sales and consumption and explain the heritage of whiskey. Similar to this is the establishment of food trails that are themed according to certain regional cuisines. The 'Taste of the Tropics' food trails in Australia are a nice example of this trend where trail-goers can taste local cuisines of fresh fruit, vegetables and seafood. The Cassoulet Trail in France connects farmers, restaurants, wine makers, hotels and food processing companies in a region that specializes in cassoulet, a popular casserole dish in the southwestern part of France. Trail followers can taste variations in cassoulet and meet the people who grow its ingredients.

The sixth perspective is culinary festivals that focus on agricultural harvests or food-ways. Strawberry festivals, cheese day celebrations, chili cook-offs and barbecue competitions are commonplace examples of festivities that celebrate food as an important part of a place-bound heritage.

SUMMARY AND CONCLUSION

While tourists' tastes are becoming more sophisticated today, they are increasingly dissatisfied with well-worn tourist attractions and destinations that focus on the grandiose elements of human heritage. In addition to wanting to see castles, palaces and other momentous attractions, people now desire to supplement their experiences with visits to heritage sites that are more realistic in terms of their relationships to everyday men, women and children. To see elements of life as they really were, not just how the aristocracy lived, people are turning to rural villages, farms, barns, schools, petrol stations, humble homes, gardens, docks, mines and other features to understand the human condition in the past.

REVIEW QUESTIONS

1. Why do you think castles, cathedrals, fortresses and other elitist heritages have long been the most salient cultural heritage attractions?

2. What do you think is causing a shift from people being interested only in the grandiose to a greater interest in the landscapes of the commoner and his/her past?

3. What will it take for rural areas to succeed in developing their cultural tourism industries?

4. For what reasons do you think the National Trust in the US is becoming more interested in traditional, rural landscapes of the mundane?

5. How can agritourism also be seen as a form of heritage tourism?

6. In what ways are food and cuisine part of the heritage milieu?

RECOMMENDED READING

Andrews, M. (1978) Recreation and the stately home. *Landscape Design* 124, 29–35.

Benfield, R.W. (2001) 'Good things come to those who wait': Sustainable tourism and timed entry at Sissinghurst Castle Garden, Kent. *Tourism Geographies* 3(2), 207–217.

Bošković, D. (1999) Market possibilities for the development of agrotourism in Istria. *Tourism and Hospitality Management* 5(1/2), 23–38.

Carpio, C.E., Wohlgenant, M.K. and Boonsaeng, T. (2008) The demand for agritourism in the United States. *Journal of Agricultural and Resource Economics* 33(2), 254–269.

Carr, A. (2008) Cultural landscape values as a heritage tourism resource. In B. Prideaux, D.J. Timothy and K.S. Chon (eds) *Cultural and Heritage Tourism in Asia and the Pacific* (pp. 35–48). London: Routledge.

Derrett, R. and St Vincent Welch, J. (2008) 40 sheds and 40 kilometers: Agricultural sheds as heritage tourism opportunities. In B. Prideaux, D.J. Timothy, and K.S. Chon (eds) *Cultural and Heritage Tourism in Asia and the Pacific* (pp. 73–83). London: Routledge.

Dromard, C. (1985) 'Stately homes on holiday' or the conquest of a foreign market. *Espaces* 77, 33–36.

Dromard, C. (1987) Enhancing the value of stately homes and residences. *Espaces* 85, 9–10.

Francis, L.J., Williams, E., Annis, J., and Robbins, M. (2008) Understanding cathedral visitors: Psychological type and individual differences in experience and appreciation. *Tourism Analysis* 13(1), 71–80.

Frost, W. (2008) Heritage tourism on Australia's Asian shore: A case study of Pearl Luggers, Broome. In B. Prideaux, D.J. Timothy, and K.S. Chon (eds) *Cultural and Heritage Tourism in Asia and the Pacific* (pp. 305–314). London: Routledge.

Garrod, G. and Willis, K.G. (2002) Northumbria: Castles, cathedrals and towns. In S. Navrud and R.C. Ready (eds) *Valuing Cultural Heritage: Applying Environmental Valuation Techniques to Historic Buildings, Monuments and Artifacts* (pp. 40–52). Cheltenham: Edward Elgar.

Groth, P. and Bress, T.W. (1997) *Understanding Ordinary Landscapes*. New Haven: Yale University Press.

Harris, S. and Berke, D. (1997) *Architecture of the Everyday*. New York: Princeton Architectural Press.

Haven-Tang, C. and Jones, E. (2008) Who's king of Monmouthshire's castles? Using royal heritage in tourism businesses to develop a sense of place. In P. Long and M.J. Palmer (eds) *Royal Tourism: Excursions around Monarchy* (pp. 181–193). Clevedon: Channel View Publications.

Jolliffe, L. and Aslam, M.D.M. (2009) Tea heritage tourism: Evidence from Sri Lanka. *Journal of Heritage Tourism* 4(4), 331–343.

Karabati, S., Dogan, E., Pinar, M. and Celik, L.M. (2009) Socio-economic effects of agritourism on local communities in Turkey: The case of Aglasun. *International Journal of Hospitality and Tourism Administration* 10(2), 129–142.

Laws, E. (1998) Conceptualizing visitor satisfaction management in heritage settings: An exploratory blueprinting analysis of Leeds Castle, Kent. *Tourism Management* 19(6), 545–554.

Loureiro, M.L. and Jervell, A.M. (2005) Farmers' participation decisions regarding agrotourism activities in Norway. *Tourism Economics* 11(3), 453–469.

Loverseed, H. (2009) Gastronomic tourism – international. *Travel and Tourism Analyst* 4, 1–42.

Lowenthal, D. (1998) *The Heritage Crusade and the Spoils of History*. Cambridge: Cambridge University Press.

Meinig, D. (ed.) (1979) *The Interpretation of Ordinary Landscapes: Geographical Essays*. New York: Oxford University Press.

Muresan, A. and Smith, K.A. (1998) Dracula's castle in Transylvania: Conflicting heritage marketing strategies. *International Journal of Heritage Studies* 4(2), 73–85.

Oliver, T. and Jenkins, T. (2003) Sustaining rural landscapes: The role of integrated tourism. *Landscape Research* 28(3), 293–307.

Powe, N.A. and Willis, K.G. (1996) Benefits received by visitors to heritage sites: A case study of Warkworth Castle. *Leisure Studies* 15(4), 259–275.

Price, C. (1994) Donations, charges and willingness to pay: Aesthetic values for cathedrals and countryside. *Landscape Research* 19(1), 9–12.

Shackley, M. (2002) Space, sanctity and service: The English cathedral as *heterotopia*. *International Journal of Tourism Research* 4(5), 345–352.

Shackley, M. (2006) Costs and benefits: The impact of cathedral tourism in England. *Journal of Heritage Tourism* 1(2), 133–141.

Sharpley, R. (2002) Rural tourism and the challenge of tourism diversification: The case of Cyprus. *Tourism Management* 23(3), 233–244.

Shen, F.J. and Cottrell, S.P. (2008) A sustainable tourism framework for monitoring residents' satisfaction with agritourism in Chongdugou Village, China. *International Journal of Tourism Policy* 1(4), 368–375.

Stroud, H.B. (1985) Changing rural landscapes: A need for planning and management. *Land Use Policy* 2(2), 126–134.

Sznajder, M., Przezbórska, L. and Scrimgeour, F. (2009) *Agritourism*. Wallingford: CAB International.

Terry, A. (2008) Claiming Christmas for the tourist: 'Living history' in Dundurn Castle. *Journal of Heritage Tourism* 3(2), 104–120.

Tweeten, K., Leistritz, L. and Hodur, N. (2008) Growing rural tourism opportunities. *Journal of Extension* 46(2), 2–4.

Vadillo Lobo, E. (2001) The use of historic buildings (paradores) for housing tourists in Spain and the cultural heritage. *Estudios Turísticos* 150, 83–111.

Voase, R. (2007) Visiting a cathedral: The consumer psychology of a 'rich experience'. *International Journal of Heritage Studies* 13(1), 41–55.

Westwood, M. (1989) Warwick Castle: Preparing for the future by building on the past. *Tourism Management* 10(3), 235–239.

Willis, K.G. (1994) Paying for heritage: What price for Durham Cathedral? *Journal of Environmental Planning and Management* 37(3), 267–278.

Winter, M. and Gasson, R. (1996) Pilgrimage and tourism: Cathedral visiting in contemporary England. *International Journal of Heritage Studies* 2(3), 172–182.

Woodruffe, B.J. (1990) Conservation and the rural landscape. In J. Pinder (ed.) *Western Europe: Challenge and Change* (pp. 258–276). London: Belhaven.

RECOMMENDED WEBSITES

Castle Hotels and Mansions – http://www.schlosshotels.co.at/en/castle-hotels-and-mansions/index.html

European Castles – http://www.european-castle.com/?404=Y

National Trust for Historic Preservation – http://www.preservationnation.org/

Rural Heritage Museum – http://www.ruralheritagemuseum.org/

Rural Heritage Resources – http://www.preservationnation.org/issues/rural-heritage/resources-rural-heritage.html

CHAPTER 17

THE INDUSTRIAL PAST

LEARNING OBJECTIVES

After reading this chapter, you should be able to:

1. Understand the global change from extractive and manufacturing economies to service economies, such as tourism.

2. Discover how locations of heavy industry are transforming their 'industrial archaeology' into heritage tourist attractions.

3. Identify the main classifications of industrial attractions.

4. Realize the unique human resource perspectives of industrial heritage tourism.

5. Learn why some industrial ventures adopt tourism in addition to their extractive or manufacturing goals.

INTRODUCTION

The Industrial Revolution of the 18th and 19th centuries brought about a significant change in how the world did things. Prior to the advent of the steam engine, more technologically advanced wool spinning machines and progress in the iron industry, almost all tasks had to be undertaken by hand. Until the 1800s, most economies of the world were dependent on resource-extractive activities (primary sector) that harvested and processed raw materials from the earth. These included mining, agriculture, hunting and fishing and forestry. Almost everyone lived off the land and subsisted on what they could grow or harvest themselves, and most of the world's population was rural. The Industrial Revolution wrought great changes to the methods used to produce consumer goods and merchandise. New technologies and the mechanization of previously labor-intensive tasks saw the rapid growth of factories and other industrial plants in cities and towns. People began moving to urban areas in search of work in heavy industry, resulting in larger and more congested cities. The manufacturing and mass-production economy is usually referred to as the secondary economic sector, or a Fordist (referring to Henry Ford and automobile production) economy, where mass-manufacturing of standardized products was the norm.

Following the Second World War many technologies were made even simpler, and computers began to be an important time- and human resource-saving device in the 1960s and 70s. In the post-war era, a shift occurred from an industrialized, secondary economy to one with a stronger emphasis on services and information (tertiary sector). Economies began to emphasize banking, insurance, entertainment, tourism, media and health care over more traditional resource extraction and manufacturing. Some observers have now begun to identify quaternary sectors that include government, culture, education and research. The production of intangible experiences that fall under the tertiary or quaternary economies is also referred to as post-Fordist, or post-industrialist, economic activity.

With the proliferation of the service economy and the deindustrialization process has come an abandonment of many of the infrastructures and physical facilities associated with the manufacturing and heavy-industry era. As part of the broader movement toward preserving the past for nostalgic, educational and scientific reasons, there has been a strong lobby since the 1970s to preserve the extractive and manufacturing patrimony (industrial archaeology) of places. The reach of this interest in preservation goes beyond only closed or dilapidated spaces, however, to include existing industry as well. Many currently functioning factories, mines, quarries and docklands have joined with their abandoned counterparts in an effort to promote themselves as important industrial attractions.

This chapter examines several current trends associated with industrial heritage, including the types of resource involved, the reasons many heavy industries engage in tourism endeavors, links between the industrial legacy and other tourism sectors, as well as a few unique personnel issues.

REUSING THE INDUSTRIAL PAST

With deindustrialization, many regions that were earlier known for their production abilities have found themselves with little else to sustain their economies. This has resulted in an outmigration of many younger residents and the dereliction of many communities. The idea of utilizing the industrial patrimony for tourism caught on toward the end of the 1970s and now has a firm footing. Many regions around the world realize they can use their industrial past for regional renewal, to create jobs and to invite younger generations back to work in the services sector, although community leaders must be cognizant of the fact that tourism is not a magic tool that will automatically return regions to their previous economic levels. Unfortunately, many communities believe tourism to be a fiscal savior and face considerable disappointment when the same number of jobs and tax dollars do not accrue with tourism as they did when heavy industry led the economy. Nevertheless, planners and development specialists do suggest that tourism can be part of a mixed solution for communities in decline if their resource base is adequate to draw outside visitors.

Resources and regions

The range of resources this form of tourism is based upon is considerable. It includes all relics and sites associated with manufacturing, extraction of natural resources, shipping and transport, energy production, waste disposal systems and great feats of engineering, as well as the ancillary features that go with them (e.g. ghost towns, museums, etc.) (see Table 17.1). Some of these categories necessarily overlap. For instance, a bridge can be both an engineering accomplishment as well as a transportation innovation.

Table 17.1 Examples of industrial heritage resources for tourism

Type of industrial relic	Examples
Manufacturing and processing	Factories, assembly plants, smelters, mills, glassblowing works, textile plants, leatherworks, breweries, wineries, mints, printing presses, potteries and kilns, diamond workshops, fish and animal processing plants
Resource extraction	Open-pit mines, underground mines, quarries, lumber yards and sawmills
Shipping and transport	Railroads, canals, aqueducts, bridges, shipyards, docks, warehouses, airplane museums
Engineering	Bridges, dams, aerospace facilities
Energy production	Hydroelectric plants, nuclear energy stations, dams, windmills
Disposal systems	Sewer systems, landfills, incinerators
Other related attractions	Ghost towns, waterfronts, brownfields, museums

In their evaluation of tourism based on mining and quarrying attractions, Edwards and Llurdés i Coit (1996) outlined several types of mine features that become part of the attraction base (see Figure 17.1). These include features associated with production, processing, transportation and the social life of mine workers and management. According to the authors, production sites are the mines and quarries themselves, which are the sources of raw materials and can have long-lasting, even eternal, visible imprints on the landscape, depending on whether or not they are open-pit or underground mines. Processing attractions include smelting works, crushing areas and even demonstrations of traditional techniques at 'site-serving' locations. Transportation aspects comprise shaft elevators,

369

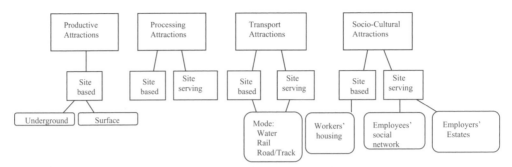

Figure 17.1 A typology of mine-based industrial attractions

Source: Based upon Edwards and Llurdés i Coit (1996: 352)

trains, trams and ports, which are all important in the production and distribution of raw and processed materials. The socio-cultural features of mining areas are those that were not directly part of the extraction and processing procedures but were an essential component of mining culture. Housing quarters, resource towns/villages, taverns and shops and even the intangible elements of mining life, such as identity, kinship, family relations and values systems, are important elements of the socio-cultural appeal of mining heritage.

An additional perspective on classifying the mechanized heritage is that of functioning versus relict industrial sites. The field of industrial archaeology includes ancient sites, such as quarries and bronze smelting areas, as well as modern but disused sites and structures. These are useful venues for tourism and create much of the appeal of places. However, industrial heritage tourism is also interested in present-day functioning sites. Operating factories, mints, mines, canals, dams and other such places are some of the most popular tourist attractions today where the production process, the equipment, workers' skills and methods are all important ingredients in the experience. The Denver and Philadelphia mints in the USA provide self-guided tours that funnel visitors through the coin-production process as the coins are actually being minted (see Plate 17.1). They also have interpretive displays that illustrate numismatic (money-related) history. Car assembly plants and open-pit mines throughout the world offer guided tours that allow visitors to see and experience the course of production, and tourists can watch glass blowers, potters and brewers do their crafts (see Plate 17.2).

Functioning plants can be further viewed in terms of their scale of reach and impact. Primary sites are those that are well known and draw visitors in their own right. Examples include some of the UNESCO-designated sites listed above but also many living factories and mines, such as Hershey's Chocolate factory in Hershey, Pennsylvania, and Cadbury World's two locations in England and New Zealand. At Hershey's, visitors used to tour the factory itself but these tours have been replaced with simulated experiences and variety shows at Hershey's Chocolate World. Tours at Cadbury World in England are

Plate 17.1 The US Mint is an important industrial attraction in Philadelphia

Plate 17.2 This crafter in Denmark demonstrates the ancient glass-making industry

based on a visitor center with explanatory displays and recreated locations associated with the history of chocolate and Cadbury, but it also includes visits to the packaging part of the plant where chocolates are wrapped and boxed for commercial distribution. At the New Zealand plant in Dunedin, tours include more areas of the operational factory. Likewise, world renowned sites like Itaipu Dam on the border of Paraguay and Brazil (see Plate 17.3), and Kennecott Copper Mine (also known as the Bingham Canyon Mine) in Utah, USA (see Plate 17.4), act as primary or anchor attractions in their respective locales, as do several resource-based ghost towns in the American west and Australian outback.

Secondary industrial attractions are those that do not necessarily draw tourists to a region but are effective ancillary enticements once a person is already in the area. Small-scale cheese-making factories (see Plate 17.5), sawmills, nuclear energy generators and historic underground sewage systems are a few examples. In a critical mass, these minor attractions can become an important part of a destination's cultural heritage milieu.

Today several regions are especially dependent on industrial heritage for their tourism economies. In the United Kingdom, Wales is home to dozens of slate, coal and lead mines, and Cornwall has a deep-rooted heritage of tin and copper mining. Both regions

Plate 17.3 Itaipu Dam on the border of Paraguay and Brazil draws visitors interested in its construction and energy-generation functions

emphasize their excavating legacy, including mining-related railways and canals, in their tourism planning and promotional efforts. The Rust Belt region of the USA, including parts of the upper midwest and the northeast, is home to many industrial relics that have become salient tourist attractions, and the copper, silver and gold mines of the western US are an important part of that region's appeal (see Plate 17.6). The bush and outback of Australia are peppered with intriguing mining ghost towns that draw visitors from the country's coastal cities. While these areas tend to have higher than normal concentrations of industrial heritage given their history of resource extraction and heavy manufacturing, industrial archaeology is located nearly everywhere in the world with essential tourism implications.

Despite the widespread global distribution of manufacturing plants and related relics, there is a disproportionately high concentration of industry-based tourist attractions in Europe – in countries such as the United Kingdom, the Netherlands, Germany, Austria, Finland, Hungary, Spain and many others. These nations have identified this branch of heritage as a lucrative partial means of stabilizing or enhancing industrial economies. In recognition of the importance of industrial heritage for tourism, the United Kingdom

Plate 17.4 The Kennecott Copper Mine is an 'anchor' attraction near Salt Lake City

marketed the Industrial Heritage Year in 1993 to build public awareness of the value of preserving and visiting this element of the past. Based on the success of the UK's efforts, the Netherlands held its own Industrial Heritage Year in 1996.

In addition, several industrial heritage routes have been developed in Europe to highlight the region's mechanized past and present. The European Route of Industrial Heritage is a themed route that links manufacturing and extraction landscapes of Germany, France, Belgium, Luxembourg, the Netherlands and the United Kingdom. There are many shorter regional industrial routes scattered throughout Europe as well, especially in the industrial heartlands of Great Britain, France, Belgium, Germany, Poland and the Netherlands. The Path of Progress National Heritage Tour Route in Pennsylvania, USA, provides a similar backdrop as it focuses on the industrial heritage and cultural landscapes of southwestern Pennsylvania.

The universal and intrinsic value of manufacturing and extractive traditions has been recognized on an international level. UNESCO began listing industrial heritage in the 1990s and has continued this reach with a large handful of sites being inscribed in the early 2000s (see Table 17.2). There are also many industrial complexes on UNESCO's Tentative List awaiting nomination to World Heritage List by their state parties.

Plate 17.5 This cheese factory lends supporting appeal to the area of Bern, Switzerland

Plate 17.6 This ghost town is all that remains of a 19th century mining operation in the western USA

Table 17.2 A selection of industrial heritage sites on the World Heritage List, 2010

Country	Site	Year of inscription
Austria	Semmering Railway	1998
Canada	Rideau Canal	2007
Finland	Verla Groundwood and Board Mill	1996
Germany	Völklingen Ironworks	1994
Germany	Zollverein Coal Mine Industrial Complex	2001
Netherlands	Ir. D.F. Woudagemaal	1998
Norway	Røros Mining Town	1980
Oman	Aflaj Irrigation Systems of Oman	2006

Poland	Wieliczka Salt Mine	2008
Spain	Vizcaya Bridge	2006
Sweden	Engelsberg Ironworks	1993
United Kingdom	Blaenavon Industrial Landscape	2000
United Kingdom	Pontcysyllte Aqueduct and Canal	2009

Source: UNESCO (2010b)

Why does heavy industry choose tourism?

As noted above, sites that currently function in an industrial capacity often take on additional tourism-related responsibilities, becoming both a source of production and a tourist attraction. There are several reasons communities and working plants elect to become involved in industrial tourism. First is to bolster their financial bottom line. A number of industrial establishments have fallen on hard times as world markets change, and demand for their products becomes more volatile. Others simply want to increase their profit margins for shareholders, owners and employees. Tourism is seen as a way of supplementing production-related income via entrance fees, guided tours and souvenir sales. Research shows that most industrial sites either break even or make a notable profit in their tourism endeavors, and in most cases there is little overhead risk involved because the attraction itself already exists. While many industrial locations have gift shops and cafes, some sites are more conducive to retail sales and boutique shopping. For instance, cheese-making factories are known for outlet shops where tourists can buy a variety of cheeses and related products, some made on site and others imported from elsewhere. Winery and distillery shops do well in selling wines and whiskeys, particularly after visitors have toured the facilities and observed the process. Retail shops are a natural fit with glass, textile, leather and ceramics works and even copper mines, and all have had considerable success in linking tourist sales with mass production.

A second reason is to increase visibility and stature among existing and potential new markets. Free or paid tours through a factory that makes consumer items (e.g. shoes, clothing, food, cars) can help stimulate consumer interest in the product and help strengthen customer brand loyalty. Seeing the assembly of Volkswagen automobiles in a German plant can create positive memories that are triggered when visitors consider purchasing a car later. Demonstrations of quality assurance and efficiency at the factory reinforce loyalty and influence buyer behavior later.

A related concept is branding, where destinations brand themselves, or create a marketable image, not only for their own self-identity but also as a visible identifier to the general public, based on their industrial past and present. Shawinigan, Quebec, for instance, brands itself as the City of Energy because it is one of Canada's largest hydroelectricity-producing locales.

The third purpose in being involved in tourism has political undertones. Many examples exist of tourism being used as a public relations tool to build public confidence with manufacturing or mining operations. Open-pit mining, quarrying, large-scale energy plants, factories and widespread timbering often fail in the court of public opinion. Concerns are frequently voiced about the ecological problems associated with clear-cutting, air and water pollution and esthetic problems such operations can create. Tourism is sometimes adopted as a tool for alleviating public fears and offsetting negative images in the public mind by providing tours and explanatory video presentations that extol the virtues of the site and what the company is doing to clean up the environment or minimize the operation's impact. Often, in this kind of situation, there are not entrance fees; rather than tourism being used as a profit-making tool, it becomes a public relations operational expense.

Fourthly, regional identity plays a prominent role in some places deciding to develop tourism based on their industrial past. In mining towns it is common for the entire community's identity to be wrapped up in their resource-extracting heritage. Their social, economic, religious and political lives often revolve around the singular reason for their existence. The mining narrative of Cornwall and Wales for many people has become a defining element of their 'Cornishness' or 'Welshness', and tourism can be used to help firm up that identity for future generations.

Finally, industrial tourism can provide a justification for urban renewal and waterfront development. This was already discussed in Chapter 9 but is worth reiterating again in this specific context. Most heavy industry of the 18th and 19th centuries was located on seashores, lakeshores and riverbanks, because of the need to bring in raw materials and export finished products by ship or boat. As a result, many waterfronts of the world developed rapidly as industrialization accelerated in the 1800s. Later, with the con-comitant growth in post-Fordist economic sectors and the decline of heavy industry, however, many shoreline industrial complexes were abandoned and remained neglected far into the 20th century.

During the latter 1900s, a social awareness of city decay began to grow resulting in a host of urban renewal projects all over the world. One of the driving forces behind this redevelopment movement was tourism. Industrial zone revitalization creates a leisure ambience that is important for urban dwellers and tourists. It increases community pride and confidence, and improves quality of life for living, working and recreating, in most cases encompassing reused industrial buildings and complexes as apartments, shops, fitness centers, cafes, cinemas, museums, bars and hotels. In some cases, brownfields, or derelict industrial wastelands, have also been regenerated and put to recreational and touristic uses, in the form of parks and outdoor theaters.

CROSSOVER WITH OTHER SECTORS

While all elements of cultural tourism have crossovers with other subsectors of tourism, there are a few that are particularly pertinent to industrial heritage. One of these is cruises. The links between cruises and industry are at least threefold. First, the ship-building trade often provides a unique resource or attraction for tourists. Old shipyards and contemporary ship-construction facilities are part of the industrial resource base in many coastal areas. Second, some of the docks and harbors where cruises land are often good examples of regenerated industrial landscapes, where even customs buildings, souvenir malls and restaurants that serve cruise visitors are renovated factories or warehouses. Finally, famous industrial sites sometimes function as relevant cruise destinations. The most famous of these is probably the Panama Canal which sees more than 13,000 vessels passing through each year, of which a small handful (usually less than 200) are cruise ships, providing a unique industrial heritage experience for a few hundred thousand passengers annually.

An unassuming but important link also exists between industrial heritage and health tourism. Schofield (2004) discusses the notion of 'subterranotherapy', or underground spa treatments, in the salt mines of Kyrgyzstan and notes the mines' unique microclimates that make this specialized form of therapy possible and popular. Other examples can be found in Europe of humid salt mining cave systems providing contemporary therapeutic care for chronic respiratory problems.

UNIQUE HUMAN RESOURCE PERSPECTIVES

There are a couple of unique staffing points that should also be noted in this discussion. It is common practice for retired or laid-off/redundant mine or factory workers to be employed as guides in heritage complexes. Some companies are able to keep some of their workers on the payroll, even when times are lean, by employing them in interpretive centers or as tour guides.

Former employees have a unique perspective on the history and operations of the plants where they once worked. Their hands-on experience allows them to connect personally to the places being shown and they can reveal much about their own past in relation to the mines, factories or other locations, lending a higher degree of authenticity to most visitors' experiences.

Many retirees volunteer to guide visitors in the factories or mines where they were once employed. For some it is an extension of their past careers and highly nostalgic, while it may also be a hobby that allows them to continue to be involved in something they grew to enjoy. These volunteers are an important part of some companies' tourism outreach efforts.

SUMMARY AND CONCLUSION

Despite the economic and physical decay suffered by traditional extractive and manufacturing sectors during the mid- and late-20th century and the populations that depended on them, tourism has brought new hope to many declining communities throughout the industrialized world. While it is not a sure answer to every community's woes, tourism should be considered a logical part of the redevelopment mix when there are enough resources upon which it can be based. Linking communities and their industrial resources together into drivable themed routes is one way of accomplishing development goals.

Industrial sites and destinations choose to become involved in tourism for a wide variety of reasons: economic, public relations, promotional effort, identity-confirming and urban redevelopment. In addition, this form of cultural tourism has unique linkages to other forms of tourism, including cruises and health treatments, and there are special personnel considerations for industrial site managers. Industry-oriented tourism is a complex and varied type of heritage tourism that appeals to serious enthusiasts and casual visitors alike. It can be an important tool for communities and companies in their efforts to create sustainable businesses, build community spirit and repair physical infrastructures, and it is an important part of the industrial past.

REVIEW QUESTIONS

1. How might ghost towns be considered part of the industrial heritage of a region?

2. Why do many functioning heavy industries, such as active mines, today take on tourism as another function of their business?

3. Why would the historical remnants and landscapes of mining and heavy industry merit being added to UNESCO's World Heritage List?

4. What are some of the unique links between industrial heritage and other forms of tourism?

5. What unique human resource characteristics differentiate industrial heritage tourism from other types of cultural tourism?

RECOMMENDED READING

Alfrey, J. and Putnam, T. (1992) *The Industrial Heritage: Managing Resources and Uses.* London: Routledge.

Alonso, A.D., O'Neill, M.A. and Kim, K. (2010) In search of authenticity: A case examination of the transformation of Alabama's Langdale Cotton Mill into an industrial heritage tourism attraction. *Journal of Heritage Tourism* 5(1), 33–48.

Avery, P. (2007) Born again: From dock cities to cities of culture. In M.K. Smith (ed.) *Tourism, Culture and Regeneration* (pp. 151–162). Wallingford, UK: CAB International.

Bazin, C.M. (1995) Industrial heritage in the tourism process in France. In M.F. Lanfant, J.B. Allcock, and E.M. Bruner (eds) *International Tourism: Identity and Change* (pp. 113–126). London: Sage.

Cameron, C.M. (2000) Emerging industrial heritage: The politics of selection. *Museum Anthropology* 23(3), 58–73.

Chen, J.S., Kerstetter, D.L. and Graefe, A.R. (2001) Tourists' reasons for visiting industrial heritage sites. *Journal of Hospitality and Leisure Marketing* 8(1/2), 19–31.

Cole, D. (2004) Exploring the sustainability of mining heritage tourism. *Journal of Sustainable Tourism* 12(6), 480–494.

Conlin, M. and Jolliffe, L. (eds) (2010) *Mining Heritage and Tourism: A Global Synthesis.* London: Taylor and Francis.

De Bres, K. (1991) Seaside resorts, working museums and factory shops: Three vignettes as British tourism enters the nineties. *Focus* 41(2), 10–16.

Dicks, B. (2008) Performing the hidden injuries of class in coal-mining heritage. *Sociology* 42(3), 436–452.

Dodman, D. (2008) Commerce and cruises: A comparative study of Jamaican waterfront transformations. *Local Environment* 13(7), 571–587.

Doorne, S. (1998) Power, participation and perception: An insider's perspective on the politics of the Wellington waterfront redevelopment. *Current Issues in Tourism* 1(2), 129–166.

Gibson, C. and Hardman, D. (1998) Regenerating urban heritage for tourism. *Managing Leisure* 3(1), 37–54.

Goodall, B. (1993) Industrial heritage and tourism. *Built Environment* 19(2), 93–104.

Green, S. (1994) Industrial tourism: An overview. *Environmental Interpretation* 7, 16–17.

Hospers, G.J. (2002) Industrial heritage tourism and regional restructuring in the European Union. *European Planning Studies* 10(3), 397–404.

Hoyle, B. (2002) Urban waterfront revitalization in developing countries: The example of Zanzibar's Stone Town. *Geographical Journal* 168(2), 141–162.

Jansen-Verbeke, M. (1999) Industrial heritage: A nexus for sustainable tourism development. *Tourism Geographies* 1(1), 70–85.

Jansen-Verbeke, M. and van de Wiel, E. (1995) Tourism planning in urban revitalization projects: Lessons from the Amsterdam waterfront development. In G.J. Ashworth and A.G.J. Dietvorst (eds) *Tourism and Spatial Transformation* (pp. 129–158). Wallingford, UK: CAB International.

Jones, A.L. (2007) On the water's edge: Developing cultural regeneration paradigms for urban waterfronts. In M.K. Smith (ed.) *Tourism, Culture and Regeneration* (pp. 143–150). Wallingford, UK: CAB International.

Kerstetter, D.L., Confer, J.J. and Bricker, K.S. (1998) Industrial heritage attractions: Types and tourists. *Journal of Travel and Tourism Marketing* 7(2), 91–104.

Landorf, C. (2009) A framework for sustainable heritage management: A study of UK industrial heritage sites. *International Journal of Heritage Studies* 15, 494–510.

Larner, C. (1994) Scenes from the past. *Leisure Management* 14(5), 24–26.

Leung, M.W.H. and Soyez, D. (2009) Industrial heritage: Valorizing the spatial-temporal dynamics of another Hong Kong story. *International Journal of Heritage Studies* 15(1), 57–75.

Llurdés I Coit, J.C. (2001) Heritage tourism and textile "model villages": The case of River Park, Barcelona, Spain. *Tourism Recreation Research* 26(1), 65–71.

Mann, R.B. (1988) Ten trends in the continuing renaissance of urban waterfronts. *Landscape and Urban Planning* 16(1/2), 177–199.

McCarthy, J. (1998) Waterfront regeneration: Recent practice in Dundee. *European Planning Studies* 6(6), 731–736.

Page, S.J. (1989) Tourist development in the London Docklands in the 1980s and 1990s. *GeoJournal* 19(3), 291–295.

Patijn, S. (1990) Revitalization of inner cities: The recognition of hidden possibilities. *World Leisure & Recreation* 32(2), 36–39.

Prentice, R., Witt, S. and Hamer, C. (1993) The experience of industrial heritage: The case of Black Gold. *Built Environment* 19(2), 137–146.

Pretes, M. (2002) Tourism mines and mining tourists. *Annals of Tourism Research* 29(2), 439–456.

Ritchie, W. (1980) On the waterfront. *Geographical Magazine* 52(12), 810–816.

Rudd, M.A. and Davis, J.A. (1998) Industrial heritage tourism at the Bingham Canyon Copper Mine. *Journal of Travel Research* 36(3), 85–89.

Ruiz Ballesteros, E. and Hernández Ramírez, M. (2007) Identity and community: Reflections on the development of mining heritage in southern Spain. *Tourism Management* 28(3), 677–687.

Speakman, L. and Bramwell, B. (1992) *Sheffield Works: An Evaluation of a Factory Tourism Scheme*. Sheffield: Sheffield Hallam University.

Stanton, C. (2005) Serving up culture: Heritage and its discontents at an industrial history site. *International Journal of Heritage Studies* 11(5), 415–431.

Stevens, T. (1987) Going underground. *Leisure Management* 7(10), 48–50.

Tunbridge, J.E. (2008) Malta: Reclaiming the naval heritage? *International Journal of Heritage Studies* 14(5), 449–466.

Varlow, S. (1990) Oiling the wheels of industry. *Horizons* 1, 8–12.

Wanhill, S. (2000) Mines – a tourist attraction: Coal mining in industrial South Wales. *Journal of Travel Research* 39(1), 60–69.

Worden, N. (1996) Contested heritage at the Cape Town Waterfront. *International Journal of Heritage Studies* 1(1/2), 59–7.

Xie, F.F.P. (2006) Developing industrial heritage tourism: A case study of the proposed Jeep Museum in Toledo, Ohio. *Tourism Management* 27(6), 1321–1330.

RECOMMENDED WEBSITES

Association for the Industrial Archaeology – http://industrial-archaeology.org/

Association québécoise pour le patrimoine industriel – http://www.aqpi.qc.ca/

European Route of Industrial Heritage – http://www.erih.net/

Industrial Heritage Association of Ireland – http://www.ihai.ie/

International Committee for the Conservation of the Industrial Heritage – http://www.mnactec.cat/ticcih/

Ironbridge Gorge Museum – http://www.ironbridge.org.uk/

Museum of Our Industrial Heritage – http://www.industrialhistory.org/

Smithsonian Industrial Archeology Exhibit – http://americanhistory.si.edu/archives/e-2.htm

Society for Industrial Archeology – http://www.sia-web.org/

The International Committee for the Conservation of the Industrial Heritage – http://www.ticcih.org/

CHAPTER 18

RELIGIOUS SITES AND PILGRIMAGE

LEARNING OBJECTIVES

After reading this chapter, you should be able to:

1. Be aware of the common debate about the difference between tourists and pilgrims.

2. Understand the characteristics of religious tourists/pilgrims in terms of behavior and experiences.

3. Know about the significant magnitude of religious tourism in many parts of the world.

4. Discover the most salient religious tourism destinations.

5. Know the role of pilgrimage travel in various religious traditions.

6. Be familiar with the main issues facing religious site managers.

7. Learn about the current trends that are unique to this type of cultural tourism.

INTRODUCTION

One of the most important manifestations of heritage tourism today is travel for spiritual or religious purposes. Religious tourism, or pilgrimage, in fact is the underlying motive for some of the world's largest tourist gatherings, and many destinations rely almost entirely upon it for their economic well-being. The hajj pilgrimage undertaken by Muslims to Mecca, Saudi Arabia, every year is the second largest tourist gathering in the world with more than two million religious adherents gathering in one small space for a short period of time. This event is exceeded only by the Hindu Khumba Mela, which involves approximately 20 million people (some estimates suggest even 75 million) every few years in a handful of locations in India. Today, almost all of the world's religions either encourage or require some form of travel for salvation or spiritual enlightenment, resulting in millions of people traveling for a variety of religious reasons.

Pilgrims are defined as people who travel for spiritual enlightenment or who seek a closer relationship with a deity. For some, it is a religious obligation while for others it is an outward manifestation of their piety and level of spiritual development. This chapter examines various concepts, debates and issues surrounding the notion of religious tourism in the context of heritage. It first looks at what pilgrimage means and how it manifests in tourism terms. It then highlights the magnitude of religious tourism and examines some of the trends and management issues facing administrators of sacred sites.

TOURISTS AND PILGRIMS

Most tourism scholars today agree that religiously-motivated travel was among the earliest forerunners of modern-day tourism. Some even suggest that it was the earliest form, discounting travel for hunting and trading, with people traveling some 3000 years ago in search of Buddha and even earlier in search of other forms of nature gods. Following the death of Jesus Christ, Christian followers traveled *en masse* from Europe and around today's Middle East to worship at the sites most closely associated with their savior's life and venerated by the churches of the time. Likewise some of the earliest forms of travel in Cyprus, Greece, Turkey and other parts of Europe were based on itineraries aimed at tracing the lives of the apostles or saints and visiting places they lived and worked. In short, many tourism historians maintain that religious or spiritual pilgrimages were the essential foundations of what we know today as tourism.

Pilgrimage or religious tourism entails people traveling away from home to places or events of a sacred nature and includes the activities, rituals and ceremonies undertaken in the destination. They do this out of a deep religious conviction and a desire to placate God and receive blessings in their lives. Some observers and scholars today have tried to conceptualize the relationship between pilgrimage and tourism and between pilgrims and tourists. Some argue that pilgrims are not tourists because they travel for spiritual or religious reasons, while tourists travel for pleasure or other hedonic reasons. However, this is essentially a false assumption and reflects a misunderstanding of who a tourist is.

From the perspective of the World Tourism Organization, the global tourism academy in general and most destinations, pilgrims are tourists because a tourist is anyone who travels away from home for at least one night but not more than a year. Tourists are not defined by their motives and activities and are not inherently pleasure-seeking hedonists. People traveling for business, to attend a funeral, to participate in a sporting event or to take part in a large pilgrimage event are tourists of one form or another. Several scholars have argued that aside from motives for traveling there is no difference between pilgrims and tourists as even pilgrims use public transportation, eat at restaurants and cafes, stay in hotels, motels or campgrounds and shop for souvenirs or mementos. Thus, not only are they statistically part of the tourism phenomenon, most also demonstrate leisure tourist-like tendencies and behaviors while in transit and in the destination.

Regardless of the underlying conceptual debate, religious tourists and pilgrims can be seen on a continuum of piousness (see Figure 18.1). On the most pious, or sacred, extreme are true pilgrims, who are spiritually moved or required to travel to sacred places

Sacred space   Secular space

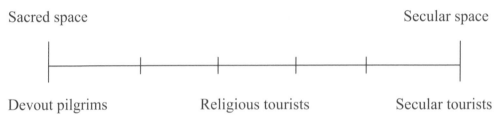

Devout pilgrims   Religious tourists   Secular tourists

Figure 18.1 Scale of religiosity in visits to sacred sites

Source: After Smith (1992)

in an effort to demonstrate their devotion to God. With heartfelt devotion they travel, often with great difficulty and suffering, to sites and events they hold to be extremely sacred. In some extreme cases they avoid all commercial aspects of tourism. On the opposite end of the spectrum are curious cultural tourists, or 'secular tourists' (Smith, 1992), who happen to visit sacred sites as part of a broader itinerary. These people tend to visit sites that are holy to others, out of curiosity or an interest in culture (see Plate 18.1). Between these two ends of the spectrum are people who might be pilgrims but also

Plate 18.1 This small church in Aruba is one of the island's main cultural attractions

participate in secular activities while on their pilgrimage, such as dining out, playing golf, seeing an opera, shopping and sightseeing. While both pilgrims and secular tourists are tourists, this spectrum illustrates that there are different levels of spirituality or religiosity motivating people to travel or visit sacred sites.

Like the continuum just noted, it is also possible to align religious travelers along a spectrum of experience and motivation. On one end of the spectrum are faithful travelers who are required to visit sacred sites in order to gain salvation in the afterlife. The most prominent example of this is Islam, whose adherents are required, if at all possible, to undertake the pilgrimage to Mecca. On the other end of the spectrum are religions that discourage pilgrimage-like activities altogether. Sikhism is one of the most notable of these faiths, wherein pilgrimage is discouraged as a waste of time and effort, bearing no fruit for the individual traveler. Between these two extremes are a vast array of Christian and non-Christian faiths that encourage varying degrees of pilgrimage. Judaism officially has no pilgrimage doctrine and does not encourage or discourage religiously-motivated travel. Most Catholic and Protestant Christian churches encourage their members to visit Biblical sites, church headquarters or historic sites associated with their faith, but these are not essential for salvation. Instead, they provide personal blessings by way of increased faith, spiritual growth, a firmer witness of God and a better appreciation of the history of their religion. Hindus and Buddhists are avid pilgrims, but it is not required of them. Instead, visits to holy sites are considered highly auspicious and beneficial for reaching their goals of various levels of spiritual consciousness.

This is in essence a theoretical debate, but what matters on the ground is the number of tourists (whether pilgrim tourists or other tourists) who visit a site, their experiences and their impacts in the destination. Many traditional pilgrimage destinations are now learning to adapt to a wider audience by providing services and experiences beyond the traditional pilgrim experience.

RELIGIOUS TOURISM: ITS MAGNITUDE

Estimates by the World Religious Travel Association (2009) place international religiously-motivated trips at around 600 million per year, taken by 300 million international religious travelers. While this is probably a conservative estimate, it does illustrate the serious magnitude of religious tourism throughout the world. Several countries and regions have become extremely significant pilgrimage destinations, whose economies are dependent upon this special tourism niche and whose social networks are significantly affected by pilgrimage tourism. Examples include Spain, France, Italy and Bosnia-Herzegovina in Europe, as well as Israel and Saudi Arabia in the Middle East and India and Nepal in South Asia. Table 18.1 illustrates some of the most significant pilgrimage destinations among five major religions of the world.

Table 18.1 Various major pilgrimage sites for five world religions

Religion	Country	Holy site or city
Buddhism	Bhutan	Taktsang Monastery, Gangtey Gompa
	China	Yung-Kang and Lung-men Caves
	India	Bodh Gaya, Sarnath, Kushinagar
	Myanmar	Bagan, Mandalay, Inlay Lake
	Nepal	Lumbini, Patan, Kathmandu Valley
	Sri Lanka	Anuradhapura, Kandy, Sri Pada
	Thailand	Wat Phra Kaeo, Wat Phra Chetuphon
	Tibet	Patola Palace (Lhasa), Jokhang Monastery
	Vietnam	Huong Pagoda Complex, Tran Quoc Pagoda
Christianity	Egypt	Mount Sinai
	France	Lourdes
	Ireland	Knock, St Patrick's grave
	Israel/Palestine	Bethlehem, Jerusalem
	Italy	Rome
	Portugal	Fatima
	Spain	Santiago de Compostela
	Turkey	Hagia Sophia
	Vatican City	St Peter's Basilica
Hinduism	Cambodia	Angkor Wat
	India	Ayodhya, Benaras, Davaraka, Haridwar, Puri
	Indonesia	Prambanan Temples
	Nepal	Pashupatinath Temple, Bhaktapur
	Thailand	Erawan Shrine
Islam	Egypt	Masjid Ra's al-Husayn, Sit Zainab
	Iran	Mashad, Qom
	Iraq	Najaf, Karbala, Moosayab
	Palestine	Jerusalem, Hebron (Khalil al-Rahman)
	Saudi Arabia	Mecca, Medina
	Syria	Great Mosque of Damascus
Judaism	Austria	Judenplatz Memorial
	Germany	Memorial to the Murdered Jews of Europe
	Iraq	Ezekiel's Tomb
	Israel/Palestine	Western Wall, Temple Mount, Cave of the Patriarchs
	Morocco	Tombs of Rabbis
	Tunisia	Djerba Island
	Ukraine	Uman
	United States	Bialystoker Synagogue, Touro Synagogue

While real numbers are difficult to ascertain at the global level, many countries that depend largely on the religious tourism niche have seen some success in measuring the magnitude of religious tourism within their boundaries. For example, in 2007, 2.27 million tourists arrived in Israel; 44% were Jews, although this does not necessarily mean they were on a pilgrimage or other religious trips, but it is likely that many were. In total, some 23% (more than half a million) of all arrivals in 2007 were counted as pilgrims (Central Bureau of Statistics, 2008), which included Christians and Jews and could have, in theory, included Muslims as well since Jerusalem is considered the third holiest place in Islam.

Saudi Arabia keeps tabs on tourist arrivals and pilgrim arrivals, although the government classifies these separately, issues separate hajj visas and has special hajj terminals at its major airports. Table 18.2 shows yearly pilgrim numbers at Mecca. As already noted, the annual hajj is considered one of the largest tourist gatherings in the world, and as the data show, it is increasing in numerical strength. At Mecca, sacred rituals are performed that symbolize personal cleansing and the casting out of evil. Prayers and sacrifices are offered, fasting is done and millions of pilgrims circumambulate the Kaaba – the holiest edifice in all of Islam, believed to have been built by Adam.

Table 18.2 Arrivals of hajj pilgrims in Saudi Arabia, 1996–2006

Year	Pilgrims from Mecca	Pilgrims from other areas of Saudi Arabia	Pilgrims from outside Saudi Arabia	Total
1416 AH (1996 CE)	126,739	658,030	1,080,465	1,865,234
1417 AH (1997 CE)	121,516	652,744	1,168,591	1,942,851
1418 AH (1998 CE)	113,928	585,842	1,132,344	1,839,154
1419 AH (1999 CE)	127,146	648,122	1,056,730	1,831,998
1420 AH (2000 CE)	105,369	466,230	1,267,555	1,839,154
1421 AH (2001 CE)	108,463	440,808	1,363,992	1,913,263
1422 AH (2002 CE)	110,592	479,984	1,354,184	1,944,760
1423 AH (2003 CE)	116,887	493,230	1,431,012	2,041,129
1424 AH (2004 CE)	119,364	473,004	1,419,706	2,012,074
1425 AH (2006 CE)*	n/a	629,710**	1,534,769	2,164,469
1426 AH (2006 CE)	n/a	573,147	1,557,447	2,130,594

Source: Kingdom of Saudi Arabia (2009)

* Under the Islamic calendar, it is possible to have two Zul-Hijja months (or part months) in the same Gregorian year (e.g. 1973), or the hajj being split between years

** In 2006 all Saudi pilgrims were enumerated together

According to a domestic tourism study undertaken by the Indian Ministry of Tourism and Culture (2003), pilgrimage was the most salient form of domestic tourism in India in 2002 with more than 100 million trips taken of a religious or spiritual nature to religious sites and events. The study further illustrated that almost half of all domestic package tours and some 20% of day trips were for pilgrimage or religious purposes. Most Hindu pilgrimages focus on rivers or temples dedicated to the lives of gods or holy men, usually built on sites believed to have been where hallowed events occurred.

While at the national level, Saudi Arabia, Israel and India might be host to the largest proportion of pilgrim tourists in the world, several other regions have become important destinations as well on an international, regional or local scale. Lourdes, France; Fatima, Portugal; Santiago de Compostela, Spain; Rome, Italy; Medjugorje, Bosnia and Herzegovina, have all become important destinations for the world's 1.1 billion Roman Catholics. Many other national shrines exist in countries that have significant Catholic populations, including most countries in Central and South America, North America and Western Europe. In addition to the Jesus-related sites in the Holy Land, other Christian denominations have their own sacred sites that dominate the tourism landscapes of certain places, such as the Mormons in Salt Lake City, Utah, Palmyra, New York, and Nauvoo, Illionois. Likewise, Trondheim, Norway, is a popular pilgrimage destination for Norwegian Lutherans and Catholics, owing to its association with Saint Olaf, the patron saint of Norway. Hagia Sophia Church (now a museum) in Istanbul, Turkey, and Mt Athos, Greece, are extremely important pilgrimage sites for Greek Orthodox Christians, and the grave of St Patrick in Downpatrick, Northern Ireland, is an important sacred side for Irish Catholics.

For Buddhists, Lumbini, Nepal, symbolizes the epitome of sacred space. This is where the Lord Buddha was born sometime around 565BC (see Plate 18.2). Thousands of pilgrims from all over the Buddhist world travel to Lumbini each year to experience the sacredness of this place and to pay their respects to Buddha. In India, other sites (Bodh Gaya, Sarnath and Kushinagar) are believed to have been associated with his enlightenment, his ministry and his death, and have become important pilgrimage destinations for Buddhists and Hindus from all over the world (see Plate 18.3). There are other significant Buddhist sacred sites in India, Sri Lanka, Thailand, China, Bangladesh, Bhutan, Indonesia, Vietnam, Laos, Tibet and Myanmar that draw local, regional and international pilgrims (see Table 18.1).

In the Jewish religion, pilgrimage itself is not necessarily encouraged but many Jews undertake pilgrimages of various sorts (known sometimes as mitzvahs of nostalgia) to grave sites of famous Jews and ancient prophets, to the Western Wall in Jerusalem and to well-known synagogues in the Middle East, North America and Europe (see Plate 18.4). Likewise, Jews traveling to holocaust sites in Europe and holocaust museums in the USA and Israel are also on a pilgrimage of sorts which, while secular in many respects, also has a religious undertone and may be spiritually moving.

Plate 18.2 The location of Buddha's birthplace in Nepal draws many visitors each year

Plate 18.3 Kushinagar, India, is known as the place where Buddha died and is one of Buddhism's holiest sites

Plate 18.4 Local worshippers and tourists alike pray at the Western Wall in Jerusalem

RELIGIOUS TOURISM AS HERITAGE TOURISM

While pilgrimage is a unique tourism niche in its own right, it can also be seen as a form of heritage tourism. Such an overlapping classification is not problematic because the two concepts are not mutually exclusive. Religious tourism can be seen as heritage tourism from at least four perspectives: religious buildings are historic sites for the general public; holy places are heritage sites for religious adherents; rituals, ceremonies and sacred experiences are a spiritual heritage for devotees; and traditional pilgrimage routes and trails have become important cultural routes for pilgrims and other heritage tourists.

First, the buildings, shrines and other sacred spaces being visited are fascinating heritage sites in their own right. As has already been noted in previous chapters, religious places and structures, such as temples, churches, cathedrals, mosques and synagogues, are among the most important heritage sites in the world. They appeal not only to religious adherents but also to cultural tourists, who seek nothing more than to photograph the sites and fulfill their own curiosity. St Peter's Basilica in the Vatican City, the Dome of the Rock (*Qubbat as-Sakhrah*) (see Plate 18.5) and the Western Wall in Jerusalem, the Salt Lake Temple in Salt Lake City, Borobudur and Prambanan temples in Indonesia, Temple

Plate 18.5 The Dome of the Rock in Jerusalem is one of Islam's holiest sites

of the Emerald Buddha (*Wat Phra Kaew*) in Thailand and the Golden Temple of Amritsar, India, are just a handful of famous examples.

The second perspective is holy sites as sacred heritage places for religious adherents and includes the sites mentioned in the previous paragraph. In this case, however, the ground, structures or natural features (e.g. caves/grottos, forests, rivers or mountains) are considered sacred by the religions that venerate them. In this regard, human cultural values have been implanted on natural features to create a unique heritage that is both natural and cultural. For most Protestant Christians, the Garden Tomb and its grounds in East Jerusalem is one of the holiest places on earth, recognized as the burial place of Jesus Christ and site of his resurrection (see Plate 18.6). Such a site features prominently on Christian itineraries but is much less prominent, if it exists at all, on general heritage tours in Israel. In the Holy Land, Christians visit other sites associated with the birth, ministry and death of Jesus Christ (see Plate 18.7), as well as the ancient prophets of the Old Testament, while secular tours tend to visit sites more closely associated with Jewish-Roman conflict or the remains of successive empires.

Mecca and the Great Mosque (*Masjid al-Haram*), the holiest place on earth for Muslims, would be of considerable interest to general heritage tourists, but they are accessible only

Plate 18.6 Among many protestant Christians, the Garden Tomb in Jerusalem is thought to be the burial chamber of Jesus

to Muslims for sacred rituals. Roman Catholics have many shrines and grottos that likely appeal only or primarily to Catholics. Likewise, members of the Church of Jesus Christ of Latter-day Saints (Mormons or LDS) hold certain mountains, hills and forest groves close to their spiritual hearts as a result of certain sacred events that occurred at these places during the faith's formative years.

Related to the second point, from the perspective of the religious adherents, the rituals and faith-building experiences that accompany them are a form of spiritual heritage, an experience that only comes through religious devotion and personal preparation for visiting sacred places and participating in rituals. For Jewish travelers undertaking various mitzvahs, participating in religious events or worshiping at synagogues or the Western Wall in Jerusalem are all part of an intangible heritage experience that can build their faith and create memorable experiences based on their ritual past. The same is true of Muslims undertaking the hajj in Mecca or Hindus bathing in the Ganges River (see Plate 18.8). The rituals and rites of those experiences have been passed down from generation to generation, are written in historic books of scripture and are an important element of the intangible heritage of believers.

Plate 18.7 Christian tourists at the ruins of the synagogue of Capernaum

The final relationship between religious tourism and heritage tourism is the use of pilgrimage routes and trails. In traditional religions, pilgrimage was a ritual that required outward demonstrations of devotion and hardship as a way of humbling oneself, making the pilgrim worthier of forgiveness, more teachable, and more prone to spiritual influences (see Plate 18.9). Several famous pilgrimage routes developed during the medieval period as an important part of the cleansing process before arriving at the final destination. In many traditions, the travail associated with the pathway itself was often considered more important than the final destination. Camino de Santiago, Spain and France, is one of the most famous of these and is used not only by Catholic pilgrims but also by nature and cultural tourists who desire to see the landscapes of southwestern France and northwestern Spain.

MANAGEMENT ISSUES AT HOLY SITES

Sacred sites are somewhat different from other heritage attractions from a management perspective. First, it is one of the few types of heritage places where worshippers intermingle with leisure tourists, creating what Bremer (2001: 3) referred to as a 'duality of

Plate 18.8 The ritual bath in the Ganges at Varanasi, India, is an important part of Hindu religious heritage

place' (cited in Olsen, 2006), or an overlapping of sacred and secular spaces simultaneously. This has the potential to create many problems as irreverent curiosity-seekers photograph, make noise, eat and drink and disrespect local mores (e.g. not taking off shoes in a Buddhist temple). This is disturbing for true pilgrims and local worshippers and creates contention between residents and tourists. Care should be taken to control the effects of non-worshipping visitors on those who are trying to have spiritual experiences. Restricting times and spaces when and where non-pilgrim tourists are allowed to visit a site, and utilizing interpretive media (e.g. signage) to direct visitors away from the most sensitive areas or provide reminders of appropriate behavior have proved to be useful management approaches (see Plate 18.10).

Secondly and similarly, some forms of pilgrimage, such as those undertaken by New Age spiritualists, have a tendency to be riddled with conflict and political undertones. Native American and other indigenous cultures are often exploited for financial gain, and self-appointed medicine men, gurus and chiefs are considered insulting by native groups. Likewise, the ecological impact of some pilgrim activities in natural surroundings, including ritual litter and disturbing natural ecosystems, creates contentious relations with

Plate 18.9 Catholic pilgrims, retracing the footsteps of Jesus with a cross in Jerusalem

public lands agencies, such as the National Forest Service in the USA or the National Trust and English Heritage in the United Kingdom. Destination managers must consider ways in which sacred space, which is claimed by multiple stakeholders, can be utilized in fair and equitable ways and how its social and ecological impacts might best be mitigated.

Another concern is the commodification of religion at holy sites. Many religious attractions rely on the goodwill of pilgrims and other visitors to donate money for maintenance and renovations. Increasingly, however, such funds are insufficient to meet the needs of sometimes centuries-old buildings. To survive economically, many shrine and holy site managers have had to turn to commercial endeavors, such as selling souvenirs, serving food in restaurants and cafes, charging for performances or offering commercial lodging for pilgrims and non-pilgrims alike. In addition, some sites have opted to charge entrance fees which is abhorrent to many site managers given the holy nature of the place, but they are beginning to realize the need for this in order to save their religious icons. Perhaps the overarching concern of everyone involved is the loss of meaning and spiritual sense of place that can occur when sacred sites become over-commercialized and when the sacred is put up for sale. At places where religious organizations are the sole monetary source of support for maintenance, interpretation and management, there is a notable

Plate 18.10 A reminder for tourists to respect local religious traditions and sacred space

lack of commodification but a stronger emphasis on 'spreading the word' and 'saving souls'.

A fourth management issue is the utilization of tourism as a proselytizing tool. While many religious caretakers see non-pilgrimage visits to their sacred sites as an unavoidable trend, sacrilege in some cases, opinions and attitudes towards non-believer tourists are beginning to change. Visits by secular tourists are now seen by some Christian groups as an opportunity to share their faith, to proselytize and perhaps even convert non-believers to the faith. Their role as pastoral caregivers is also an important part of the new role of site managers and religious leaders for believers and non-believers.

Finally, there is a notable lack of tourism-related management training among sacred site caretakers. Of course their primary concern is maintaining the spirit of the place and the physical property, as well as carrying out their ecclesiastical duties, but, with the realization that sacred spaces are now part of the mainstream tourism supply, more and more site managers are beginning to recognize the need for an increased business-oriented approach that is more inclusive of believers and non-believers and which caters to pilgrims and non-pilgrims at the same time and in the same place.

NEW AND CURRENT TRENDS

There are several interesting trends occurring in the realm of religious tourism that have an impact on heritage management and the travel experience. The first of these is the modernization of traditional pilgrimage. As already noted, most traditional pilgrimages were undertaken with much hardship. The journeys were arduous and tiring, and the lodging and sustenance were marginal at best; they had to be for individuals to earn penance and to make themselves more in tune with the spirit of the destination. Today, however, we are seeing a major shift from uncomfortable, penitent journeys to pilgrimages that in some cases resemble luxury vacations. This change is occurring in all religious traditions, not just a few.

While the very poor still arrive in Mecca by foot, camel, horse, bicycle or car, after a long and difficult journey, wealthier Muslims from around the world are choosing to fly to Saudi Arabia, take luxury, air-conditioned motor coaches to their four- or five-star hotels in Mecca and Medina and dine in world-class restaurants. Some even hire guides to help them through the religious rituals and procedures at the *Masjid al-Haram* and nearby areas. Large tour companies and individual travel agencies have also begun offering hajj packages from North America, Europe and Asia, facilitating more comfortable and inclusive pilgrimage experiences. Large tour companies, such as Thomas Cook, now offer domestic pilgrimage packages in India. Many affluent Hindu pilgrims prefer to stay in upmarket hotels, and the demand for such products and experiences is growing. The same changes are happening in Christian pilgrimage where far fewer pilgrims walk or cycle the pilgrimage trails but instead prefer to fly or drive to the final destination, and typically enjoy shopping, dining out, sightseeing, playing a round of golf or seeing a movie on the same journey.

Another type of change is the popularization of virtual or proxy pilgrimages. In some religions, it is now possible to pay someone to undertake a pilgrimage on another person's behalf. While in the eyes of many people this practice nullifies and denigrates the importance of the pilgrimage, people who are too busy to undertake the journey themselves see it as the next best option. Likewise, virtual pilgrimages can also now be done as a last resort for people who are immobile or who might otherwise be constrained from traveling. These online events also allow outsiders to observe the rites and rituals associated with various religious traditions.

Another important trend is the growth in New Age pilgrimage. New Age adherents typically belong to no formal religion, but instead seek personal spiritual growth and harmony with nature. The New Age movement, which began in the 1950s and 60s in response to an increased desire to be harmonious with nature and a dissatisfaction with traditional religion, is growing in importance and number throughout the developed world. The movement is extremely popular in the United Kingdom, the USA, Western Europe and Japan. Devotees embrace indigenous or animist views of the earth, neo-pagan beliefs and practices and individualism, and they seek harmony with the cosmos in terms of mind, spirit and body. Their practices are often referred to as alternative spirituality, self spirituality or secular religion. New Agers are devoted travelers as they seek to explore places that exude spiritual power and that are known for nature spirits, earth energies, extra-terrestrial visitations and ancient spiritual traditions. This abstract notion of spirituality challenges many traditional views of religion, but its manifestation in terms of tourism is equally important from a heritage perspective. Among the most important destinations in the world for these spiritualists are sites of ancient worship, such as Stonehenge, Machu Picchu and the Egyptian Pyramids. As mentioned earlier, they also utilize the cultural and religious traditions of native peoples, which in some cases causes considerable discord between the faithful and indigenous groups around the world.

Finally is the recognition of what some people call 'secular pilgrimage' – a form of travel that in many ways resembles traditional religious pilgrimage but which does not necessarily have a spiritual foundation. Prominent examples of this include die-hard fans traveling to the grave sites of famous celebrities, such as Elvis Presley fans visiting his home (Graceland) and grave in Memphis, Tennessee, or admirers of Princess Diana visiting her grave in Northampton, England. Other experiences include visits to patriotic or nationalistic sites, such as Arlington National Cemetery and the Vietnam Veterans Memorial in the USA; the National Monument (Monas) in Jakarta, which has very deep patriotic undertones for Indonesians; holocaust museums in Europe, North America and Israel for Jews; and Mont-Saint-Michel and its abbey for the French. Visits to such places might stir feelings of patriotism, which some might describe as spiritually moving.

SUMMARY AND CONCLUSION

The religious past is a crucial part of cultural heritage in many parts of the world and it is big business, with many traditional manifestations giving way to postmodern conveniences and non-traditional forms of pilgrimage. Few places exist today that do not have some religious or spiritual significance for organized religions, new age spiritualism or secular pilgrimage. At the very least, most destinations have historical religious structures that appeal to general cultural tourists, who may not be motivated by a spiritual drive but who might have an interest in seeing the religious element of a destination's heritage.

The largest tourist gatherings in the world today are religious in scope and must be managed carefully for security, health and ecological reasons. Religious destinations are no less prone to the management concerns and issues than other types of heritage. In fact, there is sometimes an additional layer of concern owing to the active worship that takes place on site and because commercial endeavors tend to be shunned by the stewards of religious places because it is incongruent with their overall goal of satisfying the spiritual needs of pilgrims.

REVIEW QUESTIONS

1. When a tourist is not defined by motive but rather the fact that he/she travels away from home, why do some scholars try to differentiate between pilgrims and tourists?

2. Why would religious organizations also want to differentiate between pilgrims and tourists?

3. Can you identify a religion that requires pilgrimage travel in order to gain salvation? Are you aware of any that discourage or prohibit it?

4. What are the main underlying motives for people who travel for spiritual or religious purposes?

5. In what ways can pilgrimage and pilgrim destinations be considered part of heritage tourism?

6. Are management challenges different at holy sites than at other cultural attractions? If so, how and why?

RECOMMENDED READING

Ahmed, Z.U. (1992) Islamic pilgrimage (Hajj) to Ka'aba in Makkah (Saudi Arabia): An important international tourism activity. *Journal of Tourism Studies* 3(1), 35–43.

Alderman, D. (2002) Writing on the Graceland Wall: On the importance of authorship in pilgrimage landscapes. *Tourism Recreation Research* 27(2), 27–33.

Badone, E. and Roseman, S.R. (2004) *Intersecting Journeys: The Anthropology of Pilgrimage and Tourism*. Chicago: University of Illinois Press.

Bhardwaj, S.M. (1998) Non-Hajj pilgrimage in Islam: A neglected dimension of religious circulation. *Journal of Cultural Geography* 17(2), 69–87.

Brown, M. (1998) *The Spiritual Tourist*. London: Bloomsbury.

Cohen, E. (1998) Tourism and religion: A comparative perspective. *Pacific Tourism Review* 2, 1–10.

Cohen-Hattab, K. (2010) Struggles at holy sites and their outcomes: The evolution of the Western Wall Plaza in Jerusalem. *Journal of Heritage Tourism* 5(2), 125–139.

Collins-Kreiner, N. (1999) Pilgrimage holy sites: A classification of Jewish holy sites in Israel. *Journal of Cultural Geography* 18(2), 57–78.

Collins-Kreiner, N. and Kliot, N. (2000) Pilgrimage tourism in the Holy Land: The behavioural characteristics of Christian pilgrims. *GeoJournal* 50, 55–67.

Collins-Kreiner, N., Kliot, N., Mansfeld, Y. and Sagi, K. (2006) *Christian Tourism to the Holy Land: Pilgrimage During Security Crisis*. Aldershot: Ashgate.

Digance, J. (2003) Pilgrimage at contested sites. *Annals of Tourism Research* 30, 143–159.

Din, A. and Hadi, A. (1997) Muslim pilgrimage from Malaysia. In R.H. Stoddard and A. Morinis (eds) *Sacred Places, Sacred Spaces: The Geography of Pilgrimages* (pp. 111–182). Baton Rouge: Louisiana State University.

Eade, J. (1992) Pilgrimage and tourism at Lourdes, France. *Annals of Tourism Research* 19, 18–32.

Fish, J.M. and Fish, M. (1993) International tourism and pilgrimage: A discussion. *The Journal of East and West Studies* 22(2), 83–90.

Graham, B. and Murray, M. (1997) The spiritual and the profane: The pilgrimage to Santiago de Compostela. *Ecumene* 4(4), 389–409.

Gupta, V. (1999) Sustainable tourism: Learning from Indian religious traditions. *International Journal of Contemporary Hospitality Management* 11(2/3), 91–95.

Hobbs, J.J. (1992) Sacred space and touristic development at Jebel Musa (Mt. Sinai), Egypt. *Journal of Cultural Geography* 12(2), 99–112.

Holmberg, C.B. (1993) Spiritual pilgrimages: Traditional and hyperreal motivations for travel and tourism. *Visions in Leisure and Business* 12(2), 18–27.

Hudman, L.E. and Jackson, R.H. (1992) Mormon pilgrimage and tourism. *Annals of Tourism Research* 19, 107–121.

Ioannides, D. and Cohen Ioannides, M.W. (2004) Jewish past as a 'foreign country': The travel experiences of American Jews. In T. Coles and D.J. Timothy (eds) *Tourism, Diasporas and Spaces* (pp. 95–110). London: Routledge.

Ivakhiv, A. (1997) Red rocks, 'vortexes' and the selling of Sedona: Environmental politics in the new age. *Social Compass* 44(3), 367–384.

Ivakhiv, A. (2003) Nature and self in New Age pilgrimage. *Culture and Religion* 4(1), 93–118.

Jackowski, A. and Smith, V.L. (1992) Polish pilgrim-tourists. *Annals of Tourism Research* 19, 92–106.

Jackson, R.H. and Hudman, L. (1995) Pilgrimage tourism and English cathedrals: The role of religion in travel. *The Tourist Review* 4, 40–48.

Jutla, R (2002) Understanding Sikh pilgrimage. *Tourism Recreation Research* 27(2), 65–72.

Kaelber, L. (2002) The sociology of Medieval pilgrimage: Contested views and shifting boundaries. In W.H. Swatos and L. Tomasi (eds) *From Medieval Pilgrimage to Religious Tourism* (pp. 51–74). Westport, CT: Praeger.

Kaur, J. (1985) *Himalayan Pilgrimages and the New Tourism*. New Delhi: Himalayan Books.

MacWilliams, M.W. (2002) Virtual pilgrimages on the Internet. *Religion* 32, 315–335.

Metreveli, M. and Timothy, D.J. (2010) Religious heritage and emerging tourism in the Republic of Georgia. *Journal of Heritage Tourism* 5(3), 237–244.

Morinis, E.A. (1992) Introduction: The territory of the anthropology of pilgrimage. In A. Morinis (ed.) *Sacred Journeys: The Anthropology of Pilgrimage* (pp. 1–28). Westport, CT: Greenwood.

Nolan, M.L. and Nolan, S. (1992) Religious sites as tourism attractions in Europe. *Annals of Tourism Research* 19, 68–78.

Olsen, D.H. (2003) Heritage, tourism, and the commodification of religion. *Tourism Recreation Research* 28(3), 99–104.

Olsen, D.H. (2009) "The strangers within our gates": Managing visitors at Temple Square. *Journal of Management, Spirituality and Religion* 6(2), 121–139.

Olsen, D.H. and Timothy, D.J. (1999) Tourism 2000: Selling the Millennium. *Tourism Management* 20, 389–392.

Peters, F.E. (1994) *The Hajj: The Muslim Pilgrimage to Mecca and the Holy Places*. Princeton: Princeton University Press.

Pfaffenberger, B. (1983) Serious pilgrims and frivolous tourists: The chimera of tourism in the pilgrimage of Sri Lanka. *Annals of Tourism Research* 10, 57–74.

Poria, Y., Butler, R.W. and Airey, D. (2006) Tourist perceptions of heritage exhibits: A comparative study from Israel. *Journal of Heritage Tourism* 1(1), 51–72.

Pruess, J.B. (1976) Merit-seeking in public: Buddhist pilgrimage in northeastern Thailand. *Journal of the Siam Society* 64(1), 167–206.

Rana, R.P.B. (2003) *Where the Buddha Walked: A Companion to the Buddhist Places of India*. Varanasi: Indica Books.

Reader, I. (2007) Pilgrimage growth in the modern world: Meanings and implications. *Religion* 37, 210–229.

Reisinger, Y. (2006) Travel/tourism: Spiritual experiences. In D. Buhalis and C. Costa (eds) *Tourism Business Frontiers: Consumers, Products and Industry* (pp. 148–156). Oxford: Butterworth Heinemann.

Rinschede, G. (1990) Religionstourismus. *Geographische Rundschau* 42(1), 14–20.

Rinschede, G. (1992) Forms of religious tourism. *Annals of Tourism Research* 19, 51–67.

Ron, A.S. (2009) Towards a typological model of Christian travel. *Journal of Heritage Tourism* 4(4), 287–298.

Ron, A.S. and Feldman, J. (2009) From spots to themed sites – the evolution of the Protestant Holy Land. *Journal of Heritage Tourism* 4(3), 201–216.

Ron, A.S. and Timothy, D.J. (forthcoming) *Contemporary Christian Travel.* Bristol: Channel View Publications.

Santos, X.M. (2002) Pilgrimage and tourism at Santiago de Compostela. *Tourism Recreation Research* 27(2), 41–50.

Shackley, M. (1999) Managing the cultural impacts of religious tourism in the Himalayas, Tibet and Nepal. In M. Robinson and P. Boniface (eds) *Tourism and Cultural Conflicts* (pp. 95–112). Wallingford: CAB International.

Shackley, M. (2001) *Managing Sacred Sites: Service Provision and Visitor Experience.* London: Continuum.

Shackley, M. (2001) Sacred world heritage sites: Balancing meaning with management. *Tourism Recreation Research* 26(1), 5–10.

Shackley, M. (2006) Costs and benefits: The impact of cathedral tourism in England. *Journal of Heritage Tourism* 1(2), 133–139.

Sharpley, R. and Sundaram, P. (2005) Tourism: A sacred journey? The case of Ashram Tourism, India. *International Journal of Tourism Research* 7, 161–171.

Shoval, N. (2000) Commodification and theming of the sacred: Changing patterns of tourist consumption in the "Holy Land". In M. Gottiener (ed.) *New Forms of Consumption: Consumers, Culture, and Commodification* (pp. 251–264). Oxford: Rowman & Littlefield.

Singh, Rana P.B. (1999) Sacredscape, manescape and cosmogony at Gaya, India: A study in sacred geography. *National Geographical Journal of India* 45(1), 34–63.

Singh, Rana P.B. and Rana, P.S. (2002) *Banaras Region: A Spiritual and Cultural Guide.* Varanasi: Indica Books.

Singh, S. (2004) Religion, heritage and travel: Case references from the Indian Himalayas. *Current Issues in Tourism* 7(1), 44–65.

Sizer, S.R. (1999) The ethical challenges of managing pilgrimages to the Holy Land. *International Journal of Contemporary Hospitality Management* 11(2/3), 85–90.

Smith, V.L. (1992) Introduction: The quest in guest. *Annals of Tourism Research* 19, 1–17.

Sopher, D.E. (1987) The message of place in Hindu pilgrimage. *National Geographical Journal of India* 33(4), 353–369.

Stoddard, R.H. and Morinis, E.A. (eds) (1997) *Sacred Places, Sacred Spaces: The Geography of Pilgrimages.* Baton Rouge: Louisiana State University Press.

Timothy, D.J. (2002) Sacred journeys: Religious heritage and tourism. *Tourism Recreation Research* 27(2), 3–6.

Timothy, D.J. (2007) Introduction. In D.J. Timothy (ed.) *The Heritage Tourist Experience: Critical Essays* (pp. ix–xxi). Aldershot, UK: Ashgate.

Timothy, D.J. and Olsen, D.H. (eds) (2006) *Tourism, Religion and Spiritual Journeys*. London: Routledge.

Turner, V. and Turner, E. (1978) *Image and Pilgrimage in Christian Culture*. New York: Columbia University Press.

Vukonić, B. (1992) Medjugorje's religion and tourism connection. *Annals of Tourism Research* 19, 79–91.

Vukonić, B. (1996) *Tourism and Religion*. Oxford: Elsevier.

RECOMMENDED WEBSITES

Abbayes et Sites Cisterciens d'Europe – http://www.cister.net/EN/homepage.aspx

Al-Mu'adhdhan Hajj Group – http://www.makehajj.com/

Buddhisttourst.net – http://www.buddhisttours.net/

Catholic Pilgrimage Centers – http://www.catholicpilgrimagecenter.com/

Churches Conservation Trust – http://www.visitchurches.org.uk/

Faith Based Tourism – http://www.religioustravelassociation.com/

Hajj-USA – http://www.hajjusa.com/

India Pilgrimages – http://www.india-pilgrimages.com/hindu-pilgrimage.html

Indian Religious Tours – http://www.indianreligioustours.org/

Israel Ministry of Tourism – http://www.goisrael.com/tourism_eng

Kingdom of Saudi Arabia, Ministry of Hajj – http://www.hajinformation.com/

LDS Travel Study – http://ldstravelstudy.org/

Pilgrimage Tours – http://www.pilgrimages.com/

Totally Jewish Travel – http://www.totallyjewishtravel.com/tours/kosher/

World Religious Travel Association – http://www.wrtareligioustravel.com/WRTA

CHAPTER 19

DIASPORAS, ROOTS AND PERSONAL HERITAGE TOURISM

LEARNING OBJECTIVES

After reading this chapter, you should be able to:

1. Understand the meaning of diaspora and how it manifests in tourism terms.

2. Be aware of the different types of diasporas and how their migration experiences can affect their need to travel.

3. Recognize the two main forms of diaspora travel, namely return visits and roots tourism.

4. Be familiar with secondary forms of diaspora travel.

5. Know about ways in which migrant groups create cultural attractions in their new lands.

INTRODUCTION

Millions of people each year travel in search of their roots, to experience a portion of their own patrimony. Some observers believe this is because the rapid pace of life and overdependence on new technologies in the modern world creates a degree of anxiety among western populations. The same observers suggest that people of certain ethnic or racial backgrounds also feel unsettled in their current homelands, caught in between old and new identities or uncomfortable in their present surroundings. Thus, some African-Americans do not feel African or American, and many Scottish-Americans feel more connected to Scotland than to America. Traveling to places associated with one's own personal past is said to help people feel more grounded in their lives, helping them to reaffirm their fluid identities and overcome the angst associated with hyper-modernity.

Chapter 4 explained the issue of scale of heritage appeal, ranging from global at its broadest to personal at its most basic. The majority of the content of this book draws attention to regional, national and global heritage attractions and touristic activities that revolve around them. This chapter, however, narrows the scope of heritage tourism to examine personal motives, destinations and experiences that cause people to undertake various forms of travel related to their own personal or familial past. It examines the notion of diasporic return visits, sometimes referred to in the literature as 'ethnic tourism', genealogy-based or roots travel, youth solidarity travel to motherlands and the importance of immigrant landscapes and cultures as part of a destination's heritage appeal.

DIASPORAS AND TOURISM

Diasporas are nations or ethnic groups living outside their traditional homelands but which are being bound together either literally or figuratively by spatial concentration, culture, religion, ethnicity or national identity. The most commonly studied and best understood are probably the African and Jewish diasporas, but Irish, Chinese, Scottish, Welsh, Italian, Hungarian, Polish, Ukrainian, Lebanese, Palestinian, Greek and Indian émigré movements are examples of other well-known diasporas as well. Most countries of the 'old world' (e.g. Asia, Africa and Europe) saw significant waves of emigration of their own people to the 'new world' (e.g. North and South America, the Caribbean, Australia, New Zealand) during the 18th, 19th and 20th centuries, creating settler and immigrant societies that are far more diverse culturally, ethnically and racially than most of the countries where they originated.

There are many reasons why entire nations of people, or at least large portions of them, depart their homeland. Robin Cohen (2008) outlines several types of diasporas based upon the common experiences and socio-political and economic processes involved in triggering the diasporic movement. Victim diasporas are caused by force and traumatic displacement. The Jews' expulsion from their homeland by the ancient Babylonians and Romans is a good example. The enslavement and forced transshipment of Africans to Europe, the Caribbean, South America and North America between the 17th and 19th centuries was one of the largest victim diasporas ever to occur.

The second form of diaspora is labor (or proletarian) diasporas, which entailed people scattering in search of employment or as indentured workers. Greeks in Australia, Italians in the USA, Chinese in Canada and many Indians in the UK are good examples. Third, imperial/colonial diasporas occurred as colonizers from Europe claimed and settled overseas territories, such as the British in India, the Dutch in Indonesia and the Portuguese in Brazil. Trade diasporas are the fourth of Cohen's types and include population movements for purposes of business, buying and selling of goods and services. The concentration of Chinese merchants throughout the cities of Southeast Asia is a notable example, as are the Lebanese in Africa and Latin America. Lastly, Cohen highlights what he calls deterritorialized diasporas, which are groups of people who relate with one another culturally or religiously but have little connection to any original homeland. The Roma people of Europe provide an evident example, as do several ethnic groups in India.

Many diasporic groups maintain strong ties to their homelands, including people of later generations who have never visited the mother country before. Many Irish-Americans, whose ancestors several generations earlier migrated to the USA for economic reasons, or African-Americans, whose ancestors were brought to America in shackles and chains, are still innately connected to their homelands. Some theorists argue that a people's emigration experience and life conditions in the new land can be an important factor in their sense of belonging and their personal connections to the old country. Many immigrant groups see themselves as 'halfway populations', plagued with a sense of in-betweenness, not really belonging to the original homeland or to the new country (Hollinshead, 1998). As a result, many suffer from a sense of restlessness, confusion and unease in their adopted countries. There is some evidence to suggest that this unsettledness might be magnified if the émigrés and their descendents are part of a victimized diaspora, such as one provoked by slavery, war or famine. Regardless of diasporic origin or reason, many people have an innate need to seek their origins, discover or reaffirm their identities, satisfy a sense of nostalgia or come to terms with a difficult past, which they sometimes do by traveling to the lands of their ancestors.

First-generation immigrants in most cases are especially connected to their homeland, because they themselves were born there and migrated somewhere else. For most of these people, the travel experience aims to connect with living relatives and friends. Some second- and third-generation immigrants (those born in the new land) fall into the same category, but for many subsequent generations the experience becomes more of a nostalgic one, where visits are characterized by attempts to discover themselves by connecting with places and events known to their ancestors.

Return visits

Return visits are temporary trips to an immigrant's original homeland or to another area where he/she has strong social connections. It sometimes fits within the broader framework of visiting friends and relatives (VFR) tourism, as it tends to entail more of a social network function than simply a day-to-day touristic activity (Duval, 2004). The return visitor has close familial or other personal connections to the destination and an intimate first-hand experience with it. The experience functions to strengthen, solidify and rekindle family and other social relationships and is therefore an important manifestation of one's personal heritage. Such visits are typically also seen as a way to reinforce parental cultural identities among the children of immigrants.

Return visitors encounter many family meetings and reunions and help build social capital in the destination. While personal relationships and social networks are enhanced by these visits, diasporic visitors also augment local economies through donations to families, local charities or solidarity movements. They are also often known as generous investors in local companies and development efforts.

Several studies of return visitors from various diasporas traveling back to the Caribbean, Lebanon, China, Mexico and Vietnam have found characteristics akin to other VFR tourists in terms of the activities they undertake, whom they visit and where they stay. Returnees' length of stay is usually longer than most typical tourists and, even though many return visitors stay in the homes of relatives, they tend to be big spenders, not just on investments and donations but also on shopping, dining and other leisure activities.

For some groups of first-generation émigrés, return trips to the homeland open up new vistas into the past and can change images of the places they departed from earlier. Among Vietnamese refugees, for instance, the war-torn memories of Ho Chi Minh City (formerly Saigon) are being tempered by their touristic images of a modern, thriving city. Their knowledge of the city has changed from the images they left behind in the 1970s to a place of some reconciliation.

Genealogy-based travel

Rapid modernization and technological development have begun to cause a degree of uneasiness about the future in developed societies, especially among middle-aged and older populations. As a result, many people are turning to the past as a way of grounding themselves to something enduring in a frenetic world that sometimes seems to pass them by too quickly. One contemporary manifestation of this is the growing interest in genealogy and family history research. While many people have had an interest in their own personal heritage via genealogy for many years, this phenomenon is becoming even more pervasive today with the widespread availability of many immigration, residence, demographic, employment and property ownership records becoming available on the internet.

For many people, the desire to learn of their roots leads to an increased interest in travel to their ancestral homelands, which is sometimes referred to as genealogy travel, roots tourism or personal heritage tourism. This is an extremely important form of heritage tourism and is most pervasive in countries or regions from which large emigration movements occurred at some point in history. Although some people travel domestically to hometowns or rural areas where ancestors lived, most attention to this form of tourism in scholarly research and in industry marketing efforts focuses on the international perspective of diasporic group members or others traveling to ancestral lands outside their current home countries.

Personal heritage tourism is deeply connected to places that are associated with a traveler's own familial and personal past. Thus, visits to personal heritage locations and the genealogy-related activities that accompany them can be quite different from the experiences of many other cultural tourists because of the personal and emotional attachments to the places and artifacts being viewed. Several unique activities and attractions are prevalent in roots travel. First is the dominance of family history research. Many people who travel to discover their roots, or at least experience the places connected to their kindred past, engage in various genealogical research or family history pursuits. Research in local libraries and archives, gathering information from cemeteries and gravestones (see Plate 19.1) and copying family documents, such as marriage or baptismal certificates, are important family history-related activities that often take place in

Plate 19.1 Roots tourists often visit and gather information from old cemeteries such as this one in England

conjunction with guided tours or independent travel on a broader roots itinerary. Some destinations, such as Ireland, Wales and Scotland, which are salient roots destinations for Canadian, American and Australian personal heritage tourists, are sated with 'heritage houses', 'houses of names' and genealogical centers, and they employ many professional genealogists on site (see Plate 19.2). Rather than being just a component of a broader tour, family history research in many cases is the sole reason some people travel. One of the most popular destinations for this is Salt Lake City, Utah (USA), where the Church of Jesus Christ of Latter-day Saints operates the world's largest genealogical library, to which hundreds of thousands of people travel each year from all over the world to investigate their familial past.

Second, encountering distant relatives and spending time in their homes is an important component of roots tourism. Reunions are a salient part of this and may entail large clan assemblies of thousands of people or smaller, intimate gatherings of a few distant cousins. These meetings are crucial for exchanging stories, life histories, photographs and other memorabilia that help reinforce kindred linkages.

A third common activity is touring ancestral villages and farmlands, including clan burial grounds (see Plate 19.3). Religious edifices (e.g. churches and synagogues) are

Plate 19.2 Genealogy libraries and heritage centers are an important part of the experience of roots tourists

important in this regard, for they may possess original membership records that are useful in family history research. They are very durable elements of the cultural landscape in ancestral regions that can mark sites where progenitors actually worshipped, and they might help provide a spiritual experience if descendents still practice the religion of their forebears.

Finally, there is a variety of miscellaneous activities that seem to be common in most personal heritage tourism experiences. Shopping for period antiques, visiting local museums, dining at local food establishments and collecting local foods are good examples of this.

Timothy (2008) identified three key players in the personal heritage tourism phenomenon and their roles in producing and consuming the roots experience. The remainder of this section follows Timothy's work in understanding the main genealogy tourism stakeholders.

The foremost player is the genealogy tourist. He or she is usually keen to visit ancestral lands, as there is some kind of connection to it. Geographers have long studied human connections to land and realized the natural human inclination to revere the land of their ancestors. Many genealogy tourists note that during their experience they felt a deep

Plate 19.3 Clan burial grounds such as this one in Scotland are important attractions for personal heritage tourists

sentiment for, and natural connection to, the ancestral land. For many visitors, the familial homeland becomes idealized in their own minds and in the lore of their families or diasporic networks. Homelands are often viewed as idyllic places that represent a simpler past, distanced from the anxiety and troubles of the present time and location. The primordial soil, then, is sanctified as sacred ground by émigrés – a sentiment that often transcends many generations. Thus, travel to filial homelands becomes a form of pilgrimage, journeys to the venerated spaces of the past. By standing on, touching, seeing and smelling the ancestral soil, ties to particular territories become stronger. Likewise, the activities undertaken by roots tourists, including reunions, clan festivals, family history research and storytelling, also strengthen connections to the homeland.

In addition to the land itself, roots tourists often report an increased bond between themselves and their deceased progenitors. This is especially apparent in studies undertaken among African American tourists in West Africa and Scottish Canadians in Scotland. One genealogy traveler noted:

It is impossible to describe the emotions of love and kinship I have felt for my ancestors as I have visited the areas where they lived. A treasured moment in my life

412

came when, on a trip to Sweden, I came upon a fallen-down stone building. Some-how, I knew I was standing on sacred family ground. Later research confirmed my impression – those stone ruins had been a chapel in which some of my ancestors were married. (Jorgensen, 1988: 23)

Such journeys are commonly described as spiritual, emotional or otherwise deeply personal.

Genealogy travel can be a therapeutic experience for people whose ancestors were part of a victim diaspora, where they were maltreated by those in positions of power, including imprisonment and torture. Descendents of African slaves, who live throughout the world, most notably in South America, Western Europe, North America and the Caribbean, are a good example. For many of them, journeys to Africa can be very cathartic as they begin to forgive past colonial transgressions and undergo a nascent sense of closure to the trauma and abuse suffered by their forebears. For others, however, diasporic journeys to the African homeland have an opposite effect, typically based on visits to sites associated with slavery. They come away even more embittered against the transgressors, desiring vengeance in one form or another. Travelers from the African diaspora are also some-times disappointed upon their arrival in Africa to realize that they are not always embraced by Africans as children of the motherland but instead are treated simply as any other foreign tourists – welcomed if they have money to spend.

The desire to be connected to one's ancestral homeland runs so deeply that some people desire not only to consume their homeland figuratively – sightseeing and taking photographs – but also literally in various ways. For instance, genealogy tourists some-times drink water from wells on family farms or from rivers where ancestors might have fished or bathed. Similarly, roots tourists commonly collect artifacts from ancestral places to preserve a portion of their experience and to stake a claim to owning a piece of the homeland. Soil, wood, pottery pieces, river or well water, stones or leaves are seen as sacred materials that can be displayed in family albums or on mantels at home. Some genealogy tourists even desire to leave something of themselves behind to mold them-selves symbolically into the homeland. One genealogy pilgrim in Paul Basu's (2004) study placed her ring among the stones of a wall near her ancestral home and noted that 'by putting my cheap ring inside the walls, I felt I was giving a humble offering ... almost begging to be part of it forever ... I wanted to leave a part of "me" there ... when I did it, I felt extremely good, extremely relieved' (p. 167).

The second group of main stakeholders is tour operators and other service providers. While many people organize their own genealogy trips, there are multitudes of tour com-panies offering personal heritage tours to roots seekers. In addition to tour companies, professional genealogists, lodging and food service providers as well as transportation providers promote their services to this lucrative market. Genealogy tours can be purchased on an individual basis or in medium-sized groups. In Europe, most tours cater to individuals' needs or the needs of small groups. This allows participants to undertake family history research in archives and churches, during cemetery visits and home site stopovers.

Genealogy tour companies put packages together that include lodging and transportation, as well as the services of professional genealogists. These companies have become particularly well versed in playing to the emotions of their potential customers by using catchy slogans like 'walk in the footsteps of your ancestors', which tug at the heartstrings of diasporic progeny. Personal heritage operators provide orientation tours of ancestral regions wherein visitors learn about the climate, geography and culture of the place and its people, both historically and contemporarily. This is a key part of the product, as it allows the tourists to tour villages and traverse the rural landscapes that their antecedents might have known. They also arrange farm and homestead visits if original properties can be located. Teaching diaspora tourists about how their ancestors lived, including work accoutrements, agricultural techniques, cooking methods and recipes, enriches the experience and helps customers appreciate their heritage better. Some tour companies also provide opportunities to meet distant relatives with whom stories and photographs can be exchanged and where personal relationships can be developed. Finally, family history operators facilitate genealogy research with consultants at public and private libraries and provide archived data and visits to cemeteries and churches.

The third stakeholder in the personal heritage travel experience is government agencies. National tourism organizations in countries from which large migrations have departed for other parts of the world have learned to capitalize on personal heritage travel by targeting members of their diasporic peoples abroad. The tourism boards of Ireland, Wales, England and Scotland have all actively promoted genealogy tourism to emigrants and their posterity in Australia, New Zealand and North America. Hungary, Poland, Ghana, Ukraine and Germany are examples of other countries that have made concerted efforts to promote return visits, roots routes and other types of family history-based tourism.

Even though the main underlying motive for these promotional campaigns is economic (e.g. tourist expenditures, investments and remittances), there is certainly a political element as well. In producing these crusades many countries also desire to build global solidarity for the homeland among their diasporas, which is something Croatia has done since its independence in the early 1990s to help build the country politically and economically and to lend support for its independence from Yugoslavia.

Other forms of diaspora tourism

There are other diaspora-related programs that result in important travel volumes between original homelands and adopted homelands. Several countries and ethnic organizations have initiated 'homecoming' programs for diasporic youth as a way of building solidarity with the original homeland abroad and getting the world's youth to understand the cultures, histories, politics and ways of life of the old country. Israel and China are probably the best examples of this phenomenon, although other countries have similar agendas.

These return programs are funded and operated largely by philanthropic organizations, with assistance from national governments. The 'Birthright Israel' and 'Israel Experience' are two prominent examples where Jewish youth from across the diaspora are taken to Israel on educational trips to experience culture, religious ceremonies and sites, language use opportunities and the history and heritage of Israel in an effort to solidify their Jewish identity and increase solidarity for Israel within the Jewish diaspora (see Plate 19.4). Since its inception in 2000, Birthright Israel has facilitated free travel for more than 230,000 Jewish youth from around the world. The Birthright experience is funded partly by the government of Israel, as well as private philanthropists and non-profit organizations in Europe and North America.

Birthright Armenia has similar goals to that of Birthright Israel, but it focuses more on providing internship and volunteer opportunities in Armenia for that country's global diaspora. Efforts are also under way to establish similar programs for youth of the Greek and Irish diasporas to spend time in Greece and Ireland doing internships and

Plate 19.4 A Birthright Israel bus waits for Jewish-American youth tourists near Tel Aviv

volunteer work. The China Youth Travel Service and the Chinese Youth League of Australia take Chinese young people from various parts of the world to visit important places in China that illustrate what it means to be Chinese and to appreciate better the Chinese motherland.

Ethnic attractions in the new land

Waves of immigrants to a new homeland bring with them inevitable imprints on the cultural landscapes of the adopted home region. Architectural styles, village and town layouts, languages and signage, foodways and dress, specialty shops, agricultural patterns, economic activities, religious organizations and buildings, community centers and various media are all part and parcel of the cultural landscapes that develop in areas of heavy in-migration. Many cities throughout the world are home to immigrant and diasporic groups that settled in relatively well delineated and identifiable urban neighborhoods. The impressive and large-scale Chinatowns of North America, Australia and Southeast Asia testify to large influxes of a cohesive nationality living together in compact spaces and having an important historical impact on the urban milieu (see Plate 19.5). Other popular

Plate 19.5 Sydney, Australia's Chinatown is popular for locals and tourists for its dining and shopping

ethnic enclaves include Little Italies, Little Tokyos, Greektowns, Little Indias, Little Saigons and Irishtowns.

In addition to the urban immigrant enclaves, rural ethnic islands were also settled by various diasporic groups. Hundreds of thousands of northern European immigrants, largely from Sweden, Finland, Germany, the Netherlands, Denmark and Norway, migrated to the USA and Canada in the 19th and 20th centuries, but most of these groups settled in the rural areas of the Great Lakes, the upper Midwest, the Northeast and Texas. Likewise, several European groups (e.g. Germans and Welsh) settled in rural areas of South America in an effort to start a new life in agriculture. These rural communities, like their urban counterparts, also developed unique cultural landscapes that are often more discernable than those in the city. These more rural or small-town ethnic islands, together with the ethnic enclaves of the cities, have become very important cultural destinations.

The architectural heritage of these migrant neighborhoods and villages adds a unique appeal to places where they stand out from the normative human landscape. The Finnish hay barns and churches of the Great Lakes region of Canada and the USA, the tidy Welsh farmsteads in Patagonia, Argentina, and the Bavarian facades in German settlements in Brazil and Venezuela are part of those regions' tourist appeal. Many communities have branded themselves as notable ethnic villages or urban neighborhoods and have exaggerated the ethnic esthetic of buildings, streetscapes and farmlands. Shops and bakeries sell ethnic products to residents and tourists, and souvenir shops with mementos imported from the original homeland cater to the visitor's need to take home a piece of their experience. Restaurants serve cultural cuisines that might have originated in the dominant group's homeland or that were invented and stylized in the adopted country. By way of example, Frankenmuth, Michigan, is replete with shops selling German souvenirs and European-oriented Christmas decorations. Similarly, cafés and bakeries in Gaiman, Argentina, serve up feasts of Welsh foods, such as roasted lamb and Welsh cakes, and the multitudes of restaurants in Chinatowns all over the world compete for local and tourist patronage.

Many immigrant regions try hard to sustain their ethnic appeal even after the original émigrés and their descendants no longer live there, such as the case with some Little Italies and Greektowns. In addition, as part of their efforts to grow tourism, many places are fabricated to look like authentic immigrant settlements, even when nobody from the homeland being portrayed actually ever lived there. Perhaps the best example of this in the research literature is Leavenworth, Washington, which touts itself as an 'authentic' Bavarian village, even though few, if any, Germans migrated there.

Finally, there are some immigrant groups that have lived in the host land for many generations and succeed in keeping much of their original culture intact, not because of tourism but because of strong social networks and diligent efforts not to become assimilated. Oftentimes these groups have little desire to become a tourist attraction but, by virtue of their preserved culture, they become a curiosity to outsiders. Amish and

Mennonite communities in the USA and Canada are prime examples of such communities that have survived for centuries and generations. Their living culture of electricity-free farmsteads, horse and buggy transportation, conservative dark clothing, manual farm work, one-room schoolhouses, unique churches, handicrafts and traditional cuisine remains a significant draw for tourists in the US Midwest, the eastern states and Ontario, Canada (see Plate 19.6). While many Amish and Mennonites would rather be left alone by tourists, others have realized their ability to capitalize on visitors by offering buggy rides and selling honey, candy, blankets, fresh farm produce and cheese along roadsides and at farmers' markets.

In addition to the living culture and physical imprint of various diaspora groups, festivals and celebrations are an important component of the adopted-land ethnic tourism product. There are many kinds of festivals throughout the world, but among immigrant groups the most common are religious celebrations and commemorative cultural festivals. The Mela Festival in Edinburgh, Scotland, each year celebrates the Indian diaspora in the UK through music, food, dance and other forms of entertainment. Likewise, Tulip Time in Holland, Michigan, celebrates that community's Dutch patrimony in parades,

Plate 19.6 The Amish landscape of Pennsylvania shows the group's rejection of most modern conveniences

competitions, food, dress and music. St Patrick's Day parades and other celebrations emphasize the Irish diaspora, and Greek festivals held throughout Australia celebrate that country's Greek immigrant heritage.

While some visitors to the urban and rural ethnic islands are tourists from the original homeland (e.g. Germans visiting German villages in Brazil), the majority of visitors are general cultural tourists who have little or no ethnic ties to the immigrant enclave being visited. The heritage experience associated with ethnic islands is primarily one of differentness or curiosity; people visit these places to encounter cultural elements that differ from those with which they are familiar and that surround them on a daily basis.

SUMMARY AND CONCLUSION

Diasporas and other varieties of inter-generational migration have long laid the groundwork for the development of two unique types of heritage tourism – personal heritage travel and ethnic or cultural tourism at places that demonstrate distinctive immigrant landscapes and living cultures. Personal heritage is the least understood scale of heritage, 'probably because it is more elusive than other forms and the experience more nostalgic, personal, subjective, and sometimes spiritual' (Timothy, 2008: 119). People traveling to experience sites associated with their own genetic past typically immerse themselves in genealogical research at churches, archives, libraries and cemeteries. In addition, they seek out the farmlands and villages of their ancestry and desire to meet distant relatives and partake of regional cuisines. For some destinations, from which large waves of emigrants departed, genealogy tourism is a significant element of their broader tourism offering, and several countries have become well-known destinations for return visits from the diaspora. Many stakeholders have come to be involved in this form of heritage tourism, including government offices, ministries of tourism, tour operators and other service providers.

Tourism in many rural areas and urban neighborhoods of countries where immigrant societies dominate (e.g. Australia, New Zealand, Canada, the USA, the Caribbean and much of Latin America) also benefits from the existence of urban immigrant enclaves and rural ethnic islands. These communities provide a taste of 'foreignness' to domestic tourists without their having to cross political boundaries and, in some cases, they even appeal to visitors from the original lands where the enclaved cultures originated. Festivals, village esthetics, rural landscapes, urban forms and foodways are among the most salient enticements for visitors to diasporic islands in the adopted land.

Roots tourism is a lucrative market for 'old world' countries, and the cultural tourism associated with urban and rural ethnic enclaves that are well preserved or still living are important features of cultural tourism in the 'new world' countries. Demand for this diasporic set of products will continue into the future as long as immigration continues and members of society desire to know their ancestors or feel restless in their present home surroundings.

REVIEW QUESTIONS

1. How do rapid modernization and a harried lifestyle create a need within people to discover their roots?

2. What are the main types of diaspora, and how does each of them manifest uniquely in tourism?

3. In what ways do immigrant groups contribute to the national landscape and thereby create an ethnic tourist appeal in their new countries?

4. What is the meaning of return visits and how does this correspond to visiting friends and relatives (VFR) tourism?

5. What are the most common genealogical activities undertaken by roots tourists?

6. What do people see as the most salient intrinsic rewards of visiting the lands of their ancestors?

7. Can you recognize any cultural festivals and ethnic communities in your home region that draw local recreationists and tourists from afar?

RECOMMENDED READING

Akhtar, S. (1999) The immigrant, the exile, and the experience of nostalgia. *Journal of Applied Psychoanalytic Studies* 1(2), 123–130.

Ali, A. and Holden, A. (2006) Post-colonial Pakistani mobilities: The embodiment of the 'myth of return' in tourism. *Mobilities* 1(2), 217–242.

Ari, L.L. and Mittelberg, D. (2008) Between authenticity and ethnicity: Heritage tourism and re-ethnification among diaspora Jewish youth. *Journal of Heritage Tourism* 3(2), 79–103.

Asiedu, A. (2005) Some benefits of migrants' return visits to Ghana. *Population, Space and Place* 11(1), 1–11.

Bandyopadhyay, R. (2008) Nostalgia, identity and tourism: Bollywood in the Indian diaspora. *Journal of Tourism and Cultural Change* 6(2), 79–100.

Basu, P. (2001) Hunting down home: Reflections on homeland and the search for identity in the Scottish diaspora. In B. Bender and M. Winer (eds) *Contested Landscapes: Movement, Exile and Place* (pp. 333–348). Oxford: Berg.

Basu, P. (2005) Pilgrims in the far country: North American 'roots-tourists' in the Scottish Highlands. In C. Ray (ed.) *Transatlantic Scots* (pp. 286–317). Tuscaloosa: University of Alabama Press.

Basu, P. (2005) Roots-tourism as return movement: Semantics and the Scottish diaspora. In M. Harper (ed.) *Emigrant Homecomings: The Return Movement of Emigrants, 1600–2000* (pp. 131–150). Manchester: Manchester University Press.

Bruner, E.M. (1996) Tourism in Ghana: The representation of slavery and the return of the black diaspora. *American Anthropologist* 98(2), 290–304.

Butler, R.W. and Hajar, R. (2005) After the war: Ethnic tourism in Lebanon. In G.J. Ashworth and R. Hartmann (eds) *Horror and Human Tragedy Revisited: the Management of Sites of Atrocities for Tourism* (pp. 211–223). New York: Cognizant.

Carruthers, A. (2008) Saigon from the diaspora. *Singapore Journal of Tropical Geography* 29(1), 68–86.

Cave, J. (2009) Embedded identity: Pacific Islanders, cultural economics, and migrant tourism product. *Tourism, Culture and Communication* 9(1/2), 65–77.

Chazan, B. (1997) *Does the Teen Israel Experience Make a Difference?* New York: Israel Experience, Inc.

Cohen, E.H. (1999) Informal marketing of Israel Experience educational tours. *Journal of Travel Research* 37(3), 238–243.

Coles, T. and Timothy, D.J. (eds) (2004) *Tourism, Diasporas and Space*. London: Routledge.

Collins, J. and Jordan, K. (2009) Ethnic precincts as ethnic tourism destinations in urban Australia. *Tourism, Culture and Communication* 9(1/2), 79–92.

Collins-Kreiner, N. (2000) Pilgrimage holy sites: A classification of Jewish holy sites in Israel. *Journal of Cultural Geography* 18(2), 57–78.

Dikomitis, L. (2004) A moving field: Greek Cypriot refugees returning home. *Durham Anthropology Journal* 12(1), 7–20.

Duval, D.T. (2002) The return visit-return migration connection. In C.M. Hall and A.M. Williams (eds) *Tourism and Migration: New Relationships between Production and Consumption* (pp. 257–276). Dortrecht, Netherlands: Kluwer.

Duval, D.T. (2003) When hosts become guests: Return visits and diasporic identities in a Commonwealth Eastern Caribbean community. *Current Issues in Tourism* 6(4), 267–308.

Essah, P. (2001) Slavery, heritage and tourism in Ghana. *International Journal of Hospitality and Tourism Administration* 2(3/4), 31–49.

Feng, K. and Page, S.J. (2000) An exploratory study of the tourism, migration-immigration nexus: Travel experiences of Chinese residents in New Zealand. *Current Issues in Tourism* 3(3), 246–281.

Frost, W., Reeves, K., Laing, J. and Wheeler, F. (2009) Villages, vineyards, and Chinese dragons: Constructing the heritage of ethnic diasporas. *Tourism, Culture and Communication* 9(1/2), 107–114.

Goodrich, J.N. (1985) Black American tourists: Some research findings. *Journal of Travel Research* 24(2), 27–28.

Hall, C.M. (2005) Reconsidering the geography of tourism and contemporary mobility. *Geographical Research* 43(2), 125–139.

Hasty, J. (2002) Rites of passage, routes of redemption: Emancipation tourism and the wealth of culture. *Africa Today* 49(3), 47–76.

Horst, H.A. (2004) A pilgrimage home: Tombs, burial and belonging in Jamaica. *Journal of Material Culture* 9(1), 11–26.

Hughes, H. and Allen, D. (2010) Holidays of the Irish diaspora: The pull of the 'homeland'? *Current Issues in Tourism* 13(1), 1–19.

Ioannides, D. and Cohen Ioannides, M. (2002) Pilgrimages of nostalgia: Patterns of Jewish travel in the United States. *Tourism Recreation Research* 27(2), 17–26.

Josiam, B.M. and Frazier, R. (2008) Who am I? Where did I come from? Where do I go to find out? Genealogy, the Internet, and tourism. *Tourismos* 3(2), 35–56.

Karlsson, L. (2006) The diary weblog and the travelling tales of diasporic tourists. *Journal of Intercultural Studies* 27(3), 299–312.

Kelly, M.E. (2000) Ethnic pilgrimages: People of Lithuanian descent in Lithuania. *Sociological Spectrum* 20(1), 65–91.

King, B. (1994) What is ethnic tourism? An Australian perspective. *Tourism Management* 15(3), 173–176.

Lew, A.A. and Wong, A. (2002) Tourism and the Chinese diaspora. In C.M. Hall and A. Williams (eds) *Tourism and Migration: New Relationships between Production and Consumption* (pp. 205–220). Dordrecht: Kluwer.

Lew, A.A. and Wong, A. (2005) Existential tourism and the homeland – the overseas Chinese experience. In C. Cartier and A.A. Lew (eds) *Seductions of Place: Geographical Perspectives on Globalization and Touristed Landscapes* (pp. 286–300). London: Routledge.

Morgan, N., Pritchard, A. and Pride, R. (2002) Marketing to the Welsh diaspora: The appeal to *hiraeth* and homecoming. *Journal of Vacation Marketing* 9(1), 69–80.

Nash, C. (2002) Genealogical identities. *Environment and Planning D: Society and Space* 20, 27–52.

Nguyen, T.H. and King, B. (1998) Migrant homecomings: Viet kieu attitudes towards traveling back to Vietnam. *Pacific Tourism Review* 1(1), 349–361.

Nguyen, T.H. and King, B. (2002) Migrant communities and tourism consumption: The case of the Vietnamese in Australia. In C.M. Hall and A.M. Williams (eds) *Tourism and Migration: New Relationships between Production and Consumption* (pp. 221–240). Dordrecht: Kluwer.

Otterstrom, S. (2008) Genealogy as religious ritual: The doctrine and practice of family history in the Church of Jesus Christ of Latter-day Saints. In D.J. Timothy and J.K. Guelke (eds) *Geography and Genealogy: Locating Personal Pasts* (pp. 137–151). Aldershot: Ashgate.

Rains, S. (2003) Home from home: Diasporic images of Ireland in film and tourism. In M. Cronin and B. O'Connor (eds) *Irish Tourism: Image, Culture and Identity* (pp. 196–214). Clevedon: Channel View Publications.

Safran, W. (1991) Diasporas in modern societies: Myths of homeland and return. *Diaspora* 1(1), 83–99.

Schramm, K. (2004) Coming home to the motherland: Pilgrimage tourism in Ghana. In S. Coleman and J. Eade (eds) *Reframing Pilgrimage: Cultures in Motion* (pp. 133–149). London: Routledge.

Stephenson, M.L. (2002) Travelling to the ancestral homelands: The aspirations and experiences of a UK Caribbean community. *Current Issues in Tourism* 5(5), 378–425.

Teye, V.B. and Timothy, D.J. (2004) The varied colors of slave heritage in West Africa: White American stakeholders. *Space and Culture* 7(2), 145–155.

Timothy, D.J. (1997) Tourism and the personal heritage experience. *Annals of Tourism Research* 34(3), 751–754.

Timothy, D.J. (2002) Tourism and the growth of urban ethnic islands. In C.M. Hall and A.M. Williams (eds) *Tourism and Migration: New Relationships Between Production and Consumption* (pp. 135–151). Dordrecht, Netherlands: Kluwer.

RECOMMENDED WEBSITES

African Diaspora Tourism – www.africandiasporatourism.com

Birthright Armenia – www.birthrightarmenia.org/

Birthright Israel – www.birthrightisrael.com

Diaspora Travel and Tours – www.diaspora-travels.com

Little Italy NYC – www.littleitalynyc.com

Visit Scotland, Ancestral Scotland – www.ancestralscotland.com

CHAPTER 20

INDIGENOUS CULTURE

LEARNING OBJECTIVES

After reading this chapter, you should be able to:

1. Know the important role of native cultures in some destinations' tourism offerings.

2. Understand the notion of cultural property rights.

3. Be cognizant of the misappropriation of culture that commonly leads to conflict in tourism settings.

4. Be aware of how indigenous cultures become commodified by outsiders.

5. Realize the importance of cultural centers in disseminating heritage information about native peoples.

INTRODUCTION

Indigenous people go by many names, including natives, indigenes, aboriginals, aborigines, original inhabitants and first nations. All of these terms will be used interchangeably in this chapter. Regardless of the terms that describe them, native peoples provide one of the most enduring and endearing tourist spectacles in the world. Their traditions, livelihoods, folklore, folkways and cultural landscapes create a significant appeal for travelers, for they offer something beyond the ordinary, something reminiscent of days gone by, and this appeals to outsiders. Visiting and observing living cultures is the other definition of 'ethnic tourism' where ethnicity and cultural differences become the primary attraction.

Despite efforts by many colonial superpowers between the 16th and 20th centuries to quell indigenous cultures or assimilate indigenes into European society, as well as rapid modernization and globalization, there are many aboriginal peoples still living much the same way their ancestors did. Hundreds of millions of people still live off the land, observe traditional religions and practice customary lifestyles. In places where antiquated indigenous built heritage is largely absent, owing to impermanent building materials and the vagaries of climate (e.g. the Australian aborigines, the Carib Indians of the Caribbean Basin and many Pacific Island cultures), living culture has become the dominant heritage attraction.

This chapter explains the use of living indigenous heritage as a tourism resource and explicates the notion of empowerment in relation to cultural appropriation, conservation and intellectual property rights. While most examples are negative in that many destination natives have lost ownership and/or control of their own heritage to outside interests, there are signs that the situation is improving and people are becoming more empowered. Nonetheless, there is a long history of traditional cultures being commercialized for tourist consumption at the expense of authenticity and ownership.

LIVING CULTURE AS TOURISM RESOURCE

Native heritage ranges from villages and ancient ruins to music and modern dance. Since other parts of the book have already looked at the built environment, this chapter is most concerned with the living cultures that mark the everyday life and past living traditions of the world's indigenes. What elements of native life are of interest to tourists? In short, all features combine to create an alluring cultural landscape. Sometimes it is simply being able to see people in their native settings doing what they do on a day-to-day basis that appeals to tourists (see Plate 20.1). Thus, the local people themselves and their ways of life

Plate 20.1 These Panama natives are a salient part of the cultural product

become the focal point of the tourist 'gaze'. This was noted already in Chapter 19 in relation to the Amish. More specifically, Table 20.1 suggests features of everyday life that visitors consider most important in having an authentic or satisfying cultural experience in indigenous settings.

Table 20.1 Examples of living culture elements that appeal to tourists

Cultural feature	Examples
Traditional dances	• folk dances • rain dances • animal dances • storytelling through dance
Traditional music	• singing • musical instruments • religious rituals • musical forms • language use
Villages and related structures	• houses • animal shelters and barns • drying racks • granaries • boats and boat houses • baking ovens • communal centers and open space • religious edifices
Food and eating traditions	• wild foods • food preparation (e.g. drying fish and meat) • cultivated specialty foods • recipes • sampling • opportunities to buy
Handicrafts	• carvings, stone work, leather goods, masks • clothing • religious icons and offerings • pottery • rugs and wool products • hunting accoutrements
Artisan demonstrations	• metalwork • making cheese or butter • sewing clothes • painting with natural dies • carving spears and arrows

Folklore	• storytelling • poetry • legends • genealogy • oral histories • popular beliefs
Festivals	• religious celebrations • harvest parties • birthdays • coming of age celebrations • battle re-enactments
Ceremonies and rituals	• circumcision rituals • communicating with spirits • healing ceremonies • sweat lodges • funerary and burial rituals • storytelling
Traditional livelihoods	• dog sledding • hunting and fishing • gathering • farming and agricultural patterns • making leather and clothing
Culture-based nature activities	• whale watching • viewing mountain, plains or desert scenery • canoeing • rainforest and mountain trekking • fishing and hunting • dog-sledding • horseback riding

Valene Smith (1996a) proposed a fourfold framework for understanding aboriginal heritage as a tourism resource. She suggested that indigenous ethnic tourism can be encompassed in four Hs: habitat, heritage, history and handicrafts. Habitat includes natives' homes, communities and surrounding environment within which their cultures developed and currently exist. Nature and humankind's relationship with it is what has shaped indigenous cultures everywhere. Heritage in this context refers to the knowledge, skills, languages, religious beliefs and other learned behavior that defines ethnic groups and how they live their lives. The third H, history, Smith uses to refer to contact and subsequent dealings between the natives and westerners. Finally, handicrafts are the arts and traditional handworks that have now become a commodity for tourist consumption. For many native peoples, handicrafts are the most important of the four Hs as they are offered not only to tourists but exported abroad as well to be sold on world markets.

In some destinations, native cultures are such an important part of the tourism product that observing them becomes a 'must do' part of any package tour or independent trip, even among people who otherwise have little interest in cultural heritage. Visiting Maori performances and cultural centers on the North Island of New Zealand is a good example of something that is simply expected as part of a tour of that part of the country (see Plate 20.2). Similarly, visiting hill tribes and villages is almost a standard itinerary item in and around Chiang Mai, Thailand, these days, as are excursions to Maasai villages in Kenya.

These living resources provide a crucial part of the attractiveness of place among heritage tourists in many parts of the world, wherever there are indigenous people or ethnic minorities. According to a study by McIntosh (2004), tourists have certain expectations from their encounters with native peoples that help them appreciate indigenous cultures. These include the ability to gaze or look upon indigenes and their everyday lives, to observe how people live and work. They also desire authenticity in their encounter, whatever that means to each individual. A study by Yang and Wall (2009) in China suggested that most domestic tourists who visit ethnic parks enjoy staged events and are indifferent to whether or not they are 'authentic'. Foreign tourists at the same parks, on

Plate 20.2 This Maori cultural center in Rotorua is a popular stop on New Zealand tours

the other hand, expect experiences to be as authentic as possible. Personal interaction with a native person or persons is also important, as are informal learning opportunities wherein visitors discover something new about an ethnic group. According to Turco's (1999) study, tourists to the Navajo Nation in the southwestern USA desired most to experience aboriginal culture, purchase handicrafts and artworks and admire the natural beauty of the area.

INDIGENOUS CULTURAL RIGHTS AND THE MISAPPROPRIATION OF HERITAGE

The above discussion illustrates the need for sustainable approaches to cultural tourism. The importance of local people's control over their own cultural resources that are utilized as tourist attractions cannot be overstated. As the participatory principle in the PIC planning model denotes in Chapter 11, control of cultural heritage by the people whose heritage it is, is vital to sustainable tourism development. Control has several connotations in this context. The most important meaning for this discussion, though, assumes that ideas, plans and projects will originate with the natives rather than being imposed upon them from government officials, outside investors or other commercial interests. Traditions of 'participatory development' have assumed that local people should be consulted and given a voice in tourism development endeavors. However, today, this is an inadequate view. Instead, because of higher levels of empowerment, it is thought that the people most affected (positively or negatively) by tourism should be the ones conceptualizing and initiating tourism plans, not just acting as the hurdles for others to overcome in the planning process. By being in control they can choose what elements of their culture should be shown to tourists and which parts should remain hidden.

Another aspect of control is economic empowerment, which suggests that sustainable tourism allows residents and ethnic minorities to benefit financially from the industry. This seems obvious, but in many places indigenous people have gained little but suffered much because of tourism. Employment and social services are important outcomes of cultural tourism and should be a normal expectation for any native group that chooses to become involved in tourism. All too often, tourism businesses are owned by wealthy foreigners and employ local natives for pennies a day. Such situations should not happen when people are justly empowered.

The Taos Indians of New Mexico, USA, have a very high degree of control over their culture, which is among the top attractions in the southwestern USA. They have opted to keep the pueblo closed to tourists at certain times of the year when they practice religious rituals and other important celebrations. Likewise, the Hopi natives of Arizona, USA, restrict what celebrations and rituals tourists are allowed to see or participate in, and even what physical parts of their nation are completely off limits to outsiders. By way of various agreements between the New Zealand government and the Maori, the Maori have been able to retain a considerable degree of control over their culture, its signs and its symbols. They are much more empowered than the indigenes of many areas of the world in that they are heavily involved in cultural tourism, where their culture is on display, and Maori tourism must operate on their terms. Maori-based tourism functions according to values and native principles of hospitality that promote cultural sensitivity. These include transparency, alignment, solidarity, affectionate hospitality, guardianship, kinship relations, Maori diversity, spirituality, self-determination and an emphasis on best outcomes (McIntosh *et al.*, 2004).

Unfortunately, many first nations are not as empowered as some Native American and New Zealand tribes are today, although the process of empowerment from tokenistic participation to true control is gaining ground throughout the world. One of the current issues of vital importance today is intellectual property rights in relation to indigenous culture, such as music, dance, artifacts, symbols, beliefs and architecture. Although there are some 164 signatory countries to the Berne Convention, an international treaty that covers copyright and intellectual property rights, and various United Nations accords (e.g. the 1993 Declaration on the Rights of Indigenous Peoples and the 1993 Principles and Guidelines for the Protection of the Heritage of Indigenous Peoples) that try to offer protection for native people's cultural property rights, many member states do not enforce it when it comes to the intangible heritage of their indigenes.

This has led to many groups' cultural heritage being exploited for tourism and other purposes. For instance, many souvenirs for sale are mass-manufactured copies of indigenous products and designs, sold by non-natives, usually without their consent (see Plate 20.3). There has been a longtime practice of selling imitation Native American tomahawks (hatchets), tribal chief headdresses, moccasins (shoes), spears, bows and arrows and sundry other European-conceived symbols of American Indians at American heritage sites and even in the national parks. This commoditization of culture (discussed in more depth below) has long been a point of contention for aboriginal Americans, for not only does it pilfer aspects of their patrimony, it perpetuates mythological 'cowboy-and-Indian' stereotypes of them as bloodthirsty savages intent on fighting the Anglos.

An additional manifestation of the misappropriation of first nations culture has emerged strongly since the mid-20th century with the development of the New Age movement (see Chapter 18). New Agers participate in a spiritual society that is not part of any organized religion but rather accepts elements of many religious traditions, including East Asian spiritual philosophies (e.g. Taoism), Buddhism, Hinduism and Paganism. The movement looks to nature worship, self-deification, Gaia, psychic powers, extraterrestrial visitations and indigenous people's animist beliefs for its spiritual inspiration. New Agers are passionate travelers and are known for their pilgrimages to ancient sites of worship, such as Machu Picchu, the Pyramids of Giza, Stonehenge and many more sites where they believe the earth's energies are most powerful or where extraterrestrial encounters have occurred. This includes participation in various aboriginal rites and rituals, as well as pilgrimages to places all over the world that indigenes hold sacred.

Plate 20.3 Copycat indigenous crafts are sold at this tourist shop in Mexico

Herein lies the problem. In the USA, New Age pilgrims worship at sacred Native American sites, leaving burnt candles, stone circles, campfires, crystal offerings and other types of ritual litter. This, according to Navajos and Hopis, demonstrates disrespect for hallowed ground and is environmentally injurious, but what is more concerning in many respects for Native Americans is the commercialization of their cultural practices and objects by the New Age faction, particularly for profit-making. This is done without aboriginal consent and involves the use of sweat lodges, self-appointed medicine men, shamans, pipe ceremonies, nature dances, herbal treatments, chants and sage smudges. Many self-appointed New Age shamans claim to be able to communicate with Native American spirits and perform native rites. Such activities are seen by indigenous groups as fraudulent profiteering, with spiritual leaders making millions of dollars on seminars and books, while the natives from whom they appropriated the culture live in relative poverty.

There is growing discontent among many native peoples about the official use of their heritage symbols and cultures for tourism promotion by ministries of tourism, travel companies and destination management organizations. Not too long ago, government offices of tourism commonly utilized aboriginal symbols as agency logos. Air New Zealand uses the Maori koru design on its aircrafts. Various operators in the American

431

southwest use images of the Kokopelli, the hunch-backed, flute-playing fertility god of the Southwest Indians in their advertising, and many provinces in China utilize ethnic minority symbols and depictions of culture in their promotional campaigns. Brochures and websites promoting tourism in Peru and Brazil have for a long time adopted pictures of native peoples in traditional dress, doing traditional activities. Much of the time, pictures are taken by professional photographers and sold to marketing agencies for a profit, without the subjects' knowledge that they would appear in various promotional media. Lawsuits in several countries have been filed against companies or individuals who have appropriated aboriginal cultural symbols and images without the people's consent based primarily on copyright infringement laws or other cultural protective legislation.

Another concern about aboriginal control is outside efforts to conserve native cultures. One common complaint that natives have is that conservation planning and tourism development efforts in relation to their built and/or living culture are done by outsiders, usually non-natives, based on European concepts of what is good or what is best. This 'neocolonialist' approach, outsiders deciding what is best for natives, is no longer acceptable practice in a world where indigenous peoples are becoming more powerful and in control of their heritage resources.

Many of the early efforts by Europeans in colonial societies to preserve native artifacts and cultures were done without regard to existing cultural sensitivities or social mores. Even though they thought they were acting in the best interest of the aboriginal peoples, decisions and projects were undertaken in ignorance regarding non-western heritage values. Some non-native 'conservation' efforts were, and continue to be, offensive to the indigenes. By creating museums of native peoples, sacred relics were removed from hallowed spaces, secularized and placed into profane displays for the entire world to view. Writing about Pacific Islanders' perceptions of European colonial museums about the islanders, Mané-Wheoki (1992: 35) noted that placing cultural artifacts in museums 'far away from the people for whom [they] had originally been carved and built, was tantamount to keeping a brain-dead body artificially alive on a life-support system; tantamount to freezing the corpse; tantamount to placing one's dead grandmother's body on permanent exhibition'.

Signs of improvement

As noted earlier, in the cases of the Maoris and Native Americans, the situation for ethnic minorities is improving, although there are still many original peoples who have essentially no basic human rights in the tourism and sustainable development context at all, let alone in the realm of cultural self determination. The Shan and Karen people of Myanmar are two good examples (see Plate 20.4).

Indigenous knowledge is finally being recognized as a critical ingredient in sustainable development as it pertains to cultural and natural heritage. Conventional thinking by

Plate 20.4 The Karen people of Myanmar (Burma) have little control over their role in tourism

public officials and other so-called experts suggested that native people were a threat to heritage and biodiversity because of their herding and agricultural practices, and that they knew very little about conserving their living culture. Rather than basing cultural tourism planning on the advice of outside politicians and consultants, who live far from the real-life indigenous situation, first nations are finally being considered worthy guardians of their own cultural past because of their ecological knowledge, their oneness with nature, their oral traditions and their proclivity to focus much of their learning on their ancestral past. Indigenous knowledge is equal to, or more important than, scientific knowledge in preserving and presenting their culture.

The US National Park Service and other public land agencies now have a policy to incorporate aboriginal concepts and management concerns in public lands management where Native American culture is involved. Similarly, in Australia, national parks that have an aboriginal element are being co-managed by native groups and various state departments of the environment. Based upon a blend of *piranpa* (scientific knowledge) and *tjukurpa* (aboriginal law), places such as Uluru-Kata Tjuta National Park (Ayers Rock), a UNESCO World Heritage Site and an exceedingly important sacred location for

Australia's first peoples, are being jointly managed in a way that achieves the goals of both sets of values.

Another sign of self-determination is the proliferation of native casinos in the USA and Canada. In the US, the Indian Gaming and Regulatory Act of 1988 established the right of many aboriginal American tribes to establish high-stakes casinos on their reservation lands, depending on the state where their land is located. There are approximately 425 Indian gaming facilities (not all are casinos) operated by 233 tribes in 28 states of the USA. Canada has similar first nations legislation that allows native peoples the ability to determine whether or not they desire economic development through casino gaming. There are currently 18 first nations casinos in Canada, with several more being planned (World Casino Directory, 2010). The casino movement was supposed to bring increased prosperity to traditionally impoverished reservations. Casinos have improved many people's standard of living, but they have a good share of critics who argue that the wealth remains concentrated in the hands of a few and that gaming now exceeds culture in touristic importance and has taken over as the new image of indigenous tourism in the USA.

THE UBIQUITOUS CULTURAL CENTER

One consistent trend throughout the world today is the establishment of cultural centers, wherein native peoples demonstrate elements of their living heritage. When these centers are conceived, planned and established by the aboriginal peoples themselves, they are seen as viable opportunities to demonstrate their patrimony to outsiders, to create jobs for their people, to reinforce cultural identity and bring money into tribal coffers. Cultural centers take on many styles and often resemble the living outdoor museums discussed in Chapter 14 in that natives in traditional attire might re-enact or demonstrate customary crafts, skills, music and dances for tourists (see Plate 20.5). They interpret their intangible traditions and field questions that visitors might have about their customs and rituals. In most cases, tangible structures and artifacts at indigenous cultural centers are reproductions based on archaeological evidence of the originals, although some have been known to be brought on-site from archaeological areas or existing villages.

Many indigenous cultural centers have been developed in busy tourist destinations. The natives of Japan, the Ainu, have set up the Shiraoi Ainu Museum in Hokkaido, where traditional music and dances are shown. The Bedouin people of Egypt built the Beyt Ababda Heritage Center to educate visitors about their traditional nomadic lifestyles and the difficulties of life in the desert. Several cultural centers have been established in Taiwan that exhibit various elements of the island's native peoples. These are also plentiful in Australia, New Zealand, and the USA. In China, many centers have been built to commemorate and interpret the 55 officially-recognized ethnic groups in that country. In short, native peoples everywhere have a vested interest in how their cultures are shared

Plate 20.5 Emiratis performing a modified traditional camel dance in a shopping mall in Dubai

to tourists; while these are frequently established by central governments because of the lucrative cash-earning potential. Often, actors are not 'authentic' natives – a fact that in some cases drives a wedge between the people being portrayed, the actors portraying them and the investors who initiated the project.

Like the criticisms of outdoor living museums everywhere, these cultural centers have a good share of opposition. Critics suggest that these undertakings are exploitative and superficial. They bring little money into the clan or community because most of it leaks back to national governments or non-local investors, and they never address the real-life problems of poverty, drug abuse, teenage pregnancy and lack of education that often accompany aboriginal minority life in certain countries. Obviously, however, people want to portray the positive aspects of life, not the negative, so to suggest that native centers portray all aspects of life, positive and negative, is an unrealistic expectation. The notion of exploitation can be overcome in part at least by allowing the indigenes themselves to conceptualize, plan, initiate and manage the cultural center. This level of empowerment is the best assurance that equitable relationships will be created, the most accurate stories will be told from their perspective and programs will be developed that are least offensive.

COMMODIFICATION OF CULTURE

If outsiders (i.e. New Agers, governments, tour companies and airlines) are busy com-modifying indigenous cultures, the natives themselves are too, sometimes in the context of the cultural centers discussed above. Cultures are dynamic. They change through time and with varying social, economic, environmental and political pressures. One of the most salient of these pressures, however, is tourism. As tourism grows in a destination, art forms, lifestyles, rituals and celebrations have a tendency to change to adapt to the social nuances that tourism brings with it.

Obviously handiworks, religious rites and social celebrations were originally done out of devotion, tradition, sense of duty and gratitude for the bounties of the land. They were utilitarian in purpose and enhanced the quality of people's lives. As tourists began to arrive, however, their demand for cultural performances and artworks brought about changes in these attractions. Realizing that profits could be made by selling culture to outsiders, lifestyles and all their elements were commodified for tourist consumption. In the process, their meanings, forms and functions changed, some of them being lost almost completely or altered permanently. With the growth of tourism, demand for native culture has also grown. Many dances, musical performances, ceremonies, rites, rituals and artworks have changed so dramatically they would hardly be recognized by earlier generations. Thus, cultural traditions change to meet the demands of tourists; artworks and celebrations are produced for tourist consumption the way tourists think they ought to be created or celebrated.

Carved masks are now sold in Kenya as authentic native art, when anthropological records indicate that carved masks were not used in Kenya. Carvings of giraffes are sold in Indonesia and carved crocodiles in Fiji, when giraffes and crocodiles were non-existent in Indonesia and Fiji. There are multitudinous examples of native peoples offering so-called 'traditional' artworks and ceremonies that were invented specifically for tourist consumption. Similarly, many traditional material and nonmaterial arts have changed form considerably since the introduction of tourism. Simple pottery that was originally made for utilitarian purposes is now elaborately adorned with colorful paintings of images that were foreign to the indigenes but desired by tourists. These have now become the touristic version of 'authentic' and 'traditional' arts. 'Airport art' or 'tourist kitsch' is created when items that may have their roots in original designs and functions are now mass-produced for outside consumption. Native rituals and dances performed in hotel lobbies or on a tourist stage are altered for sound, time and fit. The content and deep social meaning behind some celebrations are altered considerably because tourism demands shorter stories, more elaborate costumes and better lighting.

What makes this most negative in the eyes of cultural specialists is that by being mass-produced and mass-consumed, celebrations and handicrafts lose their original spiritual, social or utilitarian value because they are made by unskilled people who know little about the original cultural context and who have little or no personal connection to the craft. These elements of native culture become cheapened versions of heritage that depict non-existing or falsified settings but are offered as realistic depictions of what used to be. Native Americans performing pow-wow dances in casinos and Maoris performing the POI dance on a hotel stage have a good share of opponents for being over-commercialized, altered in form and performed outside their authentic environments. The aboriginals, however, argue for their right to exercise their own culture the way they want to, including performing before large audiences in touristic settings.

SUMMARY AND CONCLUSION

Heritage tourism based on living culture does have the potential to help alleviate poverty, provide educational opportunities, build community pride and preserve local cultures if it is initiated and managed in a sustainable fashion with native management philosophies and in accordance with native desires. Unfortunately, however, the people who should benefit most have not seen large dividends from the use of their native culture for tourism, which stems from the lack of self-determination and ownership of cultural property that has plagued indigenes throughout the world for centuries.

There is evidence to suggest that the situation is improving as more communities are empowered to control their own tourism futures. Unfortunately some of this self-determination has led to cultural exploitation, commodification and demise, as well as the growth of some forms of 'indigenous tourism', such as casino gaming, that detract from the cultural vitality and living heritage long upheld by indigenes everywhere.

REVIEW QUESTIONS

1. Why might some indigenous peoples desire to avoid tourism or at least control tourist access to their traditions and ceremonies?

2. In what ways could native groups utilize Smith's four Hs for managing their cultural heritage?

3. Why are some native groups iconic and very visible parts of the tourism landscape in some places, while other groups are relatively unknown?

4. What are some steps indigenes can take to assure that their culture is sold and consumed on their own terms, not on the terms set by outsiders?

5. How have public agencies begun to adopt indigenous views of the environment and integrate those views in their management plans? How do such approaches contribute to more sustainable forms of cultural tourism?

6. What are the linkages between native culture and authenticity? Can native peoples influence the authenticity of tourist experiences by managing their cultural resources in a certain way?

RECOMMENDED READING

Al-Oun, S. and Al-Homoud, M. (2008) The potential for developing community-based tourism among the Bedouins in the Badia of Jordan. *Journal of Heritage Tourism* 3(1), 36–54.

Aldred, L. (2000) Plastic shamans and Astroturf sun dances: New Age commercialization of Native American spirituality. *American Indian Quarterly* 24(3), 329–352.

Altman, J. and Finlayson, J. (2003) Aborigines, tourism and sustainable development. *Journal of Tourism Studies* 14(1), 78–91.

Amoamo, M., Pringle, R. and Sibson, R. (2007) Maori tourism: image and identity – a postcolonial perspective. *Annals of Leisure Research* 10(3/4), 454–474.

Ardren, T. (2004) Where are the Maya in ancient Maya archaeological tourism? Advertising and the appropriation of culture. In Y. Rowan and U. Baram (eds) *Marketing Heritage: Archaeology and the Consumption of the Past* (pp. 103–113). Walnut Creek, CA: AltaMira Press.

Balenquah, L.J. (2008) Beyond stone and mortar: A Hopi perspective on the preservation of ruins (and culture). *Heritage Management* 1(2), 145–162.

Bos-Seldenthuis, J.E.M.F. (2007) Life and tradition of the Ababda nomads in the Egyptian desert, the junction between intangible and tangible heritage management. *International Journal of Intangible Heritage* 2, 31–43.

Bulilan, C.M.R. and Peterson, J.A. (2007) Experiencing cultural heritage and indigenous tourism in Banaue. *Philippine Quarterly of Culture and Society* 35(1/2), 100–128.

Butler, R.W. and Hinch, T. (eds) (2007) *Tourism and Indigenous Peoples: Issues and Implications*. Oxford: Butterworth Heinemann.

Chang, J. (2006) Segmenting tourists to aboriginal cultural festivals: An example in the Rukai tribal area, Taiwan. *Tourism Management* 27(6), 1224–1234.

Chang, J., Wall, G. and Chu, S.T. (2006) Novelty seeking at aboriginal attractions. *Annals of Tourism Research* 33(3), 729–747.

Cheung, S.C.H. (2005) Rethinking Ainu heritage: A case study of an Ainu settlement in Hokkaido, Japan. *International Journal of Heritage Studies* 11(3), 197–210.

Chhabra, D. (2010) How they see us: Perceived effects of tourist gaze on the Old Order Amish. *Journal of Travel Research* 49(1), 93–105.

Chibnik, M. (2008) Advertising Oaxacan woodcarvings. *Human Organization* 67(4), 362–372.

Clark, I.D. (2002) Rock art sites in Victoria, Australia: A management history framework. *Tourism Management* 23(5), 455–464.

Clark, I.D. (2009) Naming sites: Names as management tools in indigenous tourism sites – an Australian case study. *Tourism Management* 30(1), 109–111.

Cohen, E. (1988) Authenticity and commoditization in tourism. *Annals of Tourism Research* 15, 371–386.

Cohen, E. (1989) The commercialization of ethnic crafts. *Journal of Design History* 2(2), 161–168.

Collins, J. and Jordan, K. (2009) Ethnic precincts as ethnic tourism destinations in urban Australia. *Tourism, Culture and Communication* 9(1/2), 79–92.

English, A. (2002) More than archaeology: Developing comprehensive approaches to Aboriginal heritage management in NSW. *Australian Journal of Environmental Management* 9(4), 218–227.

Fagence, M. (2001) Cultural tourism: Strategic interventions to sustain a minority culture. *Journal of Tourism Studies* 12(2), 10–21.

Fagence, M. (2003) Tourism and local society and culture. In S. Singh, D.J. Timothy and R.K. Dowling (eds) *Tourism in Destination Communities* (pp. 55–78). Wallingford: CAB International.

Friedl, H.A. (2008) Western money for southern sympathy: How the Tuareg from Timia are instrumentalizing tourists to support their 'exotic' village. In P. Burns and M. Novelli (eds) *Tourism Development: Growth, Myths and Inequalities* (pp. 39–51). Wallingford: CAB International.

Glow, H. and Johanson, K. (2009) Instrumentalism and the 'helping' discourse: Australian indigenous performing arts and policy. *International Journal of Cultural Policy* 15(3), 315–328.

Graburn, N. (1984) The evolution of tourist arts. *Annals of Tourism Research* 11, 393–419.

Guttentag, D. (2009) The legal protection of indigenous souvenir products. *Tourism Recreation Research* 34(1), 23–34.

Hall, C.M. (2000) Tourism, national parks and aboriginal peoples. In R.W. Butler and S.W. Boyd (eds) *Tourism and National Parks: Issues and Implications* (pp. 57–71). Chichester: Wiley.

Hall, C.M., Mitchell, I. and Keelan, N. (1993) The implications of Maori perspectives for the management and promotion of heritage tourism in New Zealand. *GeoJournal* 29, 315–322.

Henderson, J., Teck, G.K., Ng, D. and Tan, S. (2009) Tourism in ethnic communities: Two Miao villages in China. *International Journal of Heritage Studies* 15(6), 529–539.

Hueneke, H., Baker, R., Davies, J. and Holcombe, S. (2009) Tourist behaviour, local values, and interpretation at Uluru: 'The sacred deed at Australia's mighty heart'. *GeoJournal* 74(5), 477–490.

Hume, D.L. (2009) The development of tourist art and souvenirs – the arc of the boomerang: From hunting, fighting and ceremony to tourist souvenir. *International Journal of Tourism Research* 11(1), 55–70.

Johnston, A.M. (2003) Self-determination: exercising indigenous rights in tourism. In S. Singh, D.J. Timothy and R.K. Dowling (eds) *Tourism in Destination Communities* (pp. 115–134). Wallingford: CAB International.

Johnston, A.M. (2006) *Is the Sacred for Sale? Tourism and Indigenous Peoples.* London: Earthscan.

Kreps, G.M., Donnermeyer, J.F., Hurst, C., Blair, R. and Kreps, M. (1997) The impact of tourism on the Amish subculture: A case study. *Community Development Journal* 32(4), 354–367.

Kuo, S., Chen, C.Y. and Hsieh, C.J. (2009) Aboriginal culture and tourist development: The case of the Amis people of Fongbin township, Taiwan. *Canadian Journal of Development Studies* 28(3/4), 589–601.

Lew, A.A. and van Otten, G.A. (eds) (1998) *Tourism and Gaming on American Indian Lands.* New York: Cognizant.

Loverseed, H. (1998) Aboriginal tourism in North America. *Travel and Tourism Analyst* 6, 42–61.

McIntosh, A.J. and Johnson, H. (2004) Exploring the nature of the Maori experience in New Zealand: Views from hosts and tourists. *Tourism* 52(2), 117–129.

Morais, D.B., Dong, E.W. and Yan, G.H. (2006) The ethnic tourism expansion cycle: The case of Yunnan Province, China. *Asia Pacific Journal of Tourism Research* 11(2), 189–204.

Moscardo, G. and Pearce, P.L. (1999) Understanding ethnic tourists. *Annals of Tourism Research* 26(2), 416–434.

Müller, D.K. and Huuva, S.K. (2009) Limits to Sami tourism development: The case of Jokkmokk, Sweden. *Journal of Ecotourism* 8(2), 115–127.

Notzke, C. (2004) Indigenous tourism development in southern Alberta, Canada: Tentative engagement. *Journal of Sustainable Tourism* 12(1), 29–54.

Nyaupane, G., White, D.D. and Budruk, M. (2006) Motive-based tourist market segmentation: An application to Native American cultural heritage sites in Arizona, USA. *Journal of Heritage Tourism* 1(2), 81–99.

Peers, L. (1999) "Playing ourselves": First Nations and Native American interpreters at living history sites. *The Public Historian* 21(4), 39–59.

Piner, J.M. and Paradis, T.W. (2004) Beyond the casino: Sustainable tourism and cultural development on Native American lands. *Tourism Geographies* 6(1), 80–98.

Porter, J. (ed.) (2007) *Place and Native American Indian History and Culture.* Oxford: Peter Lang.

Riseth, J.Å., Johnson, J.T., Cant, G., Howitt, R. and Peters, E. (2007) An indigenous perspective on national parks and Sámi reindeer management in Norway. *Geographical Research* 45(2), 177–185.

Ryan, C. and Huyton, J. (2000) Aboriginal tourism: A linear structure relations analysis of domestic and international tourist demand. *International Journal of Tourism Research* 2(1), 15–29.

Simons, M.S. (2000) Aboriginal heritage art and moral rights. *Annals of Tourism Research* 27, 412–431.

Spark, C. (2002) Brambuk Living Cultural Centre: Indigenous culture and the production of place. *Tourist Studies* 2(1), 23–42.

Tahana, N. and Oppermann, M. (1998) Maori cultural performances and tourism. *Tourism Recreation Research* 23, 23–30.

Timothy, D.J. and Conover, P.J. (2006) Nature religion, self-spirituality and New Age tourism. In D.J. Timothy and D.H. Olsen (eds) *Tourism, Religion and Spiritual Journeys* (pp. 139–155). London: Routledge.

Timothy, D.J. and White, K. (1999) Community-based ecotourism development on the periphery of Belize. *Current Issues in Tourism* 2(2/3), 226–242.

Turco, D.M. (2000) Tourism in Amish communities. *Parks and Recreation* 35(9), 138–144.

Waldroup, H. (2008) Musée Gauguin Tahiti: Indigenous places, colonial heritage. *International Journal of Heritage Studies* 14(6), 489–505.

Whitford, M. (2008) Oaxaca's indigenous Guelaguetza festival: Not all that glistens is gold. *Event Management* 12(3/4), 143–161.

Xie, P.F. (2003) The bamboo-beating dance in Hainan, China: Authenticity and commodification. *Journal of Sustainable Tourism* 11(1), 5–16.

Yang, L. and Wall, G. (2008) Ethnic tourism and entrepreneurship: Xishuangbanna, Yunna, China. *Tourism Geographies* 10(4), 522–544.

Yang, L., Wall, G. and Smith, S.L.J. (2008) Ethnic tourism development: Chinese government perspectives. *Annals of Tourism Research* 35(3), 751–771.

Zeppel, H. (1998) "Come share our culture": Marketing aboriginal tourism in Australia. *Pacific Tourism Review* 2(1), 67–81.

Zeppel, H. (1999) Touring aboriginal cultures: Encounters with aboriginal people in Australian travelogues. *Tourism, Culture and Communication* 2(2), 123–139.

RECOMMENDED WEBSITES

Aboriginal Tourism Association of BC – http://www.aboriginalbc.com/

American Indian Alaska Native Tourism Association – http://www.aianta.org/

Indigenous Tourism – http://www.indigenoustourism.com/

Indigenous Tourism Australia – http://www.indigenoustourism.australia.com/

Maasai Association – http://www.maasai-association.org/opinion.html

National Indian Gaming Association – http://www.indiangaming.org/

National Indian Gaming Commission – http://www.nigc.gov/

Native Tourism – http://www.nativetourism.org/index.htm

New Zealand Maori Tourism Council – http://www.maoritourism.co.nz/

Peoples of the World Foundation – http://www.peoplesoftheworld.org/thailand.jsp

Toledo Ecotourism Association – http://www.southernbelize.com/tea.html

CHAPTER 21

DARK TOURISM: ATROCITY AND HUMAN SUFFERING

LEARNING OBJECTIVES

After reading this chapter, you should be able to:

1. Understand some of the motives for visiting places of darkness.

2. Conceptualize the notion of morbidity and how this plays out in people's travel patterns.

3. Be familiar with the different types of human suffering and death that appeal to tourists.

4. Know about the transformation of war from tourist deterrent to tourist attraction.

5. Appreciate the management challenges and opportunities associated with thanatourism attractions.

INTRODUCTION

Millions of people each year visit a wide range of attractions that satiate an interest in risk, morbidity and death. Some locales rely on 'dark' attractions for the majority of their tourism economies. Visits to spots linked to death, suffering, destruction, disaster and other manifestations of human tragedy, which every country possesses, are known by a variety of names. Among the most common of these are dark tourism, thanatourism, morbid tourism, tourism of death and macabre tourism. Thanatourism refers specifically to death sites, whereas dark and macabre tourism include thanatouristic places but encompass a broader sense of human anguish. Regardless of the exact terminologies used, what they all have in common is an interest in seeing and experiencing places known for human suffering.

This chapter briefly describes some of the motives associated with visits to macabre locations and examines the vast assortment of resources that draw in dark tourists. Based on an understanding of the nature of resources and motives of tourism, management implications unique to dark tourism are presented.

THE APPEAL OF DARKNESS

Human beings have an innate and morbid interest in shocking situations, destruction and human suffering. Throngs of people gathering to witness the aftermath of a car accident, a flash flood or a house fire are evidence of this phenomenon.

Some observers believe that people visiting sites where death occurred are motivated by a morbid curiosity about death, or uneasiness about their own mortality. Other on-lookers may have an innate desire to experience fear, to face their fears or to find novelty in their lives. For some, tragic events and their associated markers provide enlightenment: education, knowledge and a resolve never to let it happen again. Travel to certain sites takes on the aura of a spiritual pilgrimage, where seekers remember the fallen, honor a soldier's sacrifice, undergo catharsis, mourn and grieve the loss of life, volunteer to assist the destitute and pay respects to the deceased or injured. In Dann's (1998) estimation, some people simply want to satisfy their 'bloodlust' by visiting sites of death and destruction – much the same way they would by watching an execution or beheading on the internet.

Seaton (1996) understands that not all dark experiences derive from the artifacts being visited. Instead, they are an amalgam of site characteristics and people's motives, interests and desires. From this perspective he attempted to conceptualize demand for sites associated with death by suggesting a five-part taxonomy. First is travel to witness the actual killing or death of an individual. Although this is not common today, it was in the past with public decapitations and hangings. In some places capital punishment (death) is still practiced for the punishment of murderers, adulterers and committers of treason. Seaton's second type is people visiting sites of death or murder after it has occurred. Battlefields and genocide camps are suitable examples. Visiting monuments to death, such as cemeteries and war memorials, is Seaton's third example. Fourth is viewing tools of symbolic death, such as weapons and armaments in museums. Lastly, Seaton noted that some people travel to view or participate in imitation death performances, such as war reenactments or re-creations of infamous murders.

There are many other forces that cause people to visit sites of human suffering. The media is fundamental in promoting dark tourism, directly and indirectly. Television, print media and the internet all report scenes of destruction, which at a local scale draw crowds of news-watchers. Such events are usually one-off and short lived. At a larger scale, well-covered stories about globally-significant tragedies can bring people from much farther away for months and years to come. The pop-culture media also contributes by popularizing celebrities so that no part of their lives remains private. When celebrities and public figures die, the media is engrossed in covering the story. By doing so, they venerate the deceased and sanctify the places where the untimely demise occurred, resulting in waves of devoted fans on quasi-pilgrimages.

History books valorize the people and places associated with mass destruction in an effort to build a national identity and sense of ethnic pride. The Glencoe Massacre in

17th century Scotland helped solidify the Scottish national identity and is still commemorated as one of Scotland's darkest days. In the Winter War of 1939–40, the Finnish army successfully defended itself against the much more powerful Soviet army. While Finland lost approximately 11% of its national territory to Soviet advances, the smaller army succeeded in staying off the larger Soviet forces, compelling the USSR to sign a peace treaty in 1940. Finland's fight against the USSR has always been a matter of civic pride. The battlefields and war memorials commemorating the Winter War on both sides of the present border are key ingredients in Finnish nationalism.

The glorification of national achievements via official narratives, such as these, ensconce within people a desire to visit dark places of national pride. When we grow up reading about these events in school textbooks or newspapers, or see documentaries or movies about them on television, they become second nature to us. For many people they are necessary places to visit.

While we understand fairly well the attributes of places of atrocity and suffering that draw people to them, and people's outward expressions of motive, we know relatively little about what deeper emotions and psychological underpinnings drive people to seek out these places and crave these experiences. Perhaps a pervasive air of sensationalism fuels the fire of curiosity. Maybe some people come to terms with their own fear of death and pain by immersing themselves in others' suffering. Research is currently being undertaken by scholars to understand better the innate desires of large segments of the population to experience places of dark heritage and what socio-psychological conditioning takes place in people's lives to stimulate such interests.

DARKNESS ABOUNDS

Although we do not know much about people's innermost, even subconscious, stimuli that cause a fascination with death and suffering, we do know that hundreds of millions of visits are made each year to locales of darkness. There are plenty of sites of atrocity to fulfill the demand.

There is a growing discussion in academic and industry circles about the need to clarify dark tourism. A current line of thinking suggests that there are different 'shades' of darkness in attractions based upon sites' characteristics and political influence, as well as the visitors' expectations, desires and experiences.

Richard Sharpley (2009: 19–20) proposed a useful model of dark tourism demand and supply to help conceptualize the 'shades of grey' relationships between the attractions and people's interest in visiting them (see Figure 21.1). It takes into account the type of attraction in terms of whether it is purposeful (built specifically for tourist consumption) or accidental (became an attraction only after the event occurred). It also views the degree to which a fascination with death or suffering is a factor of consumption. When these two

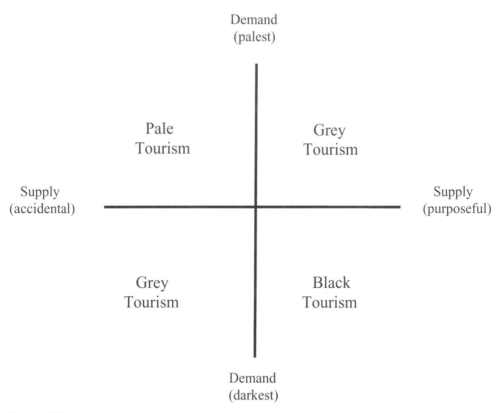

Figure 21.1 Dark tourism demand and supply matrix

Source: After Sharpley (2009)

elements combine (supply and demand), four shades of grey appear. First is pale tourism, or people with limited interest in death and destruction visiting places unintended to be attractions (e.g. graves of famous people). Second, grey tourism demand is comprised of tourists who have an interest in death, visiting sites that were not intended to be attractions. The third shade is grey tourism supply. This includes sites developed intentionally to highlight darkness (e.g. museums or monuments) that are visited by people with limited interest in death. Finally, 'black tourism' is defined as disaster-interested people visiting sites intended to be dark attractions.

Stone (2006, cited in Sharpley, 2009) developed a similar model that attempts to distinguish different attractions along a spectrum of darkness (see Figure 21.2). He suggests that attractions built for the purpose of drawing dark tourists, that are less authentic in location and interpretation, that have a well developed tourism infrastructure and which wield less political clout are the lightest of the dark attractions. Places that were not purpose-built for tourism, are more authentic in location and interpretation, more politically viable and are much less commercialized are Stone's darkest attractions.

Higher political
influence & ideology

Lower political
influence & ideology

Sites *of* death
and suffering

Sites *associated with*
death and suffering

Darkest	Darker	Dark	Light	Lighter	Lightest

Characteristics:
- Education focused
- History focused
- Perceived authenticity
(interpretation and location)
- Event more recent
- Accidental supply
- Less tourism infrastructure

Characteristics:
- Entertainment focused
- Heritage focused
- Perceived inauthenticity
(interpretation and location)
- Event longstanding
- Purposeful supply
- More tourism infrastructure

Figure 21.2 Dark tourism spectrum

Source: After Stone (2006) and Sharpley (2009)

Several different types of dark tourism have been identified by scholars and the travel industry, and various people have tried to categorize them. Table 21.1 is a classification of the most common types of dark tourism attractions for the purposes of this book, but the list is certainly not exhaustive. Instead it highlights some of the primary supply themes and provides supportive examples or subtypes of each one. An important point to note in an exercise such as this is that there will inevitably be overlap between the categories listed; each one is not mutually exclusive. For example, concentration camps may be associated with war heritage, human incarceration and death simultaneously.

Table 21.1 Types of dark tourism attractions

Type of attraction	*Examples*
Places of human incarceration	Prisons, jails, detention centers, slave forts, other slavery sites, concentration camps, penal colonies, leper colonies
War and conflict-related attractions	Concentration/internment camps, historic battlefields, war memorials, active war zones, fortified borders, sites of genocide, political instability

Natural disasters	Earthquakes, tornados, hurricanes, floods, volcanic eruptions, mudslides, bridge collapses, oil spills
Sites connected to death	Cemeteries, graves, crypts, catacombs, funerals and funerary rituals, murders, suicides, terrorist attacks, Body Worlds exhibit, famous accidents, museums, animal attacks
Crime scenes	Bank robberies, kidnappings, rapes, murders
Other morbid attractions and places of human suffering	Haunted houses, séances or exorcisms, mental hospitals and sanitariums, sunken ships, expected future events

Human incarceration

Holding people against their will simply because they are members of an ethnic minority, or because they are deemed inferior or ill, has unfortunately been a common practice throughout history. Although it still occurs in some places, it is much less common today than it was a century ago. Justifiable though, people are still held against their will because they were judged guilty of a punishable crime. Sites of human imprisonment have become tourist attractions, some of them deemed important enough to achieve World Heritage status, while thousands of others are of equal importance but on a more local scale.

Concentration camps and internment camps can be found in many parts of the world. While they existed in large number in the Soviet Union and still do in isolated states, such as North Korea, these have not been exploited for tourism purposes, for obviously political reasons. However, concentration camps associated with the Jewish Holocaust and the Japanese-American internment camps in the USA, also established during the Second World War, are now part of the dark tourism product. Dozens of concentration camps, extermination camps, transit camps, prison camps and ghettos were established all over Europe by the Nazis in their efforts to purify the Arian race by eliminating Jews and other 'undesirables' (e.g. homosexuals, Romanis, Freemasons, dissidents and people with mental and physical disabilities). While exact numbers are disputed, it is certain that millions of people were murdered or died directly because of camp conditions in the 1930s and 40s. Regarding this horrifying heritage, Lennon and Smith (2004: 16) note:

> Concentration camps have left deep scars on the landscape of Europe. They are the physical testaments to the Nazi ideals of racial superiority, and their approach to annihilating the Jewish race. Despite the negative connotations associated with the camps, several have become major tourist 'attractions'. It is suggested that approximately six million visitors each year visit six of the major museums and former camps connected with the holocaust.

448

Table 21.2 A selection of Holocaust memorials in various parts of the world

Memorial	Location
Yad Vashem	Jerusalem, Israel
Centre de la mémoire d'Oradour	Oradour-sur-Glane, France
Holocaust Memorial Center	Detroit, USA
Memorial to the Murdered Jews of Europe	Berlin, Germany
Museo della Deportazione	Prato, Italy
Stockholm Holocaust Monument	Stockholm, Sweden
Montreal Holocaust Memorial Centre	Montreal, Canada
Judenplatz Holocaust Memorial	Vienna, Austria
Cape Town Holocaust Centre	Cape Town, South Africa
Hyde Park Holocaust Memorial	London, UK
Jewish Holocaust Museum and Research Centre	Melbourne, Australia
Kalevi-Liiva Memorial	Jägala, Estonia
Budapest Holocaust Memorial Center	Budapest, Hungary
Museo del Holocausto	Buenos Aires, Argentina

This most depraved of human atrocities has been commemorated all over the world with the development of museums, monuments, parks, libraries, research centers and other memorial sites devoted to the lives lost during the Holocaust (see Table 21.2). The goals of most of these establishments are to remember the deceased, to educate younger generations and to facilitate research.

Around the same time, nearly 113,000 Japanese-Americans were held in internment camps because of public prejudice and government fear they might be loyal to Japan during the Second World War. Known as 'relocation centers', 10 of these were located in Arkansas, Wyoming, Idaho, Utah, Arizona, Colorado and California. Some of them presently lie in ruins, while others have been well preserved and managed by the National Park Service as National Historic Sites (see Plate 21.1). All of these sites are now pilgrimage centers for survivors and their descendants. It is one of America's most

Plate 21.1 The Topaz Japanese internment camp in Utah lies in ruins

shameful acts against its own citizens, and in 1988 the US government officially apologized to the Japanese-American community.

Prisons and jails, particularly those associated with famous criminals or national heroes who were wrongfully incarcerated, are now being promoted as heritage attractions. Robben Island, South Africa, is a UNESCO World Heritage Site and important attraction because it is where political prisoners, including Nelson Mandela, who fought against the injustices of apartheid, were locked away. Hoa Loa prison in Hanoi, Vietnam, was used by the French for political prisoners; later, the Viet Cong used it to house prisoners of war (POWs) during the Vietnam War; American POWs dubbed it the 'Hanoi Hilton'. These are three examples of well-known prisons but, as noted earlier, there are thousands more prisons and small-town jails where local bandits or famous inmates were incarcerated. Heritage jails usually draw three types of crowds: local visitors, people visiting friends and relatives in the location and looking for something to do, and history buffs who might be aware of a famous person's imprisonment or hobbyists who enjoy visiting jails and learning about the criminal past.

Penal colonies, like prisons and jails, were home to criminals and other social undesirables, although they had more comfortable amenities than prisons and internment camps. They were self-contained settlements where larger groups of convicts were kept in isolation away from mainstream society. In most cases they were located on islands or in otherwise remote areas to minimize outside contact. Penal colonies essentially functioned as overseas territories, governed by wardens. Many of these communities were used as free labor camps for growing produce or manufacturing goods for export. Many historians suggest that penal labor was simply a glorified term for slave labor in many of these colonies.

Penal colonies have been abandoned over the years as convicts eventually intermingled with the rest of society, and their original purpose was fulfilled. Many of them lie in ruins today, have been destroyed by human actions or weather or have been conserved for heritage purposes. Several well-known penal settlements have become tourist attractions. Perhaps the main obstacle in developing these as tourist attractions is their relative isolation. Those located on small islands near mainlands have tended to receive the most tourist attention, while those located in extremely remote areas have not had the same opportunities. Port Arthur, Australia, was a former penal settlement in Tasmania. It is one of Tasmania's most important heritage attractions and has been placed on UNESCO's Tentative List of World Heritage Sites for future consideration. Devil's Island is a historical penal colony off the coast of French Guiana, in South America. Its penal functions ceased in the 1950s, but its structures have since been restored and become a significant cultural attraction in French Guiana. Another of the best-known penal colonies was remote Norfolk Island, Australia, which was home to convicts between the late 1700s and mid 1800s. Much of the original settlement lies in preserved ruins, while other parts have been restored and marked as heritage sites (see Plate 21.2).

Similar to penal colonies, leper colonies were established in isolated areas to quarantine people with leprosy (Hansen's disease), which was a much feared disease and believed to be highly contagious. Although the disease can be treated nowadays with effective drugs,

Plate 21.2 Remnants of the penal colony of Norfolk Island

it is still feared among many people of the less-developed world. Today functioning leper colonies exist in Asia, Africa and even one in Europe (Romania), and residents are generally not permitted to leave the compound or settlement. Several historical and now-defunct leprosariums are catching the interest of tourists who have an interest in the heritage of diseases or human imprisonment.

Slavery, another of the world's darkest institutions, has always existed, but the trans-Atlantic slave trade from Africa to Europe, North America, the Caribbean and South America is the most notable (see Plate 21.3). It was massive and involved the capture, transport, death and enslavement of approximately 12 million people between the early 1500s and the mid-1800s. The trans-Atlantic slave industry stole most of its people from the northwestern parts of Africa, an area that today comprises the countries of Cameroon, Nigeria, Togo, Benin, Ghana, Cote d'Ivoire, Liberia, Sierra Leone, Guinea, Guinea Bissau, Senegal, The Gambia and a few others. European perpetrators of slavery sailed to Africa and commissioned Africans to round up and capture their own people, who were kept in shackles and chains in fortress dungeons built by the Europeans (called slave forts or slave castles), in some cases for many months. When ships arrived, the captives were led out to sea, where they spent weeks at a time in crowded cells that were disease-ridden, strewn with human effluent and dead bodies, with little room to move about. Once in the new land they were bought and sold like merchandise to the highest bidder. Slaveholders frequently mistreated their slaves with beatings, confinement, forced

Plate 21.3 Ruins of a sugar plantation in French Saint Martin is a testimony of Caribbean slavery

Table 21.3 A selection of slavery-related heritage sites

Slave site	Country
Elmina Castle	Ghana
Slave Route Heritage Trail and Tour	Barbados
International Slavery Museum	United Kingdom
Rose Hall Plantation House	Jamaica
Slavery and Civil War Museum	United States
Island of Gorée	Senegal
James Island	The Gambia
Point of No Return Monument	Benin
Village of Juffure	The Gambia
Emancipation Memorial	United States
Slavery Monument	Tanzania
Abolition of Slavery Monument	Mauritius
Ruins of Sugar Plantations and Processing	St Kitts and Nevis

family separations or even death in many cases. Since that time, people of African descent in the New World have faced discrimination and various other forms of continued abuse.

Descendants of this forced migration, or victim diaspora, are spread all over the world and many are avid travelers. There is a strong desire among many African-Caribbean people and African-Americans, for instance, to visit the motherland of Africa where slave forts (where some of their ancestors might have been brutally imprisoned), slavery museums and the Slave Route are part of their tour itineraries (see Table 21.3).

Several emotional outcomes derive from visits to these sites, which are conditioned by the site itself, the interpreter and guide narratives, and the expectations and desires of the tourists. In a study of African-American experiences at one of the slave forts in Ghana, Timothy and Teye (2004) found some interesting patterns. Positive outcomes included catharsis and forgiveness for the perpetrators of slavery, a sense of coming home, spiritual feelings associated with the place and nearness to ancestors. Those who had negative reactions felt a deep sense of grief and pain. Some were stirred to anger against the events that went on there many years ago, and others swore revenge upon the 'white man'. White visitors at the same sites experience a range of emotions from simple curiosity to a deep sense of regret for the grievous acts their ancestors committed.

Slavery-related sites in the USA (e.g. plantations, slave cabins, sites of famous African-American events in history) have a long history of tourism, but only recently has a more balanced story been told in their interpretation. Traditionally, only the white people's stories were told at southern plantations and Civil War battlefields, but the public is holding interpreters and managers more accountable for accuracy in presenting a less-biased past. An increase in black American historical museums and other sites attests to a changing awareness in the USA.

Other miscellaneous heritage settings can also be classified as human confinement against their will. The indigenous African townships in South Africa prior to 1994, Soweto being one of the most infamous, were sites of considerable human suffering and oppression. Under the repressive apartheid regime Soweto was a popular spot for tourists, and it still is. The Trail of Tears National Historic Trail in the USA marks the route several Native American tribes traversed when they were forcibly relocated from their homelands in the southeastern part of the country in the 1830s to newly-designated land in 'Indian Territory', now Oklahoma.

War-related sites

The Nazi concentration camps and Japanese-American internment camps described above could just as well fit in a discussion of war heritage. They are indeed among the most significant war-related attractions of all, but because of their long-term incarceration aspects they were included above. This section looks at other elements of war that appeal to tourists.

War affects everyone, whether they believe it does or not. It is one of the most violent acts of humankind against other human beings and involves killing, imprisonment, violations of human rights, destruction of resources and disruption of everyday life. Large-scale wars are commemorated for generations because of the lives lost and other impacts on the society and politics of place. Small-scale wars remain fresh in people's minds for one or two generations, and they are recorded in history books, but are usually not commemorated to the same extent on a global level. There seems to be a relationship between the level of violence and the attractiveness with a site, with the most violent hostilities exuding the most appeal. Many war-connected places have come to be important visitor attractions in literally every corner of the globe.

Valene Smith (1996b) proposed a useful classification of different war-related attractions. 'Lest we forget' attractions remind visitors of the reasons battles were fought in the first place. They are aide memoires of what should or should not occur again. The concentration camps and holocaust memorials described earlier are examples of these places. 'Heroic' war sites are designed to honor famous war heroes, politicians who provoked or ended war, heads of state or military officers. Smith's third type is 'reliving the past' locales, which consist of battle reenactments at battlefields and forts. Re-creating Civil War battles is a particularly trendy leisure activity among many war enthusiasts in the USA; some tourists from abroad come to the USA specifically to participate in these reenactments. 'Remember the fallen' sites are considered sacred ground where lives were sacrificed for a good cause. War memorials, battlefields and cemeteries are prominent features of this form of attraction.

Battlefields are one of the most prominent remnants of war; they are the front lines, where the fighting occurred and which are marked to commemorate combat and its impact. Many battlefields are devoid of buildings and large-scale infrastructure. They tend to be located in pastures, wooded areas, mountains or valleys – usually open or wooded areas where battles could be fought more easily, leaving nothing in the landscape to testify to their happening, except bullets, blood and mass graves. Other battles are waged in urban areas, with wanton destruction of homes, schools, synagogues, churches and other structures. Most cities rebuild after urban warfare; others remain in ruins. Several battlefields have become extremely popular attractions.

The Gallipoli Campaign, a decisive battle during the First World War in Turkey, which cost over 11,000 Australian and New Zealand lives, as well as many British, Turkish, French and Indian lives, is held in very high regard in New Zealand and Australia even today. Anzac Day celebrations in the two countries mark the anniversary of the battle, and thousands of people congregate to the battlefield at Anzac Cove, Turkey, every April 25th to attend remembrance services. The Isandlwana Memorial marks the site of the Anglo-Zulu War of 1879 and several monuments at the Spioenkop battlefield indicate the location of the Boer Wars of 1899–1901 between the British and Dutch in South Africa. Besides these, there are multitudes of battlefields that attract local visitors and foreign tourists: Civil War and Revolutionary War sites in the US (see Plate 21.4); First and Second World War sites in Verdun, Somme, Flanders, Utah Beach and Omaha Beach, France; War of 1812 sites in the US and Canada; and the Waterloo Battlefield, Belgium. In addition to these rural battlefields there are multitudinous others that represent urban warfare, such as the Nagasaki Peace Park, the Hiroshima Peace Memorial and Pearl Harbor and the USS Arizona Memorial in Hawaii.

Realizing that battlefields sell, several small island countries in the Pacific have begun to market themselves as battlefronts of the Second World War. In a few cases, wreckage of allied or Japanese airplanes or ships is their only, or nearly only, tangible heritage resource. The tiny island nations of Tuvalu and Kiribati both have remnants of Pacific battle vessels and bunkers located on their shores, and they promote these to war buffs and veterans.

455

Plate 21.4 Site of the westernmost battle of the US Civil War in Arizona

War monuments and memorials may exist on historic battlefields, but more often they are located in cities and towns elsewhere to commemorate the wars of yesteryear. The Boer Wars monument in Johannesburg, South Africa; the Australian War Memorial in Canberra; the National War Memorial in Ottawa, Canada; the War Museum in Pyongyang, North Korea; and several war memorials on the National Mall in Washington, DC, are representative of such sites. Visits to war locations and memorials can invoke highly emotional, even spiritual, feelings for some people, especially war veterans who remember their fallen comrades and the battles they fought.

The Nazi concentration camps of Europe are good examples of genocide locales, but there are many others. The Killing Fields of Cambodia, where upwards of 2 million people were executed by the Khmer Rouge regime in the 1970s, and the Tuol Sleng Genocide Museum in Phnom Penh are illustrative of that country's perilous political past. The sites of mass extermination campaigns in Rwanda in 1994 are indicative of inter-ethnic wars fought over racial supremacy.

A related war product is returning veterans. Visits to battle sites in Vietnam among Vietnam War veterans are a popular trend these days. Less visible, perhaps because of their advanced age, but nonetheless noteworthy, are trips to battle sites of the Korean

War and Second World War. For veterans these trips bring back upsetting and happy memories. They are very nostalgic and can help veterans overcome emotional problems brought on by the war. In fact, such visits are often endorsed by psychiatrists as therapy for post-traumatic stress disorder.

One of the riskiest forms of war tourism is visiting active war zones. While this is not widespread, there are people who undertake such journeys. Viewing scars on the landscape, destroyed villages, mass graves or enemy encampments are among the highlights of people's travels. At present consumers can purchase risky tours of Afghanistan, which visit abandoned Taliban and Al Qaida training camps, gutted villages and hideout caves. Independent travelers have been known to wander the war-torn streets of Baghdad in recent years, some of whom were kidnapped, imprisoned or beheaded.

There are many forms of political instability, full-blown war being only one of these. Political conflicts appeal to a wide range of onlookers, and some destinations have succeeded in promoting 'conflict tourism'. Media coverage of years of fighting between the Irish republicans (Roman Catholic) and Irish unionists (Protestant) in Northern Ireland brought a considerable amount of 'free advertising' and global visibility to the conflict. Tourists have been visiting Belfast and its dividing fences/walls between Protestant and Catholic sides of the town, known as the Peace Lines, for many years, even during the conflict. In addition to the fences, spots of death and destruction linked to 'the troubles' are important sites on city tours. Even coups d'etat and other forms of political upheaval draw considerable visitor interest.

Fortified borders and security infrastructure present another interesting case of war-related dark tourism when people are separated from family members, traditional communities, left in harsh political regimes or suffer otherwise by their existence. Characteristic of these types of borders is the inability of the citizens on one side to cross to the other. The Berlin Wall, which lasted from the 1960s until its dismantlement in 1989, and the Demilitarized Zone (DMZ), which divides North and South Korea, are such barriers. Historically, the East-West Germany border separated and currently the DMZ separates family members and people from their traditional lands. The Berlin Wall was an important tourist attraction, where people could stand on platforms and look across to the other side. The DMZ today also has such a function. It is an important political attraction on both sides of the border, but its interpretation is different depending on whether the North Koreans or the South Koreans are telling the story.

A more recent development is the 'security fence' built in the West Bank by the Israeli government. Among Palestinians, their Arab neighbors and other supporters across the globe, building the wall is seen as a malevolent maneuver to subjugate the Palestinians and prevent them from accessing their jobs, family members and farmland on the other side. The Israelis argue the wall is necessary to prevent attacks on their citizens. Regardless of one's own position on the matter, the wall is a favored stop among solidarity tourists who support either the cause of Palestine or the cause of Israel (see Plate 21.5).

Plate 21.5 Israel's security wall separating Jerusalem from Bethlehem

Natural disasters

While being tourist attractions for a select few, political instability, active warfare and natural disasters deter many more people than they attract. Tourism is extremely volatile, and even mere mention of illnesses, political unsteadiness or natural calamities causes arrival numbers to plummet. There is a tendency, however, for natural disaster areas to recuperate more quickly than locations associated with human-induced disasters, probably because the former are 'acts of God' or Mother Nature – not perpetrated intentionally by humankind, so that people are not specifically targeted for destruction. People hastening to view natural disasters while they are happening or shortly afterward is evidence of this phenomenon; visits to terrorist sites and war zones tend to come a bit later.

Hundreds of thousands of natural disasters happen each year that attract local crowds. Mudslides, overflowing rivers, floods and fires are a few examples. Some natural catastrophes, though, are seen nationwide or internationally, drawing particular attention to the event and its aftermath. Visitors to such sites come in waves. At first, there is a rush of local onlookers who are shocked and excited by what they see. Later, media crews, rescue personnel and other gazers from further afield begin to arrive; this may last for weeks or months. Finally the most momentous events are marked and interpreted as permanent sites of calamity that may be visited for years to come.

Within hours of the powerful 1989 Loma Prieta Earthquake in San Francisco, which killed 63 people, injured almost 4000 and destroyed highways, buildings and other infrastructure, newspapers and television reported substantial increases in visitor arrivals to the San Francisco area. People came to see the destruction and mayhem. The large earthquake that rocked Haiti in January 2010 became a hotbed for volunteer tourists, reporters and health workers. Because air travel into the country was severely disrupted, it took a while before 'disaster tourists' were able to enter the country, but enter they did. As of early 2011, Haiti's earthquake still functions as a very important attraction in the Caribbean.

The famous explosion of Mount St Helens (Washington, USA) in 1980 drew tens of thousands of gawkers right away and millions in later months and years to see the famous volcano and its devastating impact. That it killed almost 60 people, annihilated 250 homes and destroyed hundreds of miles of highways, rail lines and bridges, made the mountain all the more appealing. The recent eruption (April–May 2010) of the Eyjafjallajökull volcano in Iceland not only affected many people's lives, including air travelers throughout Europe, it became Iceland's biggest tourist attraction in 2010. The explosion of Soufrière Hills volcano in Montserrat not only wiped out the small island's capital city, it drew thousands of tourists. Additional eruptions in 2010 brought even more people to the island to view its pyroclastic flows and plumes of ash.

Mega-floods have in recent years also drawn considerable attention by the traveling public. The December 2004 tsunami that destroyed many communities and tourist destinations in Indonesia, Thailand and Sri Lanka drew a significant crowd of voyeurs and volunteers soon after the tidal waves. Most of the places affected have almost completely recovered, but they are still visited by curiosity-seekers hoping to catch a glimpse of the damage. The floods caused by Hurricane Katrina in New Orleans in 2005 were a devastating blow to the people of the US Gulf coast. Thousands of people lost their homes, just under 2000 people were killed and the storm exacted billions of dollars in damage. While tourism came to an immediate standstill in the city, it began to grow little by little with the assistance of hundreds of thousands of volunteers who outnumbered pleasure tourists several fold. Today, the visitor industry in New Orleans has recovered and surpassed previous levels, owing largely to the disaster. Gray Line Tours offers the Hurricane Katrina Tour, where participants can have an 'eyewitness account of the events surrounding the most devastating natural – and man-made – disaster on American soil!' The narrative continues:

> We'll drive past an actual levee that "breached" and see the resulting devastation that displaced hundreds of thousands of U.S. residents ... Your tour guide will give a "local's" chronology of events leading up to Hurricane Katrina and the days immediately following the disaster. This tour will travel through neighborhoods such as Lakeview, Gentilly, New Orleans East, St. Bernard, and the Ninth Ward. (Gray Line, 2010).

The US Gulf Coast was hit yet again in 2010 with one of the world's largest oil leaks from a BP platform off the coast of Louisiana. While authorities expected a decrease in tourism, which did happen in terms of traditional beach tourists, a new type of tourist emerged – disaster tourists, who desired to see the oil in the water and the tar balls on the beach. Bushfires, bridge collapses, tornados, oil spills and mudslides are important resources for tourism, at least in the short-term.

Death attractions

All of the attractions described so far are associated with death. However this section highlights particular cases of infamy in terms of gravity and celebrity, where well-publicized murders, assassinations, suicides or accidental deaths capture significant public attention either because they are exceedingly gruesome and scandalous or because they involve a person with celebrity status. Such sites are probably considered to be the most morbid and appeal to people's specific socially-ingrained fear or fascination with dying. Another motive commonly noted is adoration or respect for famous people who meet an untimely demise.

A quick scan through the internet reveals list after list of homes, apartments, public establishments and other locations where celebrities committed suicide, were murdered or died accidentally. Many of them provide addresses, maps and driving instructions to these places. The majority of such locations do not memorialize the tragic events that occurred there, but the tourists continue to visit – often proving to be a nuisance at residences and businesses that are privately owned.

Locations linked to famous murders draw much media attention and, by default, tourist attention. While in most cases visitor flows might not last long, famous murders and murderers can become fodder for destination theming. For instance, tourists in London can purchase Jack the Ripper guided walking tours that aim to scare, excite and entertain participants. A tantalizing advertising narrative for one of the tours goes something like this:

> As the night sets in and the long shadows fall, we delve into the crooked, cobbled alleyways of Whitechapel to follow the Ripper's bloodstained trail of terror. Step by bloodcurdling step you are spirited back to that spine-chilling era of gaslit horror, to join the Victorian police as they hunt the Ripper through a warren of crumbling backstreets. Through the menacing shadows you weave, visiting and inspecting the murder sites, sifting through the evidence, and eliminating suspect after fascinating suspect. (Jones, 2002)

This is a famous example of a series of unsolved murders as an attraction that has lasted for several generations and will likely continue into the future, owing to its popular culture appeal and because it is so well ensconced in the world's memory. There are countless other locations of murder that do not have the same level of acclaim but are nonetheless important sites at local or regional levels.

Plate 21.6 The spot where Yitzhak Rabin was assassinated in Tel Aviv is a popular attraction for Israelis

Assassinations have an appeal as well (see Plate 21.6). Ford's Theater, where Abraham Lincoln was assassinated in 1865, is one of the most popular attractions in Washington, DC, and is owned and operated by the National Park Service. The precise spot on Elm Street in Dallas, Texas, where John F. Kennedy was assassinated in 1963 is marked by a large X, and the exact position where Pope John Paul II was shot and nearly died in 1981 is marked with an embedded white plaque in the cobblestones of St Peter's Square. The Lorraine Motel in Memphis, where Martin Luther King was shot and killed, is a tourist attraction and now part of the National Civil Rights Museum.

Another form of thanatoptic tourism focuses on cemeteries and graves. From a supply perspective these become visitor attractions for a few different reasons:

- Cemeteries are tourism resources when they exude some kind of historicity or architectural appeal. 'Scenic' graveyards may be unique examples of an architectural period or historical era that is exemplified in the physical layout or crypt design.
- Nationalistic cemeteries help shape a national psyche and build patriotism, so that there is a pilgrimage-like tendency to visit sacred burial grounds where soldiers or national heroes are interred (see Plate 21.7).

Plate 21.7 The hallowed grounds of Arlington National Cemetery enliven the patriotic spirit of American tourists

- Graves of famous people project an unmistakable allure for fans who go to pay their respects, mourn or satisfy curiosity.

Three of the most visited graves include those of Elvis Presley, Princess Diana and Marilyn Monroe. Michael Jackson's tomb at Forest Lawn Memorial Park in Glendale, California, is closed to most visitors because of a fear of vandalism and crowdedness by masses of admirers. For many fans, these celebrity graves are the ultimate destination-cum-pilgrimage aspiration (see Plate 21.8).

Death reenactments may be seen as socially deviant behavior, but they appeal to some people. Crucifixions, where people are actually nailed to crosses, take place in various Christian locations (e.g. the Philippines), where people re-create the death of Jesus in an effort to connect better to him or demonstrate penitence. There are even demonstrations of dismemberment and disembowelment at some houses of horror, where people can either participate or observe as a way of fulfilling their own fantasies about killing or being killed. Some of these activities take place in various museums of death, several of which have been established in North America and Europe.

Plate 21.8 Fans of Eva Peron adorn her Buenos Aires tomb daily with flowers and messages of admiration

Table 21.4 A selection of famous terrorist attacks

Site	*Year*	*Location*
Ground Zero	2001	New York City, USA
Crash site of Flight 93	2001	Rural Pennsylvania, USA
Mumbai Bombings	2008	Mumbai, India
Oklahoma City Bombing	1995	Oklahoma, USA
Madrid Train Bombings	2004	Madrid, Spain
7/7 London Bombings	2005	London, UK
Bali Bombings	2002	Bali, Indonesia
Lockerbie Bombing	1988	Lockerbie, UK

Finally, terror attacks have an immediate deterrent effect on tourism, but after the dust settles there is a tendency for curiosity-seekers to visit the site, photograph it and meditate on its importance (see Table 21.4). The Oklahoma City bombing in 1995 destroyed a federal government building and killed 168 people. Following the initial shock, onlookers began to appear with cameras, flowers and binoculars. The 1988 bombing of Pan Am Flight 103 over Lockerbie, Scotland, is still fresh in the minds of many Americans and Brits for its senselessness, destruction and loss of life. A memorial now marks the spot in Lockerbie where most of the airplane's parts landed. The September 11, 2001 terrorist assaults in the USA created one of the world's worst human-induced disasters in history. The public response was quick in assisting survivors and lending support for the families who lost loved ones. The public was equally quick to travel to Manhattan to see the devastation first hand. Today there is a National Memorial in rural Pennsylvania to mark the crash site of Flight 93, and a massive new memorial is currently under construction at Ground Zero.

Crime scenes and events

Crime scenes abound but, unless the perpetrator is a famous personality, visitation to most crime spots is relatively short-lived. Places related to well-known outlaws like Bonnie and Clyde, Butch Cassidy and the Sundance Kid and Jesse James are often marked and marketed as tourist commodities. 'Butch Cassidy slept here' type attractions abound, even in places he never visited, but it makes good marketing. Jails, cowboy towns, motels and saloons all have a stake in the claim to notorious bandit heritage.

Much to the world's horror, in April 2008, newspapers, the internet and television news reported the story of a man in Austria, Josef Fritzl, who had locked up his own daughter for 24 years, raped her repeatedly and fathered seven children with her. Just two years earlier in Austria the story of Natasha Kampusch made world headlines. At the age of 10 she was abducted by a stranger and held prisoner in his house for eight years. A similar story broke in California in August 2009, when Jaycee Lee Dugard was rescued from her kidnapper after being confined in his backyard for 18 years. These sensationalist stories and their media coverage stir people's penchant for witnessing excitement and 'houses of horror'. While the interiors of these locations are usually off limits to visitors, people are drawn to the locations to catch a glimpse and to photograph the places made famous by the media.

Other morbid attractions

Besides the multiplicity of sites and events already described, there are a few anomalous ones that defy categorization. Haunted houses, hotels, schools and various other places said to be possessed by spirits of the dead are an exciting prospect for many people. To be able to sleep in a haunted mansion house or hotel adds value to the overnight experience. Rose Hall mansion in Jamaica is said to be haunted by Annie Palmer, the White Witch of Rose Hall, which lends appeal to the plantation house as an attraction. Historic hospitals, such as sanitariums and psychiatric hospitals, may appeal to people with an interest in medical history or the stigma associated with diseases or mental illness. Such places are often believed to be haunted by the ghosts of patients from the past, such as the Waverly Hills Sanatorium in Kentucky. Sunken ships are another unique attraction that are sometimes said to be haunted, but people might also visit as a way of experiencing a notorious disaster or to look for treasures.

The final resource is quite unique but has fairly negative connotations. There are some places in the world where mega-tragedies are expected to happen and therefore draw significant tourist crowds. Every year, hundreds of thousands of religious tourists in Israel descend upon or overlook the Jezreel Valley, where it is believed by Christianity that the epic Battle of Armageddon will take place at the end of the world, where evil will be defeated by good and will usher in the second coming of Christ. Visits to the valley and the study of events to come are a salient part of many religious tours in the Holy Land.

MANAGEMENT IMPLICATIONS

Dark tourism is unique in many respects. Its inherent differentness from other types of heritage tourism creates distinctive management situations that must be addressed in a sensitive manner. Based upon knowledge of managing dark destinations, this section briefly examines several administrative principles that are crucial in making difficult sites palatable to the public.

Balance and sensitivity

Because of its sensitive nature, dark tourism is a highly politicized subsector. There are, without fail, divergent views, or dissonance, between stakeholders involved in planning, developing, managing and viewing morbid resources. Management must be done carefully and in a sensitive way that provides a balanced view of the past or the resource in question.

One aspect of balance is providing an acceptable weighting between education and entertainment. All heritage sites wrestle with this concern, but the hypersensitivity of disaster and death sites makes it all the more urgent. Some dark sites thrive on entertainment, such as Jack the Ripper tours or haunted mansions, while others are exceedingly solemn, eschewing even the slightest semblance of 'entertainment' owing to a perceived incompatibility between leisure and human suffering. The entertainment factor should never be overemphasized at the expense of education or commemoration.

Another view of balance is assuring that dissonant views of events are represented. While biases are inherent in all thanatoptic spaces, every effort toward objectivity should be made to represent both sides of the debate. Who killed whom? Where or when did it occur? Who was at fault? Was she guilty or innocent? These are some of the plethora of questions that stir considerable debate at sites of death and murder. Facts should guide good interpretation, but alternative opinions might also be considered an important part of an interpretive program.

Sensitivity is required in every aspect of site management (interpretation, maintenance, entrance fees, human resource training, marketing). This is especially true with regard to victims and family members of victims. Their state of mind is very different from that of other visitors, and extra care should be taken to assure that the use of sites is done tastefully and in a way that is not upsetting to those most personally affected. In this regard, site and interpretive planning would benefit by the participation of direct stakeholders, including victims, family members, perpetrators and the visitors themselves.

Know the audience

It is important to know the consumers of dark heritage. International tourists, domestic visitors, tour guides, veterans, victims, victim families, perpetrators and hobbyists are part of the large market for morbid destinations. Each of them has a different perspective on the past and different expectations from their visits. It is important to know what these diverse views and interests are so that visitors will be able to have memorable, educational, spiritual, nostalgic or cathartic experiences if they so desire.

Audiences for atrocity sites change over time. While many attractions will live on for a very long time, others will fade in public memory within a generation or two. Even with regard to the Holocaust, it is difficult for some young Israelis to identify with its magnitude, and they have little interest in visiting sites that commemorate its atrocities. Although time does not always erase personal or public memory, it does change the need for new forms of interpretation and marketing to meet the needs of newer generations – either to get them to visit or to make the tragedy relevant.

Making an impact

One guiding principle that seems to hold true at many sites is impact. The shock factor has been mentioned before, but sometimes it is a viable way of getting people's attention or providing an entertaining experience. Interpretation can be a valuable tool in this regard. It might be used as a way to emphasize suffering and horrible human rights abuses, or it can be used to downplay the significance of certain occurrences. Since the goal of some sites is to assure that such atrocities never happen again, the shock factor can help the gravity of certain events sink deep and create a resolve within people to do their part in assuring that the tragedy does not repeat itself. For some visitors, shocking interpretation is repulsive and horrifying but for others it makes the visit worthwhile. While at many locales the heritage of violence is watered down to pacify the audiences, others thrive on being blunt – telling the story how they feel it should be told.

A question of ethics

A final concern deals with ethics. Many people question the ethics of using death, disaster and other forms of human pain to turn a profit. The concern lies within the notion of exploiting the suffering of others for personal or institutional gain. The Katrina tours mentioned earlier are seen by some critics as exploiting displaced peoples and a devastated region for their own financial benefit. Some people have related ethical concerns about the quasi-voyeuristic behavior of tourists watching people at their most vulnerable moments. The paparazzi taking pictures of Princess Diana as she was dying in a tunnel in Paris and the public buying into it is a prominent example. Learning about private aspects of peoples lives (e.g. diseases, incidents of rape, drug overdoses) without their permission, even after they are dead, is seen by many as an immoral and degenerative act. Destinations and site management must come to terms with these concerns and decide how best to mitigate any problems that might arise.

SUMMARY AND CONCLUSION

It is clear that people are fascinated by destruction, death and human suffering, but each type of event is different in its impact. Natural disasters attract tourists much quicker than human-caused tragedies do, and their negative effect on arrivals is of a much shorter duration. The media is largely responsible for this, and is especially skilled at fuelling dark tourism through its sensationalist rhetoric.

This chapter has unashamedly taken a primarily supply-side view. We know relatively little about the demand, or underlying deeper motives, spurred and encouraged by social baggage and culturally-conditioned psychological drives that cause people to be interested in viewing tragedy. We suspect, however, that many people are pushed by a need for catharsis, altruism, grief, education, civic identification and a change of pace. One thing is certain, however; dark places are among the most pervasive tourist sites on earth and will continue to be as long as there is death and mayhem in the world.

REVIEW QUESTIONS

1. How do jails, prisons and penal colonies fit within the broader framework of dark tourism?

2. What are some of the underlying life experiences or motives that cause people to want to visit sites of death and human suffering?

3. Are there elements of past tragedies that should not be visited or promoted as tourist attractions? Why?

4. How might the experiences of victims or their families be different from the experiences of general tourists visiting crime scenes or sites of disaster?

5. Why might some people desire to visit active war zones? What kinds of liability issues might come into play for agencies and service providers who sell tickets or packages to such places?

6. What are the reasons human-caused disasters dissuade tourists for longer periods of time than natural disasters do? Does it have anything to do with predictability?

7. Should managers and other personnel at dark attractions receive different training than workers at non death-related heritage attractions? Why? What do they need to know?

RECOMMENDED READING

Ashworth, G.J. (2004) Tourism and the heritage of atrocity: Managing the heritage of South African apartheid for entertainment. In T.V. Singh (ed.) *New Horizons in Tourism: Strange Experiences and Stranger Practices* (pp. 95–108). Wallingford: CAB International.

Ashworth, G.J. and Hartmann, R. (2005) *Horror and Human Tragedy Revisited: The Management of Sites of Atrocities for Tourism.* New York: Cognizant.

Austin, N.K. (2002) Managing heritage attractions: Marketing challenges at sensitive historical sites. *International Journal of Tourism Research* 4(6), 447–457.

Beech, J. (2000) The enigma of holocaust sites as tourist attractions: The case of Buchenwald. *Managing Leisure* 5(1), 29–41.

Blom, T. (2008) Morbid tourism: The case of Diana, Princess of Wales and Althorp House. In P. Long and N.J. Palmer (eds) *Royal Tourism: Excursions around Monarchy* (pp. 142–158). Clevedon: Channel View Publications.

Brandt, S. (2003) Advertising journeys to hell or pilgrimages? Battlefield tourism to the Western Front from 1914 until today. *Tourismus Journal* 7(1), 107–124.

Charlesworth, A. (1994) Contesting places of memory: The case of Auschwitz. *Professional Geographer* 51, 91–103.

Collins-Kreiner, N. (2007) Graves as attractions: Pilgrimage-tourism to Jewish holy graves in Israel. *Journal of Cultural Geography* 24(1), 67–89.

Cooper, M. (2006) The Pacific War battlefields: Tourist attractions or war memorials? *International Journal of Tourism Research* 8(3), 213–222.

Dann, G.M.S. and Seaton, A.V. (eds) (2001) *Slavery, Contested Heritage and Thanatourism*. New York: Haworth.

Donnelly, K.J. (2005) 'Troubles tourism' – the terrorism theme park on and off screen. In D. Crouch, R. Jackson, and F. Thompson (eds) *The Media and the Tourist Imagination: Converging Cultures* (pp. 92–104). London: Routledge.

Foley, M. and Lennon, J. (1996) JFK and dark tourism: Heart of darkness. *International Journal of Heritage Studies* 2(4), 198–211.

Fyall, A., Prideaux, B. and Timothy, D.J. (2006) War and tourism: An introduction. *International Journal of Tourism Research* 8(3), 153–155.

Gibson, D.C. (2006) The relationship between serial murder and the American tourism industry. *Journal of Travel and Tourism Marketing* 20(1), 45–60.

Gut, P. and Jarrell, S. (2007) Silver lining on a dark cloud: The impact of 9/11 on a regional tourist destination. *Journal of Travel Research* 46(2), 147–153.

Hall, C.M., Timothy, D.J. and Duval, D.T. (2003) *Safety and Security in Tourism: Relationships, Management and Marketing*. New York: Haworth.

Henderson, J.C. (2000) War as a tourist attraction: The case of Vietnam. *International Journal of Tourism Research* 2(4), 269–280.

Henderson, J.C. (2007) Remembering the Second World War in Singapore: Wartime heritage as a visitor attraction. *Journal of Heritage Tourism* 2(1), 36–52.

Hughes, R. (2008) Dutiful tourism: Encountering the Cambodian genocide. *Asia Pacific Viewpoint* 49(3), 318–330.

Knox, D. (2006) The sacrilised landscapes of Glencoe: From massacre to mass tourism, and back again. *International Journal of Tourism Research* 8(3), 185–197.

Lennon, J. and Foley, M. (2000) *Dark Tourism: The Attraction of Death and Disaster*. London: Continuum.

Logan, W. and Reeves, K. (eds) (2009) *Places of Pain and Shame: Dealing with "Difficult Heritage".* London: Routledge.

Lunn, K. (2007) War memorialisation and public heritage in Southeast Asia: Some case studies and comparative reflections. *International Journal of Heritage Studies* 13(1), 81–95.

Mansfeld, Y. and Pizam, A. (eds) (2006) *Tourism, Security and Safety: from Theory to Practices.* Oxford: Butterworth Heinemann.

Miles, W.F.S. (2002) Auschwitz: Museum interpretation and darker tourism. *Annals of Tourism Research* 29(4), 1175–1178.

Muzaini, H., Teo, P. and Yeoh, B.S.A. (2007) Intimations of postmodernity in dark tourism: The fate of history at Fort Siloso, Singapore. *Journal of Tourism and Cultural Change* 5(1), 28–45.

Pezzullo, P.C. (2009) "This is the only tour that sells": Tourism, disaster, and national identity in New Orleans. *Journal of Tourism and Cultural Change* 7(2), 99–114.

Pizam, A. and Mansfeld, Y. (eds) (1996) *Tourism, Crime and International Security Issues.* New York: Wiley.

Poria, Y. (2007) Establishing cooperation between Israel and Poland to save Auschwitz Concentration Camp: Globalising the responsibility for the Massacre. *International Journal of Tourism Policy* 1(1), 45–57.

Ratz, T. (2006) Interpretation in the house of terror, Budapest. In M. Smith and M. Robinson (eds) *Cultural Tourism in a Changing World: Politics, Participation and (Re)presentation* (pp. 244–256). Clevedon: Channel View Publications.

Rittichainuwat, B.N. (2008) Responding to disaster: Thai and Scandinavian tourists' motivation to visit Phuket, Thailand. *Journal of Travel Research* 46(4), 422–432.

Robbie, D. (2008) Touring Katrina: Authentic identities and disaster tourism in New Orleans. *Journal of Heritage Tourism* 3(4), 257–266.

Ryan, C. and Kholi, R. (2006) The Buried Village, New Zealand: An example of dark tourism? *Asia Pacific Journal of Tourism Research* 11(3), 211–226.

Seaton, A.V. (1999) War and thanatourism: Waterloo 1815–1914. *Annals of Tourism Research* 26, 130–158.

Seaton, A.V. (2002) Thanatourism's final frontiers? Visits to cemeteries, churchyards and funerary sites as sacred and secular pilgrimage. *Tourism Recreation Research* 27(2), 73–82.

Seaton, A.V. and Lennon, J. (2004) Thanatourism in the early 21st century: Moral panics, ulterior motives and alterior desires. In T.V. Singh (ed.) *New Horizons in Tourism: Strange Experiences and Stranger Practices* (pp. 63–82). Wallingford: CAB International.

Sharpley, R. (2005) Travels to the edge of darkness: Towards a typology of "dark tourism". In C. Ryan, S. Page and M. Aitken (eds) *Taking Tourism to the Limits: Issues, Concepts and Managerial Perspectives* (pp. 217–228). Oxford: Elsevier.

Sharpley, R. and Stone, P.R. (eds) (2009) *The Darker Side of Travel: The Theory and Practice of Dark Tourism*. Bristol: Channel View Publications.

Slade, P. (2003) Gallipoli thanatourism: The meaning of ANZAC. *Annals of Tourism Research* 30, 779–794.

Stone, P.R. and Sharpley, R. (2008) Consuming dark tourism: A thanalogical perspective. *Annals of Tourism Research* 35(2), 574–595.

Strange, C. and Kempa, M. (2003) Shades of dark tourism: Alcatraz and Robben island. *Annals of Tourism Research* 30, 386–405.

Teye, V.B. and Timothy, D.J. (2004) The varied colors of slave heritage in West Africa: White American stakeholders. *Space and Culture* 7(2), 145–155.

Timothy, D.J. and Teye, V.B. (2004) American children of the African diaspora: Journeys to the motherland. In T. Coles and D.J. Timothy (eds) *Tourism, Diasporas and Space* (pp. 111–123). London: Routledge.

Timothy, D.J., Prideaux, B. and Kim, S.S. (2004) Tourism at borders of conflict and (de)militarized zones. In T.V. Singh (ed.) *New Horizons in Tourism: Strange Experiences and Stranger Practices* (pp. 83–94). Wallingford: CAB International.

Winter, C. (2009) The shrine of remembrance Melbourne: A short study of visitors' experiences. *International Journal of Tourism Research* 11(6), 553–565.

Winter, C. (2009) Tourism, social memory and the Great War. *Annals of Tourism Research* 36, 607–626.

Yankholmes, A.K.B., Akyeampong, O.A. and Dei, L.A. (2009) Residents' perceptions of Transatlantic slave trade attractions for heritage tourism in Danish-Osu, Ghana. *Journal of Heritage Tourism* 4(4), 315–329.

RECOMMENDED WEBSITES

Arlington National Cemetery –
http://www.arlingtoncemetery.org/visitor_information/monuments.html

Auschwitz-Birkenau Memorial and Museum – http://en.auschwitz.org.pl/m/

Bodyworlds Exhibit – http://www.bodyworlds.com/en.html

Dark Tourism Forum – http://www.dark-tourism.org.uk/

Ghost Tourism Portal – http://ghosttourism.informe.com/portal.html

Grief Tourism – http://www.grief-tourism.com/

Ground Zero Museum – http://www.groundzeromuseumworkshop.com/

Judenplatz Museum Vienna –
http://www.wien.info/en/vienna-for/jewish-vienna/museum-judenplatz

United States Holocaust Memorial Museum – http://www.ushmm.org/

Yad Vashem – http://www.yadvashem.org/

CHAPTER 22

CONCLUSIONS: THE FUTURE OF THE PAST

LEARNING OBJECTIVES

After reading this chapter, you should be able to:

1. Examine some of the major themes and trends discussed throughout the book.

2. Be familiar with emerging patterns and future directions of cultural tourism.

3. Understand the value of natural heritage and its connections to cultural heritage.

4. Realize the trend in heritage trails being developed all over the world.

5. Comprehend the political, demographic and technological forces shaping the future of cultural heritage tourism.

There should be no doubt about the importance of cultural heritage as a tourism resource. It has been a foundation upon which travel has been based for many centuries, even millennia, and today hundreds of millions of visits are undertaken to heritage sites each year. The enormity of the earth's cultural resources is a testimony of humankind's ability to adapt to natural environments, disasters, disease and political upheaval. That heritage was being preserved several centuries ago and continues to be conserved today illustrates its significance in successive societies going back thousands of years.

There is a long research tradition looking at cultural tourism supply and demand. Likewise, conservation of the past and interpretation have long led destinations and individual attractions in their efforts to plan, manage and market heritage tourism. Geographers have a long tradition of examining the spatial aspects of heritage, and many heritage scholars have delved into the nuances of authenticity and the politics of the past. We know a great deal about these foundation elements of heritage, as this book has shown. However, there are areas beyond these normative themes that have yet to be fully studied within the tourism context. This concluding chapter highlights some contemporary concerns and issues facing heritage managers and cultural destinations in the postmodern world, some of which were touched upon in the previous chapters and some of which were not. In particular, heritage tourism scholars need to pay special attention to at least the following trends: authenticity, volunteer human resources, nature as heritage, the crossover between heritage and other tourism sectors, heritage trails and routes, demographic changes and demand, heritage education, unconventional resources and locations for cultural tourism, cross-border resources and heritage and national identity.

THE FUTURE OF THE PAST: WHERE DO WE GO FROM HERE?

This book has touched on a few topics that deserve a little more elaboration in the concluding chapter. These are critical issues, which few scholarly publications, including this book, have considered in enough depth. Owing to space constraints, most of them have not had their own chapters, but they are important factors to consider.

Authenticity

Much has been said about authenticity in cultural contexts. Most of the literature focuses on whether or not tourists intentionally seek out authentic experiences and places or whether or not they seek contrived places that provide entertainment and fun. While this debate is an important one, we must move beyond this basic notion of authenticity. There are now nascent efforts to delineate how different stakeholders view authenticity – museum curators and site managers. There is an urgent need to continue to understand heritage stewards' perceptions of genuineness and what makes artifacts and experiences authentic. It is quite possible that their views of authenticity will be quite different from those of the visitors who attend their attractions. The debate also needs to be extended to the realm of the destination community, for what community members see as authentic might not be in tune with what tourists or curators perceive. In many less-developed parts of the world, it is difficult for destination residents to conceive of the fact that outsiders would have any interest in seeing their everyday lives. From their perspective, life is mundane. In 1996 in Indonesia, after finding out about Yogyakarta Province's plan to develop tourism around her village, an old woman asked the author, 'Why would anybody want to come here? What makes us so special?' She failed to realize that her everyday life, the home she lived in, the food she prepared and the clothes she wore, emanated an authentic cultural charm for foreigners, who desired to see common folk going about their daily lives. Her 'mundane' existence was all but mundane for outsiders. There is much work to be done to understand the meanings of authenticity to different people in different places and whether or not it can truly be examined objectively.

Volunteerism

The management chapters did not deal much with human resource issues, primarily because they resemble those issues so prevalent in other tourism settings, and this information is readily available in tourism management textbooks. Nonetheless, there are a few employment differences between heritage sites and other types of tourist attractions. Perhaps, as noted early on in the book, one of the most salient is the reliance on

474

volunteers. Most heritage places are owned either by the public sector or not-for-profit organizations. With budget shortfalls, these establishments are becoming ever more reliant on volunteers to help them accomplish their dual mission of conserving and educating. With proper training, volunteers can work in on-site excavations or preservation efforts. They can act as guides or other information brokers, such as costumed actors or interpreters. Many museum cafeterias and gift shops are staffed by volunteers who enjoy interacting with visitors and gaining on-the-job experience.

Volunteer tourism is a vast arena and takes on many forms and occurs in many venues. Historic sites and archaeological digs are among the most commonplace today. What differentiates volunteer tourists who work short-term in archaeological settings from those in other volunteer settings, such as building homes for the poor? Why do volunteers spend their weekends, summer holidays or their retirement years volunteering for the national parks agencies? In the absence of pay, what do they get in return? Some volunteerism scholars believe their reward is often the altruistic satisfaction of finding themselves in the service of others. Others believe volunteering is merely an extension of visiting. Perhaps there are different motives associated with volunteer staff in heritage settings that are different from other settings. Likewise, maybe short-term archaeology volunteer tourists are motivated differently than volunteer tourists in other settings. Much future research is needed to understand the motives and outcomes of heritage human resources.

Natural heritage

Almost always without fail, when scholars write of heritage tourism, they are referring to cultural heritage. Nevertheless, it is important to remember that heritage can be both cultural (of human origins) or natural, as both elements are inheritances from the past that are used for the present as tourism or recreational resources. The physical processes that created the Copper Canyon in northern Mexico, the volcanoes of Iceland or the deserts of North Africa are every bit as important to the earth's history, and that of humankind, as language, beliefs, architecture and foodways. Humans are unequivocally connected to nature and its processes. Thus, in most parts of the world, cultural heritage is molded to some degree by the type of environment where it developed.

There are many books today that focus on the natural elements of heritage that are used in tourism contexts, zeroing in on concepts such as ecotourism and nature-based tourism, as well as specific natural settings: geological areas, fluvial systems, forests, mountains and coastal zones. Despite the inseparability of culture and nature noted above, the focus of this book is the cultural past as a tourism resource – but we need to know more about the crossover between nature and culture in the tourism context. How natural processes, climates and various ecosystems affect the development of human culture was examined early on in geographical studies under the notion of environmental determinism. While this concept has a fair number of critics in the way it was conceived in the early 1900s, environment arguably has a bearing on how cultures develop.

There is a tendency among the traveling public and marketers to conceive of a heritage experience simply as visiting a built or living cultural attraction, clearly distinguishable from its natural surrounds. Likewise, nature-based experiences are typically seen by consumers, promoters and caretakers as taking place in the outdoors, usually in the wilderness, devoid of any cultural features to detract from nature. The truth is there simply is no clear-cut separation between nature-based and culture-based resources, for even the establishment of nature preserves, national parks and wilderness areas, no matter how remote, is a cultural exercise in designation, policy, management and interpretation. Likewise, all cultural sites exist within the natural realm, which in many cases determined the site's development and degree of decay. There are many heritage destinations where nature and culture simply are more inseparable than others. Mongolia's primary appeal, for instance, is the inseparability and oneness of nature and culture. The same is true of Bhutan, even in the cities, where urban development and the human landscape blur into the natural realm without clear-cut distinctions.

There is an urgent need among scholars to assess the commonalities between these two broad types of heritage. How are and should nature and culture be interpreted differently, or similarly? Are the methods for each equally effective? Does the public value nature over culture, depending on location and cultural context? Are there instances where managers should treat a cultural site in isolation from its natural surroundings? These are all important questions that we know very little about. There is considerable scope for knowledge creation about natural realms as heritage resources.

Cultural heritage and other tourism sectors

As the nature discussion above highlights, there is considerable overlap between cultural heritage and other forms of tourism – but we know relatively little about only a few perspectives. For example, we do know that heritage tourists are more likely to shop while traveling than many other types of tourists. There is a close link between shopping and heritage, because it seems that cultural tourists have a keener interest in taking home a memento of what they have seen. Most museums and heritage sites now play into this truism by offering on-site shopping. It brings in extra revenue to help meet the conservation goals of the site, and some say it might help prevent visitors from taking relics home as souvenirs.

Wine and cuisine tourism are also closely linked to heritage, as in many places viticulture and foodways are an important manifestation of their regional cultures. Understanding the relationships between wine tourism and heritage tourism is crucial; destinations could do well by couching their wine and food patrimony within the broader framework of heritage demand. It would be interesting to know more about destination residents' perceptions of the heritage value of wines and foodways, and such questions could be fruitfully brought to bear in future research.

Some scholars have begun merging sport tourism research with heritage tourism studies in recent years as well, as they have identified sport stadiums as tangible heritage and sporting events as an intangible past. In fact, sport is one of the most ancient elements of culture we have on record and clearly has major implications for heritage tourism development. Stadiums, arenas, race tracks and museums are important material elements of sport heritage, while sporting events, traditions and world records are features of the intangible past. The heritage of sport is an extremely important cultural resource in many destinations – golf in St Andrews, Scotland; ice hockey in Canada and Finland; the Baseball Hall of Fame in Cooperstown, New York; and various venues of the World Cup and the Olympics.

Chapter 3 identified several elements of tourism supply that double as heritage attractions; historic hotels and railways are relevant examples. Heritage experiences that derive from normal tourism services have not been examined well by scholars. There is much room for additional research to look into the conflicts associated with the modern use of heritage resources. Balancing heritage values and functional needs is an important consideration for managers. What other types of ancillary services might also double as heritage resources? Presumable there are many. Several older amusement/theme parks have an age worth because they have been functioning for decades, or even centuries in a few cases. According to historians, amusement parks began in Europe in the 12th century with pleasure gardens and periodic fairs that provided entertainment, food, rides and freak shows. The world's oldest amusement park is Bakken in Denmark, which opened in 1583 and continues to function as a theme park with rides, food and shows. Other parks developed in Europe (Prater in Vienna in 1766; Tivoli Gardens in Denmark in 1843) and North America (on Coney Island in the mid-1800s). While their main purpose is still to entertain the public, there certainly is an important heritage element associated with places like Bakken and Coney Island. There is much scope for understanding better how attractions and services not normally viewed as part of cultural tourism can in fact emanate a heritage appeal.

Heritage trails and routes

Cultural routes and heritage trails are one of the most interesting trends in heritage tourism nowadays. Some individual sites by themselves would not survive as a singular attraction, so many are now being linked together into linear streams of attractions that, when taken as a whole, become a viable tourist draw. Many of these are loosely put together with their only commonality being their geographical location, for instance the Heritage Trail of Iron County (Michigan). Other heritage trails develop, as sites that are conceptually linked under a common theme are connected into a linear set of point attractions. For instance, the Boston Freedom Trail is an urban pedestrian trail that links the city's historic buildings, cemeteries and other sites of importance to early Colonial America and its struggle for independence. Still other trails are manifested as long-distance routes that originally did function as a linear route, so its theme remains intact. Camino de Santiago (Way of St James), the pilgrimage route through southern France and northwestern Spain, has been used by pious pilgrims for more than a thousand years. It is still a crucial pilgrim path used by thousands of religious tourists each year. Hadrian's Wall Path National Trail is a 135km footpath that parallels the ancient Roman wall.

There is also a matter of scale involved in understanding trails and routes. Most long-distance trails are best traveled by car, with the exception of several well known footpaths like Hadrian's Wall noted above and the Appalachian Trail. In North America, long-distance trails can stretch thousands of miles. The Lewis and Clark National Historic Trail traverses 6,068km and 11 states to commemorate the route of these early explorers. While small segments can be hiked or undertaken on horseback, clearly automobile is the only probable option for those wishing to navigate the entire route or significant portions of it.

From a management perspective, generally, the larger the scale, the more difficult a trail is to manage because of the need to negotiate multiple landowners, local site stakeholders and individual state land agencies. Also, monitoring visitor use is difficult on long distance routes because of a lack of entry points where visitors can be enumerated or fees levied. Likewise, there are vast distances between stations where vandalism can occur, which might not be discovered for some time given remote locations or distance from funnel points. More and more tourist destinations are seeing the potential value of creating heritage routes and trails to link specific sites and nodes together as a more comprehensive cultural resource.

Demographic changes

Mentioned in Chapter 2 is an issue often ignored by heritage tourism observers: demographic shifts in market populations. Humans are more mobile today than ever before in history. One manifestation of this is migration from one country to another. Several countries that traditionally have had fairly closed doors for immigration (e.g. Finland, Denmark) are now more open because of the requirements for their membership in supranational alliances such as the European Union. Similarly, a thriving economy in the USA (until 2007) drew multitudes of immigrants from Latin America between the 1970s and 2000s. Initial reports suggest that different ethnic groups often have different desires when it comes to vacation travel. For example, given their close-knit family connections and their special affinities for their homeland, first-, second-, and third-generation Mexican-Americans often elect to travel back to Mexico to visit relatives rather than spend time camping in the mountains, laying out on a beach or visiting an amusement park. Other groups that have much deeper roots in the new homeland have fewer connections to their ancestral lands and may therefore prefer to visit cultural sites in their own countries or other places where they have no familial connections.

Likewise, there is a demographic shift in aging populations, with greater numbers of retirees having an interest in visiting heritage places all over the world. This includes an increase in people desiring to undertake personal heritage travel for genealogical reasons or simply to see sites they have heard about their whole lives. In also entails war veterans visiting former battlegrounds, war memorials or villages with which they were once familiar. It will be interesting to see what future demographic transformations will occur and how they will affect demand for cultural heritage.

Technology

A topic that arose several times in the book but which was not well developed is that of modern technology. This is a vital consideration for everyone involved in cultural tourism. Technology has the ability to promote visitation to heritage sites, de-market sensitive areas, allow planners to prepare sites for development and measure the impacts of visitors. Owing to space limitations this section does not delve deeply into technology's relations with heritage, but it does reiterate a few interesting trends mentioned in Chapter 10 that are beginning to manifest in heritage tourism.

The first is hand-held interpretive guides. Audio guides have existed in museums and at heritage sites for decades, but the new trend involves people searching for information about a specific spot simultaneously with their visit. Satellite-based technology extends this further to allow visitors to search additional sources of information while at historic places. If they want to see how the stories are told from other people's perspectives, they can search the internet while standing before a monument or museum display. Various global positioning devices allow visitors to access the comments and experiences of previous visitors, including suggestions about which elements of a site are must-see attractions and which ones can be skipped without missing much.

Similar contraptions are now starting to be used as research tools. Satellite-tracking devices allow heritage managers and researchers to track the locations of visitors. In large areas, such as historic city centers or sizeable archaeological complexes, as well as in museums and historic houses, this can be a valuable way of tracking people's behavior. Which spots are the most visited? How long do visitors spend at each display? How well does pedestrian traffic flow during busy times? Are there areas that are almost entirely ignored? All of these questions are important for planners and managers and can be helped by modern technical devices.

Just as the internet and GPS apparatuses allow people to find 'volunteered geographic information', such as reviews of restaurants, hotels or car rental agencies, they are now being used to elicit information about potential cultural destinations and sites. Globe-trotters now use social media like Twitter, Flickr, Youtube and Facebook to keep in touch with family and friends at home, to blog and offer travel advice live while they are traveling. Some of them have amassed a significant following, who cling to the traveler's every 'tweet' not only for travel advice but because of their admiration for the person.

Travel bloggers in the field heavily influence their readers' decisions by offering advice and sharing their own experiences, good and bad.

The idea of virtual travel has been discussed for more than ten years, with some people forecasting that virtual experiences may replace real-life experiences for some people, perhaps those with budgetary or time constraints. While it might seem a bit far-fetched, virtual vacations could become a normative practice for some people who would enjoy an afternoon at the Taj Mahal without having to travel to India. We can already see the beginnings of this in the virtual pilgrimages mentioned in Chapter 18. It is too soon to know the degree to which this will replace actual vacations, but whenever such technology is made available to the public there will no doubt be a cohort willing to invest in it.

Heritage education

Heritage management for tourism and other uses has become an important part of the social milieu today. In recognition of this, increasingly more universities and colleges are offering courses, undergraduate degrees, post-graduate degrees and certificates in heritage management, cultural studies, industrial archaeology, conservation and museology. Conservation, funding, visitor management, marketing, planning, interpretation and archival research are all important components of these courses. Most cultural sites have traditionally been operated by people lacking knowledge of theoretical issues such as authenticity, scale, politics and place attachment, let alone more applied skills such as interpretation, marketing planning and conservation techniques. The recent trend towards formalized heritage-related curricula will go far in supporting the principles of sustainability and in creating heritage places that are both protective of resources, educative for visitors and enjoyable for all.

Unconventional heritages

Several chapters discussed various unconventional heritages, but some of these deserve reiteration here. To return to the discussion in Chapter 16, vernacular landscapes are rather unconventional attractions. While many people have speculated on the sophistication of visitors and their dissatisfaction with the normative privileged past as being one motive for this, we know little about the true re-orientation of heritage. It is clear that aristocratic heritage will continue to attract people; castles, cathedrals and fortresses will always have an appeal. However, the resource base is now being extended far beyond that to include features that would never have been considered important just a couple of generations ago. Barns, fences, outhouses, fishermen's cottages, factories, coal mines, schools, jails and cemeteries all qualify as non-traditional cultural resources that have become the vogue in recent years.

Unconventional might also refer to heritage location. The most visited heritage sites are, obviously, located in the most visited countries and regions. Europe, the most significant destination region as regards international arrivals, is also home to some of the most prominent heritage attractions. They are easily accessible and world famous. The living and built heritage in the less-developed world is also a valuable resource for tourism, but visitation levels often depend upon how accessible a country is. Until fairly recently, Cambodia was off the tourist radar screen, but today it is a mainstream destination on well-trodden tourist routes because of its living culture and built heritage. Other countries have not come as far in their development, even though they have a wealth of resources. Ethiopia, for instance, has one of the richest cultural resource bases in Africa, and while Addis Ababa is within rich, much of the country is less accessible.

Almost all corners of the globe are within reach of tourists. Essentially the only space left is sub-oceanic territories, although even these are now being exploited for tourism. Shipwrecks and treasure hunts are becoming trendier. These heritage resources have essentially been left alone by tourists for decades or centuries, except for a handful of divers, but now they are being visited by larger groups of explorers. Arctic and Antarctic regions are also common destinations that were atypical until recently. Cruises now ply Arctic and Antarctic waters, with hundreds of passengers at one time descending on fragile tundra. While nature is still the core of the Antarctic experience, there are two primary types of human heritage: remains of early expeditions and scientific research centers. Both are important parts of the Antarctic experience, and they are currently being preserved by the international community via the Antarctic Treaties. Other Arctic destinations, such as Svalbard, Greenland, Baffin Island and Ellesmere Island, are now fully-vested cultural destinations in addition to being nature-based destinations. They have long been off the tourist radar screens but are now on many people's must-see lists.

Cross-border resources

There is a unique geographical setting that has not been well examined by heritage scholars, and that is cultural (and natural) resources divided by political boundaries. On the UNESCO World Heritage List are 24 sites or areas that straddle international borders. Some of these are small in scale, such as sets of ancient petroglyphs, while others cover large regions that are linked across the border by their common ecosystems or cultural features.

There are multitudes of examples of living cultures divided by international boundaries; they are especially plentiful in Africa and parts of Asia, where colonial superpowers took no thought to align their administrative boundaries along cultural or ethnic lines. When the European colonies of Africa gained independence between the 1950s and 1980s these internal boundaries became international boundaries, dividing tribes and cultural communities between two or more countries. Not only has this resulted in various political sensitivities over the years, but it has had other cultural and heritage implications, including groups on one side of a border being vigorously assimilated into the majority society, while on the other side cultures have remained relatively intact. Some borders have been somewhat closed, so that common cultural groups have been less able to interact across the frontier, thereby losing much of the holistic cultural connectivity that once existed.

A prominent tourism example from South America of a cultural group and its natural surroundings divided by a border is the Quechua-speaking people of Lake Titicaca, which straddles the border of Bolivia and Peru. While these people can freely cross the border, there are other groups in the world who cannot. Peru and Bolivia each manages its native people differently and has a different set of policies for tourism development, all within a cohesive cultural area.

Another view of this issue is tangible heritage resources that literally lie across a political boundary or adjacent to it. Several examples can be highlighted here. The small Roman fort (50m × 50m) at Panissars, near Perthus, France, lies precisely on the border-line of France and Spain. In fact one of the official state boundary markers lies in the ruins. The fort was originally built as a check station for this critical Roman route over the Pyrenees Mountains before France and Spain existed as modern states. Today the structure sits in ruins and is a fascinating heritage attraction accessible by road from the French side. Another example, but not as geographically compact as the Roman ruins, is the Stone Circles of Senegal and The Gambia. This World Heritage Site is located in both countries and encompasses four groups of 93 stone circles and many burial mounds that represent a rare and ancient sacrosanct landscape over a 100km area along the Gambia River.

The Preah Vihear temple complex in Cambodia lies adjacent to the Thai border, and the temple and its surrounding area has been a hotbed of dispute between the two countries for decades. Thailand claims that Preah Vihear is located inside its boundaries while Cambodia argues otherwise, based on the original boundary established by the French-Siamese (Thai) Commission in 1907. The matter went to arbitration in 1962 at the International Court of Justice, which determined that the site is in fact located in Cambodia. Thailand still disputes this verdict and armed clashes between the Thai and Cambodian military occasionally materialize over the disputed territory, with the most recent fighting being in 2010–11. The temple is an important cultural attraction in Cambodia, but it is presently accessible only by foot from the Thai side of the border.

To be inscribed on the UNESCO List, neighboring countries have to work together across their common borders, giving up a modicum of sovereignty, to assure the protection and attention of their cross-frontier resources. Some, as in the case of Preah Vihear, are at the center of cross-border conflict. Others are hardly impacted at all by the existence of a border, as at Lake Titicaca. Nonetheless they are cross-border resources, jealously guarded by individual nation states, and individual polities must work together for the common good to protect valuable resources and develop tourism surrounding them. We still know next to nothing about cross-border relations and cooperative efforts in the heritage context. What makes them work? What hinders their success? How can these barriers be overcome? Comparative studies have yet to be accomplished to analyze differences in legislative actions, policy development and management of trans-frontier resources. Such studies can help lead to bi-national or multi-national policies that will help protect living cultural, built and ecological heritage resources in a much more sustainable way.

Heritage and national identity

The past being used to bolster national pride and personal identity is a common thread in heritage studies today. The national identities of countries are rooted in their cultural heritage, primarily their built patrimony, as this provides a tangible element that helps them come to terms with the past – sometimes a very difficult past. Some states have only come into existence recently and are still struggling to find their own identity, or fit, in a world filled with well-established nation-states. Montenegro, Macedonia, Eritrea and Namibia are a few examples. Some nations have weak, or even nonexistent, heritage that defines who they should be; this was very much the case in the French colonies of West Africa shortly after their independence in the 1950s and 60s. As the previous section noted, the French drew seemingly arbitrary boundaries throughout their African territories, dividing cultures and ethnic homelands. The post-colonial countries of French West Africa (e.g. Togo, Benin, Cote d'Ivoire, Chad, etc.) had to create new heritages – their own national identities – since traditional societies were defined by tribal or ethnic affinity, not by superimposed state boundaries.

In a like manner, many regional entities are trying to separate from their current states to become independent countries or autonomous regions. There are well over 300 secessionist movements in all parts of the world, some being more official or legitimate than others, and some even achieving a degree of independence from the surrounding state to become what political geographers refer to as 'de facto states', or entities that function much like independent countries but do not enjoy widespread recognition by the international community. Some of the most prominent de facto states include:

- Nagorno-Karabakh (declared independence from Azerbaijan in 1992).
- Transnistria (declared independence from Moldova in 1990).
- Turkish Republic of Northern Cyprus (declared independence from Cyprus in 1983).
- Abkhazia (declared independence from the Republic of Georgia in 1992).
- Kosovo (declared independence from Serbia in 2008).

Other well-known regions that have significant internal public and political support for their independence, and which have an active separatist faction, include Quebec (Canada); South Tirol (Italy); Frisia (Netherlands); Chechnya (Russia); Tatarstan (Russia); Basque Country (Spain and France); Catalonia (Spain); Wales (United Kingdom); Scotland (United Kingdom); Shan States (Myanmar); Tibet (China); West Papua (Indonesia); Reunion (France); Caprivi (Namibia); and Zanzibar (Tanzania). There are dozens more.

Common among breakaway movements and de facto states are their use of national heritage – language, religion, ethnicity, built patrimony, history of being a cohesive nation at some point in the ancient past – as justification for their cause of independence. Most argue the need for complete independence or greater autonomy within their present polity because they do not receive due recognition by the state or rights equal to those of other groups. Some simply believe that history has dealt them a bad hand by lumping them together with other nations within a single state. Regardless of history, heritage is the most common pawn in the secessionist movement of the world today.

Numerous secessionist regions are also noteworthy tourist destinations. While many heritage intellectuals have provided valuable discourse on politics and heritage, it lacks attention by tourism scholars. This is an outstanding deficiency in tourism studies. How these secessionist movements affect tourism is a critical consideration. Some groups use violent means in attempting to establish their legitimate self-rule (e.g. the Basques in Spain), while others rely more on peaceful or legislative actions. These clearly have implications for demand, but do they also have implications for supply? Like other conflicts noted in Chapter 21, many independence movements may be viewed as attractions, not only for solidarity tourists but for people interested in global politics. The heritage of separation in Catalonia is a very essential element of tourism promotion and interpretation in that region. The same could be argued for Scotland and Wales.

FINAL WORD

Heritage tourism is highly inclusive – probably the most encompassing type of tourism yet to be identified. It revolves directly around living cultures, the built environment, faith traditions, folklore, arts and handicrafts, music and the everyday life of people. We often speak of different types of tourism, including ethnic tourism, cultural tourism, religious tourism and industrial tourism, which all fit snuggly under the heritage tourism umbrella. Even other forms of tourism, such as visiting friends and relatives, sport tourism, eco-tourism, shopping tourism, agritourism, volunteer tourism, wine tourism, educational travel and health tourism, overlap a great deal with heritage tourism, for many of the resources upon which they are based are inherited from the past and are cultural resources. Simply put, heritage is everywhere – and it is not always old.

There are other aspects of heritage and tourism that were not discussed at great length in this book, owing primarily to space constraints. Volumes of work have been written in the past about heritage and culture, and many more tomes will be written in the future. However, we will have only started scratching the surface in understanding what moves people to partake of the past and preserve it. Cultural heritage is a multidimensional phenomenon that exists everywhere and is one of the most salient resources for tourism development. It is also one of the most fragile resources upon which tourism can be based and must be managed with utmost care so that it remains viable for generations to come.

REVIEW QUESTIONS

1. Can almost anything be considered heritage? How?

2. What are some future directions associated with globalization and heritage?

3. How will technology affect access to cultural sites and popularize heritage travel?

4. What kinds of current and future political trends are taking place or will likely take place to influence heritage and its use as a tourism resource?

5. What are the interrelationships between cultural heritage and other tourism subsectors?

RECOMMENDED READING

Davis, S.G. (1996) The theme park: Global industry and cultural form. *Media, Culture and Society* 18, 399–422.

Herbert, D.T. (ed.) (1995) *Heritage, Tourism and Society*. London: Mansell.

Joliffe, L. (ed.) (2007) *Tea and Tourism: Tourists, Traditions and Transformations*. Clevedon: Channel View Publications.

Jolliffe, L. (ed.) (2010) *Coffee Culture, Destinations and Tourism*. Bristol: Channel View Publications.

Kalay, Y.E., Kvan, T. and Affleck, J. (eds) (2008) *New Heritage: New Media and Cultural Heritage*. London: Routledge.

Macleod, D. and Carrier, J.G. (eds) (2010) *Tourism, Power and Culture: Anthropological Insights*. Bristol: Channel View Publications.

McKercher, B. and du Cros, H. (2002) *Cultural Tourism: The Partnership between Tourism and Cultural Heritage Management*. New York: Haworth.

Ramshaw, G. and Gammon, S. (2005) More than just nostalgia? Exploring the heritage/sport tourism nexus. *Journal of Sport and Tourism* 10(4), 229–241.

Russo, A.P., Clave, S.A. and Shoval, N. (2010) Advanced visitor tracking analysis in practice: Explorations in the PortAventura theme park and insights for a future research agenda. In U. Gretzel, R. Law and M. Fuchs (eds) *Information and Communication Technologies in Tourism 2010* (pp. 159–170). Vienna: Springer-Verlag.

Shoval, N. and Isaacson, M. (2007) Tracking tourists in the digital age. *Annals of Tourism Research* 34, 141–159.

Shoval, N. and Isaacson, M. (2009) *Tourist Mobility and Advanced Tracking Technologies*. London: Routledge.

Stamer, D., Guo, C. and Lerall, K. (2008) Managing heritage volunteers: An exploratory study of volunteer programmes in art museums worldwide. *Journal of Heritage Tourism* 3(3), 203–214.

Timothy, D.J. and Boyd, S.W. (2003) *Heritage Tourism*. Harlow: Prentice Hall.

Timothy, D.J. and Boyd, S.W. (2006) Heritage tourism in the 21st century: Valued traditions and new perspectives. *Journal of Heritage Tourism* 1(1), 1–17.

Timothy, D.J. and Boyd, S.W. (forthcoming) *Cultural Routes, Nature Trails, and Scenic Byways: Tourism and Linear Resources*. Bristol: Channel View Publications.

World Bank (2001) *Cultural Heritage and Development: A Framework for Action in the Middle East and North Africa*. Washington, DC: World Bank.

REFERENCES

Alexander, E.P. and Alexander, M. (2008) *Museums in Motion: An Introduction to the History and Functions of Museums*. Lanham, MD: AltaMira Press.

Archaeological Digs (2010) Tel Dor: Archaeological Riches by the Sea. Available at http://archaeologydigs.blogspot.com/2009/12/tel-dor-archaeological-riches-by-sea.html. Accessed January 30, 2010.

Arreola, D.D. (1999) Across the street is Mexico: Invention and persistence of the border town curio landscape. *Yearbook of the Association of Pacific Coast Geographers* 61, 9–41.

ASEAN Secretariat (2009) ASEAN Declaration on Cultural Heritage. Available at http://www.aseansec.org/641.htm. Accessed December 5, 2009.

Ashworth, G.J. and Tunbridge, J.E. (1990) *The Tourist-Historic City*. London: Belhaven.

Ashworth, G.J. and Tunbridge, J.E. (2000) *The Tourist-Historic City: Retrospect and Prospect of Managing the Heritage City*. New York: Pergamon.

Barthel, D. (1990) Nostalgia for America's village past: Staged symbolic communities. *International Journal of Politics, Culture, and Society* 4(1), 79–93.

Basu, P. (2004) Route metaphors of 'roots-tourism' in the Scottish Highland diaspora. In S. Coleman and J. Eade (eds), *Reframing Pilgrimage: Cultures in Motion* (pp. 150–174). London: Routledge.

Boorstin, D. (1961) *The Image: A Guide to Pseudo-Events in America*. New York: Harper and Row.

Boyd, S.W. (2002) Cultural and heritage tourism in Canada: Opportunities, principles and challenges. *International Journal of Tourism and Hospitality Research* 3(3), 211–233.

Bremer, T.S. (2001) *Religion on Display: Tourists, Sacred Place, and Identity at the San Antonio Missions*. Doctoral dissertation, Princeton University, Princeton, New Jersey.

Budruk, M., White, D.D., Wodrich, J.A. and Riper, C.J. (2008) Connecting visitors to people and place: Visitors' perceptions of authenticity at Canyon de Chelly National Monument, Arizona. *Journal of Heritage Tourism* 3(3), 185–202.

Butler, R.W. (1999) Sustainable tourism: A state-of-the-art review. *Tourism Geographies* 1(1), 7–25.

Canadian Heritage (2009) Legislation Related to Canadian Heritage. Available at http://www.pch.gc.ca/pc-ch/legsltn/index-eng.cfm. Accessed December 3, 2009.

Canadian Tourism Commission (2009) *Tourism Snapshot, 2008*. Ottawa: Canadian Tourism Commission

Central Bureau of Statistics (2008) *Tourism in Israel 2007*. Tel Aviv: Central Bureau of Statistics.

Chakravarty, I. (2008) Heritage tourism and community participation: A case study of the Sindhudurg Fort, India. In B. Prideaux, D.J. Timothy and K.S. Chon (eds) *Cultural and Heritage Tourism in Asia and the Pacific* (pp. 189–202). London: Routledge.

Chhabra, D. (2009) Proposing a sustainable marketing framework for heritage tourism. *Journal of Sustainable Tourism* 17(3), 303–320.

Cohen, E. (1979) Rethinking the sociology of tourism. *Annals of Tourism Research* 6, 18–35.

Cohen, R. (2008) *Global Diasporas: An Introduction*. London: Routledge.

Compendium (2009) Cultural Policies and Trends in Europe. Available at http://www.culturalpolicies.net/web/. Accessed November 1, 2009.

Corsane, G., Davis, P., Elliott, S., Maggi, M., Murtas, D. and Rogers, S. (2007) Ecomuseum performance in Piemonte and Liguria, Italy: The significance of capital. *International Journal of Heritage Studies* 13(3), 224–239.

Cox, J. (1994) Interpretation for persons with a disability. In R. Harrison (ed.) *Manual of Heritage Management* (pp. 353–355). Oxford: Butterworth Heinemann.

Craig-Smith, S.J. (1995) The role of tourism in inner-harbor redevelopment. In S.J. Craig-Smith and M. Fagence (eds) *Recreation and Tourism as a Catalyst for Urban Waterfront Redevelopment: An International Survey* (pp. 15–35). Westport, CT: Praeger.

Daniels, R. (2004) *Prisoners with Trial: Japanese Americans in World War II*. New York: Hill and Wang.

Dann, G. (1998) *The Dark Side of Tourism*. Aix-en-Province: CIRET.

DeLyser, D. (1999) Authenticity on the ground: Engaging the past in a California ghost town. *Annals of the Association of American Geographers* 89, 602–632.

Department of Environment, Water, Heritage and the Arts (2009) Legislation. Available at http://www.environment.gov.au/about/legislation.html. Accessed November 10, 2009.

Douglas, N. and Douglas, N. (1991) Where the tiki are wired for sound and the poi glow in the dark: A day at the Polynesia Cultural Center. *Islands Business Pacific* 17(12), 60–64.

Duval, D.T. (2004) Conceptualizing return visits: A transnational perspective. In T. Coles and D.J. Timothy (eds) *Tourism, Diasporas and Space* (pp. 50–61). London: Routledge.

Earthwatch (2010) Archeology and Paleontology Expeditions. Available at http://www.earthwatch.org/exped/camilli.html. Accessed March 30, 2010.

Edwards, J.A. and Llurdés i Coit, J.C. (1996) Mines and quarries. *Annals of Tourism Research* 23, 341–363.

English Heritage (2009) English Heritage: Making the Past Part of Our Future. Available at http://www.english-heritage.org.uk/. Accessed October 19, 2009.

Fyall, A. and Garrod, B. (1998) Heritage tourism: At what price? *Managing Leisure* 3, 213–228.

Government of Australia (2010) Smartraveller: The Australian Government's travel advisory and consular assistance service. Available at http://www.smartraveller.gov.au/. Accessed July 18, 2010.

Gray Line (2010) City Tours: Hurricane Katrina Tour. Available at http://www.graylineneworleans.com/katrina.shtml. Accessed July 5, 2010.

Halewood, C. and Hannam, K. (2001) Viking heritage tourism: Authenticity and commodification. *Annals of Tourism Research* 28, 565–580.

Hall, C.M. (1994) *Tourism and Politics: Policy, Power and Place.* Chichester: Wiley.

Hall, C.M. and McArthur, S. (1993) The marketing of heritage. In C.M. Hall and S. McArthur (eds) *Heritage Management in New Zealand and Australia: Visitor Management, Interpretation, and Marketing* (pp. 40–47). Auckland: Oxford University Press.

Herbert, D.T. (1995) Heritage as literary place. In D.T. Herbert (ed.) *Heritage, Tourism and Society* (pp. 32–48). London: Mansell.

Hollinshead, K. (1998) Tourism and the restless peoples: A dialectical inspection of Bhabha's halfway populations. *Tourism, Culture and Communication* 1(1), 49–77.

ICOMOS (2009) About ICOMOS. Available at http://www.international.icomos.org/about.htm. Accessed December 3, 2009.

Indian Ministry of Tourism and Culture (2003) *Domestic Tourism Survey: 2002–2003.* New Delhi: National Council of Applied Economic Research, Ministry of Tourism.

Ioannides, D. and Timothy, D.J. (2010) *Tourism in the USA: A Spatial and Social Synthesis.* London: Routledge.

Jamal, T. and Hill, S. (2004) Developing a framework for indicators of authenticity: The place and space of cultural and heritage tourism. *Asia Pacific Journal of Tourism Research* 9, 353–371.

Jansen-Verbeke, J. and Lievois, E. (1999) Analysing heritage resources for urban tourism in European cities. In D. Pearce and R.W. Butler (eds) *Contemporary Issues in Tourism Development* (pp. 81–107). London: Routledge.

Jones, R. (2002) On the Trail of Jack the Ripper. Available at http://www.jack-the-ripper-walk.co.uk/walk.htm. Accessed July 5, 2010.

Jorgensen, L.W. (1988) A 'roots' vacation. *Ensign* 18(6), 23.

Kim, S.S., Timothy, D.J. and Han, H.C. (2007) Tourism and political ideologies: A case of tourism in North Korea. *Tourism Management* 28, 1031–1043.

Kingdom of Saudi Arabia (2009) Hajj and Umrah Statistics. Available at http://www.hajinformation.com/main/l.htm. Accessed September 22, 2009.

Kirchberg, V. (2000) Die McDonaldisierung deutscher Museen: Zur Diskussion einer Kultur- und Freizeitwelt in der Postmoderne. *Tourismus Journal* 4(1), 117–114.

Knudson, D.M., Cable, T.T. and Beck, L. (1995) *Interpretation of Cultural and Natural Resources*. State College, PA: Venture.

Ku, M. (2003) Gendered bodily performance in historic museums. *Tourism Recreation Research* 28(2), 13–19.

Leiper, N. (1990) Tourist attraction systems. *Annals of Tourism Research* 17, 367–384.

Lennon, J. and Smith, H. (2004) A tale of two camps: Contrasting approaches to interpretation and commemoration in the sites at Terezin and Lety, Czech Republic. *Tourism Recreation Research* 29(1), 15–25.

Light, D. (1992) Bilingual heritage interpretation in Wales. *Scottish Geographical Magazine* 108(3), 179–183.

Light, D. (1995) Heritage as informal education. In D.T. Herbert (ed.) *Heritage, Tourism and Society* (pp. 117–145). London: Mansell.

Lord, G.D. (1999) The Power of Cultural Tourism. Keynote presentation at the Wisconsin Heritage Tourism Conference, 17 September, 1999.

Lowenthal, D. (1985) *The Past is a Foreign Country*. Cambridge: Cambridge University Press.

MacCannell, D. (1973) Staged authenticity: Arrangements of social space in tourist settings. *American Journal of Sociology* 79, 589–603.

MacCannell, D. (1976) *The Tourist: A New Theory of the Leisure Class*. New York: Schocken.

Mané-Wheoki, J. (1992) Sacred sites, heritage and conservation: Differing perspectives on cultural significance in the South Pacific. *Historic Environment* 9(1/2), 32–36.

Markwick, M.C. (2001) Tourism and the development of handicraft production in the Maltese Islands. *Tourism Geographies* 3(1), 29–51.

McIntosh, A.J. (2004) Tourists' appreciation of Maori culture in New Zealand. *Tourism Management* 25(1), 1–15.

McIntosh, A.J., Zygadlo, F.K., and Matunga, H. (2004) Rethinking Maori tourism. *Asia Pacific Journal of Tourism Research* 9(4), 331–351.

McKercher, B., Weber, K. and du Cros, H. (2008) Rationalising inappropriate behaviour at contested sites. *Journal of Sustainable Tourism* 16, 369–385.

Moscardo, G. (1996) Mindful visitors: Heritage and tourism. *Annals of Tourism Research* 23, 376–397.

National Trust (2009) Our History. Available at http://www.nationaltrust.org.uk/main/w-trust/w-thecharity/w-thecharity_our-past.htm. Accessed November 10, 2009.

National Trust (2010) BARN AGAIN! Available at http://www.preservationnation.org/issues/rural-heritage/barn-again/. Accessed January 3, 2010.

National Trust for Historic Preservation (2009) National Trust. Available at http://www.preservationnation.org/. Accessed November 15, 2009.

National Trust for Historic Preservation (2010) Cultural and Heritage Tourism – The Same or Different? Available at http://culturalheritagetourism.org/resources/documents/CulturevsHeritage_000.pdf. Accessed April 19, 2010.

Nelis' Dutch Village (2010) Welkom! Experience a Bit of Old Holland without Leaving the States. Available at http://www.dutchvillage.com/. Accessed January 3, 2010.

Newton, C. (2010) 21 of 30 state parks will be closed. *Arizona Republic* 16 January, B1, B6.

New Zealand Ministry of Tourism (2008a) Tourist Activity: Maori Cultural Tourism. Available at http://www.tourismresearch.govt.nz/Documents/Tourism%20Sector%20Profiles/Maori%20Culture%2003-2008.pdf. Accessed September 20, 2009.

New Zealand Ministry of Tourism (2008b) Tourist Activity: Museum Tourism. Available at http://www.tourismresearch.govt.nz/Documents/Tourism%20Sector%20Profiles/MuseumTourismApril2008.pdf. Accessed September 20, 2009.

Nurick, J. (2000) Heritage and tourism. *Locum Destination Review* 2, 35–38.

Oliver, P. (2001) Re-presenting and representing the vernacular: The open-air museum. In N. Al Aayyad (ed.) *Consuming Tradition, Manufacturing Heritage: Global Norms and Urban Forms in the Age of Tourism* (pp. 191–211). London: Routledge.

Olsen, D.H. (2006) Management issues for religious heritage attractions. In D.J. Timothy and D.H. Olsen (eds) *Tourism, Religion and Spiritual Journeys* (pp. 104–118). London: Routledge.

Out of Africa Wildlife Park (2010) African Bush Safari. Available at http://www.outofafricapark.com/african_bush_safari.html. Accessed January 3, 2010.

Packer, J. and Ballantyne, R. (2005) Solitary vs. shared learning: Exploring the social dimensions of museum learning. *Curator: The Museum Journal* 48(2), 177–192.

Pearce, D.G. (1997) The roles of the public sector in conservation and tourism planning. In. W. Nuryanti (ed.) *Tourism and Heritage Management* (pp. 88–100). Yogyakarta, Indonesia: Gadjah Mada University Press.

Pearson, M. and Sullivan, S. (1995) *Looking after Heritage Places: The Basics of Heritage Planning for Managers, Landowners and Administrators.* Carlton: Melbourne University Press.

Plog, S. (1991) *Leisure Travel: Making it a Growth Market … Again!* New York: Wiley.

Poria, Y. and Gvili, Y. (2006) Heritage site websites content: The need for versatility. *Journal of Hospitality and Leisure Marketing* 15(2), 73–93.

Poria, Y., Reichel, A. and Biran, A. (2006) Heritage site perceptions and motivations to visit. *Journal of Travel Research* 44(3), 318–326.

Prentice, R.C. (1995) Heritage as formal education. In D.T. Herbert (ed.) *Heritage, Tourism and Society* (pp. 146–169). London: Mansell.

Prideaux, B. and Kininmont, L.J. (1999) Tourism and heritage are not strangers: A study of opportunities for rural heritage museums to maximize tourism visitation. *Journal of Travel Research* 37(3), 299–303.

Reisinger, Y. and Steiner, C.J. (2006) Reconceptualizing object authenticity. *Annals of Tourism Research* 33, 65–86.

Richards, G. (2001) The market for cultural attractions. In G. Richards (ed.) *Cultural Attractions and European Tourism* (pp. 3–29). Wallingford: CAB International.

Ritzer, G. and Liska, A. (1997) 'McDisneyization' and post-tourism: Complementary perspectives on contemporary tourism. In. C. Rojek and J. Urry (eds) *Touring Cultures: Transformations of Travel and Theory* (pp. 96–110). London: Routledge.

Schofield, P. (2004) Health tourism in the Kyrgyz Republic: The Soviet sale mine experience. In T.V. Singh (ed.) *New Horizons in Tourism: Strange Experiences and Stranger Practices* (pp. 135–146). Wallingford: CABI.

Seaton, A.V. (1996) Guided by the dark: From thanatopsis to thanatourism. *International Journal of Heritage Studies* 2(4), 234–244.

Seward County Museum (2009) Seward County Historical Museum. Available at http://www.sewardcountymuseum.com/. Accessed December 5, 2009.

Sharpley, R. (2009) Shedding light on dark tourism: An introduction. In R. Sharpley and P.R. Stone (eds) *The Darker Side of Travel: The Theory and Practice of Dark Tourism* (pp. 3–22). Bristol: Channel View Publications.

Smith, V. (1992) The quest in guest. *Annals of Tourism Research* 19, 1–17.

Smith, V. (1996a) Indigenous tourism: The four Hs. In R. Butler and T. Hinch (eds) *Tourism and Indigenous Peoples* (pp. 283–307). London: International Thomson Business Press.

Smith, V. (1996b) War and its tourist attractions. In A. Pizam and Y. Mansfeld (eds) *Tourism, Crime and International Security Issues* (pp. 247–264). New York: Wiley.

Stebbins, R.A. (1996) Cultural tourism as serious leisure. *Annals of Tourism Research* 23, 945–948.

Stone, P.R. (2006) A dark tourism spectrum: Towards a typology of death and macabre related tourist sites, attractions and exhibitions. *Tourism* 54(2), 145–160.

Taylor, J. (2009) Ten ways to ruin an old building. Available at http://www.buildingconservation.com/articles/ten/tenways.htm. Accessed October 20, 2009.

Terrisse, M. (2007) Les facteurs de réussite. *Espaces, Tourisme & Loisirs* 250, 44–52.

Tilden, F. (1957) *Interpreting Our Heritage*. Chapel Hill: University of North Carolina Press.

Timothy, D.J. (1997) Tourism and the personal heritage experience. *Annals of Tourism Research* 34(3), 751–754.

Timothy, D.J. (2007) Empowerment and stakeholder participation in tourism destination communities. In A. Church and T. Coles (eds) *Tourism, Power and Space* (pp. 199–216). London: Routledge.

Timothy, D.J. (2008) Genealogical mobility: Tourism and the search for a personal past. In D.J. Timothy and J. Kay Guelke (eds) *Geography and Genealogy: Locating Personal Pasts* (pp. 115–135). Aldershot: Ashgate.

Timothy, D.J. and Boyd, S.W. (2003) *Heritage Tourism*. Harlow: Prentice Hall.

Timothy, D.J. and Emmett, C.F. (forthcoming) Jerusalem, tourism and the politics of heritage. In M. Adelman and M. Elman (eds) *Jerusalem across Disciplines*. Syracuse, NY: Syracuse University Press.

Timothy, D.J. and Nyaupane, G.P. (2009) *Cultural Heritage and Tourism in the Developing World: A Regional Perspective*. London: Routledge.

Timothy, D.J. and Teye, V.B. (2004) American children of the African diaspora: Journeys to the motherland. In T. Coles and D.J. Timothy (eds) *Tourism, Diasporas and Space* (pp. 111–123). London: Routledge.

Timothy, D.J. and Teye, V.B. (2009) *Tourism and the Lodging Sector*. Oxford: Butterworth Heinemann.

Timothy, D.J. and Tosun, C. (2003) Appropriate planning for tourism in destination communities: Participation, incremental growth and collaboration. In S. Singh, D.J. Timothy, and R.K. Dowling (eds) *Tourism in Destination Communities* (pp. 181–204). Wallingford: CAB International.

Tourism Research Australia (2009) *Cultural and Heritage Tourism in Australia, 2008*. Belconnen: Tourist Research Australia.

Travel Industry Association of America (TIA) (2003) *The Historical/Cultural Traveler*. Washington, DC: Travel Industry Association.

Travel Industry Association of America (TIA) (2007) *Domestic Travel Market Report, 2007*. Washington, DC: Travel Industry Association.

Turco, D.M. (1999) Ya' 'at 'eeh: A profile of tourists to Navajo Nation. *Journal of Tourism Studies* 10(2), 57–61.

UNESCO (2009a) World Heritage. Available at http://whc.unesco.org/en/about/. Accessed December 2, 2009.

UNESCO (2009b) List of World Heritage in Danger. Available at http://whc.unesco.org/en/danger. Accessed December 2, 2009.

UNESCO (2010a) Rice Terraces of the Philippine Cordilleras. Available at http://whc.unesco.org/en/list/722. Accessed February 11, 2010.

UNESCO (2010b) UNESCO World Heritage List. Available at http://whc.unesco.org/en/list. Accessed July 2, 2010.

UNWTO (2006) *Compendium of Tourism Statistics*. Madrid: World Tourism Organization.

UNWTO (2008) *Tourism Highlights, 2008 Edition*. Madrid: World Tourism Organization.

UNWTO (2009) *Tourism 2020 Vision*. Madrid: World Tourism Organization.

UNWTO (2011) *Tourism Highlights, 2010 Edition*. Madrid: World Tourism Organization.

Upitis, A. (1989) Interpreting cross-cultural sites. In D.L. Uzzell (ed.) *Heritage Interpretation, Vol. 1: The Natural and Built Environment* (pp. 153–160). London Belhaven.

Urry, J. (1995) *Consuming Places*. London: Routledge.

US Department of Commerce (2005) *Cultural and Heritage Tourism in the United States*. Washington, DC: US Department of Commerce.

US National Park Service (2011) NPS Stats, Annual Summary Report for 2010. Available at http://www.nature.nps.gov/stats/viewReport.cfm. Accessed March 16, 2011.

van Aalst, I. and Boogaarts, I. (2002) From museum to mass entertainment: The evolution of the role of museums in cities. *European Urban and Regional Studies* 9(3), 195–209.

VisitBritain (2008) Taking part survey results. *Foresight* 56, 1–8. Available at http://www.visitbritain.org/Images/Foresight%20Issue%2056_tcm139-167379.pdf. Accessed September 15, 2009.

VisitBritain (2010a) *Investing in Success: Heritage and the UK Tourism Economy*. London: VisitBritain.

VisitBritain (2010b) *Overseas Visitors to Britain: Understanding Trends, Attitudes and Characteristics*. London: VisitBritain.

Wall, G. (1989) An international perspective on historic sites, recreation, and tourism. *Recreation Research Review* 14(4), 10–14.

Wall, G. (1997) Tourism attractions: Points, lines and areas. *Annals of Tourism Research* 24, 240–243.

World Casino Directory (2010) Welcome to the United States. Available at http://www.worldcasinodirectory.com/american-casinos.asp. Accessed July 20, 2010.

World Commission on Environment and Development (1987) *Our Common Future*. Oxford: Oxford University Press.

World Monuments Fund (2009a) World Monuments Fund. Available at http://www.wmf.org/. Accessed November 30, 2009.

World Monuments Fund (2009b) World Monuments Fund 2010 Watch List. Available at http://www.wmf.org/watch. Accessed November 30, 2009.

World Religious Travel Association (2009) Five-step introduction to faith-based travel and hospitality. Available at http://www.wrtareligioustravel.com/WRTA. Accessed October 16, 2009.

WTTC (2008) *Tourism Satellite Accounting: The 2008 Travel and Tourism Economic Research Executive Summary*. London: World Travel and Tourism Council.

Yang, L. and Wall, G. (2009) Ethnic tourism: A framework and an application. *Tourism Management* 30, 559–570.

INDEX